THE CAST OF CHARACTER

THE CAST OF CHARACTER

STYLE IN GREEK LITERATURE

NANCY WORMAN

UNIVERSITY OF TEXAS PRESS AUSTIN

This book has been supported by an endowment dedicated to classics and the ancient world and funded by the Areté Foundation; the Gladys Krieble Delmas Foundation; the Dougherty Foundation; the James R. Dougherty, Jr. Foundation; the Rachael and Ben Vaughan Foundation; and the National Endowment for the Humanities. The endowment has also benefited from gifts by Mark and Jo Ann Finley, Lucy Shoe Meritt, the late Anne Byrd Nalle, and other individual donors.

Copyright © 2002 by the University of Texas Press

First edition, 2002

Requests for permission to reproduce material from this work should be sent to Permissions, University of Texas Press, Box 7819, Austin, TX 78713-7819.

♾ The paper used in this book meets the minimum requirements of ANSI/NISO Z39.48-1992 (R1997) (Permanence of Paper).

LIBRARY OF CONGRESS CATALOGING-IN-PUBLICATION DATA
Worman, Nancy Baker, 1963–
The cast of character : style in Greek literature /
Nancy Worman.— 1st ed.
p.   cm.
Includes bibliographical references and index.
ISBN 0-292-79155-0 (alk. paper)
1. Greek literature—History and criticism.
2. Greek language—Style.   I. Title.
PA3052 .W67   2002
880.9′001—dc21
2002028636

FOR MY PARENTS,
EUGENIA CUYLER WORMAN
AND NATHANIEL WORMAN

All cleverness, whether in the rapid use of that difficult instrument the tongue, or in some other art unfamiliar to villagers, was in itself suspicious; honest folk, born and bred in a visible manner, were mostly not overwise or clever—at least, not beyond such a matter as knowing the signs of the weather; and the process by which rapidity and dexterity of any kind were acquired was so wholly hidden, that they partook of the nature of conjuring.

GEORGE ELIOT, *SILAS MARNER*

CONTENTS

Acknowledgments
xi

List of Journal and Textual Abbreviations
xiii

Introduction
1

1. *Kosmos* and the Typical Casts of Character
17

2. Oral Performance, Speech Types, and Typical Styles in Homer
41

3. Visible Types and Visualizing Styles in Archaic Poetry
82

4. Verbal Masquerade and Visual Impact in Tragedy
108

5. Manipulating the Senses in Rhetorical Set Pieces
149

Conclusion
193

Notes
197

Bibliography
239

General Index
252

Index Locorum
264

This book is a distant descendant of a dissertation written in the Department of Classics at Princeton University, under the direction of Froma Zeitlin. Froma has my deepest gratitude for her guidance and encouragement. I have benefited immeasurably from her intellectual breadth, her keen eye for cultural nuance, and her profound knowledge of ancient literature. Andrew Ford, André Laks, and Josh Ober, members of my committee, offered many invaluable suggestions from standpoints that deepened my awareness of the theoretical complexity of the project. My fellow graduate students—especially Kathy McCarthy, Daniel Mendelsohn, and André Lardinois—consistently provided both intellectual encouragement and emotional support.

A grant from the National Endowment for the Humanities funded the year in which I completed the dissertation. I also benefited from Barnard College's Special Assistant Professor's Leave program, which gave me a semester free from teaching duties to complete a rewrite of the book.

A number of my colleagues at Barnard and Columbia offered much-needed advice on different revisions of this study. I thank Suzanne Saïd, Debbie Steiner, and especially Helene Foley, whose interest in and support of my research has been repeatedly supplemented by her wise suggestions on particular projects. Other colleagues in the field have also been generous with their time and knowledge: I owe special thanks to Claude Calame, Lowell Edmunds, Nancy Felson, Richard Martin, Laura McClure, Piero Pucci, Seth Schein, and Eva Stehle.

I also want to thank those who shepherded the manuscript through the various stages of its publication at University of Texas Press: the Classics editor Jim Burr; manuscript editor Lynne Chapman; and copyeditor Nancy Moore. All were admirably attentive and helpful. In addition, the judicious suggestions of the anonymous readers made this a better book.

I am enduringly grateful to my friends and family for their sustained patience and humor. I single out Andrea Schulz, whose steady friendship and editor's eye have bolstered me from early on in this project. Finally, I thank my husband Iakovos Vasiliou, who has been an unfailingly thoughtful, inspiring companion and an incisive reader at all stages of the book's progress.

An article in the volume *Making Silence Speak: Women's Voices in Greek Literature and Society,* edited by André Lardinois and Laura McClure, partially coincides with material in the section "Helen as Guest and Host" in chapter 2. Sections of articles published in the journals *Classical Antiquity* (16.1) and *Helios* (26.1) have been revised and incorporated into various discussions in chapters 2, 4, and 5.

Andrew Ford's book *The Origins of Literary Criticism* regrettably appeared too late for consideration here.

LIST OF JOURNAL AND
TEXTUAL ABBREVIATIONS

AJP	*American Journal of Philology*
Anc. Soc.	*Ancient Society*
C	F. D. Caizzi, ed. *Antisthenis Fragmenta*. Milan, 1966.
CA	*Classical Antiquity*
CJ	*Classical Journal*
CP	*Classical Philology*
CQ	*Classical Quarterly*
CW	*Classical World*
DK	H. Diels and W. Kranz, eds. *Die Fragmente der Vorsokratiker*, 12th ed. Berlin, 1966–67.
G&R	*Greece & Rome*
GRBS	*Greek, Roman, and Byzantine Studies*
HSCP	*Harvard Studies in Classical Philology*
ICS	*Illinois Classical Studies*
IG	*Inscriptiones Graeci, 1873–.*
JHS	*Journal of Hellenic Studies*
K-A	R. Kassel and C. Austin, eds. *Poetae Comici Graeci*. Berlin.
LIMC	*Lexicon Iconographicum Mythologiae Classicae*. Zurich, 1981–.
L-P	E. Lobel and D. L. Page, eds. *Poetarum Lesbiorum Fragmenta*. Oxford, 1955.
N²	A. Nauck, ed. *Tragicorum Graecorum Fragmenta*, 2nd ed. Heidelscheim, 1964.
NJb	*Neue Jahrbucher für klassische Altertum*
PG	*Patrologiae cursus completus, series Graeca*, ed. J. P. Migne. Paris, 1857–66.
PMG	*Poetae Melici Graeci*, ed. D. L. Page. Oxford, 1962.
Radt	S. Radt, ed. *Tragicorum Graecorum Fragmenta*, vol. 3 (Aeschylus, 1985), vol. 4 (Sophocles, 1977). Göttingen.
REG	*Revue des Études Grecques*
RhM	*Rheinisches Museum für Philologie*

SEG	J. J. E. Hondius, ed. *Supplementum Epigraphicum Graecum.* Leiden, 1923–.
SPh	*Studia Philologica*
Stu. Urb.	*Studi Urbinati*
TAPA	*Transactions of the American Philological Association*
W^2	M. L. West, ed. *Iambi et Elegi Graeci,* 2nd ed. Oxford, 1989–92.
YCS	*Yale Classical Studies*

INTRODUCTION[1]

In Patricia Highsmith's claustrophobic and morally ambiguous novel *The Talented Mr. Ripley*, the eponymous antihero faces a situation in which he has to appear before the same policemen as two different people. In his second interview with them he must play himself rather than the dashing and entitled young man whom he had been impersonating. His solution to this dilemma is a simple one: instead of wearing a literal disguise, he alters his tone of voice, his posture and general deportment, the quality of his clothes, and his speaking style. Except for the addition of a pair of glasses and a slight darkening of his hair color, he is still the same person, as far as the concrete aspects of his physical appearance are concerned. But because he so successfully acts the part of his own timid and insignificant self, the policemen do not even think to compare him to the elegantly casual man they had interviewed the first time around.

Tom Ripley has altered what I shall refer to as his visible type or "cast" of character. These are the elements that make up one's typical style, the physical and linguistic mannerisms that mark a speaker as a type conforming to a set of socially familiar categories. Important to the apprehension of type are those visible elements that a speaker engages at the moment of self-performance, when he most wants to convince another that he is a particular kind of person. The eyewitness experience of the performer is essential to the audience's conviction that he is a certain type: the policemen must see Ripley speak a certain way and watch the droop in his ill-clothed shoulders

1

that finishes his own brief and deferential sentences or, conversely, the languid gesture of a beringed hand that punctuates the phrases of the wealthy man he impersonates. The playwright John Guare may have been aware of the similarities that Paul "Poitier" bore to Ripley when he brought to the stage the graceful impersonator of *Six Degrees of Separation*. Paul learns to charm upper-class couples into taking him in by altering his speaking style, deportment, and dress to resemble their own. The female protagonist of Wilkie Collins' novel *No Name* indulges in more concrete physical disguises to gain her ends, as befits her richly layered Victorian character. Nevertheless, her successful deceptions depend just as much on changes in vocal tone, posture, and speaking style, techniques she perfected while working as a small-time actress.

Numerous examples of such misleading strategies exist in modern literature, of course. I hope merely to suggest the scope and significance of the ideas explored in this book by recalling a few familiar modern characters whose manipulations of effect depend largely on changes in typical styles rather than on concrete disguises. These characters show how weighty an impact such seemingly ephemeral elements as facial expression, vocal timbre, vocabulary choice, or style of dress can have on the reception of the speaker. The techniques that this book analyzes developed in an ancient setting, the performative nature of which lent even more importance to the visible type the speaker appears to be than modern literary settings might be expected to do.

In the predominantly oral culture of ancient Greece, the character of the individual was conceived of as a visible entity, something that could be assessed from witnessing his public actions, daily deportment, and manner of speaking. In fifth-century Athens the centrality of oral arenas to the democratic city-state, including the theater, the courts, and the Assembly, insured that this increasingly literate culture nevertheless continued to be largely oriented around oral practices. This singular circumstance gave rise among the writers of the period to a perception of the overarching differences between oral and written styles and to a concern about the dangerously compelling effects of both. During the political upheavals that marked the end of the fifth century in Athens, this contested linguistic territory fostered suspicions that the grand, visualizing[2] style associated with oral performance and the overly precise, polished style associated with written composition could each have their detrimental effects on audiences.

As Cicero, Dionysius of Halicarnassus, Demetrius, and Aristotle before them demonstrate in detail, verbal style—the form and arrangement of words—plays an influential role in persuasive and appealing composition. These writers also acknowledge (Aristotle reluctantly) that the speaker's physical appearance, deportment, and the character he projects also contribute to the force of his arguments, all of which may in some sense be understood as aspects of style.[3] Just how this works begs the question of what style is and how conceptions of style may have changed from antiquity to the present. I am concerned here with elucidating earlier ideas about style that made a serious contribution to later stylistic concepts. The philosophically oriented thinking of Plato and Aristotle did much to obscure these ideas, during the rise of rhetoric as a field of study.[4]

This book explores the beginnings of an awareness of style in archaic and classical Greek literature and assesses the tendency of poets and early prose writers to treat verbal techniques and visual effects as interrelated. It centers around a number of famous depictions of Helen and Odysseus, two figures who uniquely focus ideas about the impact of the visibly persuasive character type and the impressive oral style. Like Tom Ripley, both figures also reveal the potentially distracting or misleading effects of such versatile self-performance and thus of style itself.

STYLE AS A SOCIAL PERFORMANCE

The French sociologist Pierre Bourdieu has argued that one cannot understand social practices without understanding the relationship between how the body is socialized and the use of language. For Bourdieu, this linguistic usage is predominantly physical, since it is the body that engages certain verbal habits, themselves learned through socialization. Style, from this perspective, comprises the interaction between word usage and bodily deportment, as both are molded and regulated by class and gender.[5] Bourdieu terms this interaction bodily *hexis*, the ancient Greek word for habit or typical state of being. In Aristotle, *hexeis* designate the dispositions that are formed over time by habitual action and that constitute different character types.[6] For Bourdieu, bodily *hexis* itself is molded by the set of entrenched beliefs and attitudes (the *habitus*) that delineates the given social group.[7] As Bourdieu puts it, *hexis* is "political mythology realized, *em-bodied*, turned into a permanent disposition, a durable way of standing, speaking, walking, and thereby of feeling and thinking."[8] Thus the verbal style of the individual cannot be apprehended apart from its physical enactment. This is itself a product of inculcation—the result of a bodily memory whose visible manifestations (re)produce attitudes and beliefs molded over generations.[9] Bourdieu further points out that these stylistic schemes are value-laden; an honorable type comports himself in a particularly honorable manner, from the steady, regulated way he eats his meals to the firm, rhythmic way he speaks in public.[10]

In the second volume of his history of sexuality, Michel Foucault emphasizes that a stylized and visually oriented attitude toward behavior informed the ancient Greek understanding of character type and ethics.[11] Foucault argues that the Greek writers of the classical period display a concern with regimen rather than injunction, aiming at the regulation of pleasures according to what is judged to be suitable behavior in relation to such type markers as age, health, and status of the individual.[12] For the Greek citizen, Foucault argues, the principles that govern such regulation are based on ideas about proportion and timing, a pervasive emphasis on fitting measure that he terms "a stylization of attitudes and an aesthetics of existence."[13] The corollary associations (which Foucault does not pursue) between Greek ideas about character and the physical regimens that he terms "techniques of the self" contribute to an awareness of style as an interconnected patterning of verbal conduct, deportment, and daily activity, that is, as the visible organization of character type.[14]

Judith Butler has argued for a similar understanding of self-presentation as stylized, most prominently in her elaborations of the "performative" nature of gender identification. Butler's notion of "corporeal style"—consisting of the inflections, deportment, and dress that signal participation in particular social categories—clearly parallels Bourdieu's ideas about bodily *hexis*.[15] Butler's emphasis on identity as a social performance rather than a natural phenomenon accords with the work of such anthropologists as Michael Herzfeld, who has studied the performance of gender identity in modern Greek communities as a "poetics of social interaction."[16] Herzfeld focuses on a social semiotics similar in general outlook to those of Bourdieu and Butler, in which the self is performed by engaging the tropes particular to a given identity category.

Performance theory in general has influenced thought about ancient social institutions, as well as studies of the body in antiquity.[17] The methodological perspective that informs this "cultural poetics" tends to embrace both signifying practices in daily life and those schematized by artistic media, a blurring of distinctions that can be problematic for the analysis of literary semiosis. Nevertheless, the recognition that character is formulated by means of the visible engagement in a stylistics of identity supports an approach more useful for addressing how style operates in oral settings.

Indeed, all these scholars' observations about self-presentation as a social, regularized, embodied, and therefore visible phenomenon uniquely suit the public, performative context in which ancient ideas about style developed. Rather than focusing on the individual, as a modern phrase like "personal style" implies, the ancient concepts of style were elaborated with a focus on visible behavior within the community, on the categories of character type that organized this behavior, and on the kinds of speech that suited different types in different settings.[18] Thus all styles of self-presentation would have been assessed in relation to normative notions of the fit between character type and typical setting: what was suitable for the bedroom, for example, would not be so for the dinner table. Similarly, the locutions suited to the warrior would not be those suited to the concubine or to the keeper of pigs.

These are value-laden, hierarchized distinctions; and whatever power a given speech possesses is conferred from outside, in effect, that is, from the way in which the speech successfully engages in discourses already acknowledged as authoritative (e.g., locutions typical to priests or warriors).[19] Bourdieu himself emphasizes that the scepter (*skêptron*) of the ancient Greek kings is a visible emblem of linguistic *habitus*. Handed from speaker to speaker in archaic assemblies, the *skeptron* thereby confers on successive warriors the authoritative status necessary to public persuasion. We might compare the example that the literary theorist Kenneth Burke makes of Thomas Carlyle, when discussing the distinctive features of an individual's self-presentation. Burke terms these features "stylistic identifications" and quotes Carlyle on the similarly emblematic nature of clothing: "Has not your Red hanging-individual a horsehair wig, squirrel-skins, and a plush gown; whereby all mortals know that he is a JUDGE?—Society, which the more I think of it astonishes me the more, is founded upon Cloth."[20] In his lectures on rhetoric, Aristotle remarks in blander fashion, "It is necessary to consider what indicates an old man as a red cloak does a young man, for the same clothing does not suit (πρέπει) both."[21]

Most earlier Greek poets and prose writers judged a speaker's ability primarily on the manner in which he told his story, including his presentation of himself as a particular type, from the formation of his words to the drape of his cloak. Ancient ideas about the visibility of style and character type make use of a physically based scheme that opposes (in general terms) heroic to deformed or degraded statures. In archaic and classical poetry and prose, terms like *kosmos, tropos,* and *schêma* most often trace this kind of bodily geometry, triangulating speaking style, visible actions, and deportment, which together can either genuinely indicate a person's type or prove a false indicator of that type. Deportment and stature may betray birth, as Ion notes of Creusa in Euripides' eponymous play (γενναιότης σοι, καὶ τρόπων τεκμήριον / τὸ σχῆμ' ἔχεις τόδ', *Ion* 237–238). Fancy talk and a nice outfit may, on the other hand, prettily conceal wrongdoing, the trick with which Hecuba charges Helen in the *Trojan Women* (τὸ σὸν κακὸν κοσμοῦσα, 982). The *tropos* or "turn" of a man may denote his visible manner, his verbal style, or even his dress,[22] while a word like *schêma* ("shape") points most insistently to the disposition of the body and its visible actions, as Simon Goldhill has noted.[23] *Kosmos* is a term that early in archaic poetry suggests the crucial balancing of all these elements in the projection of a winning style. It most centrally denotes a pleasing integration of parts, a fitting adornment that one can see both literally and in the mind's eye.

The word *kosmos* thus embraces the elements that make up what I am referring to (quite untechnically) as the "cast" of character: the interactions among dress, deportment, and verbal strategies that in the act of self-presentation crystallize as one's typical style. This is the style a person assumes in the moment of performing as a recognized type, where witnesses to her self-enactment can actually visually assess who she is (or who she purports to be). A typical style in this context is thus not so much an individual, unique manner of engaging that projects who one "really" is. Rather, since ancient notions of character type are much more schematic and performative, one's typical style is just that—typical, conforming to accepted behavioral patterns and recognizable categories of type.[24] Thus Odysseus' typical style in Homeric depiction adheres to the conventional cast of the versatile, clever type, versions of which he engages very convincingly, even when he is not playing himself.

This "typical style," then, is the combination of socially categorized verbal and visual habits that Bourdieu calls bodily *hexis*. The Greek word *tupos* eventually came to mean speaking style among the rhetoricians, but its earlier uses embrace broader notions of things visibly familiar, recognizable, or of the same general character.[25] Similarly, Greek terms central to rhetorical theory such as *prepon* (suitability) and *eikos* (probability) reveal a concern with regularized patterns of visible type, the roots of which are much older than the treatises in which these concepts figure prominently.[26] Modern scholars have recognized the importance of these concepts to Greek rhetorical theory, probability for its usefulness in forensic arguments about factual details, and suitability for its centrality to stylistic issues. But they have not noticed that both depend crucially on a schematized awareness of social habits and are associated with visibility.[27] What a person is likely to do or what it is fitting that he do can only be assessed by means of witnessing that he is a particular type (i.e., of a given status, stature, disposition) in a particular setting. Notions of probability and suitability thus engage the audience's understanding of typical characters and their likely behavior. Probability itself depends on suitability, and suitability, again, pertains primarily to style, to the deportment, dress, and language that make one recognizable as a given type. Any exploration of notions of style in ancient Greece should thus embrace this broader understanding of its purview.

STYLE BEFORE ARISTOTLE

Most previous discussions of ancient conceptions of style address the subject from a much narrower perspective than that outlined above, in part because of assumptions about when the awareness of stylistic effect first developed. Although some recent studies of the origins of Greek rhetoric do consider fifth-century discussions, the few scholars who address stylistic issues most often treat as introductory any material that predates the fourth century.[28] Their analyses begin in earnest with Aristotle's recommendations in the *Rhetoric* for formulating a persuasive style, which means that his treatment of the topic largely determines how it is defined. Consequently, discussions are usually restricted to style in prose writing, which is regarded as coming into Greek consciousness with the advent of rhetorical theory. Scholars therefore either ignore earlier conceptions of stylistic type or treat them as not rigorously defined enough to be helpful.

This way of setting the parameters for the study of style in writing is certainly defensible. A number of studies of early rhetorical theory as a technical discipline have included cogent analyses of the development of prose style.[29] The scope of such studies often depends, however, on the largely uncontested thesis that unless the ancient sources have a technical word for a category of inquiry, no awareness of the topic can be usefully identified and explored.[30] Yet most important discussions of the origins of rhetoric, while they frequently engage in this kind of debate, nevertheless look to earlier periods for evidence of an awareness of rhetorical concepts.[31] If scholars agree that it is useful to consider archaic and classical literature before Plato in analyzing the development of rhetorical theory, then surely the same can be argued for stylistic theory before Aristotle. Acknowledging the importance of earlier depictions of persuasive strategies has occasionally led to the recognition of how this material might bear on topics like style.[32] Indeed, Richard Enos has gone so far as to suggest that earlier ideas about language centered around distinctions of style.[33] To my knowledge, however, only Neil O'Sullivan's consideration of Aristophanic conceptions of style has significantly broadened the chronological parameters of the discussion.[34]

Sensitivity to stylistic effect can be identified as far back as Homer, along with an attention to persuasive techniques more generally.[35] Dramatic, oratorical, and historical texts reveal a heightened awareness of the impact of style in the late fifth century, which may indeed be influenced by the advent of prose writing. Yet most instances of this awareness revolve around reaction to an individual's style of delivery in oral performance. They thus center on the apprehension of the speaker's adherence to a typical character profile, which usually includes such visual details as dress and deportment. Earlier treatments of oral performance that are no longer extant may well have addressed the topic of style from this broader perspective. As commentators on ancient rhetoric and literary criticism always note, handbooks existed in the fifth century that offered instruction in oratorical technique. None of these have survived, but it is likely that they contained set speeches (i.e., speeches on set themes, about and/or in the voice of paradigmatic mythohistorical figures). They may also have included analyses of different styles of composition and delivery.[36] There is further evidence that such lesser-known intellectual figures as Polus and Antisthenes wrote books on style or "types" (*charaktêres*) of speakers; both were said to be students of the sophist Gorgias, the famous proponent of an elaborate oral style.[37]

It thus appears that before Aristotle defined style as verbal embellishment in prose writing and sought to ignore elements of oral performance, ideas about style did include the visual aspects of a speaker's type. These ideas centered around the eyewitnessing of speakers and were inseparable from an understanding of character as importantly visible and performative.[38] Beginning a discussion of ancient ideas about style with Aristotle would seem to distort the picture quite seriously. As some scholars have recognized in relation to other aspects of rhetorical theory, this narrower focus minimizes the influence of ideas developed during the period in which prose was being invented and the transition from a predominantly oral attitude toward language was underway.[39]

Indeed, the later discussions themselves show evidence of this influence. Aristotle and Isocrates both closely connect verbal style (*lexis*) and delivery (*hupokrisis*) (Arist. *Rhet.* 1403b–1404a; Isoc. 5.25–27). This suggests, as Thomas Cole has noted, that they could explain what effect *lexis* should have in a text only by analogy to that of *hupokrisis* in performance.[40] The association of *lexis* and *hupokrisis* reveals an understanding of style as somehow bound up in the spoken word, as an *oral* technique, which Aristotle is attempting to revise for use in the written text.[41] One might even suspect that Aristotle, with his analytical and readerly orientation to his subject matter, was reacting against these more oral and visually oriented conceptions of style. In his view, such visual elements—which he relegates rather tellingly to a "vulgar" (φόρτικον, *Rhet.* 1404a35) category borrowed from theater (*hupokrisis*)—possess an illegitimate impact in the performance or persuasive setting because of the "corruption" (μοχθηρία) of the audience (*Rhet.* 1403b35, 1404a8).[42] He notes, however, that the actor Theodorus and the dramatist Euripides both offer useful indications of how to cover up (κλέπτεται) the fact that one is suiting one's speech to subject and audience (*Rhet.* 1404b20–26).

This suspicion of oral performance informs much of what Aristotle has to say about style and character type. It had, moreover, a weighty effect on subsequent theory and scholars' attempts to analyze that theory. Adhering to narrower definitions of style may reflect accurately (if uncritically) Aristotle's own parameters. Yet even analyses of Aristotle's ideas, as well as those of later rhetorical theorists, could usefully pay more attention to the interaction of style and character type, and the importance of appearing to be a certain kind of person in the persuasive setting. Aristotle's vexing and often elliptical treatment of the speaker's self-presentation in the *Rhetoric*, for example, repeatedly skirts the issue of delivery and stops just short of an admission that character and style are mutually determining.

This circumspect treatment of the topic echoes an awareness that Plato sought to raise regarding the pleasures of speech performance. In the *Gorgias*, for example, Socrates argues that tragedy aims at pleasure (ἡδονήν) and that, stripped of its music and meter, tragic poetry is essentially public oratory (δημηγορία) (502b–d). This awareness of the distractingly pleasurable (and therefore potentially dangerous) power of oral performance unquestionably predated both Plato and Aristotle. Thucydides and the tragic poets themselves express concern that a crowd-pleasing, sweet-speaking, attractive character might sway an audience to commit unscrupulous and immoral acts.[43]

In fifth-century Athens ideas about style did not, then, develop in a morally neutral and uncharged setting. Rather, they surfaced coincident with a growing realization among elites of how much power any sophist or demagogue might accumulate by the display of a winning style in public settings.[44] This style made use of conventional notions of type to forge a speaking style and visible character that would seem familiar and therefore persuasive to citizens.[45] In an oral culture like that of the archaic period and later in a "performance culture" like Athens,[46] the attributes of a person that one could literally witness in his deportment, speech habits, and significant actions would have loomed larger than more abstract conceptions of his character.[47]

STYLE IN LITERARY REPRESENTATION

Most of the oral settings that this study analyzes are embedded in literary narratives and are products of a mythohistorical tradition. These literary depictions anticipate many distinctions drawn in later technical discussions, but they do not necessarily adhere to narrower understandings of stylistic type. In his book on Greek prose style, Kenneth Dover makes a useful distinction between lexical style and what he calls "style at the level of invention."[48] This involves broader choices about approach and presentation in written composition than those that could be strictly categorized as lexical. It thus includes elements important to an analysis of style in literary settings that predate Aristotle. A poet or prose writer may depict a character's style by giving him certain figures of speech and phrasing, but his style may also be indicated by certain types of arguments, structuring devices, and techniques of characterization such as slander or, conversely, self-praise.[49] In earlier literature, speeches often borrow effects from ritual contexts, such as the cadences of prayer (or curse) or the elegiac lyricism of lamentation. These portrayals of a character's speaking style sometimes also include visual details such as facial expression, gesture, or dress.

Because these verbal and visual cues contribute importantly to the reception of the speaker by the audience internal to the narrative, addressing them should bring us closer to capturing the wide range of stylistic effects in predominantly oral settings. Indeed, it should not be surprising that most of the literary depictions considered here utilize broader, more fluid, and more emblematic categories of stylistic type than those of the fourth-century theorists and later writers. Since this study looks beyond discussions that isolate style as an area of inquiry as such, it is not restricted to or even primarily concerned with vocabulary that seems technical in any narrow sense.[50] Instead, it explores in detail the vocabulary and imagery that poets and prose writers employ in representing verbal and visual elements in speech performance. More precisely, this book considers how internal narrators and characters in performed texts make use of and react to style: what strategies they undertake to insure their good reception; how they characterize what they are doing; when they call attention to this process; and what conclusions about moral worth or status they draw from it.

This is, moreover, an essentially literary study. Although it makes use of concepts from sociological and performance theory, for the most part it emphasizes representations rather than reality and understands literature as a refraction (rather than a reflection) of lived life. Its discussions trace the semiotic patterns in literary depictions that pertain to ideas about style and character type and elucidate the ways these depictions arrange significant objects and verbal imagery around the apprehension of style in oral performance. From this perspective, Helen is less a character with a history and "lifelike" personality than a trope for the sensory impact of style, while Odysseus signifies an authorial function in the suitable alternation of stylistic types. In addition, the literary representations on which I focus embed attitudes toward actual performers in settings that highlight schematic differences among types. Homologies are thus repeatedly suggested between the author-performers and those characters in their compositions who serve some sort of stylistic function, whether as an active formulator or an object of discourse. In the classical period, such homologies evolved into the use of Homeric characters in particular as types emblematic of different oratorical styles. This highly literate schema would suggest that even the performances of historical figures were assessed in relation to the tropes of oral composition and that whatever constituted the "real" features of those performances were organized by the tradition in relation to ideas about visuality and persuasive style.

I am thus less concerned with such historical details than with the uses that poets and prose writers make of those figures who stand in for ideas about style. Some of these uses offer little evidence of the actual styles of performers but instead highlight the visual patterns that structure ancient

thinking about style and moral type. Nevertheless, because these oral performances are depicted as social phenomena, and thus are organized by
social habits and hierarchies, Bourdieu's observations (and to a lesser extent
those of Butler and Foucault) offer helpful guidelines for assessing the semiotic patterns that organize the literary representations. The literary imagery
clearly treats everyday life as structured by such public performances and
embraces larger ideas about self-presentation, about the body as a visible
map of social status and about speech as an instrument of power.

THE RELEVANCE OF HELEN AND ODYSSEUS

One of the central paradoxes of style in the ancient setting is that those
figures who are depicted as speaking against type, as combining types, or
as using types as disguises best crystallize ideas about the interaction of
style and character in the speaker's self-presentation.[51] Any transgressions
of type or setting that the speaker might commit often result in suspicious or
negative reactions from the interlocutor or internal audience. Thus the ways
in which gender and class categories contribute to molding typical styles
come into focus at these moments of transgression. It is then that a speaker
effectively reveals the mechanics of stylized self-performance by combining
conventional locutions or alternating familiar stances, which the audience
may apprehend as a mismatch between speaker and type. This itself may
lead to a recognition that style is mutable and therefore not to be trusted as
an accurate measure of moral or social status, let alone identity.

In earlier literature this emphasis on visual assessment did not necessarily entail a general devaluation of visible details as distracting or deceitful, although certain female characters in archaic poetry do suggest the
dangers that may lie in being distracted by bodily adornment. Especially
in Homer, heroes for the most part look as they are: they wear their forceful types like their armor, as a set of visually identifiable attributes. Thus it
is the unusual mismatch between how one presents oneself and who one
is that arouses concern about typical style as a distracting or misleading
cloak for one's character. Changeable and attractive types such as Helen
and Odysseus embody this concern. It is only in the literature of the late
fifth century, however, that any widespread anxiety can be detected among
Athenian writers about the ramifications of the potential for appearances to
be deceptive. Before then, internal audiences react to the visual and verbal

mannerisms of a speaker's self-presentation as clearly affecting the meaning of his speech, but with only the rare acknowledgment that this style may have been assumed for the occasion.

In Greek literature, the figures of Odysseus and Helen increasingly serve to focus anxiety about the potential for distraction or outright deception inherent in this visually oriented means of identifying a speaker as a particular type. I am not proposing that the depictions of these two figures in Greek poetry and prose comprise all that is said about style in any of these periods. This is not true by any means. But their depictions include some of the most essential clues to the development of ideas about style and visible type. They also demonstrate forcefully the connection of these ideas in fifth-century Athens to a concern that the versatile character may also "dress up" in some way and thus dissemble as to his true type to win his (possibly immoral) way.[52]

These depictions of Helen and Odysseus thus provide the most useful indicators of how ancient writers thought about visible style and character for a paradoxical reason: the motivations and sometimes even the identities of both tend to be obscure, difficult to pin down, changeable, and contradictory. They are liars and imitators, effective storytellers, and adept users of costume. Perhaps precisely because the sophist Gorgias and his students champion them, for the dramatic poets, Helen and Odysseus embody doubts about how speaking style, dress, and deportment may distract from the true or precise recounting of events. These doubts arise from the nascent awareness that style itself may be similarly changeable, detachable from the individual like the persona, the "cast" of character type. In the fifth century some of this awareness was most likely the result of exposure to sophistic ideas about effective speaking. Both the idea that virtue (*aretê*) could be taught and the practice of arguing on both sides of an issue encouraged an understanding of a speaker's character as malleable and manufactured rather than inherent or natural.[53] The dramatists for the most part seem to have agreed with the suspicion nursed by many members of the educated elite that sophistic training made dangerously versatile leaders out of citizens with strong speaking abilities and weak morals. They most often depict both Helen and Odysseus as smooth-talking purveyors of evildoing (*kakourgia, Tro.* 966–968) and profligate behavior (*panourgia, Phil.* 407–409).[54] Responses of the internal audiences to them register discomfort at the possibility that a fine speaking style may mask an inner disorder, that the beautiful (*kalos*) style may be no more than the special craft of a base (*kakos*) speaker.[55]

These familiar details are not offered as a prelude to tracing the histories of Helen and Odysseus; these have been analyzed in depth by scholars.[56] I am interested only in those details of their narratives that indicate archaic and classical attitudes toward style. Roland Barthes' distinction between character and figure may help to clarify this focus. According to Barthes, a character is a combination of semes with a proper name (or an "I") and an evolution in narrative time. A figure, in contrast, is an atemporal, impersonal entity composed of symbolic relationships.[57] The signature feature of Helen's figure is a beauty both dangerous and immortal, but she is also depicted as the embodiment of something equally threatening and attractive: an enchanting style of self-presentation. Depictions of her do not merely show her engaging in this typical style; more importantly, she is emblematic of it. The details of her figure thus indicate a visualizing scheme, a metonymic *emblem* that points to certain conceptions of style.[58] She eventually comes to signify the sensory impact of style and more particularly the visually enchanting, elaborate style typical of the grand sophistic display. Similarly, in Homer and later writers, Odysseus' figure crystallizes the recognition that one's visibly identifiable character may be detachable from who one really is. The speaker adept at donning physical disguises and dissembling verbal styles may thereby appear preeminently suitable to whatever audience he faces. Because this versatile suitability is *the* central rhetorical feature that Odysseus embodies, I address only those details of his narrative that highlight this aspect of his figure.

THE ORGANIZATION OF THE BOOK

Chapter 1, "*Kosmos* and the Typical Casts of Character," outlines the central set of associations that shapes ideas about style and character type in the archaic and classical periods. The chapter first reviews the ancient vocabulary that helps to delineate style as a "cast" of character in these periods. Three terms receive the most attention: *kosmos,* which embraces the kind of visualized ordering of parts that style entails; *êthos,* a common word for character that sometimes has moral implications; and *charaktêr,* which I argue denotes more emphatically the visible cast of type demarcated in public self-presentation.

Chapter 2, "Oral Performance, Speech Types, and Typical Styles in Homer," looks to Homeric epic for information about how the orality of early Greek literature helped to shape an understanding of the linguistic aspects of bodily *hexis* in the persuasive setting. I analyze how Homer presents Helen and Odysseus as adept controllers of sense impressions, and thus as shapers of what their audiences actually see. Homer's portraits of these characters in oral performance thus establish some early parameters for the assessment of stylistic concerns such as likeness and suitability, as well as for the way these elements might contribute to misleading an audience regarding one's motivations or one's type.

Chapter 3, "Visible Types and Visualizing Styles in Archaic Poetry," considers more extensively how the visible elements of oral performance affect the audience's reaction to the speaker. I first address broader concepts about bodily ornament and moral type and then narrow the inquiry to consider how Homer associates Helen and Odysseus with modes of costuming and disguise that parallel their elusive speaking styles. Because the archaic poets tend to associate stylistic effect especially with the visual delights of the female body, this chapter also considers how poets' depictions of the dangerous pleasures of feminine beauty ultimately contribute to an understanding of style as similarly suspect.

If the archaic poets align style with sensory delights, and especially with the titillation of the eye, writers of tragedy focus on the moral difficulties that attend the effective performance of the versatile character. In chapter 4, "Verbal Masquerade and Visual Impact in Tragedy," I examine why dramatists tend to represent Helen and Odysseus as arousing moral recoil in their interlocutors. Because of their use of dissembling and changeable self-presentations, their very appearance on stage initiates questions about the accuracy of the visual apprehension of type. In drama this concern takes on an added metatheatrical significance, since this is the genre of spectacle and enactment, where the audience can actually witness the performance of type.[59]

The rhetorical theorists treat Helen as a figure emblematic of sensual verbal appeal and Odysseus as an adept manipulator of audience perception. The fictional speeches that the sophist Gorgias and his students composed to illustrate certain aspects of their argumentative techniques continue the archaic attention to sensory impact. Chapter 5, "Manipulating the Senses in Rhetorical Set Pieces," explores the ways in which the figures of Helen and Odysseus are used to highlight the effects that showy, versatile speakers have on sense perception. This quasi-physical impact strongly influences what visible type that speaker appears to be.

A brief conclusion indicates the importance of the imagery analyzed in the book for later rhetorical theory.

CHAPTER 1

KOSMOS
AND THE
TYPICAL CASTS
OF CHARACTER

ἀνδρὸς χαρακτὴρ ἐκ λόγου γνωρίζεται.

One can recognize the character of the man
from his speech.

MENANDER, fr. 72

In *Criticism in Antiquity*, D. A. Russell argues that *lexis* has no metaphorical extension equivalent to the English word "style." Some idea of style as it is embodied by a particular model, he further notes, did exist; later writers indicate the distinctive imprint of an orator's style with the term *charaktêr*.[1] This included the character type that the speaker projects, although its usage does not seem to demarcate this aspect of style in particular. Rather, we see the use of a word that has to do exclusively with language (*lexis*) and the corresponding use of *charaktêr*, which points to a visual conception of type. This latter notion may include a person's cast of features, deportment, or use of language, that is, whatever can be witnessed by an onlooker. The term *charaktêr* also highlights the possible gaps between the "stamp" of one's surface effects and one's essential make-up. A cognate of the verb "to strike" (*charassô*), *charaktêr* was used with the advent of currency to designate the stamp on a genuine coin. The term's original meaning thus carries with it this concern about surface effects and authenticity, which continues in later usage. The narrower meaning of *lexis* as verbal style comes into use only late

17

in the classical period, appearing first in any technical sense in Aristotle's *Rhetoric* (1403b1 and *passim*).[2] Russell thus argues that the explicit discussion of verbal style arises with the development of prose writing and the growth of oratory. That is, it evolves first as an aspect of rhetorical training, in distinguishing oratorical from poetic styles.[3]

There is little reason to question the idea that a technical discussion of style first grew out of writers' attempts to distinguish prose from poetic style in the composing of theoretical and technical treatises on oratory. But this argument does not entail that no awareness of stylistic effect existed earlier, or that writers were unclear about what kind of coherence they expected between a person's verbal style and his visible type.

In discussing the development of categories of style, Luigi Salvioni has pointed to the relationship between the techniques of probability (*eikos*) that are attributed to the early sophists Corax and Teisias, and the notion of the "credible man" (*epieikês*).[4] Frances Muecke has analyzed Agathon's treatment of poetic style in Aristophanes' *Thesmorphoriazusae*, which he presents as necessarily captured in his speaking manner, in his deportment, and more precisely in how he defends his chosen costume. Discussing Agathon's intellectualization of this association between poetic style and appearance, Muecke points to the common belief that the poet and his work were interchangeable, notes that dress is the "external indication" of this connection, and regrets that we cannot recapture the sophistic or rhetorical arguments behind Agathon's defense of his effeminate look.[5] For our purposes, however, Agathon does make one crucial move: he claims that the poet who wishes to compose beautiful plays (καλὰ δράματα) must be beautiful (καλός) in nature and appearance, explicitly insisting, however silly his argument, on a match among the use of language, dress, and internal composition (*Thesm.* 159–170). One's bodily *hexis* should be, according to Agathon, emblematic of both one's artistic product and one's character.

Neil O'Sullivan has shown that certain fundamental stylistic concepts can be reconstructed from the works of Aristophanes and the fourth-century rhetoricians Isocrates and Alcidamas.[6] He centers his discussion on the distinction between the "grand" and the "plain" linguistic styles, and he suggests that such categories were recognized among poets and prose writers in the late fifth century. In one of the most crucial clarifications of his discussion, O'Sullivan maintains that these styles conform to emerging differences between oral performance and written composition, with the latter giving rise to an emphasis on linguistic precision and lucidity over emotional impressiveness and verbal embellishment. This argument helps to ground my claim that the relation between style and character type that Aristotle tentatively outlines for written oratory had its roots in earlier conceptions of what constitutes the effective and appropriate oral performance and what elements of a speaker's address most influence the listener. Aristotle and other fourth-century prose writers such as Isocrates would thus have been reacting against not only the distracting elements inherent in oral performances (e.g., the elaborate dress that the sophists were said to wear) but also the forceful and highly metaphorical style to which such displays lent themselves.

Awareness of such stylistic differences can be found in the portrayal of character types and differing speaking abilities, in the internal audiences' reactions to these speakers and occasionally in direct discussions of the power of language. O'Sullivan analyzes this awareness in Aristophanes, revealing his use of the grand-plain dichotomy especially in the *Frogs*. O'Sullivan contends that this constitutes an important distinction for fifth-century writers. For the archaic material, however, no such useful and overarching dichotomies can be isolated; rather, the forceful qualities of the spoken word are repeatedly analogized to other sensory effects in an effort to capture their texture and range. The discussions of the archaic material thus focus more on these associations and their embodiment in particular figures and less on broad distinctions between styles. This book follows not only the development of ideas about style in this relatively neutral sense but also the growth of anxiety and distrust aroused by the perceived powers of certain oral styles. In the first half of the fourth century, this apprehension culminates in the philosophers' promotion of the plainer style, which they considered more suitable for written composition.

The potentially negative aspects of the influence of stylistic elements are concentrated importantly in the characters of Helen and Odysseus. It is the hint of trouble attending them in Homer that the fifth-century writers perceive and develop into a conception of them as essential antitypes. The discussion below considers the terms that authors use when addressing how one represents oneself to others, terms that demarcate aspects of style to which the characters of Helen and Odysseus draw attention. Each of the sections on terminology also addresses the responses of Plato and Aristotle to earlier ideas about style. While this book does not focus on the ideas of either thinker, these discussions show how their influential reactions to certain aspects of persuasive effect served to obscure the less technical conceptions of style and character with which this analysis is primarily concerned.

VISUAL AIDS

The argument that archaic and classical conceptions of style depend crucially on the assessment of visible type gains support from an understanding of how central the visual analogy was to Greek thought from early on, a topic that Raymond Prier and others have explored.[7] The faculty of sight seems to represent the primary sensory experience of the world, an eyewitness emphasis that coheres with the predominantly oral nature of Greek culture in earlier periods. In the oral setting, language would have been perceived in its enactment, as an event that one could see. This visually oriented attitude may also have influenced later ways of conceiving verbal style, even when it had come to apply primarily to ideas about writing. As an obvious example, the word for stature or physical form, *eidos* (the "seen thing"), along with its cognate *idea*, later came to mean type or style of speech among the rhetoricians.[8] Similar usage exists in English, of course, but Prier explains that an important difference lies in the archaic analogies to sense perception being synesthetic and thus not metaphorical but symbolic—they "mean something in themselves."[9] Such analogies retained their visceral quality for classical writers and continued to be essential to the communication of experience.

In a still oral and performative culture, therefore, things that could not be seen in the literal sense (e.g., spoken words) nevertheless were regarded as possessing a visual quality by virtue of their witnessed utterance and their palpable effect on reality. Thus there are at least three distinct but mutually effecting ways in which language is conceived of as visual. First, the ancient treatment of language as a witnessed event accords with Bourdieu's sense that language use constitutes a central part of bodily *hexis*. Second, since archaic and classical writers analogize language to tactical experience, speech itself is conceived of and measured in visualizing terms. Finally, the visualizing power of language contributes to its association with objects of sight. As the lyric poet Simonides puts it, "Speech is the portrait of deeds" (ὁ λόγος τῶν πραγμάτων εἰκών ἐστίν).[10]

KOSMOS

In ancient Greek usage, the word *kosmos* designates a visible order of things, an appropriate, sometimes decorative, and often honorable organization of parts or integrity of traits. This order should ideally match moral disposition in the individual, which is in turn measured in concrete terms, such as neatness of appearance, orderliness in group assembly, and suitability of speech. This integrated patterning makes up what I am calling a "cast" of character: a recognizably suitable and coherent set of traits that leads those who witness a person's appearance, speech, and behavior to affirm him as a particular type.

Coherence of this sort is expected, and noted when it is absent. One should speak in the appropriate manner (*kata kosmon*) and employ suitable ornament (*kosmeô*) in the fashioning of both one's appearance and one's words. One's body (living or dead) may thus be embellished by decoration (*kosmos*) that accurately conveys one's status and fittingly enhances one's stature. A city may be similarly embellished by the wealth and deeds of its leading citizens. A man may live an orderly life through being responsible and self-controlled in public life (*kosmios*), a visible behavior that reflects the continence of his character. There is a *kosmos* of the heavens and the soul, as there is of the body and the body politic.[11]

The semantic range of *kosmos* is thus not generally restricted to word choice or cut of dress but comprises both, in addition to the deportment and visible behavior that color the perception of a particular character and therefore influence apprehension of her type. This patterning of physical attitudes and attributes and verbal tactic and tone constitutes the emblematic self-performance that Bourdieu calls bodily *hexis* and Butler, corporeal style. These conform to a set of characteristics apprehended by eyewitnesses as typical; they communicate a familiar outlook and encourage audience identification.[12] The various uses of the term *kosmos* in archaic poetry in fact anticipate later notions of suitability and likeness or probability: *kosmos* reflects a monitoring of the appropriate and orderly engagement with social categories in which the speaker is recognized as suitable for x and likely to do y. Since *kosmos* can refer to bodily adornment, negative connotations may also arise, especially when this adornment is accompanied by or associated with the use of ornate language. Audiences often regard this elaborate corporeal style as masking some fault or wrongdoing. Such a style may so stun an audience that its members do not attend properly to moral concerns, since the use of visual display and ornate imagery may promote an inaccurate, highly colored, and forcefully rearranged version of events.

Early Greek literature shows an awareness of the dangers of such verbal deceits and of the coherence that should mark a person both internally and externally. In Homeric epic the phrase *kata kosmon* denotes suitable appearance, behavior, and speaking style, an idea of orderly patterning that has its most concrete instantiation in the *Iliad*, where the phrase and its cognate verb *kosmeô* are used in remarking on the battle array.[13] In the *Odyssey*, *kata kosmon* and the related phrase *kata moiran* ("in due portion") indicate a suitability, especially of words, that demonstrates a person's attention to propriety and thus manifests the orderliness of his character. When this coherence is not maintained, others remark upon it and draw attention to the precise nature of the disorder.

Not surprisingly, Odysseus figures in one of the most famous incidents of this kind. In Phaeacia, when the handsome Euryalus hypothesizes that their weary guest is not participating in sport because he is lower class, Odysseus points out that the young man is behaving inappropriately to a guest (*Od.* 8.158ff.). His angry response is aimed at instruction in suitable speech, and he uses this notion of coherence between one's appearance and one's behavior to explain the misstep: while the god may "crown with beauty" the words even of the ugly man (ἄλλος μὲν γὰρ εἶδος ἀκιδνότερος πέλει ἀνήρ, / ἀλλὰ θεὸς μορφὴν ἔπεσι στέφει, 8.170), such grace may fail to adorn the speech of a man of godlike beauty (ἄλλος δ' αὖ εἶδος μὲν ἀλίγκιος ἀθανάτοισιν, / ἀλλ' οὔ οἱ χάρις ἀμφιπεριστέφεται ἐπέεσσιν, 175).[14] Accordingly, he deems Euryalus' words οὐ κατὰ κόσμον (8.179).[15]

As a deceitful, complex, and clever speaker, Odysseus himself sometimes tests the limits of what constitutes appropriate speech. For instance, when he meets up with the faithful Eumaeus on Ithaca he tries to convince him that he has encountered "Odysseus" in his travels (*Od.* 14.321). Although he employs a tactic that suits his mendicant disguise, the swineherd is suspicious of such an obviously ingratiating ploy and replies caustically that his interlocutor speaks οὐ κατὰ κόσμον in attempting this particular technique (*Od.* 14.363). Although the beggar's claim thus arouses some suspicion as to his ability to adhere to the truth, it also conforms with his lowly status, in that such overstepping of oneself would be expected of a man in straightened circumstances. At significant junctures in the *Odyssey* both Helen and Odysseus are praised by others as speaking appropriately (*kata* or *ou para moiran*), an assessment that seems most often to be a response to speeches whose veracity is in some question. In book 4, for example, when Helen tells Telemachus about his father's spying mission to Troy and in so doing depicts herself as loyal to the Greek cause, Menelaus praises her tale as appropriate (κατὰ μοῖραν, *Od.* 4.266) but then proceeds to contradict her version of where her sympathies lay. Similarly, later in book 14 the disguised Odysseus tells a story about "Odysseus" using a harmless lie to get a cloak. This time Eumaeus applauds his tale as in keeping with the moment (οὐ παρὰ μοῖραν, 14.509), even though he views it as a clever trick.[16]

In the Homeric Hymns the notion of *kosmos* surfaces especially in describing the activities of the two gods who serve as the divine counterparts of Helen and Odysseus: Aphrodite and Hermes. In the *Hymn to Hermes,* the trickster god makes use of his ability to sing in a suitable fashion to woo his interlocutor Apollo into forgetting the theft of his cattle. The "versatile" Hermes, who is a flatterer and a thief (πολύτροπον, αἱμυλομήτην, / ληιστῆρ', *h.Merc.* 13–14), cradles his lyre like a pro and recites poetry *kata kosmon* when he is trying to charm his brother (433; cf. 479).[17] Hermes' tricks, moreover, include the performance of type as a disguise. He uses an infantile bodily *hexis*—drawing his arms and legs close to his body, toying with his blankets, cooing, and speaking in a mild and ignorant manner—as a cover for his very grown-up theft of Apollo's cattle. That is, he pretends to be another type to persuade his brother that he is not like (οὐδέ . . . ἔοικα, 265) a cattle thief, and thus that it is not probable that he committed the theft.[18]

Persuasion and deceit are also allied in the longer hymn in praise of Aphrodite (e.g., *h.Ven.* 5.33). In it and its shorter partner, *kosmos* and *kosmeô* describe Helen's patron goddess adorning her beautiful body with help of the Charites (5; cf. *Od.* 8.364–366) or the Hours (6). The elaborate detail of the process recalls the bedecking of Pandora in Hesiod (*h.Ven.* 5.65, 162; 6.11, 12, 14), which achieves an emphatically visual and dangerously deceitful persuasion.[19] In the hymn, Aphrodite decorates her body to seduce the mortal Anchises into bedding down unknowingly with a goddess. She then lies in response to Anchises' awe-struck viewing of her decorated body (cf. χρυσῷ κοσμηθεῖσα, 65), asking why he likens her to the immortal goddesses (τί μ' ἀθανάτῃσιν ἐΐσχεις, 109). Although she has taken elaborate pains to adorn her divine form, she pretends that she is just another pretty maiden who coyly demurs when likened to the gods. In this case, bodily *hexis* suggests a type like but not exactly matching the identity of the speaker. As with Helen and Odysseus, both figures' essential traits are emblematic of stylistic deceits, but the one focuses attention on bodily beauty and decoration, the other, on the cunningly mutable corporeal style.

Pindar also uses *kosmos* to denote the form of words, but for the epinician poet *kosmos* is primarily positive, meaning something like "fitting decoration." It can thus apply to both epinician poetry and the victor's crown. The poet may build an "elaborate, speaking decoration of words" (ποικίλον κόσμον αὐδάεντα λόγων, fr. 194.2), or a "silver-colored decoration of olive leaves" (γλαυκόχροα κόσμον ἐλαίας) may be tossed upon the victor's head (*Ol.* 3.13). The hymn may add a "sweet-singing decoration" (κόσμον . . . ἁδυμελῆ) to the victor's crown (*Ol.* 11.13), or the victor himself may be an ornament (κόσμον) for the city (*Nem.* 2.8), as may the epinician poet's composition (*Nem.* 6.53).[20] Slanderous, "hateful" (ἐχθρά) tales of the gods, in contrast, are deemed "beyond due measure" (παρὰ καιρόν) by Pindar (*Ol.* 9.36–37) in a passage that recalls Homeric notions of stylistic proportion and suitability.[21] If *kosmos* designates a recognizable, accepted, or appropriate ordering of parts, *para kairon* or *moiran* would be its opposite: a manner of engaging that does not conform to acceptable (i.e., assessed and measured) modes of behavior.

For the sophist Gorgias, the leading proponent of the grand oral style, *kosmos* similarly designates positive attributes, fitting ornamentation that is therefore praiseworthy. His display piece *The Encomium of Helen* in fact takes many of its cues from praise poetry. When he employs the term *kosmos* at the outset of his elaborate speech defending Helen, he seems to be claiming for encomiastic oratory what Pindar claims for praise poetry: the support of the proper order of things, the suitable adornment of characters by laudatory words. Encomiastic speech is particularly dependent on the visual analogy, and Gorgias' theory of persuasion relates the power of things seen to verbal imagery, seeking to demonstrate how one can be overcome by a combination of visual and verbal appeal, in an elaborate confection that reflects his own oratorical style (see further in ch. 5). Again, as with Pindar, Gorgias' use of the term emphasizes its positive aspects, that is, the coherent patterning of elements to forge an orderly integration of visible type and social setting.

In some contrast, tragedy explicitly mingles the encomiastic associations of *kosmos* with the threatening and deceitful aspects of adornment. Variants of the word are most frequently deployed in arming and burial rituals, whose motives may be feigned, thus also raising questions about the masquerading nature of the genre itself. Characters in tragedy are often fitted out for combat or the tomb; in Euripides' tragedies in particular, they sometimes trick each other regarding just what it is they are dressing up to do (e.g., *IT, Hel., El., Med.*). In keeping with the grim focus of tragedy, the occasion is usually the real or apparent death of a character, or at the least a threat to his well-being. *Kosmos* takes on sinister associations precisely because it has to do with both decorum and decoration, that is, with proper suiting for the warrior or honors for the dead, finery that may mask simultaneously physical appearance and true intention.

In fact, Euripides quite generally uses *kosmos* and its cognates to denote the decorative concealment of trickery or wrong-doing.[22] Often appearance and speaking style are thereby associated, so that a decorative bodily *hexis* parades a craven character and/or betrays an internal disorder better concealed. In the *Andromache*, for instance, Hermione first appears elaborately dressed. With her haughty speaking style (cf. πνέοντες μεγάλα τοὺς κρείσσους λόγους, 189), golden adornment (κόσμος . . . χρυσέας χλιδῆς), and embroidered gown (στολμόν . . . τόνδε ποικίλων πέπλων, 147–148) she is very much her mother's daughter. Later she emerges with her dress disordered, torn open to reveal her breast (again like her mother), and complains in fulsome fashion that she has done wrong as a result of being exposed to the "embroidering" (ποικίλων, 937) female gossips in her household. The chorus responds that women should prettily cover up (κοσμεῖν) their own and other women's "feminine weaknesses" (τὰς γυναικείας νόσους, 956).[23] We might compare also a critical juncture in Sophocles' *Philoctetes*, when Odysseus, the character who trains others to speak in an embroidering fashion (ποικίλως, 130), seizes the bow of the wounded and sympathetic Philoctetes. The seizure prompts the victim of his deception to question whether this wily sophistic type, adorned (κοσμηθείς) with Philoctetes' weapon, will now strut in front of the Argive troops (1063–1064).

Plato takes the danger that tragedy so often associates with cosmetic effect to its logical conclusion: the elaborate, cunning style of the seasoned orator in itself suggests deceit. When, for example, Socrates claims in Plato's *Apology* that he will not speak in any beautifully wrought, carefully arranged style (κεκαλλιεπημένους γε λόγους . . . ῥήμασί τε καὶ ὀνόμασιν οὐδὲ κεκοσμημένους, 17b15–c1), he connects his own simple style (εἰκῇ λεγόμενα τοῖς ἐπιτυχοῦσιν ὀνόμασιν, 17c2) to just claims (δίκαια . . . λέγω, 17c2, 18a5), to that which is suitable (πρέποι, 17c3), and especially to truth-telling (τὸν τἀληθῆ λέγοντα; ἀκούσεσθε πᾶσαν τὴν ἀλήθειαν; τἀληθῆ λέγειν, 17b5, 17b8, 18a6).[24] Since Socrates also pointedly disclaims any ability to speak cleverly with a phrase that manifestly invokes the agility of sophistic tactics (δεινὸς λέγειν, 17b1, b3, b4–5), his truthful, simple style is meant to distinguish him especially from this dangerous type. Interestingly, scholars have argued that the speech is strongly influenced by Gorgias' *Palamedes*, a set piece composed by the foremost proponent of the elaborate style Socrates rejects.[25] Nevertheless, the comparatively plain forensic style of the *Palamedes*, and the fact that it emphasizes the visibility of the virtuous character, may have recommended it to Plato as a model for his depiction of Socrates and Socrates' simple, casual style. Plato clearly reacted against what he felt to be the moral implications of Gorgias' elaborate oral style, even as he was appropriating some of his forensic techniques for his own purposes.[26] In the *Phaedrus* he pillories those who compose speeches in this ornamental mode, calling the rhetorician Theodorus a "speech embroiderer" (λογοδαίδαλος, 266e4), a reference that Cicero takes to apply especially to Thrasymachus and, of course, to Gorgias (*Orat.* 39).[27]

Plato's *Gorgias* signals an important turning point in ideas associated with *kosmos*. The dialogue maintains the word's demarcation of both visible and conceptual coherence but valorizes the latter to the detriment and ultimate rejection of the former. Plato treats *kosmos* as encompassing both a physical order (i.e., health) and a psychic order (i.e., *sôphrosunê*), the latter of which he regards as far more important and relates to social and world order.[28] In a contentious and startlingly innovative move, Plato thus subjugates the *kosmos* of visible and tactile things to that of ineffable entities. For instance, he deems the body an ornament (κόσμος) of the soul that serves to inhibit just judgment in Hades (*Gorg.* 523e6). While this essentially follows Euripides' depiction of the decorative, visually oriented aspect of *kosmos* as something negative and suspect, Plato's parallel use of the adjective *kosmios* reveals a new emphasis, in that it applauds the responsible but essentially invisible private citizen.[29] While the word itself may seem to encourage comparison to Pindar's notion of the good citizen who adorns (*kosmeô*) the city, Plato's *kosmios* man resists precisely the kind of public display that Pindar praises. As a restrained and internally coherent type, the *kosmios* man is also directly opposed to the portrait of Gorgias that Plato creates: a teacher of decorative verbal techniques who does not comprehend the limitations of his superficial "knack" (*empeiria*). From Plato's perspective, Gorgias' elaborate oral style may involve a superficial type of *kosmos*, but the true kind of *kosmos*—that involving the soul—belongs to a man of quite a different sort than the sophistic teacher of rhetoric.

Aristotle also revises the semantics of *kosmos*, but he does so by emphasizing its visual (and therefore relatively superficial) application rather than by promoting its moral implications. In Aristotle's rhetorical theory, *kosmos* comes to refer specifically to an ornamental style of written speech especially associated with Gorgias. This restricted range parallels Aristotle's limitation of style to types of verbal embellishment. This kind of *kosmos* most often denotes figures of speech and more elaborate usage, a meaning retained by later writers such as Demetrius and Dionysius.[30] In the *Rhetoric* Aristotle introduces his discussion of style by criticizing those "uneducated" masses (οἱ πολλοὶ τῶν ἀπαιδεύτων) who appreciate a poetical style (ποιητικὴ . . . λέξις) in speeches; he cites Gorgias as the style's leading proponent (1404a24–28). Earlier poets, Aristotle maintains, used to adorn (ἐκοσμοῦν) their writing with unusual words, but this would be a laughable (γελοῖον) stylistic practice for oratory (1404a34). However, a few lines later he admits that this decorated (κεκοσμημένην) style can be useful when one desires to give one's subject matter a lofty quality (1404b4–8). In the section preceding this, Aristotle remarks that actors of his day have greater influence on the audience than the poets themselves and that the same is true of impressive speakers in oratory.

Since rhetoric in general is concerned with opinion (*doxa*)—that is, with how things appear—the good orator must be attentive in his oral performance to how he presents both himself and the subject at hand. The orator's careful matching of deportment and character type to audience and subject matter is all the more crucial, Aristotle suggests uncomfortably, because of the corruption (μοχθηρίαν, 1403b35, 1404a8) of both Athenian governance and the individual audience member. Democratic practice has become a spectacle similar in its appeal to dramatic performance. This lamentable circumstance has meant that such vulgar (φορτικός, 1404a35) topics as delivery must be discussed, to facilitate addressing its equivalent in writing: verbal style.

The visual imagery of such scenes in tragedy as Hermione's grandiose entrance and subsequent disheveled accusations emphasizes the connections between internal states and external appearance, an emphasis not lost on Aristotle. In the *Poetics* he remarks that a necessary aspect of tragedy is the ordering of spectacle (ὁ τῆς ὄψεως κόσμος, 1449b32). Although he carefully avoids discussing visual effect (e.g., scene-painting [*skênographia*], costumes) and the related topic of actors' delivery (e.g., gesture, vocal modulation), the representation of character in tragedy is repeatedly analogized to painting, so that objects of sight remain central to understanding dramatic effect.[31] Elsewhere in the *Poetics* Aristotle uses *kosmos* to denote embellishment, either of the tragic form by episodic and metrical alterations (1449a28) or of tragic language by a certain "ornamental" type of word (1457b2). The definition of this kind of verbal ornament may have been given in a lacuna in the text (1457b33ff.). Discussions in book 3 of the *Rhetoric* suggest that the fanciful metaphors and neologizing compounds for which Gorgias was famous constitute the core of the decorative style in writing.[32]

Thus Aristotle ultimately transforms *kosmos* and its cognates from a word group that joins social order with physical adornment, and suitable speech with good character, to one that concerns only a kind of superficial embellishment in written language. This move parallels his reduction of more inclusive notions of style to diction (*lexis*). Aristotle's disinclination to discuss issues of spectacle and delivery in both the *Poetics* and the *Rhetoric* reflects this narrowing of perspective, a turning away from the overwhelming impact of style in oral performance to its more narrowly circumscribed function in the written text. This in itself reflects a concern that the force of typical and therefore convincing styles in the moment of performance might carry too much weight with the "corrupt" crowd of Athenian citizens. Aristotle's transformation of the full impact of oratorical and dramatic effects into the thin stylistic veneer provided by pleasing verbal figures reflects in a more pragmatic form the negative reaction of his teacher Plato to oratory and poetry. Yet in the *Poetics* in particular, Aristotle's own language suggests that his thought is nevertheless informed by visual effect: he repeatedly associates character and visual patterns, implicitly reinvigorating the broader notion of *kosmos* that he seems explicitly to reject.

The importance of the word *kosmos* for this discussion lies, then, in its emphasis on visual analogy, on the notion that an order that can be seen (or at least visualized) may extend to internal states, social rankings, and perhaps especially verbal expression. But even in Homer the notion of *kosmos* also includes the possibility of its opposite, as figures like the hideous but eloquent Thersites and the beautiful but rude Euryalus suggest.[33] The characters of Odysseus and Helen especially suggest the possibility that one may be led astray, even deceived, by how things appear. This deception is the result of the combined effects of how one speaks and how one looks, the distracting bodily *hexis* that becomes a focus of concern in late fifth-century tragedy and oratory. Plato was not the only writer of the classical period to notice that both venues capitalize on the influence that powerful verbal imagery can have on human motivation, especially when combined with visual effects. This verbal and visual masquerade took its most elaborate form in tragedy, and the dramatists themselves show apprehension about this aspect of their medium. As a proponent of the flamboyant style that most frequently aroused such anxieties, Gorgias was said to have declared provocatively that deception in tragedy was an indication of the dramatist's success.[34] Tragic characters often demonstrated on stage precisely how visual effects and compelling imagery can confound right-minded argument, while the elaborate style of the sophistic orator, in combination with his fancy dress and dramatic gestures, aroused similar suspicions.[35] Dramatists and philosophical writers were both in their different ways reacting to a danger perceived as inherent in the visually persuasive oral performance.

CHARAKTÊR AND ÊTHOS

The concern in archaic and classical texts with the kosmos of one's dress and demeanor stands in rather complex relation to the ideas covered by êthos, a word that turns up in later archaic and classical usage and is commonly translated "[moral] character."[36] Unlike the visually oriented word charaktêr, êthos is more ambiguous between internal disposition and external characteristics. In this it resembles the word phusis ("nature"), which—oddly for modern readers—may designate visibly identifiable attributes or an inherited internal disposition.[37] In Homer and Hesiod êthos is used in the plural for customary places ("haunts") or social practices ("customs"). It is rare in the singular, although in one significant place, Hesiod gives it a meaning closer to that which it has later (WD 67, 78), when he refers to the deceitful disposition that Hermes gives to Pandora, the elaborately fabricated female figure whose ornamental exterior masks her deceitful type. The poet says explicitly that Hermes "put into" Pandora a "thievish disposition" (ἐν δὲ θέμεν . . . ἐπίκλοπον ἦθος, WD 67), clearly contrasting her lovely external and nasty internal features.

Among the archaic poets, Theognis offers the most interesting data for early conceptions of êthos. Sometimes, as seems to be the case in Hesiod, he uses êthos to denote an internal state that may nevertheless be revealed, as when he declares that although many men hide a counterfeit, thievish disposition (κίβδηλον ἐπίκλοπον ἦθος), the true type of each is shown forth (ἐκφαίνει) over time (965–967). In other passages, Theognis points more directly to the visible behaviors and deportments that mark one as a particular type. Once he exhorts himself (213) and once his young advisee

Kurnos (1071) to turn a variegated disposition (ἐπίστρεφε ποικίλον ἦθος) toward all friends. This treatment of *êthos* depicts it as a versatile device that matches in its effects the dissembling garments or evasive bodily deportment of a type like Odysseus.[38] Another passage seems to contradict this advice. The poet addresses an unnamed advisee with the admonition that although his body is beautiful in form (τὴν μορφὴν), a mighty and foolish crown (καρτερὸς ἀγνώμων ... στέφανος) rests upon his head (1259–1260). This crown of foolishness results, it appears, from his disposition having the mobility of a quick-wheeling bird of prey (ἰκτίνου ... ἀγχιστρόφου ... ἦθος), persuaded as he is by the words of other men (1261–1262). While versatility in typical style may protect one, inconstancy of outlook and allegiance makes one a danger to oneself and others. Theognis thus often treats *êthos* as something visible but ephemeral, a quality of mind that can be read by the attentive observer on the face and in the deportment of his fellow citizens.[39] By likening *êthos* to the changeable sheen of garments and the twisted posturings of the elusive sea creature or the hunting bird, his visual imagery suggests that the tinctures, shapes, and movements of character can be assessed and understood only by the eyewitness experience of it.

Among such visual images, the "variegated disposition" (*poikilos êthos*) of the circumspect citizen is also particularly interesting for this discussion. In archaic poetry this multifaceted quality is often viewed as an essential trait of the especially clever, agile type. In Homer Odysseus has a *poikilos* intelligence (ποικιλομήτης: *Il.* 11.482; *Od.* 3.163, 7.168, 13.293, 22.115, 22.202, 22.281), as elsewhere do Hermes (*h.Merc.* 155, 514) and Prometheus (ποικίλον αἰολόμητιν, *Th.* 511; ποικιλόβουλον, *Th.* 521).[40] The use of *poikilos* to designate the versatile and sometimes too variegated type carries over into the fifth century, during which time it also explicitly denotes speaking style and becomes increasingly negative in its application. Like *kosmos,* then, *poikilos* comes to serve as a bridging term between behavioral traits and verbal characteristics. Even more interestingly, this zeugma also ultimately spawns derogatory usage. We might note that both *kosmos* and *poikilos* take on their most negative connotations when they are used in contexts where image-laden praise speech and fancy dress focus attention on visuality. In Pindar and especially in tragedy, the very notion of adornment can spark anxiety about what that adornment may mask. The dramatic medium centers on the display of character, but this very display leads inevitably to questions about the veracity of what is seen.[41] Both *kosmos* and *poikilos* highlight this dilemma, in the emphasis they place on elaborate decoration and ornamental detail.

Pindar, for example, declares that "tales decorated with elaborate lies are deceiving" (δεδαιδαλμένοι ψεύδεσι ποικίλοις ἐξαπατῶντι / μῦθοι, Ol. 1.29–30).[42] In tragedy *poikilos* and its combined forms can designate elaborate styles of attitude, language, and dress, sometimes in the same speech. In Aeschylus' *Agamemnon* the king reacts with suspicion to his wife's offerings of richly woven materials (ποικίλοις κάλλεσιν, 923) and intricate flattery (τῶν ποικίλων / κληδών, 926–927). Elsewhere the repetition of the word similarly serves to mark a menacing connection between elaborate finery and speaking styles that both portend evil. Recall that Euripides' Hermione adorns herself with elaborately worked clothing (ποικίλων πέπλων, *Andr.* 148) but later charges that others corrupted her with their "elaborate chatter" (ποικίλων λαλημάτων, 937). Euripides' *Medea* traces a particularly threatening zeugma between mental capacity and bodily adornment. Medea describes putatively clever types as "those thinking that they know some intricate thing" (τῶν δοκούντων εἰδέναι τι ποικίλον, 300); later her gift to Creusa of poisonous elaborate clothing (ποικίλους πέπλους, 1159) suggests that it is the deadly manifestation of a clever, intricate mind.[43]

Other tragedies focus more fully on the connection between mental type and language use, revealing that the "intricate" quality of mind makes for a deceptive or at least overly flexible style of speech—the paradigmatic example of which is Odysseus. In Sophocles' *Philoctetes* Odysseus warns Neoptolemus that a henchman in disguise (who serves as a double of the hero) will speak intricately (ποικίλως αὐδωμένου, 130). In *Iphigenia in Aulis* Odysseus himself is regarded by Agamemnon as being "always subtle and with the crowd" (ποικίλος ἀεὶ ... τοῦ τ' ὄχλος μέτα, 526); in *Hecuba* he is deemed by the chorus "a subtle-minded, sweet-talking, people-pleasing wrangler" (ὁ ποικιλόφρων / κόπις ἡδυλόγος δημοχαριστής, 133). In tragedy, then, *poikilos* always carries with it the connotation of visibly suspect finery, whether of dress, attitude, or speaking style. It is the versatile, deceitful, disguise-loving characters who make use of such intricate self-performances.[44] These characters are the opposite of the intractable, virtuous heroic types, and their complex and changeable attitudes intimate their dangerously flexible, persuasive, even demagogic talents.[45]

If the *poikilos* character can be witnessed by his versatile bodily *hexis*, this visibility may also be found in fifth- and fourth-century ideas about *êthos* more generally. Christopher Gill has argued that the meaning of *êthos* in the classical period should not be conflated with modern notions of character, that is, as a term that encompasses the whole being of an individual. He stresses that the word has a much more restricted application that arises from traditional notions of types of people, denoting "character-markers" such as a person's speeches that indicate moral stances, significant actions, and type-revealing statements made by others.[46] Russell describes the use of character in fifth- and fourth-century logography with a similar emphasis on visible type: "A speech-writer—Lysias is the most celebrated—has to put himself in his client's place, make him say nothing inconsistent with his visible personality, and at the same time make him a representative of an acceptable type."[47] The singular usage that arises in this period seems still to retain some of its earlier usage (in the plural) of "customary places" or "customs," in its suggestion of behaviors and bodily attitudes that can be seen, recognized, and assessed because they are habitual and thus repeatedly witnessed. In tragedy *êthos* may denote visible attributes of the individual, sometimes as distinct from a person's nature (*phusis*).[48] The lion ode in Aeschylus' *Agamemnon* speaks of *êthos* as something that is displayed (ἀπέδειξεν, 727), while in the *Persians* the *êthê* of Darius are treated by the chorus as if they were concrete attributes: they have been buried along with the man (649). A person can also bear (φόρει) an *êthos* like a mantle (Soph. *Ant.* 705).[49]

The word *charaktêr* points more emphatically than *êthos* to a visible and schematic conception of character, and it thus more precisely matches the merging of verbal style with visible type that grounds Bourdieu's notion of bodily *hexis*. As mentioned above, the word *charaktêr* originally designated the stamp on a genuine coin, more generally connoting the visible marks that indicate authentic type. Herodotus uses the word to denote other distinctive marks, including performative ones such as those of a dialect or a facial expression.[50] A number of Euripides' choruses use *charaktêr* to designate the distinctive marks that they wish might indicate the true worth of a person.[51] One of these instances, the hymn to youth in the *Heracles*, claims that the hero's return from Hades stamps him clearly as a virtuous man (659). Subsequent events challenge this claim, when the hero is transformed from a glorious victor (καλλίνικον, 40, 180, 570, 582, 681, 788) into a "victor over no one" (καλλίνικος οὐδενός, 961), who in his madness shadow boxes with imagined enemies and turns on his own family.[52] The passage suggests that the visible stamp of *charaktêr*, like the decorative effects demarcated by *kosmos* and *poikilos*, may mislead those who have eyewitness experience of it.

There is some indication that by the mid to late fifth century, writers had begun to employ *charaktêr* to delineate distinctive style or type in a linguistic sense and that its meaning may well have overlapped with that of *lexis*. According to Diogenes Laertius, Gorgias' pupil Antisthenes wrote a treatise entitled *Peri Lexeôs ê Peri Charaktêrôn* (DL 6.15), as well as illustrations of these ideas, such as the extant set speeches *Odysseus* and *Ajax*. While Diogenes may be recording a title given to the work at some later period, it nevertheless reflects the assumption that Antisthenes was working with a notion of *charaktêr* associated with verbal style, which likely involved ideas about how different styles ought to suit different character types to be persuasive. The word probably did not denote a speaker's style in a strongly technical sense until later, however, when theorists of rhetoric attempt to delineate the distinctive speaking styles of famous orators.[53]

The relationship between linguistic style and character type thus had clearly been under negotiation before Aristotle. But as with his treatment of style, Aristotle's handling of character rejects these more fluid associations in favor of a perspective that largely restricts character to internal states.[54] He uses the word *êthos* in his discussions of character (e.g., *NE* 2.1), perhaps because *charaktêr* carries such strong connotations of visibly identifiable markings and had already come to be used to mean something like style. In the *Rhetoric êthos* designates moral qualities apprehended primarily through language. Aristotle treats the delineation of different *êthê* as a central aspect of constructing an effective speech. Here self-presentation clearly involves the projection of emotions suited to both one's subject matter and one's audience (cf. especially 1390a25–28). The key features of the persuasive character, however, are positive and calming ones: wisdom, virtue, and goodwill (φρόνησις καὶ ἀρετὴ καὶ εὔνοια, 1378a8). Aristotle insists, again, that character must be perceived "through speech" (διὰ τοῦ λόγου) and not through some preconceived notion that the speaker is "some type" (ποιόν τινα, 1356a9–a10).

The projection of *êthos* thus dovetails with the style of the speech. It is imbedded in its manner of argumentation, since certain types of people would use certain types of arguments and couch them in similarly suitable vocabulary. Moreover, *êthos* does not only involve some general impression of the speaker's goodwill, although this helps the audience to think of him as some type (ποιόν τινα) that they would trust (1366a10–12). It also helps to mold an argument that, in turn, communicates character (ἠθικὸς λόγος, 1366a9–10) and that suits both the subject at hand and the audience. In this same passage, Aristotle treats suitability (τὸ πρέπον) as ideally coordinating speaker, audience, and subject matter, so that the speaker may effect both a recognition of himself as a trustworthy, familiar type and a positive reception of his speech as an equally trustworthy and appropriate extension of this type.[55] Thus the representation of character should also shape the narrative section of the speech, where one may cast aspersions on one's opponent or highlight one's own correct decision making (προαίρεσις, 1417a15–25).[56] It is only here that Aristotle indicates his awareness that the êthos may be communicated visibly. At 1417a22–24, Aristotle uses the example of walking and talking at the same time (ἅμα λέγων ἐβάδιζεν) as a clear indication of audacity and rudeness (δηλοῖ γὰρ θρασύτητα καὶ ἀγροικίαν ἤθους).

In the *Poetics* the references to *êthos* similarly indicate that Aristotle conceives of it as inhering not in any particular person but rather in any speech that delineates a set of behaviors or attitudes (e.g., 1450b8).[57] *Êthos* constitutes an aspect of each type (*genos*) of person, which may be communicated in a speech or action (1454a15–16). This idea indicates the importance of social categories to Aristotle's analysis of character, as well as suggesting the interchangeability of type that is central to dramatic mimesis, which would clearly suggest moral issues for the orator. This underlying problem may account for Aristotle's treatment of *êthos* in the *Rhetoric* being so much more limited and elliptical than one might expect. He recommends, for example, that the orator take care to hide the artificiality and plasticity of the performance of type (διὸ δεῖ λανθάνειν ποιοῦντας, καὶ μὴ δοκεῖν λέγειν πεπλασμένως ἀλλὰ πεφυκότως, *Rhet.* 1404b18–19). The statement itself indicates an awareness that the orator's mutability in this regard resembles that of the dramatic actor. In the *Poetics,* where he similarly avoids discussion of the character's manner of delivery and appearance, Aristotle nevertheless implicitly acknowledges the importance of looking like a particular type. Here he follows most references to *êthos* with analogies to painting, suggesting that features of a type could be seen in a manner similar to the disposition of physical form traced by the visual artist (1448a1–9, 1450a18–29, 1450a38–b4). The poet is repeatedly compared to the painter (e.g., 1454b8–14, 1460b8–12); the type of poetic language that brings up images "before the eyes" (πρὸ ὀμμάτων) leads Aristotle to mention gesture and bodily deportment (τοῖς σχήμασιν) (1455a21–30) as important ways of communicating type and emotion. One wears one's character like a set of clothes, whose features are made visible by one's bodily *hexis*.

In both the *Rhetoric* and the *Poetics*, Aristotle explicitly focuses on moral disposition as a central means of counteracting this dependence on visual assessment of character. By emphasizing the linguistic projection of moral type and skirting the importance of visual effects through analogies to painting, Aristotle initiates a move away from the understanding of character as essentially visible. Character becomes instead a central component in speechmaking for the delineating of moral disposition, which Aristotle implies governs the choice of linguistic style. This treatment of character was less influential in subsequent rhetorical theory than in philosophical debate; there seems to have been some confusion and differences of opinion among later rhetorical theorists regarding what *êthos* originally denoted. Quintilian puts the problem most pointedly, when he worries that the word has no Latin equivalent, since *mores* (the closest parallel) refers to all moral behavior rather than specifically to the measured and honorable demeanor of the trust-inspiring speaker (Inst. Orat. 6.28–9). The latter is the meaning he tentatively attributes to *êthos*, which it had acquired by the first century C.E. Hermogenes treats *êthos* as one of seven stylistic categories, the one that included elements of the so-called middle style such as clarity (σαφήνεια) and beauty (καλλός) (*Peri Id.*; cf. Cic. *Orat.* 36, 134). Aristotle's handling of *êthos* as a term primarily designating moral qualities that govern stylistic choice thus eventually develops into the reverse: *êthos* becomes subordinate to style (*idea*), a category delineating some of its calmer effects.

VISUALITY AND THE WRITTEN WORD

The fifth-century sophist Prodicus told a story about Heracles' moral education, which is paraphrased by Socrates in Xenophon's *Memorabilia* (2.1.21–33). It deserves some consideration here, since it crystallizes traditional ideas about the visibility of character.[58] The narrative relates the hero's choice between Virtue (Aretê) and Vice (Kakia) in emphatically visual terms: the details of their bodily *hexeis* (i.e., speech, dress, and deportment) reflect precisely their moral types.[59] The figure of Aretê is adorned with the "deportment of moderation" (κεκοσμημένην . . . τὸ δὲ σχῆμα σωφροσύνης) and she is dressed in white. The form and deportment of Kakia is marked by artifice; her beauty is only deceptively appealing (ὥστε δοκεῖν τῆς φύσεως εἶναι, 22). The flirtatious gaze is particularly highlighted. Kakia not only

looks immoral (i.e., over-dressed and vain), but her own manner of looking is equally so (τὰ δὲ ὄμματα ἔχειν ἀναπεπταμένα), while Aretê's eyes
are "adorned" with modesty (κεκοσμημένην . . . τὰ δὲ ὄμματα αἰδοῖ, 22).
Kakia's style of speech underscores her suggestive deportment. She offers
Heracles what Aretê later terms "preludes of pleasure" (προοιμίους ἡδονῆς,
27), a string of participles that describe ongoing sensory delights, free from
challenging activity, delights that her own appearance crystallizes. Aretê's
chaste speech, in contrast, contains a series of verbal adjectives expressing
necessity, a list of duties to city and self (28). Thus these embodiments of
moral order (or its lack) deport themselves, dress, and speak in a manner
that shows the eyewitness Heracles precisely what they are.

In Xenophon's rather old-fashioned portrait, Socrates paraphrases Prodicus in support of his own argument that virtue requires strenuous effort,
but he offers little comment or criticism of the sophist's tale. He does remark
that Prodicus told the original story in fancier form, as befits the orator's
mode (ἐκόσμησε μέντοι τὰς γνώμας ἔτι μεγαλειοτέροις ῥήμασιν, 34). But
he retains the sophist's connection between visible form and moral type,
without redirecting attention to the conceptual entity. As Andrea Nightingale has discussed, Plato makes quite a different use of these intertextual
moments, in that he always frames his generic borrowings with revisions
of their emphases and aims.[60] Such appropriation and innovation is absent
from Xenophon's account; the introduction of a moral tale, which itself follows the tradition of wisdom poetry, into the philosophical dialogue arouses
little comment and is allowed to stand as a defensible portrayal of moral
attitudes.

Xenophon, like many fourth-century writers, thus adheres more closely
to traditional emphases on the visibility of character. Plato's influential rejection of visible attributes as superficial changed this easy association and
sparked open controversy about the importance of appearances. His stron-
gest opponent on many rhetorical topics was Isocrates, whose writerly attitudes nevertheless maintain a firm connection between the kind of visibility
essential to the active citizen and the embellished verbal style that con-
formed with his easily witnessed virtues.[61] Encomiastic genres in particular
fashion the portrait of the individual in terms of the external measures by
which he may be judged: actions, speech, deportment, physical appearance.
In the epilogue of his speech in praise of the Cypriot king Evagoras, for
example, Isocrates compares the praise speech to the sculpted or painted
portrait (73–75), a move that reinforces the centrality of visual analogies to

the genre.[62] The encomiast adorns his subject as might the visual artist. It is clear that this notion of visible ornament is especially suited to the praise genre; compare again Pindar's imagery of decoration.

By the fourth century, however, some writers have begun to regard this ornamentation as descriptive of written composition more generally, particularly the style that a kind of careful preparation entails. Such writerly composition—as opposed to speaking on one's feet, as Socrates supposedly does in the *Phaedrus*—is allied with Euripidean poetry and the "middle" or "thin" (μέσος, ἰσχνός) style of speech composition.[63] As a technique of the writerly type and especially the logographer (i.e., the paid speechwriter), this meticulously crafted style is viewed with suspicion by conservative writers such as Aristophanes.[64] But the grand style—Aeschylus' and Gorgias' style, the style apparently associated with oral performance—also incited reaction, particularly from Thucydides, Euripides, Plato, and Aristotle. By the late fifth century and into the fourth, any persuasive style that suggested manipulation, stunning cleverness, or deception of some kind (whether from an overabundance of fancy figures or an overly precise hairsplitting) came in for attack from one or the other direction.

A pamphlet entitled *Peri Sophistôn*, usually dated to the mid fourth century and attributed to Gorgias' student Alcidamas, focuses criticism on those who write speeches. Alcidamas defends what he considers the superior style of extemporaneous speaking, arguing that the spoken word is more powerful (i.e., closer to the "grand" style) and less susceptible to misrepresentation, because the speaker can respond, as written words cannot (cf. Pl. *Phdr.* 275d).[65] Near the end of the treatise, Alcidamas declares that written speeches should not even be called λόγοι, since they are really "copies and shapes and imitations" (εἴδωλα καὶ σχήματα καὶ μιμήματα) of speeches. Written words are thus more like statuary and paintings, themselves copies of real bodies (27). Both types of visible shapes bring delight (τέρψις) and amazement (ἔκπληξις), strong emotional reactions tht in persuasive settings distract the audience from the subject at hand.[66] For Alcidamas the ultimate danger in written words lies in their power to seem to be a mirror (κάτοπτρον) of the soul, to give deceptively easy access to human nature through this visual experience (32).[67] Alcidamas' arguments thus cleverly invert the kind of charges leveled at the grand oral style of his teacher Gorgias and for which he (Alcidamas) was also known. Where others had attacked the visual impact of the elaborate oral performance, Alcidamas claims that the written word possesses this dangerous attraction.

Alcidamas' pamphlet treats ideas more famously explored in the *Phae-drus*, where Lysias the speechwriter is roundly criticized, logography con-sidered a reprehensible craft (257c), the efficacy of the rhetorical manual (*technê rhetorikê*) questioned (266c), and Thrasymachus (the manual writer) treated as an audience manipulator (267c) and explicitly associated with Odysseus (261c).[68] Later in the dialogue, Socrates presents his own antidote to the problem with writing (i.e., composed speeches): the true art of decla-mation lies in the knowledge of the speech appropriate to the nature (φύσις) of each listener. The good speechmaker must fashion on the spot a varie-gated speech for a variegated soul and so on (ποικίλη μὲν ποικίλους ψυχῇ καὶ παναρμονίους διδοὺς λόγους, 277c2–3).[69] Decades earlier Antisthenes apparently used a similar formula for how one ought to suit speech to audi-ence (πολυτροπία καὶ χρῆσις ποικίλη λόγου εἰς ποικίλας ἀκοάς, fr. 51 C).[70] But for Antisthenes the visual type suggested by ποικίλος, which highlights a verbal elaborateness and versatility of character, provides a perceptible link between speech and character, precisely on the strength of the visual image it suggests. From Plato's perspective, in some contrast, the persuasive impact of the visible world and visual imagery on the mind of the listener must be countered by attention to an underlying truth that cannot be per-ceived by the senses, although verbal and visual representation may, as Gill notes, "play a role in leading to knowledge."[71] Perhaps even more than that of Alcidamas, Plato's attitude stands in direct contrast to Isocrates' empha-sis on visuality. For Isocrates, as for many fifth- and fourth-century writers, the elaborate portraiture of the grand oral style is central to its emotional power, its unparalleled impact. These qualities align speaking style with the strongly visual experience of life among equally self-promotional Athenians in the visibly decorated city of Athens, which must have been second only in its impact on the eye to religious sanctuaries such as Delphi and Delos.

The relation between visible type and the *kosmos* of speaking style is in fact well articulated in the speeches of Isocrates. A consummate speech-writer whose compositions are clearly closer to set speeches and pamphlets, and who may never have himself declaimed in public, Isocrates nevertheless regards language as an active, visible entity. He gently mocks the decorative properties of *poikilia* when he writes of how he "dressed up" his language (ποικιλίαις κεκοσμήκαμεν) in his youth, but he admits that without the felicities of deportment and expression to sweeten a speech, it may seem "naked" (γυμνός, 5.25–27). Further connections between adornment, style, and visible type show up in other speeches: in *Demonicus* (15) he exhorts his addressee to consider the *kosmos* appropriate to himself, an embellishing of character (*êthos*) fashioned from the virtues that would chasten it. Elsewhere he explains how suitably ceremonial dress (ἐν ταῖς ἐσθῆσι καὶ τοῖς περὶ τὸ σῶμα κόσμοις) can persuade viewers (οἱ μὲν ὁρῶντες) that one is worthy of rule (*Nic.* 32). Encomiastic speech likewise decorates (κοσμεῖν) the deeds of prominent men, as instruction for the young in the virtuous character type. While poetry has recourse to many decorative flourishes (κόσμοι), as a writer of *encomia* Isocrates will adorn his subject in a manner suitable to prose (*Evag.* 5–8).

In *Republic* 10 and *Gorgias* 465b Plato uses similar imagery, although he does so with a more negative purpose, to denigrate the poet's ability. While the poet may color his words with decorative imagery (ἐπιχρωματίζειν),[72] stripped (γυμνωθέντα) of such enchantment (κήλησιν), his words are revealed as nothing special, like a plain face once it has lost the bloom of youth (*Rep.* 601a4–b6). Compare Plato's likening of rhetoric to cosmetics in the *Gorgias* (465b1–c2), which he deems not only deceitful (ἀπατηλή) but also involving an evil cunning (κακοῦργος). Adornment of the body deceives by deportment, make-up, polish, and clothes (σχήμασι καὶ χρώμασι καὶ λειότητι καὶ ἐσθήσει ἀπατῶσα, 465b4–5). Rhetoric operates in the same manner, imitating the good work of justice, as cookery does of medicine, sophistry of lawmaking, and cosmetics of exercise. For Plato, then, the kind of verbal dress that Isocrates envisions for projecting one's character in a rhetorical display instead highlights the deceitful cover that persuasive style effects.

The delineation of character type and style in archaic and classical literature thus follows a pattern of strong correlation between the visible and the intelligible, a range of ideas embraced by the word *kosmos.* The inclusive, correlating nature of the term reveals the impossibility of separating moral states from visible behaviors. This is the same mutually affecting interaction between beliefs and the body that Bourdieu argues for in his explanations of *habitus* and bodily *hexis.* For the ancient authors, however, it is clear that these are prescriptive as well as descriptive correlations. The same orderly patterns should mark character type, speaking style, and appearance, and their mismatch or versatile altering signals deception. Plato challenged this encompassing pattern of external and internal characteristics in his rejection of rhetoric as a kind of cosmetics. Aristotle sought to reduce its range to mere embellishment in written prose. Their revisions of traditional conceptions of the interaction between character and style effectively obscured—for modern readers if not as much for ancient—how both had been perceived. While some earlier ideas about style were maintained and developed in later rhetorical treatises, they have tended to be less influential in modern scholarship than those of Plato and Aristotle.

CHAPTER 2

ORAL PERFORMANCE, SPEECH TYPES, AND TYPICAL STYLES IN HOMER

Although this century has witnessed many important developments in the study of Homeric poetry as an oral medium, scholars still sometimes show a tendency to blur the distinctions between oral and written composition.[1] Even those most influenced by oral theory often treat spoken exchanges between Homeric characters as if the situations in which they take place involved only the words uttered. Yet the characters who speak in these exchanges are presented as engaging in face-to-face experiences of each other's oral performances, the effects of which the narrator frequently emphasizes by describing the stature, deportment, dress, and/or the intimate surroundings of the speaker.

The Homeric poet thus reproduces this visual experience in the visualizing style of his narration. The emphasis on sight arises from the eyewitnessing nature of oral genres, as Egbert Bakker has pointed out.[2] The oral poet uses sensory details and vibrant metaphors to invigorate the shapes, colors, and patterns of the event witnessed. He also inserts spatial and temporal markers to orient the listener in relation to the action, and organizes the visual experience sequentially so that the listening audience can follow his eye (as it were) from point to point in the scene depicted.[3] This envisioning of events encourages the experience of the scene as crucially visible. Thus when it centers on a spoken exchange, the oral poet depicts it as if he were an eyewitness of the speeches *as they were performed*, with all the important visual details, spatial orientations, and sequential patterns of the experience intact.

This visualizing style would have been reinforced for the listening audience by the performance of the rhapsode, whose lavish robes, shifting character impersonations, and emotive delivery constituted the visible extension of the narrative's imagery.[4] Whatever account one may give of how Homeric poetry made the transition from a product of ongoing oral composition to a definitive written form, the fact remains that the original material developed out of the social practices of an oral culture and that its narratives continued to be disseminated primarily through oral performance. Thus ideas about an individual's typical style of self-presentation would have developed in relation to this eyewitness experience, and the visual impact of the speaker would have been felt to be nearly as important as his words. Homer and other archaic poets effectively preserve this experience, in that they characterize both language itself and its visible performance by means of sensory image and synesthetic metaphor.

An analysis of the oral performances depicted in Homeric poetry should somehow take account of this eyewitness experience of language. The narratological approach promoted by Irene de Jong has focused attention on the speaker's apparent success in verbal exchange, such as whether she receives a respectful response, or whether her command is carried out. This in turn would have provided both the internal and the external audiences with clues for determining the relative status of the speaker.[5] While the emphasis in narratology remains on the utterance, elements such as deportment (e.g., whether a speaker is seated or standing) may also enter into the assessment of status. Narratology's focus on the context of utterance should dovetail neatly with a focus on the speaker's style and visible character, and yet most studies have not tended to take into account other visible elements such as dress and general appearance. Nor have they usually included any more precise analyses of speaking style and its relation to individual character types than can be gleaned from attention to status and perspective. Nevertheless, Richard Martin's study of speech performance in the *Iliad* broke new ground in differentiating heroes' verbal styles; Donald Lateiner's study of nonverbal behavior in Homer has helped focus attention on appearance.[6] The linguistically based analyses of Bakker have emphasized the close relationship between Homeric poetry and everyday speech, thus calling attention to performance strategies common to both. Bakker has also pointed to the importance of deictic (pointing) words, which may indicate the kind of significant gestures that would help to delineate a speaker's deportment in verbal exchanges.[7]

My treatment of the Homeric material differs from these approaches, while benefiting from the attention they have drawn to epic speech in performance. Because of their emphasis on orality, some of these scholars tend to downplay the literariness of Homer. But while Homeric characters' oral performances contain crucial information for analyzing archaic ideas about style, this does not entail their treatment as actual performers who existed independent of the literary tradition in which they are embedded. In fact, their "real" speech habits are heavily marked by culturally entrenched character typologies and mythohistorical convention. As figures in a literary tradition, they serve any number of semiotic functions beyond their particular appearances in narrative.[8] Like many studies of Homeric speech habits, this discussion looks to the experience of oral performance, the context of utterance, and audience reception for information about characters' styles. But it also treats the literary character as a semiotic entity, as a combination of semes that can only be fully understood within the context of the literary discourse that gives the character shape.

Helen and Odysseus are, moreover, both important characters in Homeric narrative and figures that emblematize larger ideas about visible character and style. They therefore function in a more essentially literary fashion than the average character, insofar as their significant features point to ideas about the linguistic and visual effects of epic. The vocabulary, phrasing, and verbal tones typical of these speakers—as well as details of the speech settings, their clothes, and their gestures or expressions—forge semiotic patterns that not only delineate their own typical styles but also indicate central aspects of style. The external narrator and the goddesses who intermittently manipulate Odysseus and Helen also attach certain visible details (especially clothing) to them that underscore their emblematic functions. Attention to such details should insure that crucial patterns of poetic semiosis are not lost in the focus on performance. These patterns affect how the character is perceived by the external audience and inform an understanding of her semiotic function in the larger literary tradition.

While Bourdieu's notion of bodily *hexis* comprises both the verbal and visual aspects of style, in the next two chapters I consider these aspects separately. This chapter primarily addresses the verbal features of the speaker's bodily *hexis*, which include lexical choices, figures, argumentative strategies (i.e., style at the level of invention), and any indications of vocal tone or cadence. Chapter 3 gathers the details of the speaker's visual impact, including those of dress, deportment, gesture, facial expression, and intimate setting (i.e., the objects and architectural or geographical spaces associated with him). This is an admittedly artificial division of the material, especially for a thesis that argues that these details must be taken together if one is to comprehend the full impact of the oral performance. But it also enables a clearer view of how the various aspects of oral performance intersect. The visualizing, tactile way early poetry characterizes language, which itself underscores the sensory impact of the impressive speaker on an audience, parallels the visual details that the narrator describes as significant aspects of the speaker's performance.

The imagery commonly used in archaic poetry to trace the impact of words on the senses is an important aspect of this interaction. The depictions indicate that audiences may perceive this impact as overwhelming or misleading, which suggests that honey-tongued speech is not necessarily indicative of trustworthy character. In Homer this apprehension occurs most notably in reaction to Helen and Odysseus, whose significant stylistic features I explore in detail below. Particularly in settings that call for guest-host formalities, Homer depicts both characters as deploying rhetorical tactics that flatter their interlocutors and encourage a sense of familiarity and allegiance. Such strategies seek to preempt negative reactions from their hearers and to distract them from attempting to discover true motivations or even identity. These characters are also shown to be sensitive to stylistic suitability and to be adept at forging images that look like the truth.

LANGUAGE AND THE SENSES IN ARCHAIC POETRY

In archaic poetry the adjectives that describe speaking style tend to point up tactile characteristics that give a sense of the locution's look, taste, or texture. The mouth itself seems to encourage this zeugma among its activities: it is the central organ that links speech to bodily *hexis,* thereby rendering it a visible event. The mouth not only forms tender words, it also tastes sweets that render the tongue charming and kisses softly.[9] Most of the characterizations that follow are very familiar to classicists; I rehearse them here merely to point out how they highlight the relation of language to bodily sensation and thus its effects in performance, focusing attention on the sensory impact of the speaker and the reactions of the audience. This emphasis on sensory experience is also important to understanding why stylistic effect may excite anxiety, in that it helps to explain the perception of the persuasive performance as overwhelming, threatening, and potentially deceptive.

Consider a few famous images. *Meilichios* or *glukeros* speech is the honey-sweet utterance that charms or gently persuades the listener, sometimes into a dangerously lulled and forgetful state. In Hesiod the Muses give honeyed speech to good leaders and poets (*Th.* 83–84, 94–97); Nestor's voice is sweeter than honey (μέλιτος γλυκίων ... αὐδή, *Il.* 1.249) in Homer, but the sound of the Sirens is also honey-sweet (μελίγηρυν, *Od.* 12.187).[10] Odysseus and Helen both use these honeyed tones when they are looking to seduce their interlocutors into alliances that their respective appearances would seem to deny (*Od.* 6.148; *Il.* 6.343).[11] Theognis counsels his addressee always to offer the honey-sweet thing (τὸ μείλιχον) with the tongue but to keep a more acidic heart (καρδίη ὀξυτέρη, 365–366), a purposeful contrast between taste sensations that renders the behavior of the clever man tactile and concrete. Similar to the use of *meilichios*, the *malakos* ("soft") utterance indicates a kind of verbal caress, a tone and phrasing that gently bend the listener to the speaker's purpose. Helen deploys this *malakos* speech when seeking to nudge Paris into heroic action (*Il.* 6.337), as does Hesiod's good leader when persuading his people (*Th.* 90). Cicada-like old men and the Muses are also lily-voiced (*Il.* 3.152; *Th.* 41), a characterization that suggests the synesthetic intersection of the word's limpid sound (*leirioeis*) and the flower's smooth-petaled appearance; note that the word is also used of skin (e.g., *Il.* 13.830).

The speech of the able rhetor famously flows (*rheô*) from his lips like water or honey (e.g., *Il.* 1.249; *Th.* 84). In Hesiod this is a direct result of the Muses having poured (*cheiô*) honey-sweet dew on his tongue (*Th.* 83, 97). The speaker with this sweetened, fluid tongue also makes straight judgments (ἰθείῃσι δίκῃσιν, *Th.* 86) and sets things aright with his soft words (μαλακοῖσι ἐπέεσσιν, *Th.* 90). In Homer the fine speaker's syllables may drift down like snowflakes (*niphades*), and he may have a weaving way with words (*huphainô*) even when he himself is not much to look at, as is the case with Odysseus (*Il.* 3.212–224).[12] Above all, like Odysseus and Helen both, the winning speaker is adept at matching speaking style to occasion and audience, pleasing listeners with words as a central aspect of guest-friendship (*xenia*) transactions (e.g., *Od.* 4.219–264). Thus a persuasive speaking style looks, tastes, and feels good, in effect; it settles over one like a gentle snowfall or gleams like a finely wrought web. But it also has the right proportions, like a beautiful body or a good cut of beef, and is "straight," like the one who deploys it. The adept speaker often looks the part, being upright of stature and clear of eye (e.g., Diomedes).[13] If he sings well for a living, however, he may be crippled or blind; his compensation is the fine portion of meat that matches his well-proportioned song, as Odysseus insures for the blind Phaiacian singer Demodocus (*Od.* 8.480).[14]

In Homer the Sirens' sweet but *lêthê*-filled voices suggest a potential problem with this pleasing pattern, as does the gap between the verbal flurry of Odysseus and his unremarkable appearance, or Helen's soft words and her violent effect on those around her. The lowly shepherd-poet in Hesiod who is fractious and hungry nevertheless receives the gift of divine voice from the Muses (*Th.* 24–34), which connects him to Zeus on the one hand and the kings on the other. But physical want may make the clever man say what he thinks will please most, whether or not it is true, as needy characters from Homer to Hipponax show.[15] Such speakers suggest the central, insurmountable problems with style: that to aid persuasion it must be mutable; that it may not match the speaker's appearance, thereby serving as a sort of verbal disguise; and thus that the criteria (of fine proportion, lovely texture) that govern it may distract the hearer from attending properly to its moral tenor. He then may misidentify the speaker or her motives entirely, or be drawn into a verbal trap that becomes physical and inextricably entrancing.

In Homer this potentially dangerous style is marked primarily by a versatility of speech type and tone, as well as by an elusive or changeable visible type (discussed in ch. 3). As Adam Parry and others have demonstrated, the voices of many important characters in Homeric epic differ from each other in vocabulary choice, tone, and formulaic expression.[16] While occasion dictates these differences to some extent, the style of each speaker is generally true to his character type: just as Nestor's measured, honey-sweet tones and use of exempla suit his status as elder statesman, so do Andromache's mournful self-reference and admonishing use of the future tense mark her as the paradigmatic widow, even when her husband is still alive. If certain characters show a remarkable degree of consistency in their speech types, others speak in a manner that is more changeable, inclusive, and therefore difficult to categorize. The hybrid quality of their verbal styles arises from their variegated roles in Homeric narrative. These characters have their conventional extension in the figure of the rhapsode, whose impersonations of different Homeric characters would have suggested to ancient audiences the pleasures and distractions of witnessing such versatile types within the narrative setting.[17]

HELEN AS GUEST AND HOST

The Homeric poet portrays Helen not only as a central object of praise and blame; she is also sensitive to the typical locutions employed by others to describe her and careful about her own usage. She is thus repeatedly shown attempting to offset her damaged image with a versatile combination of speech types. In respect to verbal *hexis*, then, Helen's figure in Homer is emblematic of an attention to suitable style and the flattery it involves. The details of her narrative also often indicate an awareness of her type's subtly dangerous or distracting effects.

THE SELF-ABUSING GUEST

Helen's repentant character in the *Iliad* has tended to be taken at face value by scholars. They describe her rueful responses to Priam and Hector and her angry rejection of Paris and Aphrodite, often without analyzing in any detail the quality of these verbal exchanges.[18] Yet her visible deportment and the responses of others to her, in combination with her versatile and flattering verbal style, suggest that these exchanges represent the complexly layered strategies of the uninvited guest. I submit that in these exchanges (1) Helen's apparent tone often does not match her ultimate intention and (2) the speech types she uses, which range from the mournful widow's to the flyting warrior's, are transposed by the poet from their usual contexts to form locutions unique to her. Helen is also significantly aware of her centrality to the narratives of others, manifesting a concern with reputation (*kleos*) anomalous among mortal female characters in Homer, which connects her to the Muses, the Sirens, and ultimately the poet, as a number of scholars have recognized.[19] Helen's frequent references to the future also indicate this focus on her posterity, as do those of the Trojan elders when speaking of her (e.g., 3.160, 3.411, 6.352, 6.357). Moreover, her attention to reputation—both her own and her effect on that of others—indicates that her figure shows a special sensitivity to how she is represented and how she represents herself. While some aristocratic female characters in Homer do manifest some awareness of their reputations (e.g., Penelope, who positions herself as Helen's opposite in book 23 of the *Odyssey*), only Helen is consistently portrayed as focusing on her public role as an object of blame.

In the scene at the Trojan wall, for example, Helen is both the renowned beauty who flutters the hearts of old men and Priam's partner in the viewing of heroic physiques. The first time Priam asks her to name a warrior, Helen identifies Agamemnon but quickly shifts attention to her own past, thus substituting her story for his biography. Her reply does not seem particularly suited to the context and in fact somewhat resembles in content Andromache's mournful speech in book 6, when the latter bewails her widow's fate to her living husband. Andromache's voice is consistently mournful, however, and her use of the mourner's *topoi* coheres with her role as loyal wife.[20] At the wall, when Priam asks Helen to name Ajax, she again mourns her fate in this diversionary fashion. Her identification moves quickly from his epithets (e.g., ἕρκος Ἀχαιῶν, 3.229) to the Cretan leader Idomeneus. As guest-friend of Menelaus, he reminds her of her own story, and she remarks on the absence of her brothers from the battlefield (3.234–242). She then conjectures that their absence can be explained by their fears of the shame and reproach that are hers (αἴσχεα δειδιότες καὶ ὀνείδεα πόλλ' ἅ μοί ἐστιν, 3.242).

The poet thus portrays Helen as giving herself the central role in her descriptions of others. She repeatedly characterizes their actions as dependent on her own, and she uses her audience with the Trojan elders to salvage her reputation by means of rueful self-abuse. Her versatility in these instances includes the engaging of a *habitus* usually associated with male speakers: again, *kleos* is rightfully the concern of the warrior, not of the warrior's prize. Like any good warrior (and unlike her paramour), she fears the insults of others (αἴσχεα . . . ὀνείδεα, 3.242; μωμήσονται, 3.412; cf. κακὸν ἔπος οὐδ' ἀσύφηλον and ἐνίπτοι, 24.767–768) and recognizes the vulnerability of her public position.

Helen, in contrast to the chaste Andromache, treats her story as if it were the story most central to every warrior's life, which is in some sense the case. That is, while the mourning wife's story would be told only in keening over her husband, Helen's story is on the lips of everyone. It is a tale especially connected to a number of prominent warriors and generally a concern to everyone. As the precipitating, fateful figure for these heroes, who drew them across the sea and down onto the plain to their respective fates, her story is their story; her own *kleos* is inevitably bound up in the *kleos* of each.[21] Helen's masculine focus and public role signal the unique position of her character. Her story is immodestly encompassing, and her bold attempts to bolster her image (in *Iliad* 3 and *Odyssey* 4 especially) suggest a typical style that is usually the purview of men.

Thus, in keeping with her masculine concern with *kleos*, Helen tends to speak *muthoi*, an authoritative speech type that commonly marks public or formal utterances delivered by males of high status.[22] When the poet assigns such locutions to Helen, they serve to underscore the complexity and singularity of her role as a female speaker with a public presence, who seeks to mitigate the bitter character of her *kleos*. Her authoritative utterances are frequently softened by her carefully reverential responses to interlocutors and her rueful self-blame. Thus Helen's authoritative *hexis*, which is itself unusual for female characters, possesses a unique versatility in her usage. For instance, before she lapses into self-reflection in response to Priam's first inquiry, she says that he is worthy of veneration (αἰδοῖος) and fearsome (δεινός) in her eyes (172). She thereby reinforces the social hierarchy of their roles by a show of extreme respect. Her reverence implies a self-effacement that is consistent with her tendency to self-abuse; she refers to herself as "dog-faced" (κυνώπιδος, 3.180; cf. 6.344, 356) and later as "hateful" (στυγερήν, 3.404).[23] These strategies constitute a primary stylistic tendency unique to her and indicate her sensitivity to her reception, both in this public male setting and in the feminized space of her private chambers.

The excessive respect that Helen shows Priam (and later Hector) is also sustained by a tactic typical of both Helen and Odysseus.[24] The expression of regret (*ophelon*, "would that I . . .") is common in Homer and used by many different characters. But both Helen and Odysseus deploy *ophelon* phrases more often than any other speakers. They also do so in delicate guest-host situations, where the phrases are less direct, emotional responses than rhetorical strategies. In these settings, such rueful phrases serve as a means of suggesting attitudes that accord with those of interlocutors. They thus bolster the speaker's image by making him appear appropriate to his hosts and thereby encourage empathy in them. This preemptive self-blame may, however, also constitute a bedroom challenge that imitates the warrior's taunts (i.e., "flyting" speeches). The layered and oblique nature of this regretful rhetoric suggests that Helen's and Odysseus' typical styles are both marked by a versatile indirection.

Thus when Priam asks Helen to name the warriors he sees on the battlefield, she sighs, "Would that evil death had pleased me, when I followed your son here" (ὡς ὄφελεν θάνατός μοι ἀδεῖν κακός, ὁππότε δεῦρο / υἱέι σῷ ἑπόμην, 3.173–174).[25] She also employs it in a less obviously consistent manner, when scorning Paris in books 3 and 6. As mentioned, the phrase is commonly used in verbal taunts.[26] When Helen is not turning this abuse on herself, she turns it on those closest to her: Paris and Aphrodite. But, as I explore below, her reproaches of her intimates also aim at maintaining the allegiance of those men whose public, visible characters mark them as virtuous and courageous. The poet's depiction of Helen thus both transposes the use of blaming speech from typical masculine contexts to the feminized privacy of the bedroom and reveals that this same stylistic tactic may be redirected for the purposes of flattery.

Helen's complex use of blaming speech is shown first in her confrontation with Aphrodite (3.383–420). Here the goddess assumes the role of plot manipulator to save Paris from the battleground, a setting where he cannot shine. She seeks also to bring her two favorites together again by depicting his visibly charming features to a reluctant Helen. The goddess thereby inspires in Helen a passion that seems suspended between desire for the beautiful Paris whom Aphrodite describes (3.391–394) and anger at the goddess with whom she shares important characteristics.[27] Note that Helen herself calls her painful feelings ἄκριτα (3.412), the most common meaning of which is "confused, indeterminate." The word underscores both the complexity of Helen's position and (what comes to the same thing) the merging of roles in this scene, so that Helen's abuse of Aphrodite parallels her self-abuse.[28]

Helen has been referred to as a "faded Aphrodite"; theirs is a dispute between two figures who are very intimately associated.[29] The scene thus suggests an indeterminacy in Helen's figure, with its double motivations and opposing traditions. Not surprisingly, then, her rueful abuse of herself and her scornful responses to her intimates resemble each other. She exhorts both Aphrodite and Paris with dismissive imperatives (3.406, 432) and pictures each in a compromised position (3.407–409, 434–436). She also uses *ophelon* phrases of both herself and Paris.

The scornful abuse of one so intimate can sound similar to the dueling speech of warriors, with its use of negative epithets and goading imperatives. Coupled with Helen's self-abusive epithets, this speech and that in which she reproaches Paris mimic the aggressive challenge of the hero on the battlefield.[30] When Helen returns to the bedroom, as she is ordered to do by her patron goddess, her expression and tone suggest pique (ὄσσε πάλιν κλίνασα, πόσιν δ ἠνίπαπε μύθῳ, 3.427), while her taunting phrases recall the flyting warrior. "Would that you had died there," she says, "subdued by the better man, who was once my husband" (ὡς ὤφελες αὐτόθ' ὀλέσθαι, / ἀνδρὶ δαμεὶς κρατερῷ, ὃς ἐμὸς πρότερος πόσις ἦεν, 3.428–429). It is not just any flyting warrior that she recalls here: at the beginning of book 3, Hector chastises his brother on the battlefield, declaring that he wishes Paris had never been born or had died unmarried (αἴθ' ὄφελες ἄγονός τ' ἔμεναι ἄγαμός τ' ἀπολέσθαι, 3.40). Compare Helen's reproach of Aphrodite for using seductive talk (ἠπεροπεύειν, 3.399), which recalls Hector's derogatory characterization of his brother as a seducer (ἠπεροπευτά, 3.39).

In the bedroom Helen's words vacillate between direct abuse and ironic indirection: she changes tacks with brusque disdain, first telling Paris to go challenge Menelaus for a second time, then remarking that he had better not, since Menelaus would probably kill him (3.432–436).[31] Compare first Achilles, who goads Aeneas with a parallel insult in a famous flyting scene, when he urges him to retreat into the mass of soldiers (ἐς πληθὺν, 20.197) lest he be harmed. And compare again Hector, who challenges his brother similarly at the opening of book 3:

> οὐκ ἂν δὴ μείνειας ἀρηΐφιλον Μενέλαον;
> γνοίης χ' οἵου φωτὸς ἔχεις θαλερὴν παράκοιτιν·
> οὐκ ἄν τοι χραίσμη κίθαρις τά τε δῶρ' Ἀφροδίτης,
> ἥ τε κόμη τό τε εἶδος, ὅτ' ἐν κονίῃσι μιγείης.

> Won't you stay and face war-loving Menelaus?
> Then you would know what sort of man he is
> whose blooming wife you keep:
> nor will the kithara and your hair and form
> —those gifts of Aphrodite—be of much use to you
> when you make love to the dust. (3.52–55)

Both Helen and Hector contrast Paris unfavorably with Menelaus and point up the superiority of the Greek warrior in terms that suggest sexual conquest (e.g., μιχθείς, μιγείης, 3.48 and 55; δαμείς, δαμήῃς, 3.429 and 436). The centrality of the lover's role to Paris' type insures that even his encounters on the battlefield will have a tincture of the bedroom.[32] These two scornful depictions of Paris' unwarlike attitude serve to frame book 3, so that it begins and ends with Paris' sensuous presence and the bellicose types who reproach him: Hector and Helen. Helen's use of this perspective is not nearly so straightforward as her brother-in-law's, however. Hers is an imitation of his flyting speech, an anomalous use of a verbal style that belongs on the battlefield. Here, in the intimate context of the bedroom, it takes on an additional shade of meaning: a sexual challenge, perhaps, as well as a military one.

By invoking her war-loving first husband to goad her bed-loving second, Helen has brought the battle into the bedroom, where her flyting abuse takes on an erotic subtext that her words do not directly convey. The poet's depiction of her usage is thus a subtle refraction of the hero's tragic exclamation or bitter taunt. Helen turns the familiar phrase against her too-tender husband, thereby linking herself to him and both of them to Aphrodite, the other recipient of such rueful reproach. This isolates the three of them as against conventional type. The hero's despair as well as his scorn takes on a singular usage in Helen's mouth. The Homeric poet reserves this indirection for her and Odysseus, the two characters who most depend on delicate verbal negotiations and good receptions for the completion of their journeys.[33]

A scene in book 6 portrays Helen engaging in a similarly careful calibration of effect. Her tone has changed somewhat since her interaction with Paris in book 3, and now she speaks with a flirtatious combination of enticement and gentle abuse. When Hector comes to rouse Paris from his sensuous reverie in the couple's private chambers, Helen tries to get her manly brother-in-law to sit down by scorning her softer husband.[34] She engages in a delicate seduction of Hector, addressing him with "honey-sweet" words (μύθοισι . . . μειλιχίοισι, 6.343). We might note that this sweetness also characterizes Odysseus' tactics of ingratiation in an erotically charged scene (cf. *Od.* 6.143, 146, 148), and that both Nestor and the Sirens speak in a honeyed manner. The adjective thus comprises a range of speaking styles from the authoritatively but gently persuasive to the dangerously seductive.[35] In this passage Helen's verbal demeanor also indicates the variegated qualities of this style. When Hector first enters and reproaches his brother, the mild Paris responds that Helen had just been urging him to return to battle with "soft" words (μαλακοῖς ἐπέεσσιν, 6.337). This is an unusual content for beguiling tones, but like most of her utterances in book 3, it suggests the hybrid quality of her typical style. The enticing associations of *malakos* thus contrast strangely with the stringency of her message, while those of *meilichios* lend her words a potentially threatening quality. Hector's refusal to sit with her thus becomes a refusal to play the victim to her Siren, a role his brother so willingly accepts.

While the Homeric poet may repeatedly counter the recognition of this ominous seductive quality in his representation of Helen, it nonetheless resonates in the scene as the barely suppressed subtext. Some scholars have argued that its lingering presence suggests that the Homeric Helen is poised against the tradition of her blame.³⁶ I would add that it also points up the delicate style crucial to female figures who fear ill-repute. This is a style strongly marked by the necessities imposed by gender: the female speaker who fears for her reputation must use verbal indirection and deflection, rather than confrontational defense, to win over her interlocutors. Unlike her male peers, the high-born woman is not supposed to have a public reputation in the first place. The tactics of the notorious beauty must thus include an acknowledgment of so regrettable an acquisition.

From this perspective it should not be surprising that Helen begins her conversation with Hector by calling herself an "evil-devising, shudder-inspiring dog" (κυνὸς κακομηχάνου ὀκρυοέσσης, 6.344; cf. κυνός, 6.356), echoing the self-blame that she had used earlier in conversation with Priam. As she had with the father, so with the son she debases herself by uttering this abusive label. Her self-characterization calls up the image of the cur, the homeless interloper in rich and hallowed halls, who embodies righteous indignation (*nemesis*) and suffering (*pêma*) and guards the road to Hades.³⁷ The wishful phrase that follows her self-abusing epithets is an elaborate expansion of her earlier regretful remarks. Rather than simply desiring to die, she declares that she wishes that on her day of birth she had been blown away:

> ὥς μ' ὄφελ' ἤματι τῷ ὅτε με πρῶτον τέκε μήτηρ
> οἴχεσθαι προφέρουσα κακὴ ἀνέμοιο θύελλα
> εἰς ὄρος ἢ εἰς κῦμα πολυφλοίσβοιο θαλάσσης,
> ἔνθα με κῦμ' ἀπόερσε πάρος τάδε ἔργα γενέσθαι.

> Would that on the day my mother first bore me
> a rushing gust of evil wind had carried me off
> to the mountains, or into the waves of the many-voiced
> sea, where they might have finished me before these
> things happened. (6.345–348)³⁸

The elegaic tone softens her speech and matches her honeyed encouragement that her angry brother-in-law sit down with her and Paris. She further declares that (things being as they are) she would rather have a better husband (ἀνδρὸς ἔπειτ' ὤφελλον ἀμείνονος εἶναι ἄκοιτις, 6.350). She ruefully casts herself and her paramour in this less than virtuous role and then concludes that due to their passion (ἄτη, 6.356), they will both be subjects of song for future generations. As in book 3, the poet closely couples Helen's self-blame with her recognition of her damaged *kleos,* depicting her attempt to mend it as a subtle combination of flattery and self-abuse. Her lyrical, gently seductive style is thus underscored as a conscious technique at the end of her speech by its juxtaposition with her metapoetic statement that she and Paris will be figures of blame in the songs of future generations (ἀοίδιμοι, 6.358).

Helen's rhetorical maneuver is, as usual, a delicate one. She must acknowledge her alliance with Paris to show her awareness of their shame; but she also thereby isolates herself from him, since he assumes no responsibility for his actions. As in book 3, Helen brackets herself with Paris as an object of abuse and highlights their shared status by using the *ophelon* phrase (twice in book 6) to express a heroic bitterness that applies to them both. Helen's usage thus transforms a typically direct expression of regret into this unique speech act, which layers self-abuse, scorn for an intimate, and a suggestion of allegiance that aims at convincing her interlocutor of a shared outlook and intent. While Hector does not in the end sit down with Helen, neither does he speak roughly to her, instead responding with a respect that resembles his father's treatment of her. By having Helen introduce a defamatory tradition that threatens to reveal her other story and yet ultimately serves to fend off abuse of her by others, Homer represents her as successfully deflecting this blame. In Homeric epic no one else abuses Helen as she abuses herself.

At the end of the *Iliad* Helen delivers the final mourning speech over Hector's dead body. Homer gives her this surprisingly prominent status among the mourners, which supports the argument that the Homeric poet is forcefully asserting an alternate tradition that elevates Helen and rejects the tradition of blame.[39] But if we consider precisely how she mourns Hector, looking beyond her use of the mourner's standard *topos* of lament for her fate as vulnerable survivor, we can see that her lament focuses entirely on the threat of the blame she incites. This is not to say that other mourners do not fear ill-repute: Andromache certainly does, but mostly for her son Astyanax (e.g., *Il.* 22.494–501).[40] Helen's lament, in some contrast, is only about her reputation, only about her awareness of her damaged public image and her need for verbal protection. In describing her fears for the future, she makes no mention of other horrors such as slavery and remarriage, which are often voiced by newly bereft female mourners in both epic and tragedy.[41] After expressing her usual sentiment of regret (ὡς πρὶν ὤφελλον ὀλέσθαι, 24.764), Helen notes that she had never heard a debasing or disrespectful word from her brother-in-law (οὔ πω σεῦ ἄκουσα κακὸν ἔπος οὐδ' ἀσύφηλον, 24.766). She adds that if anyone else in his family ever reproached her (ἐνίπτοι), Hector would fend them off verbally (ἐπέεσσιν παραιφάμενος κατέρυκες) with his gentle mind and words (σῇ τ' ἀγανοφροσύνῃ καὶ σοῖς ἀγανοῖς ἐπέεσσι, 24.767–772). She concludes by declaring that she has no other kind and friendly person (ἤπιος οὐδὲ φίλος) in Troy and that everyone else shudders (πεφρίκασιν) in her presence (24.774–775).

Helen's entire lament thus focuses on the blame that she fears she will endure now that her primary defender is dead, and her final word in the *Iliad* (πεφρίκασιν) resonates with the dread that she inspires. Her self-abuse in Homer, while it preempts that of her interlocutors, also repeatedly reminds the audience of the difficulty of holding off blame from this notorious figure.[42] Hector, like the poet, may be gentle-minded toward Helen, but her description of his protection reveals the tenuousness of her hold on praise. Here as elsewhere in the poem her words declare one thing and suggest another—often, her connection with death, which causes a chill in those around her.[43]

If the *Iliad*'s portrait of Helen shows her repeatedly attempting to restore her reputation, this is precisely because she is a blameable type. While male characters commonly manifest this concern for *kleos*, Helen's situation is unique. She is a public figure and, as such, embodies public attitudes not only toward her ominous beauty but more importantly toward the speech types it inspires. The *Iliad* makes clear that the defense of Helen's reputation is a delicate affair. It can be achieved only by the fashioning of a versatile performance that borrows stylistic habits common to male speakers of high status and transposes them into uncommon settings as a means of deflecting blame. The anxiety aroused by her presence is not, then, a response merely to her beauty but rather to what that beauty emblematizes: a dangerous power that overwhelms the senses, the destructive attraction of which brings ill-repute, which in turn necessitates this stylistic deflection. The figure of Helen in Homeric epic thus shares associations with the stylistic effects of oral performance and its distracting force. Within the larger tradition, these associations would ultimately crystallize into an anxiety about the impact of style itself, with Helen as the trope for its threat to right-minded judgment.

THE AUTHORITATIVE HOST

The *Odyssey* portrays Helen as being in a similarly delicate position in relation to her reputation, but here she assumes the authoritative role appropriate to her reinstatement as mistress of her first husband's halls. She is no longer an unwanted and dangerous guest in an enemy city, whose fragile status must be repeatedly reinforced by deferential self-blame and flattery. The Homeric poet again shows Helen staging a series of meticulous and versatile self-performances, although in the *Odyssey* she is more direct in her attempts to control the reception of her character. Here her speeches invoke various models of authoritative speech (the Muses, the choral performer, the speaker of prophecy) and demonstrate her sensitivity to the appropriate locution in the guest-host setting.

Helen's first words to her audience seem to draw purposeful attention to her perspicuity and narrative control. When she recognizes Telemachus as the son of Odysseus, she highlights her ability to perceive likeness and questions whether she should announce her knowledge.[44] This perception of likeness (ἐοικότα, 4.141; ἔοικε, 4.143) not only highlights Helen's keen sensibilities, it also forms the core of the adept speaker's facility for the implementation of appropriate styles. Helen will later promote the suitability of her own speech in similar language (ἐοικότα γὰρ καταλέξω, 4.239; see further below). Not to be outdone, Menelaus asserts that he too noticed the likeness; as the narrator had explained earlier, he recognized Telemachus but hesitated to say anything (4.116–118). Helen, by contrast, speaks out decisively, gives shape and purpose to the conversation, and saves the dinner party by doling out to her hearers the *pharmakon* "no-pain" (νηπενθές, 4.221). This, in combination with her words, staunches the diners' flow of tears, which her husband has bumblingly encouraged.

This scene also portrays Helen as involved in the mechanics of deception, like her counterpart Odysseus. She controls guest-host interactions to deflect attention from her ill-repute, numbing the minds of her audience and then telling them "plausible" things (*eoikota*) that her husband later deems "appropriate" (κατὰ μοῖραν, 4.266) rather than true. Menelaus also depicts her as cunningly imitating (ἴσκουσ', 4.279) the voices of others. As numerous commentators have pointed out, the Homeric poet draws attention to Helen's facility for deception in this scene by juxtaposing her story of her actions and allegiances in Troy with that of her husband. Both stories, moreover, position Helen as the fitting partner or antagonist for Odysseus, underscoring their similarity to each other and their dangerous mimetic agility. Helen claims that when Odysseus entered Troy under the guise of a household slave, she saw through the disguise but did not betray him. In contrast, Menelaus claims that if it had not been for the perspicuity of Odysseus, Helen would have led the Greek soldiers to their deaths by calling to them in the voices of their wives.

In her tale, Helen first explains that she will not recount all the feats that Odysseus undertook during the war, implying that like the Muses she might be able to do so. Rather, she says, she will limit her account to his achievements within the walls of Troy. The phrase she uses in introducing her narrative of Odysseus' feats resembles one used by her husband to Nestor's son Peisistratus (ὅσ' ἂν πεπνυμένος ἀνὴρ / εἴποι καὶ ῥέξειε, 4.204–205; οἷον τόδ' ἔρεξε καὶ ἔτλη καρτερὸς ἀνήρ, 4.242); later he repeats her phrase almost exactly (4.271). Helen's use of the clause thus marks her sensitivity to conversational context. She signals the suitability of her story by sounding like her husband, who has been speaking with great warmth and familiarity about both Odysseus and Nestor.

Helen further highlights her superior status as a narrator by emphasizing again that like Telemachus' father, she possesses one of the primary attributes of the authoritative speaker: great perspicuity. She relates that when Odysseus appeared within the city walls disguised as a slave, she alone recognized him and taxed him with her knowledge. She emphasizes the extent of his disguise by repeating phrases that describe his likeness to a man of low status, a rhetorical strategy that underscores both his cleverness at deception and hers at detection:

> αὐτόν μιν πληγῇσιν ἀεικελίῃσι δαμάσσας
> σπεῖρα κάκ' ἀμφ' ὤμοισι βαλών οἰκῆι ἐοικώς
> ἀνδρῶν δυσμενέων κατέδυ πόλιν εὐρυάγυιαν·
> ἄλλῳ δ' αὐτὸν φωτὶ κατακρύπτων ἤισκε
> δέκτῃ ὃς οὐδὲν τοῖος ἔην ἐπὶ νηυσὶν Ἀχαιῶν.
> τῷ ἴκελος κατέδυ Τρώων πόλιν, οἱ δ' ἀβάκησαν
> πάντες· ἐγώ δέ μιν οἴη ἀνέγνων τοῖον ἐόντα
> καί μιν ἀνηρώτων· ὁ δὲ κερδοσύνῃ ἀλέεινεν.

> Having beaten himself with unseemly blows
> and having thrown a grimy cloak around his shoulders,

looking like some household servant with cruel masters,
he slipped into the wide avenues of Troy.
With this cover he likened himself to another man, a
beggar, a type that would never be among the ships of
the Achaeans. Looking like this, he slipped into Troy,
and everyone was fooled. But I alone recognized him even
in such a guise and I questioned him. Yet he eluded me
with his guile. (4.244–251)

In Helen's emphatic description, Odysseus disguises himself with blows
that are unbefitting (ἀεικελίῃσι, 4.244) of the hero. He is then so unlike himself—so like a household slave or a beggar (οἰκῆι ἐοικώς, ἤισκε δέκτῃ . . .
τῷ ἴκελος, 4.245, 247, 249)—that he slips into Troy (κατέδυ πόλιν, 4.246,
249) unnoticed, except by Helen herself. As Helen relates the tale, Odysseus
counters her probing eye by refusing to confirm her identification until she
has bathed and anointed him, dressed him well, and sworn a great oath of
secrecy to him.

The poet thus shows Helen characterizing her actions as like those of the
other powerful goddesses Odysseus encounters, Calypso and Circe—from
the care of the hero's body to the swearing of an oath not to harm him.[45]
Her depiction suggests that her goddesslike actions encouraged Odysseus
to take her into his confidence, while it also conveys the threat that she could
have been to him. Like Calypso and Circe, she had the power to unman him
completely, either as he sat naked and vulnerable in her bathtub, stripped
most completely of his protective disguise, or later when he was preparing
to slash his way through the streets of Troy. Hence the need for the great
oath, which Odysseus tends to swear when in positions of extreme vulnerability: trapped inside Troy in the hands of the changeable Helen, marooned
on Calypso's shore contemplating the building of a flimsy raft, or about to
enter the very beautiful and lêthê-inducing bed of Circe.[46]

Thus her story again highlights the adept speaker's ability to recognize
likeness and to deploy it in a useful manner. This use of familiar types may
also involve deception or threat, suggesting the danger inherent in such manipulation. It may fool or overwhelm the senses and thereby inhibit recognition of the truth. Because it capitalizes on the comfortable familiarity of the
plausible or suitable type, the manipulation of hexis may serve as a mask for
identity. This is Odysseus' typical style. But, once again, attention to like-

ness and suitability also constitutes the signature tactic of a versatile oral performer like Helen, in that it may distract the audience from one's bad reputation. Notice that Helen makes no direct claim to her loyalties; rather, she tells a tale that shows her ministering to a Greek hero like a benevolent goddess. Helen's story thus underscores her and Odysseus' cleverness not only in some general relation to deception but more particularly in their adept handling of this manipulation of type.

As an additional mark of her authoritative knowledge, Helen explicitly claims that after she has played the role of ministering goddess, Odysseus told her the "whole plot" (πάντα νόον, 4.256) of the Greeks. Once again she emphasizes her omniscience or at least the vast extent of her knowledge, since what this *panta noos* encompasses is left in question. She may have even been told then about the Trojan horse (as her probing response to it in Menelaus' story suggests), that is, about the device that would end the war. Helen also describes her heart's rejoicing (ἐμὸν κῆρ / χαῖρ') amid the wail (λίγ' ἐκώκυον) of the Trojan women at Odysseus' subsequent killing of Trojans (4.259–260), the destruction she has made possible by being loyal to those with whom she now dines. Sitting once again in her first husband's halls, Helen ends her story by complimenting Menelaus, as lacking "neither brains nor beauty" (οὔτ' ἀρ' φρένας οὔτε τι εἶδος, 4.264). Helen's self-performance is thus carefully calibrated both to support her claims to narrative authority and to gratify her audience; it could not be more delicately balanced or suitably told.

Her story is nevertheless thrown into some question by Menelaus' depiction of his wife's loyalties in the war (4.265–289), although how well he succeeds in doing so or even how much he desires to has been exaggerated by many readers of the scene. He initially responds to his wife's elegant story by remarking that she has told everything in a fitting fashion (ναὶ δὲ ταῦτά γε πάντα, γύναι, κατὰ μοῖραν ἔειπες, 4.266), an interesting characterization for a speech whose implicit claim he seems himself to refute. In Homer this and the related phrases *kata kosmon* and *kata aisan* mark distinctions between suitable and unsuitable speech.[47] These phrases use the concept of fitting measure to assess speaking ability, the one with reference to spatial organization (*kata kosmon*), the others to proportion or fitting amount (*kata moiran, kata aisan*). This is standard procedure in Greek aesthetic evaluation, which always has moral implications. One judges another's speech in respect to balance and timing, to a sense of proportion, both internal proportion (e.g., balance between narrative and argument) and external (e.g., consistency between the setting and the speaker's visible type). The latter is perhaps the more important: Gregory Nagy has argued convincingly that in Homer, the phrases *kata moiran* and *kata aisan* indicate conformity to epic diction in particular.[48] Helen's speech, on this account, meets not only the criteria of dinner-table etiquette but also those of the poet's genre, further supporting her status as authoritative speaker and (more importantly) as a metarhetorical figure. The implications of her emblematic *hexis* thus help delineate the boundaries of the genre itself.

In rhetorical terms, phrases such as *kata moiran* do not assess the truth of the speech but rather whether the speaker is behaving appropriately with her words. Echoing her claim that she will speak "suitable" things (ἐοικότα, 4.239), Menelaus thus approves Helen's ability to tell a story that highlights Odysseus' ingenuity and his military prowess and that thereby flatters and gratifies his son. He further affirms the stylistic elegance of her invention by using a similar frame for his own tale. He echoes one phrase of hers exactly (4.242 and 4.271) and employs a narrative strategy whose general shape resembles hers. Like Helen, he points up his own status and exclaims over the cleverness of Odysseus in the service of all the Achaeans:

> ἤδη μὲν πολέων ἐδάην βουλήν τε νόον τε
> ἀνδρῶν ἡρώων, πολλὴν δ' ἐπελήλυθα γαῖαν·
> ἀλλ' οὔ πω τοιοῦτον ἐγὼν ἴδον ὀφθαλμοῖσιν
> οἷον Ὀδυσσῆος ταλασίφρονος ἔσκε φίλον κῆρ.
> οἷον καὶ τόδ' ἔρεξε καὶ ἔτλη καρτερὸς ἀνὴρ
> ἵππῳ ἔνι ξεστῷ ἵν' ἐνήμεθα πάντες ἄριστοι
> Ἀργείων Τρώεσσι φόνον καὶ κῆρα φέροντες.

> I have seen the customs of cities and the minds
> of heroic men, and I have traveled much on the earth.
> But never have I seen with my own eyes such
> a brave heart as that which firm-minded Odysseus has.
> What a deed this mighty man achieved and dared,
> when all we nobles of the Argives were seated
> in the wooden horse, bringing murder and grim fate to the
> Trojans! (4.267–273)

Compare Helen's introduction:

ἀτὰρ θεὸς ἄλλοτε ἄλλῳ
Ζεὺς ἀγαθόν τε κακόν τε διδοῖ· δύναται γὰρ ἅπαντα·
ἦ τοι νῦν δαίνυσθε καθήμενοι ἐν μεγάροισι
καὶ μύθοις τέρπεσθε· ἐοικότα γὰρ καταλέξω.
πάντα μὲν οὐκ ἂν ἐγὼ μυθήσομαι οὐδ' ὀνομήνω
ὅσσοι Ὀδυσσῆος ταλασίφρονος εἰσιν ἄεθλοι.
ἀλλ' οἷον τόδ' ἔρεξε καὶ ἔτλη καρτερὸς ἀνὴρ
δήμῳ ἔνι Τρώων, ὅθι πάσχετε πήματ' Ἀχαιοί.

The god Zeus grants good and evil at different times;
for he is capable of all things. And now eat, seated in these
great halls, and enjoy my stories: for I shall speak suitable
things. I shall not recount or mention everything,
however many are the labors of firm-minded Odysseus.
But what a deed the mighty man achieved and dared
in the Trojan city, when the Achaeans were suffering ills!
    (4.240–243)

Recall that Helen had said she would not tell everything that Odysseus
achieved in the war, although her locution suggests that she would be able
to. Her first words also pay homage to Zeus, father of the Muses and of Helen
herself, so that she establishes her unparalleled authority as a knower and a
speaker by implied association with both.[49] In his speech Menelaus declares
that although he has encountered the strategies and mental types of many
men (like Odysseus), having traveled far (like Odysseus), he has never seen
such a one as Odysseus. Both introductory strategies seek to control the reception of the tale by pointing, either implicitly or explicitly, to the wisdom
and experience of the tellers. This grounds their authority as narrators in
types that are both familiar and also associated with Odysseus: Menelaus
is a hero-traveler, Helen, a semidivine knower. In approving the appropriateness of his wife's speech and echoing her verbal strategy, Menelaus in
effect counters the content of his own story, which after all directly contradicts Helen's representation of her loyalties. While he supports the *manner*
in which his wife speaks, he tentatively takes issue with its content.

This potential conflict is itself mitigated by Menelaus blaming his wife's
actions on Aphrodite. In his depiction, Aphrodite intended that Helen be
driven to do as the goddess wished: to bring ruin to the Trojans (κελευσέμε-
ναι δέ σ' ἔμελλε / δαίμων, ὃς Τρώεσσιν ἐβούλετο κῦδος ὀρέξαι, 4.274–

275).[50] At the end of his tale, Odysseus' protector Athena leads Helen away from the horse, so that goddesses compel both her arrival on the scene and her leave-taking. The only event not motivated by the goddesses, and for which Helen may thus be held responsible, is her imitation of the voices of the warriors' wives (φωνὴν ἴσκουσ' ἀλόχοισιν, 4.279). In this she is met and matched by Odysseus. As in her own story, here in her husband's, Helen and Odysseus are paired as singularly clever, especially in relation to the manipulation of type. If Helen can don multiple verbal disguises (something the hero does elsewhere in the *Odyssey*), Odysseus can effectively see through her disguise—as she alone saw through his—and literally stop the voice of another in his throat (ἀλλ' Ὀδυσεὺς ἐπὶ μάστακα χερσὶ πίεζε / νωλεμέως κρατερῇσι, 4.287–288).

Thus while Odysseus sits inside the Trojan horse, alone in his recognition of Helen, the perspicuous Helen literally probes its significance, fondling its sides as if touching all the Greek husbands and mouthing the voices of their wives (4.277–279). This is a mimetic ability that the female chorus is said to have, to its great glory, in the *Hymn to Delian Apollo* (162–164).[51] Like the Muses, Helen can tell the truth or not; like the rhapsode or choral performer, she can imitate the voices of others to the delight and possible danger of her audience. Helen herself merely claims before she tells her story that she will speak *suitable* things, which, if they are not true, ought to be by virtue of the extent to which they fit the context in which they are told. One might say that *eoikota* are ethically true: they suit character and situation and are thus the mainstay of the rhetorically adept speaker.

Some scholars have suggested that the scene treats Helen as the embodiment of the double story and thus of the dissimulating potential of mimesis itself.[52] While the juxtaposition of the two stories does encourage the audience to question the truth of Helen's narrative, the fact remains that Helen establishes her narrative authority by associating herself implicitly with Zeus, the Muses, and the epic poet. Moreover, Helen's husband approves her story openly and imitates the structure of her narrative frame. Even if the *Odyssey* as a whole may treat Helen as a foil for Penelope, she retains her singular status as a semidivine figure for the poet, as a possible partner for Odysseus (like Calypso and Circe), and most importantly as a double for him, since she is equally adept at deception, narrative control, and detection. Although most readers seem to accept that Menelaus' is the true version of events, Helen is depicted as being in such complete command of

verbal interaction that she quells the disturbing responses her double reputation usually arouses. Indications of her ill-repute surface briefly and cause
no reaction in her interlocutors, leaving many readers with an eerie sense
that they have been seduced by a rhetorically agile speaker.[53]

As a measure of this near-success, the defamatory tradition intrudes only
once in Helen's speech (κυνώπιδος, 4.145), and even her husband's story
avoids blaming her directly for her actions. This stands in some contrast
to the *Iliad*, where Helen spends much of her time defaming herself. There
she deploys this defamation as a means of deflection, yet her self-blaming
techniques insure that her bad reputation registers repeatedly. The reception of Helen's story by the internal audience of the *Odyssey* is milder than
one might expect precisely because it—in conjunction with the emotion-
calming drug that facilitates its reception—is so appropriate, so carefully
fashioned to suit the context of its delivery and thus to gratify her hearers.
Although as a metapoetic figure Helen does seem in this scene to represent
the doubling nature of storytelling, as an adept speaker she charms her audience and effectively overshadows her husband's potentially upsetting tale.

Consider also the scene in book 15, where the poet adds another model
of authoritative speech to Helen's repertoire. Her agile reading of the
omen that marks the departure of Telemachus and Peisistratus from Sparta
(15.160–178) precisely forecasts Odysseus' interpretation of Penelope's
dream (*Od.* 19.535–558), thereby linking Helen to both the seer's role and
Odysseus himself. Helen foreshadows Odysseus' own prophecy, which is
not really a prophecy but both a threat and a promise, and like a good seer,
she foretells what does come to pass. Most interestingly, she relates with
striking brevity the entire plot of the *Odyssey*: "Thus Odysseus, having suffered many evils and wandered much, will return home and exact satisfaction" (ὡς Ὀδυσεὺς κακὰ πολλὰ παθὼν καὶ πόλλ' ἐπαληθεὶς / οἴκαδε
νοστήσει καὶ τίσεται, 15.176–177). Once again she conflates the roles that
mark a special authority in relation to storytelling: the omniscience of the
Muses and the narrative compass of the poet. Compare especially the opening of the *Odyssey*, with its similar repetition of πολλά, its juxtaposition of
wandering and suffering, and its reference to return (*nostos*), Odysseus' primary goal:

Ἄνδρα μοι ἔννεπε, Μοῦσα, πολύτροπον, ὃς μάλα πολλὰ
πλάγχθη, ἐπεὶ Τροίης ἱερὸν πτολίεθρον ἔπερσε·

πολλῶν ἀνθρώπων ἴδεν ἄστεα καὶ νόον ἔγνω
πολλὰ δ' ὅ θ' ἐν πόντῳ πάθεν ἄλγεα ὃν κατὰ θυμόν
ἀρνύμενος ἥν τε ψυχὴν καὶ νόστον ἑταίρων.

Speak to me, Muse, of the versatile man, who wandered
very far, after he sacked the sacred city of Troy.
He saw the cities of many peoples and knew their minds,
and he suffered many griefs in his heart on the seas,
fighting for his life and the return of his companions. (1.1–5)

Where the Homeric poet holds off the end of the story, Helen includes it (with τίσεται), spanning the entire narrative in a single sentence. This breadth of perspective is notably unlike Helen's imperfect knowledge of events in the scene at the Trojan wall, which Michael Lynn-George has contrasted with the omniscient perspective that the poet attains in the Catalogue of Ships, with some help from the Muses.[54]

In *Odyssey* 15, then, Helen seems in possession of an inhuman knowledge, and as usual Menelaus is greatly overshadowed by his more mentally and rhetorically agile wife. Just as the husband stammers out his own recognition of Telemachus in book 4, here he "ponders how he might express his thoughts judiciously" (μερμήριξε δ' ἀρηΐφιλος Μενέλαος / ὅππως οἱ κατὰ μοῖραν ὑποκρίναιτο νοήσας, 15.169–170), while his wife prophesies with startling alacrity. Note that Menelaus is unsure how to speak in a context that requires an authoritative and suitable response (κατὰ μοῖραν), even though he is appealed to directly by the respectful Telemachus (15.167–169). This is precisely the kind of response that Helen is capable of, as her husband himself has acknowledged (cf. 4.266). Helen's mantic talents elicit an avowal from Telemachus that he will worship her as a goddess in his own land, as if he were pledging the establishment of a cult in Ithaca like that which did exist in the archaic period in Sparta and perhaps elsewhere.[55]

Thus the *Odyssey*'s final words on Helen acknowledge her status not merely as prophet or poet but also as herself divine, as one who might know more than the average human not just about the details of the story but about how to tell it in a deeply appropriate manner. In this scene the figure of Helen collapses the connection between poet or seer and divine authority in that she seems to play both roles at once. In book 4 her echoing of the poet's invocation of the Muses at the beginning of her own story achieves a similar conflation. Her manner is so persuasive that it effectively circumvents the obvious problem with her oral performance in the first place: that it is a *likeness*, a profoundly suitable manipulation of type that recasts her in a different role and thus masks her bad reputation. In this agile impersonation she resembles the rhapsode, the choral performer, the orator, and in the *Odyssey* her status as authoritative speaker remains relatively secure. But her ruinous story insures that the stylistic techniques she both employs and symbolizes will ultimately carry with them the same negative associations.

ODYSSEUS AS HOST AND GUEST

In the Homeric epics Odysseus' typical style frequently centers on the practice of fair exchange, whether among the Achaean leaders or among strangers. In the *Iliad* this practice tends to be addressed directly as the topic of dispute, while in the *Odyssey* the hero's careful manipulations of type demonstrate this same attention to balance and fair trade. Both epics show Odysseus reflecting this emphasis not merely in the subject matter of his speeches but also in the choice of vocabulary and images, which establish a pattern of usage that has social and rhetorical applications. This notion of proportionate exchange is also closely connected to ideas of suitability, which is to say that it is central to the techniques of the agile oral performer. The figure of Odysseus thus emerges as the paradigmatic agent of this stylistic balancing act, which also involves some apprehension that the fair-sharer may trade types with too much alacrity.

THE FAIR-SHARING HOST

In the *Iliad* Odysseus is primarily a good henchman of the sons of Atreus. He maintains order among the troops and undertakes a number of rhetorical maneuvers that suit the clever tactician. He is not, however, always a very successful word trader in the *Iliad*. At crucial junctures his insistence on balance and proportion fails to resolve the crisis of order and authority that Achilles precipitates. Odysseus nevertheless maintains his support of the hierarchies among the Achaean leaders, the fitting proportions in the division of spoils, and the orderly social rituals that preserve group cohesion. He thus frequently plays host to Achilles' guest, even in settings (like that of the embassy in *Iliad* 9) where Achilles is the actual host. Odysseus appropriates this role for himself, repeatedly referring to the fair division of food and spoils in his attempts to reintegrate the recalcitrant hero into the army hierarchy. In both of his confrontations with Achilles, and when he seeks to control the troops, his arguments center on the notion of the proportionate exchange that should govern fighting, feasting, and speaking.

In *Iliad* 2, for example, Odysseus keeps the troops in order by means of the kind of balanced style and suitable deportment that remind both the leaders and the soldiers of their respective places in the Achaean hierarchy. The kings he taxes with behaving in a low-born manner (κακόν, 2.190), with not controlling their men, and with an imperfect understanding of Agamemnon's intentions and his power. He warns them that Agamemnon may in turn behave badly toward them (κακόν, 2.195) and that the chief leader gets his power from Zeus. That is, Odysseus reminds them that they are not low-born types, that they will get as good (or as bad) as they give, and that they have still to answer to the most powerful *basileus* among them. He then accuses each of the soldiers of being unwarlike and weak (ἀπτόλεμος καὶ ἄναλκις, 2.201), of being useless (lit. "uncounted," οὔτε . . . ἐναρίθμιος, 2.202)[56] in war and council, and of all trying to be kings, when only one man holds the power. He thus uses the arithmetic of army hierarchy to hold each soldier to his duty as a follower: minus war spirit and strength, minus usefulness in council, but plus a disorderly desire to be a leader, the soldier counts for nothing. The two reproaches revolve around the notions of balance and appropriate behavior, without which the order of the army would disintegrate.

Odysseus' tone and posture in relation to each group reflect this same sense of order: when speaking to the leaders, he stands next to them and restrains each verbally with a gentle chiding (τὸν δ' ἀγανοῖς ἐπέεσσιν ἐρητύσασκε παραστάς, 2.189). Any soldier who is shouting (βοόωντα, 2.198) he propels with his scepter and commands him loudly with a *muthos* (τὸν σκήπτρῳ ἐλάσασκεν ὁμοκλήσασκέ τε μύθῳ, 2.199). Gentle words and verbal restraint are appropriate tactics for one's equals, while physical control and a loud, authoritative voice are a fitting strategy for disorderly inferiors, especially for those soldiers shouting and running about. Odysseus' tactics in this scene thus comprise both suitable words and suitable demeanor, so that his entire bodily *hexis* effects persuasion in this face-to-face context.

Odysseus' treatment of Thersites depicts the implementation of this calculating style in grim detail. The low-ranking, shrill-voiced Thersites speaks not so much badly as out of order; he is also hideous to look at, an important feature of his *hexis* that I discuss in more detail in chapter 3. But he is foremost a man with "disorderly words" (ἔπεα . . . ἄκοσμα, 2.213) in his head; Odysseus addresses him first as ἀκριτόμυθε—"indeterminate of speech"

(2.246), a label that Richard Martin has argued underscores precisely his unheroic type.[57] Odysseus emphasizes this by his expression and tone, glaring at Thersites and using an authoritative, scornful voice (καί μιν ὑπόδρα ἰδὼν χαλεπῷ ἠνίπαπε μύθῳ, 2.245); he also criticizes the rowdy soldier's blame-filled speaking style (ὀνείδεά τε προφέροις, 2.251; ὀνειδίζων, 2.255).

As G. S. Kirk remarked, Thersites is not so terrible a speaker but in fact makes a rather well polished speech; his verbal style is called *akosmos* because his behavior is out of line.[58] Not being a heroic type, he should not address a king, especially abusively, in public assembly. He not only challenges the king but also employs a different social arithmetic that, while describing accurately Agamemnon's greed, does not suit a situation in which the chief leader needs to demonstrate his power. His complaint that Agamemnon keeps most of the spoils and women for himself while the soldiers do most of the work (2.226–234) calls into question the apportionments that hold the ranks together: the man with the most power to order the troops must hold the most wealth as a fitting support of his position. This same man should also be foremost on the battlefield, but Agamemnon often seems to take more than he gives. It is this inconsistency that precipitated Achilles' withdrawal (as Thersites points out, 2.239–242) and that Odysseus has to counter by an emphasis on orderly hierarchies and proper recognition of authority.

Odysseus twice attempts to persuade Achilles (in books 9 and 19) to reenter the ranks of the Achaean leaders by highlighting the practices that make the organization of the army cohere. He takes up this task with a more elaborate attention to order and authority than that used on the troops. He effectively tries to offset Agamemnon's excesses with delicately balanced speeches, employing an argumentative style that is structured by ideas of fair exchange. In archaic poetry every feast signals a carefully apportioned détente among leaders or family members that carries with it the threatening potential of its opposite: the quarrel (*neikos*), the disintegration of balanced interaction.[59] Behind these exchanges between Odysseus and Achilles may lie the tradition of their quarrel, to which Demodocus refers in the *Odyssey* (8.72–82). Odysseus' careful treatment of Achilles in the *Iliad* thus would counter not only Agamemnon's excesses but also his own, adding an extra layer of tension and consequence to his stylistic balancing act.[60]

In the embassy scene Odysseus preempts Phoenix's prerogative to speak first as Achilles' elder and intimate (9.223), appropriating his status by the use of such paternal locutions as "my dear boy" (ὦ πέπον, 9.252) and the reiteration of Achilles' father's words in direct quotation (e.g., τέκνον ἐμόν, "my child," 9.256–257). Odysseus also effectively trades roles with his host: he opens his speech with an amiable proem, pouring out wine and greeting Achilles, commenting on the meal they have shared and giving a general sense of the pleasure of such rituals (9.225–228). He begins by affirming the shared repasts that Achilles could have in Agamemnon's tent, provisions also provided the embassy by Achilles, thereby highlighting the division of food and the meal's satisfying completion:

χαῖρ' Ἀχιλεῦ· δαιτὸς μὲν ἐΐσης οὐκ ἐπιδευεῖς
ἠμὲν ἐνὶ κλισίῃ Ἀγαμέμνονος Ἀτρεΐδαο
ἠδὲ καὶ ἐνθάδε νῦν· πάρα γὰρ μενοεικέα πολλὰ
δαίνυσθ'· ἀλλ' οὐ δαιτὸς ἐπηράτου ἔργα μέμηλεν,
ἀλλὰ λίην μέγα πῆμα, διοτρεφές, εἰσορόωντες
δείδιμεν.

Greetings, Achilles: you will not lack a fitting feast
in Agamemnon's tent, nor do you now
—for you have many heart-suiting things here for
feasting. Yet the rituals of a fine feast should
not concern us, but rather the too-great calamity,
god-nurtured one, that we fear as we look upon it. (9.225–230)

Odysseus thus shares the concept of the balanced, fitting feast (δαιτὸς μὲν ἐΐσης) between Achilles and Agamemnon; either place would provide the leader with strength-suiting meals (μενοεικέα πολλὰ δαίνυσθ'). The use of such proportional terms and the repetition of words for division (δαι-τός, δαίνυσθ') call attention to the organized distribution that proper social practice insures. This is precisely what Odysseus will try to convince Achilles that Agamemnon is prepared to undertake. In the meantime, Odysseus also aims at getting Achilles to see his own role in holding off the Trojans as part of this balanced interaction.

Accordingly, he sets this pleasant sharing (δαιτὸς ἐπηράτου ἔργα) against the terrible suffering (λίην μέγα πῆμα) of war, which—unlike the sharing of meals—Achilles alone can bring on or prevent for the Greek army. He addresses Achilles by a common but nonetheless pointedly respectful epithet (διοτρεφές) and places him syntactically between the pain feared and the fearful viewers. Odysseus makes clear that the ships are threatened (9.230–231) and that Achilles alone, by "putting on" his defensive strength (δύσεαι ἀλκήν, 9.231), can intervene to stop Hector who, exulting greatly in his own strength, rages in terrifying fashion (Ἕκτωρ δὲ μέγα σθένεϊ βλεμεαίνων / μαίνεται ἐκπάγλως, 9.237–238). He describes in striking detail the menacing proximity of the Trojans and the powerful frenzy (κρατερὴ . . . λύσσα, 9.239) that has seized their leader, juxtaposing the looming figure of Hector to the Greek ships.

Odysseus' word order thus positions Hector and the Trojans in the midst of the ships (9.231–235, 241–242), while the Achaeans' fear (9.230) and his own (δείδοικα, 9.244) hover on either side of the scene, separated from Hector by the ships.[61] The disposition of the Trojans is a deadly one for the Greeks, as the structuring of his description makes clear. In the speech, Achilles stands outside this scene (9.231, 246–251), which causes the disorder that Odysseus details. The pain (9.229) that opens the scene is answered at its end by the pain that Achilles will encounter if he does not find a remedy for the Achaean's dilemma:

> αὐτῷ τοι μετόπισθ' ἄχος ἔσσεται, οὐδέ τε μῆχος
> ῥεχθέντος κακοῦ ἔστ' ἄκος εὑρεῖν.

> There will be suffering for you yourself in the future,
> nor can you find a remedy to cure evil already done.
>   (9.249–250)

The word-play of ἄχος-μῆχος-ἄκος cleverly matches the pain to its cure, using the similarity among the words to suggest the connection that Achilles should make between the army's pain and his own, as well as their shared pain and his ability to serve as its remedy. The entire structuring of this first section of Odysseus' speech shows Achilles with a visual concreteness his proper place within the army's social and battle formation. Just as he should take his place among the leaders when food is divided, so should he balance the violent power of Hector with his own, matching the exultation in might (σθένεϊ βλεμεαίνων) of the Trojan's aggressive stance with his defensive strength (ἀλκήν). Odysseus' opening strategies thus juxtapose an intimate performance of shared rituals among leaders with a stirring portrait of their respective dispositions in public, that is, their attitudes and stances on the battlefield, when faced with the terrible Hector.

Odysseus' report of Agamemnon's offer constitutes the majority of the rest of the speech; it emphasizes what sort of stature Achilles can hope to gain by this redistribution of wealth. Although his report is basically accurate in content, it is less so in tone: he leaves out Agamemnon's assertion of supremacy (9.160–161), countering the leader's imperious speaking style with his own more balanced modulations, and his bad behavior with his typical emphasis on fair exchange.[62] Having begun his delivery with a pacifying reference to shared meals, he now moves on to the delicate business of the unfair portion that precipitated the conflict between Achilles and Agamemnon. In exchange for ceasing his anger, Achilles will receive worthy gifts (ἄξια δῶρα δίδωσι μεταλλήξαντι χόλοιο, 9.261, cf. 299), a trade-off that equates material goods and emotional states. Odysseus then echoes this division but now in relation to possible Trojan spoils (δατεώμεθα, 9.280). The speech also repeatedly employs verbs of valuing and esteeming, so that the idea of division becomes linked to that of fitting honor, as the direct result of fair apportionment (e.g., τείσει, 9.284; τιμήσουσι, 9.297; τείσουσ', 9.303).

Odysseus' speech has been analyzed for what are considered its proto-rhetorical devices: the genial introduction, the proposition, the dramatic tricolon, the concluding appeal to *pathos*.[63] Adam Parry and others have argued that it is meant to look conventional, in contrast to the newer, more personalized voice of Achilles.[64] Odysseus' speech does seem to anticipate rhetorical categories familiar to a postclassical audience. Moreover, the opposition between the two speakers may well be highlighted by their different speaking styles: the modulated, pragmatic strategies of diplomacy versus the bitter cadences of the isolated hero. But Odysseus' speech also has metarhetorical implications, since the very concepts that organize the speech (i.e., proportion, suitability) are those that underpin stylistic technique.

In fact, Odysseus' focus signifies precisely the orderliness and suitability that should characterize the agile speaker's oral performance. Indeed, the zeugmas that the speech forges between concrete effects and visible dispositions are those that ground archaic and classical assessments of style in performance. Odysseus, who is not only concerned with fair exchange but also with persuading his resistant interlocutor, again establishes an arithmetic of social order, this time calculating attitude and status in terms of material wealth. The calculus that equates status with its suitable visible effects also governs the structure and imagery of his speech. Thus *what* he argues is also *how* he argues, his orderly stylistic calibrations repeatedly making this connection between fair exchange and balanced speech.[65] Moreover, since he seeks to engage his interlocutor in the genial social rituals that articulate this same sense of balance and appropriateness, his bodily *hexis* as a whole functions as an enactment of style's dictates.

Achilles' response signals his awareness of Odysseus' tactics, of his coaxing style, and even perhaps of his metarhetorical language. Addressing Odysseus as "many-strategied" (πολυμήχανος), he declares pointedly, "It is indeed necessary to deliver *this* speech in a straightforward manner" (χρὴ μὲν δὴ τὸν μῦθον ἀπηλεγέως ἀποειπεῖν, 9.309). He warns his interlocutors not to sit by him "cooing" (τρύζετε, 9.311) and further displays his wariness of Odysseus' type with a well-aimed proverb: "Hateful to me as the gates of Hades is that man who hides one thing in his breast but says another" (ἐχθρὸς γάρ μοι κεῖνος ὁμῶς Ἀΐδαο πύλησιν / ὅς χ' ἕτερον μὲν κεύθη ἐνὶ φρεσίν, ἄλλο δὲ εἴπῃ, 9.311–312).[66] Achilles' use of the proverb indicates his awareness of how this character type operates: by a subtle set of associations that proceeds along deeply conventional lines. They thus appear familiar and thereby seem to restore balance to an unbalanced situation, while masking the speaker's attempts at coercion.

Achilles rejects these associations and the system of give-and-take that underpins them. He also employs the vocabulary of apportionment but only to refute the implications of Odysseus' speech. He states grimly, "The lot is the same for the one staying behind and the one who fights" (ἴση μοῖρα μένοντι, καὶ εἰ μάλα τις πολεμίζοι, 9.318). The declaration denies the social conventions inherent in the concept of equal apportionment (ἴση μοῖρα)— a key concept, as we have seen, for assessing both the suitability of speaking styles and the central content of Odysseus' speech (cf. δαιτὸς μὲν ἐΐσης, 9.225). Achilles thus remains isolated not only by sustaining his anger but also by scorning this style.

In book 19 a discussion takes place among the Greek leaders, as Achilles stands furiously ready to reenter the battle and avenge Patroclus' death. The scene reveals in a more concrete form Odysseus' general failure to persuade Achilles of the importance of conventional notions of balance and proportion. Once again, Achilles uses Odysseus' formulation of suitable ritual and balanced interaction to delineate his own more grim and isolated sense of measure. He refuses to engage in the practical ritual of sharing food, although he does in the end agree that the army should eat before battle and that the formal presentation of his recompense from Agamemnon might be made. Both of these activities Odysseus has urged to stage a public, ceremonial reinstitution of normality.[67] In this second verbal struggle with Achilles (19.154–183, 216–237), Odysseus attends to orderly rituals in a manner similar to his embassy speech, but here he does so with more emphasis on the public acknowledgment and assuaging of physical needs. His speech is permeated with references to sustenance and to body parts; he visualizes the hungry versus the sated body on the battlefield, comparing the ability of each to fight.[68] Echoing his mannerly prologue from the embassy speech, Odysseus asks now that Achilles allow similar appeasement, so that he might not lack his due (αὐτὰρ ἔπειτά σε δαιτὶ ἐνὶ κλισίης ἀρεσάσθω / πιείρῃ, ἵνα μή τι δίκης ἐπιδευὲς ἔχῃσθα, 19.179–180).[69] The rituals of apportioning food and drink and dividing spoils again self-reflexively color his speaking style, while his focus on the body's satisfaction draws attention to the group enactment of sharing and balance. Here he highlights the ability of sustenance to embolden the heart (θαρσαλέον . . . ἦτορ, 19.169) in a manner both physically and emotionally healthier than the morbid fire that feeds Achilles' fury.[70]

The exchange is triangulated among Agamemnon, Achilles, and Odysseus. Achilles responds directly only to Agamemnon, which suggests that he regards Odysseus as merely ancillary. But while Achilles treats Odysseus as little more than the king's mouthpiece, Agamemnon supports his adviser, complimenting his henchman as speaking "in proportion" (ἐν μοίρῃ, 19.186) and echoing Odysseus' urging of a formal, public division of food and spoils. Moreover, Achilles' speech responds directly to Odysseus' imagery; it is Odysseus' proposals that he ultimately accepts, resisting only the suggestion that his own body be involved in the sharing of food. Achilles declares that he would rather fight immediately than eat, and in bitter, elegiac tones he links the division of food to "divided" bodies of the Greek dead and especially to that of Patroclus (νῦν δ' οἱ μὲν κέαται δεδαϊγμένοι, 19.203; δεδαϊγμένος, 19.211; cf. 19.319). He vows that no food or drink will pass down his throat while his friend lies unavenged and that such activities are not a concern for him, but instead killing, carnage, and the painful groaning of men (19.214). Rather than use his own mouth for eating, he will cause the mouths of other men to emit cries of despair, as he feeds his grieving heart on their slaughter.

Achilles thus transforms the ritual apportioning of meat into an act that is inappropriate while human bodies lie dismembered by the enemy. Odysseus in reply regards this grim exchange of cutting up Trojan warriors in return for dismembered Greek corpses as a mismatch of dead and living bodies, which fatally ignores the necessary feeding of one's own vital belly.

He argues that a warrior quickly has his fill of battle (αἶψά τε φυλόπιδος πέλεται κόρος ἀνθρώποισιν, 19.221) and that the troops should not mourn the dead by fasting (γαστέρι δ' οὐ πως ἔστι νέκυν πενθῆσαι Ἀχαιούς, 19.225).

Consistent with his emphases in book 9, Odysseus strives to maintain balance in social ritual, focusing especially on the primacy of fulfilling physical need and insuring fair compensation. As before, Achilles replies to Odysseus' arguments by inverting the diplomat's orderly schema and thereby indicates his awareness of the metarhetorical import of Odysseus' tactics. He responds as much to Odysseus' stylistic patterning of communal ritual—to the scheme that orders both social behavior and suitable speech—as he does to the content of the argument. Achilles' reactions explicitly oppose his bodily *hexis* to that which Odysseus counsels. Instead of sharing food with the Greek leaders, Achilles uses his mouth vehemently to pour forth his grief (ἀδινῶς ἀνενείκατο, 19.314; cf. 19.315–337) and to cry aloud (κλαίων, 19.338). This causes the old men in the crowd to groan over their own losses (στενάχοντο, 19.338). Then, after Athena invigorates him (19.352–353), Achilles arms himself, gnashing his teeth (τοῦ καὶ ὀδόντων μὲν καναχὴ πέλε, 19.365) and eager for Trojans (ὁ δ' ἄρα Τρωσὶν μενεαίνων, 19.367).

The Greek leaders conduct as many of the restitutional rituals as they can without Achilles' full compliance. The sons of Nestor bring out the promised gifts for Achilles; Agamemnon swears publicly that he has never slept with Briseis, while all the Achaeans witness his oath sitting in orderly formation (κατὰ μοῖραν, 19.256); and, finally, the troops are fed. Order has been to some extent reestablished. But even Odysseus, the consummate host to Achilles' reluctant guest, cannot persuade the angry hero to speak or to eat in a manner that shows proper attention to group welfare, balanced exchange, and suitable community ritual. When, at the end of the book, Achilles' horses prophesy his quick death to him, they attribute it to "a mighty god" (θεός τε μέγας) and to Moira, the goddess of apportionment (19.410). Achilles responds that he knows that his lot (μόρος) is to die far from his family (19.421–422). An outsider to communal ritual, his sense of order and fair exchange recognizes only the lonesome portion he has received from the gods.

Like Helen in the *Odyssey* but with somewhat different emphasis, in the *Iliad* Odysseus serves an authorial function in the implementation of appropriate style. His bodily *hexis* in general emblematizes the notion of proportionment that underpins ideas about suitability, from his genial hosting act to his carefully balanced words. In the *Odyssey* and in later tradition, it becomes clear that this attention to fair-sharing is the trademark of the versatile self-performer, whose ability to change type may itself indicate the fundamental untrustworthiness of stylistic effect.

THE VERSATILE GUEST

In some contrast to the Iliadic Odysseus' focus on the fair portion that should also govern one's style, in the *Odyssey* the figure of Odysseus encapsulates the masquerading tactics employed by the agile trader of type. The epic has imbedded in its own narrative strategy an association between the visible characters Odysseus assumes and the way the story gets told. The *Odyssey* is structured around the numerous tales that are told of Odysseus and those that Odysseus himself constructs to convince his audiences that he is a believable type.[71] These all tend to underscore the suitability of the particular type, the authority it affords the oral performer, and the versatility of its adept use. Other characters are depicted as using the figure of Odysseus as a touchstone of this kind of verbal authority in their self-performances, and the typical styles that Odysseus himself assumes carefully mirror the attitudes and outlooks (i.e., the *habitus*) of his audiences.

Since the successes of Odysseus' assumed characters are dependent on audience reception, and since, in turn, audiences are persuaded by those viewpoints that match or resemble their own, Odysseus embodies this focus on appearing plausible by speaking appropriately and projecting a type that reflects or flatteringly offsets that of the audience. The poem's narrative strategies configure this repertoire of types as the hero's greatest strength, even as it also suggests that such masquerades may disrupt the assumed match between visible demeanor and verbal style or between visible character and true identity.[72]

The stories of Odysseus that Telemachus hears in the early books of the *Odyssey* reveal as much about the tellers as about the absent man. As the example of Helen's story discussed above shows, they demonstrate just how dependent the tale is on the teller and link the character of Odysseus to this narrative flexibility. These scenes and those in which Odysseus himself tells his stories show that the adept speaker engages in a negotiation between the type he projects and the character of the audience when determining the style of his oral performance. As a keystone of this attention to suitability, he may claim knowledge of a figure important to his audience or liken this figure to himself as a means of making his assumed type appear more authoritative and more similar in *habitus* to his hearers. For Nestor, Odysseus is thus a good advisor of men; for Helen, a careful disguiser and interpreter of others; and for Menelaus, a man of many travels and much experience. Moreover, Nestor and Helen tell stories that put them in intimate contact with Odysseus, as his special match and confidant.

These speakers all use the figure of Odysseus to shore up their own claims to authoritative speech. Since the ostensible aim in these scenes is praise of Odysseus with his son as appreciative audience, the strategy is circular and yet effective, a verbal reciprocity that mirrors the formal rituals of the guest-host relationship. If Odysseus is shown to be worthy of praise, and if he is like the speaker, then the speaker himself becomes praiseworthy and all the more capable, therefore, of praising Odysseus in appropriate and persuasive fashion. These dinner-table enactments of the mutually reinforcing strategies that structure the aristocratic *habitus* thus visibly manifest the statuses to which the speakers lay claim. Meanwhile, their authoritative oral styles and noble deportments all add status and authority, in turn, to the depictions of Odysseus in their narratives.

The subtly alternating types that Odysseus assumes in his deceptive narratives are all calculated to account for his identity and reasons for his presence in Ithaca. These are similarly chosen to reflect the outlook of the audience and similarly invoke the figure of "Odysseus" to bolster claims to authoritative speech. But for Odysseus in disguise, it is more essential that his audiences regard him as a believable type than that they believe the details of his stories. He thus employs elements that seem plausible and elicit sympathy in his audiences as well as *topoi* that give rise to a sense of familiarity without intimate knowledge. That is, he trades on likeness and probability to insure his good reception. He utilizes a character type that is similar to but not quite his own, so that his stories accurately represent the traveler's adventures he might have had if he were of a slightly lower status—a less prominent aristocrat or a wealthy merchant, perhaps, but still a wanderer and a stranger to many shores.

Odysseus' verbal *hexis* is carefully adapted both to the physical circumstances in which he finds himself (i.e., the state of his body and dress) and to his interlocutors' character types. Attention to proportion seems to govern stylistic choice here as well, in that story length is also calibrated to suit situation and audience. Only the story told to Eumaeus is of any extended length; of the other accounts, only that told to Penelope is substantial, although in comparison to the tale Eumaeus hears, it is relatively concise in its encomiastic formality. All the tales present Odysseus in a guise not unlike his identity in the *Odyssey:* a formerly affluent wanderer, adept at the invention of strategies and plots, who is continuously in the process of outwitting or being outwitted and who fought in the Trojan war with his own command, but in the carefully obscure capacity of a minor leader.[73]

Odysseus' choice of Crete as his fictional homeland, moreover, introduces an additional element of this versatile style: the *topos* of what might be termed the familiarly foreign, that is, the use of a geographical area or a population that has a sharply defined profile (i.e., its characteristics are known in a stereotyped fashion), but one striking precisely because no one has specific knowledge of it.[74] The susceptibility of an audience to the reassuring and known makes persuasive the elements that are familiarly distant, because they capitalize on the audience's satisfaction in recognizing the stereotype. Their very distance pleasurably tweaks the curiosity, and knowledge of factual detail cannot interfere either with the comforting chauvanism their use fosters in the audience or with the speaker's verbal disguise.

Each of the scenes in which Odysseus uses his Cretan tale to mask his true identity reveals his skill in the implementation of an appropriate style. For instance, since the hero is ignorant of his connection to the shepherd whom he meets on the shores of Ithaca, he does not bother to deploy the figure of "Odysseus" in his speech as a means of forging allegiance. The story he tells to the disguised Athena is condensed and pithy; he uses a tight string of causalities (οὕνεκα . . . εἵνεκα . . . οὕνεκα, 13.262–266) to draw the listener along quickly to the plot points that account for his presence on the island and his relatively healthy, well-dressed aspect. Odysseus paints his character as one fearsome to contend with: proud, shrewd, and quick-thinking (as his story is quickly devised) but not fundamentally cruel or morally suspect, which is precisely how the poet of the *Odyssey* presents Odysseus.[75]

At the outset of this story, the narrator describes the wary Odysseus as constraining his story (πάλιν δ' ὅ γε λάζετο μῦθον, 13.254). Odysseus' brief account of himself shows the calculating preparedness of a man who must "always be reviewing in his breast very shrewd thoughts" (αἰεὶ ἐνὶ στήθεσσι νόον πολυκερδέα νωμῶν, 13.255). To hold back one's *muthos*, then, indicates here a stylistic choice at the level of invention: the restriction of one's story to those elements that will most quickly paint a believable character and the economical, tightly knit phrases that suit both the character painted and the audience to whom he speaks.[76] If the shepherd had not been Athena, the device would probably have worked as he had intended. When the goddess reveals herself to her favorite, she laughs and teasingly compliments him on his capacity for such trickery (13.287–295). While this was not the effect he had anticipated, the goddess shows her appreciation of his verbal masquerade by providing the physical disguise that will help him win his way home.

When Odysseus has been transformed by Athena into a destitute and ragged older man, the poet portrays him carefully suiting his demeanor and speaking style to this new appearance. But he also alters these slightly, depending on his audience. With Eumaeus he takes his time in beginning his tale, referring to the leisurely rhythms of post-dinner performances and the pleasures of the long story (14.193–195). He thus draws attention to the enactment of rituals that cement alliances by underscoring the participants' shared behaviors, a maneuver that recalls his attempts to handle Achilles in the *Iliad*. In the *Odyssey,* however, the interlocutors are both apparently low-status older men. Odysseus' opening accordingly captures in its languorous phrases the sensual pleasure of spinning out a story when time, sustenance, and company permit (εἴη μὲν νῦν νῶιν ἐπὶ χρόνον ἠμὲν ἐδωδὴ / ἠδὲ μέθυ γλυκερὸν κλισίης ἔντοσθεν ἐοῦσιν, 14.193–194). The soothing prologue serves as a stylistic sweetener for his protracted narrative, fashioned to suit the situation and the taste of an aging, sated listener.

In his narrative Odysseus seeks to persuade his interlocutor of his sincerity by using a style that reflects in an unobtrusive and yet satisfying manner the worldview of his listener. He emphasizes the hard-luck details of a fate he knows to be not so different from that of Eumaeus, focusing particularly on the repeated threat of enforced slavery (14.296–297, 340) and couching his story in the pithy language of well-traveled old age.[77] The scene is also full of inter- and intratextual humor. For example, deploying a phrase made famous as Achilles' description of Odysseus' dissembling nature in the *Iliad*, the beggar claims to hate "like the gates of Hades" the very type he is impersonating (14.156–157). His use of the proverb thus mimes the bitter style of Achilles, so that Odysseus in this episode is shown playing against his own versatile type, condemning the *polumêchanos* character even as he impersonates a lower-status version of it.

The famous dissembler's condemnation of dissemblers while he is also disguised as one—both as a mendicant who might get food for good lies and as a native of Crete—sets up one of the most intricate instances in Greek literary tradition of the imposture of type. The beggar's narrative is also laced with pungent descriptions and comic echoes of episodes similar to those related by the Homeric poet of Odysseus' struggles. For instance, the calamities of the Cretan beggar begin with a raid gone bad, like that of the Cicones episode (9.39–59). The beggar even has himself cry out, as Odysseus did in the sea near Scheria, "How I wish that I had died and met my fate there [in Egypt / in Troy]!" (14.274–275; cf. 5.308–309). The episodes that resemble those related in quick succession to the disguised Athena turn up here in greater and more colorful detail. For instance, a supplication scene reported in a single line (13.273) is described to Eumaeus in six, with specificities of the physical position of the suppliant, his emotions, and the zealous pursuit of his attackers (13.279–282).

Later that night, when he is suffering from the cold night wind, Odysseus tells a tale that he introduces to Eumaeus and the other herdsmen as "a bit of boasting" (or "wishful talk," εὐξάμενός τι ἔπος, 14.463). This he declares has been induced by the wine he has drunk, which gives rise in general to a voluble and rowdy demeanor and speaking style (14.463–466). Faced with his body's needs and seeking cover for his exposed and shivering aspect, Odysseus claims a reason for the verbal style that suits his assumed character type: like the beggar's general demeanor, his style "wishes" for something in return for the telling. He relates how "Odysseus" tricked a young and eager soldier into giving up his cloak for the night, so that he (the beggar-narrator) would not freeze while on watch with Odysseus at Troy. The beggar gives Odysseus a line that is in fact uttered by Agamemnon in the *Iliad*, when he is telling the Greek leaders about his dream (κλῦτε, φίλοι· θεῖός μοι ἐνύπνιον ἦλθεν ὄνειρος, *Il.* 2.56; cf. *Od.* 14.495). Once again the Homeric poet depicts Odysseus quoting from Iliadic tradition, giving his character a line from a famous speech, here transposed to a humorous context. He thereby shows the beggar associating "Odysseus" with a kind of mild and witty deceit, which seeks material gain but does not really harm others. The young man whose cloak was thus appropriated went off proudly on a mission to Agamemnon.

The style of the tale and clever strategies of the central characters (i.e., the beggar and "Odysseus") suit the late hour and the wine-drinking audience, who appreciate a good trick well executed, as Eumaeus remarks wryly (οὐδέ τί πω παρὰ μοῖραν, 14.508–509). Like the tales told to Telemachus, the narrator associates himself with Odysseus as a clever speaker to raise his own status as narrator. He also uses the story about the hero's trick as a ruse to gain the same item of clothing for himself. Odysseus' telling a story about "Odysseus" while in disguise as a similarly clever type redoubles the intricacy of the rhetorical maneuver, while the pairing of the cloaks gives them a symbolic weight, suggesting the doubling of personas that help to mask the identity of the hero.[78] The scene thus calls attention to the combination of deportment and oral self-presentation that marks the speaker as a particular type and lends veracity to his speech, even as the tale he tells calls into question this same veracity.

The story that the beggar relates to Penelope in book 19 (165–202) is also attentive to suitability, and also highlights the visible details of bodily dress and deportment that may reinforce or offset the speaker's own visible type (see further in ch. 3). This time the disguised Odysseus employs a highbrow style that suits the aristocratic exchange of bloodlines. In addition, his response to Penelope's test of his claims about "Odysseus" leads to a layered depiction of the body's dress that suggests the many layers of its owner's character. The verses that open this tale use encomiastic conventions to gratify the interlocutor by heightening the speaker's status. He thereby offsets his visibly bedraggled appearance by situating his fictional persona so that it basks in the glow of formal praise of Crete (19.172–173).[79] The narrator enumerates the multitude of peoples and their languages and then focuses on the most famous city in narrative tradition, Cnossos, identifying himself as a lesser-known grandson of Minos and brother of Idomeneus, a name the beggar has already invoked in earlier tales to place himself within the Trojan war story.[80] For the noble Penelope, then, the pauper presents himself as a prince, verbally ensconcing himself at the center of an elaborate praise of his chosen homeland and genealogy and setting himself up close to the figure of Odysseus, with whom he claims the formal bond of gift exchange (19.171–185).[81] Fully two-thirds of the beggar's tale is devoted to the Odysseus of Penelope's desire; he feeds her hunger for news of a man far visibly (if not verbally) nobler than her interlocutor, detailing accurately his fine clothes and attractive type.

Homer thus shows Odysseus utilizing similar elements in his stories but altering his typical style (e.g., length of descriptions, diction, emphasized elements) so that his verbal *hexis* suits those of his hearers, even though he remains dressed in his beggar's rags. The attention to balance and proportion that so significantly characterizes Odysseus' type in the *Iliad* is complemented by this focus in the *Odyssey* on suitability. Both have to do with a notion of fitting measure, so that in Homer Odysseus' figure emblematizes this central aspect of style. However, his reception by those to whom he tells his tales reveals not only how persuasive such carefully fitting self-representations can be but also how much suspicion this versatile type can arouse. Both Eumaeus and Penelope, his two most important listeners, remain on the whole slightly wary of him, while never questioning his identity as a once-wealthy traveler reduced to begging. Recall that Eumaeus twice deems the beggar's speaking style suitable (οὐδέ τί πω παρὰ μοῖραν, 14.509; κατὰ μοῖραν, 17.580), an indication of his skill in matching his *hexis* to that of his audience.

The beggar's familiar type and ready words may themselves excite suspicion, however, if they seem too obviously altered to win material goods, as Eumaeus warns the disguised Odysseus early in their meeting (αἶψα κε καὶ σύ, γεραιέ, ἔπος παρατεκτήναιο / εἴ τίς τοι χλαῖνάν τε χιτῶνά τε εἵματα δοίη, 14.131–132). The beggar goes ahead and tries the ploy of knowing "Odysseus" anyway (14.321), which causes Eumaeus to exclaim in frustration (14.363–368) that his boast is inappropriate (οὐ κατὰ κόσμον, 14.363). Eumaeus later reports the claim to Penelope (στεῦται, 17.525) as a reason for being wary. While Penelope also tests the stranger regarding his supposed contact with Odysseus (17.215–218), both she and Eumaeus nevertheless find pleasure in the beggar's tales. This pleasure is acknowledged easily by Eumaeus when he describes the storyteller to Penelope, while his vocabulary hints that such facile storytellers might be suspect. To depict the beggar's effect on his audience, he uses the verb *thelgô* (17.514, 521), which can denote a potentially dangerous or deceptive charming of an audience. Telemachus uses the same word when, upon viewing the newly youthful stranger who claims to be his father, he suspects Odysseus' identity and guesses that he is being bewitched by a god (16.194–195).[82]

These scenes indicate a lurking suspicion of the adept speaker and of the pleasure his words may afford. The implication of παρατεκτήναιο, the word Eumaeus uses in warning the beggar off the technique of claiming to know Odysseus, is that the mendicant may use some "skill" (*technê*) in suitably fashioning his speaking style.[83] That is, he might alter his style in accordance with his sense of how he could gratify his listener, just as the traveling worker (*dêmioergos*) skilled in shoemaking might offer different fashions to different customers.

This concern about the mutable style of the skilled speaker emerges in much more explicit form in the classical period, when professional orators seek to shrug off any indications of being too obviously versatile in their speaking styles, especially in relation to the representation of character type.[84] Note also that the pleasure of the skilled oral performance becomes another cause for suspicion in the classical period, which is aroused particularly by the adept oratorical styles of the sophists.[85] In the *Odyssey* this apprehension centers on the figure of the beggar Odysseus.

CHAPTER 3

VISIBLE TYPES
AND VISUALIZING
STYLES IN
ARCHAIC POETRY

Archaic poets conjoin taste or touch with visual effect to characterize elements of verbal style, which strike the ear as they strike the eye—a conceptual synesthesia that gives physical weight to the spoken word and persuasive force to concrete detail. This sensual characterization of verbal impact has its more concrete extension in the visible features of a speaker's style. In literary depiction, the narrator may provide these details or they may be found in portraits deployed by adept and seductive performers themselves, who frequently offer visualizations of dress and deportment to flatter or entice their hearers. A speaker's use of such images also helps to delineate his own verbal and visible *hexis* and thus should display his character. But these physical details may cloak rather than reveal character, which brings into focus the central problem with stylistic elements in the first place: that they are mutable, which means that the agile oral performer can change them like a suit of clothes. Indeed, the dress and deportment of the body may also operate as a distraction, masking identity or intention.

This chapter explores the visible aspects of style and analyzes the sources of their perception as potentially deceitful, seductive, or overwhelming. Figures such as Pandora at one extreme and Thersites at the other highlight essential aspects of how the body signifies stylistically. But Helen and Odysseus illuminate subtler aspects of corporeal style, their elusive or changeable physical types matching their distracting or mutable verbal styles. The deportment and dress of these figures, as well as the significant objects and compelling images with which they are associated, thus raise more complex and disturbing questions about how one's visible manner may profoundly affect one's message.

THE BODY AS PUBLIC MEASURE

The body, especially in Homeric representation but also in Hesiod and the lyric poets, invokes ideas about order and proportion by means of concrete attributes. As an emblematic entity, it is thus essential to understanding the relationship between physical appearance and speaking style. Jean-Pierre Vernant has argued that archaic and classical representation measures the body in relation to the visible indications of one's social stature. "The Greek body of Antiquity," he explains, "appears in the manner of a coat of arms and presents through emblematic traits the multiple 'values'—concerning his life, beauty, and power—with which an individual is endowed, values which he bears and which proclaim his *timê*, his dignity and rank."[1] Vernant emphasizes that these bodies are situated within the visual field and measured along a continuum from light to dark. Just as the warrior's gleaming armor may foreshadow his victorious forays on the battlefield (e.g., *Il.* 19.365–383), so do the Furies' murky and blood-drenched forms mirror their grim role in death and retribution (e.g., A. *Eum.* 52). Physical grace, which itself may effect a visual persuasion, is also conceived of as a bright, tactile thing. The beauty enhancer *charis*, for instance, which can be poured over the body like a shining, liquid gown (e.g., Hes. *WD* 65), is associated in its Indo-European equivalents with light.[2]

There are also bodies in Greek literature that are categorized less by this public measure than by qualities that reveal their ambiguous places within the social schema. In their veiled or disguised forms, these sorts of bodies may invoke epistemological concerns similar to those that Froma Zeitlin has identified with bodies in tragedy: their visible presentations often call attention to the possibility of change, imposture, doubling, or otherwise eluding the eye.[3] Their depictions may involve touch (from soft to hard) and smell (from perfume to stench)—more intimate measures of body type.[4] When bright, a body's high-status gleam sometimes serves to mask rather than to reveal its identity. Shining garments may call attention to it, suggesting its specially luminous aspect and sometimes revealing its alluring skin.[5] Its possessor's eyes may meet the onlooker with a flashing glance, so that the viewer is himself viewed and disarmed.[6] Vernant does not differentiate in his study between depictions of male and female bodies, but in fact it is precisely at the gender divide that distinctions may be most pronounced.

As has been exhaustively documented in recent years, archaic literature traces strong symbolic and social divisions between the sexes. Those who deviate from the assigned roles and types are punished with blame (and blaming narratives) or violent ends. Gender differences are clearly important to a discussion of how archaic poets think stylistic elements operate in persuasive situations, and some of the most important of these differences coalesce around the representation of the body and visible type. Female figures are clearly more often objectified and given less agency in archaic literature, which means that their connections to ideas about style are also distinct from those of male figures. The roles of versatile types such as Helen and Odysseus may overlap to a certain extent in Homer, but even there the figure of Odysseus serves a much more consistently authorial function in relation to notions of style. As will become increasingly clear in the discussions that follow, the broader associations of their figures reveal that the beautiful female form is most often highlighted as a passive object in the deployment of stylistic effects, while the clever male performer tends to remain in an active role, in command of those effects.[7]

The apprehension inspired by certain female figures in epic is paralleled by the revulsion evident in the more practical worry of the lyric poets: that the wife may look as she is, being just as brutish in heart and mind as she is in face and body. Semonides' notorious poem on the characters of women (fr. 7 W²) repeatedly relates appearance to internal makeup by comparing different types of women to different animals and natural elements.[8] The poet lingers perversely on the hideous bodies and characters of redoubtable types like the pig woman (whose habits he deems "disorderly" [ἄκοσμα], 4), the dog woman (who cannot speak "sweetly" [μειλίχως], 18), the sea woman (whose demeanor is "unsweet" [ἀμείλιχος] to all, 35) and the monkey woman (whose visage is "most debased" [αἴσχιστα], 73). The beautiful but high-maintenance body and fastidious character of the mare woman, on the other hand, indicates that she is no better than her uglier counterparts.[9] Only the bee woman, the one potentially good type among so many bad ones, is not made to look her part. Her busy actions make her husband's life flourish; she avoids the titillating chatter (ἀφροδισίους λόγους, 91) of other women and possesses no distinguishing physical attributes. Yet the helpful wife, it turns out, may be the worst of all, her seemingly prudent type (σωφρονεῖν δοκεῖ) masking disgraceful behavior (λωβωμένη, 108–109).[10]

For Semonides, then, the appearance of the female body is a troubling thing. Strongly indicative of character type and speaking style, it provides the visual clues to which burdensome type a woman is. Whether beautiful or ugly, the female form causes disruption and heartache, since the messages it conveys about character and verbal type are always negative. The good wife has no body to be remarked upon; although she may also avoid dangerous and idle speech, she still brings grief to her husband by her ability to *appear* virtuous. Semonides ends his poem with a bitter and damning reference to Helen, whom he credits with initiating the trouble womankind embodies. She represents Semonides' equivalent of Hesiod's Pandora: the first female bane to be visited upon men, her dangerous allure precipitated mankind's fall into a post–Golden Age misery.

Among male types, shape may register public rank but usually without the ominous implications that attend the female form. Hephaestus' shambling gait (*Il.* 1.599–608) and Thersites' bow-legged, lame-footed, hunch-shouldered, pointy-headed, and fuzzy-haired aspect (*Il.* 2.217–219) stand out in Homeric epic for their general deviation from the heroic norm. The narrator describes the disorderly speech and misshapen body of the latter, in sharp contradistinction to the fine-speaking, broad-shouldered heroes. In a typically tart response to the epic tendency to insist on a match between visible stature and temperament, the iambic poet Archilochus praises a captain whom he prefers to the taller, more dapper type, pointedly describing a short, stocky man while defending his firm-footed (ἀσφαλέως . . . ποσσί), upright character (fr. 114 W²). There is, however, one character in Homer who has this short, stocky stature, who often appears to be an ill-favored type, and yet who speaks better than any of the other heroes because his mind is firm (*empedos*) and well-grounded like his step: Odysseus.[11] In Homer he most consistently embodies the possibility that the match between outward appearance and true type may not always hold up and therefore that character may not always be clearly perceptible to the eye.

This epistemological quandary surfaces primarily with such versatile types as Helen and Odysseus, and it is precisely this fact that inspires the awareness of style as distracting or changeable in the first place. The significant visible features of their figures suggest that style involves dressing up and thus may be enticingly elaborate, deceptive, or too easily altered. The roots of this suspicion of style as fancy dress can be found in archaic poets' depictions of feminine adornment and its role in scenes of seduction.

FEMININE ADORNMENT AND VISUAL SEDUCTION

In his study of persuasion in Greek tragedy, R. G. A. Buxton remarked, "To the Greeks *all peitho* was 'seductive.'"[12] In archaic literature, all kinds of speech may be compelling in some manner analogous to physical attraction. Moreover, any visually pleasing elements that a speaker may deploy are recognized as equally persuasive and therefore equally "seductive." Oral persuasion and sexual seduction are treated as intersecting, as the presence of the goddess Peitho in vase paintings of marriage and seduction scenes also attests. Poets assess the impressive oral performance in connection to such scenes, whether or not sexual desire or attraction in fact plays any obvious role in the given speech. From early in archaic depiction, this visual seduction also serves to incite apprehension that adornment may conceal and deceive, that the decorative body may mask a doggish mind.

Archaic poets often treat female bodies with apprehension precisely because of their status as highly prized objects whose shapes and garments effect a visible persuasion. Where a man's winning verbal style may conceal trickery, the suspicion aroused by physical appeal is generally reserved for women. The depictions of the epic poets indicate that women of high status do not necessarily command much verbal authority. Helen is relatively unusual in this regard, a status for which her semidivine genealogy may help to account. Yet, as a bridal figure whose repeated seizures underscore her value, Helen also embodies the paradigmatic exchanged sign that operates as a symbolic entity rather than a full-blown character.[13] Archaic depictions tend to suggest that a woman's appearance alone displays her worth; her body is decorated and praised accordingly, often as a public preparation for marriage.[14] A bride's elaborately adorned form visibly manifests her family's pride in her stature and reinforces her value for her husband. These depictions of upper-class women as prized objects encouraged the association of an eroticized, visually oriented style with the female form. This in turn fostered a connection between the decorative female body and an idea of style as a distracting, feminized, and ultimately suspect embellishment. Both Helen and Pandora suggest the dangers associated with such decorative objects, which may further confirm that from early on in the literature, the adorned bridal figure also embodies the fear that she may bring ruin.[15] The figure of Pandora is this suspicion's ultimate symbol: without parents, fabricated as a trick for men by the gods, she exists only to emblematize this conundrum.

In *Works and Days* Hesiod warns that while Zeus may straighten out human affairs (ἰθύνει, 7; cf. 9), he is also himself devious (μητιόεις, 51) and, like the gods collectively, hides things from humans (42, 47). The primary and most disastrous example of this tendency to concealment is the deceitful object Pandora, the figure who constitutes Hesiod's most important contribution to an understanding of archaic ideas about style. Her carefully crafted and well-adorned exterior masks a doggish mind and cunning character type (κύνεόν τε νόον καὶ ἐπίκλοπον ἦθος, *WD* 67). The poet does not give her direct speech, but he emphasizes the deceit (δόλον, *Th.* 589; *WD* 83) that she embodies and the lies and wheedling words that are in her heart (ψεύδεά θ' αἱμυλίους τε λόγους, *WD* 78).[16] Recall also that Hesiod primarily associates *kosmos*—the word so central to ideas about style—with Pandora (*Th.* 573, 587; *WD* 72, 76). Scholars have emphasized that Pandora is a fabricated object, whose very construction signifies her deceitful nature.[17] Cunning concealments are tricks practiced by males with deceitful minds (e.g., Zeus and Prometheus), but the decorative figure of Pandora is the trick itself. She thus manifestly embodies this masking of true type and as such symbolizes paradigmatically the disjunction between the pleasing exterior and the displeasing interior.[18]

Peitho—the goddess who, along with Aphrodite and Himeros (Desire), attends the marriage of Helen and Paris on many vase paintings—in *Works and Days* helps the Charites decorate the neck of Pandora with gold necklaces (73–74).[19] Iconographic evidence thus supports a connection between Pandora and Helen as decorated brides, and the involvement of Aphrodite and Peitho in the adornment of both.[20] The jewels—the element in the scene with which Peitho appears to be most strongly associated—indicate the added touch that achieves persuasion, the enticement to bed or to some equally dangerous activity. That is, these golden adornments serve as visible signifiers of the stylistic element in the seduction scene, directly analogous to the decorative words that charm the beloved.[21] Compare the deception of Zeus (*Il.* 14), in which Hera bathes in her bedroom built by Hephaestus, bedecks her divine body with a veil made by Athena, and fastens it with golden pins. Then, having completed her toilette (πάντα . . . κόσμον, 14.187), she goes to Aphrodite for a special belt (κεστός) that contains erotic appeal (φιλότης), desire (ἵμερος), and intimate talk (ὀαριστὺς πάρφασις, 14.216–217). This last item is a titillating verbal style, so that both visual appeal and seductive words work to persuade the beloved to bed. A scholiast glosses ὀαριστὺς πάρφασις with πειθώ; the goddess seems to lurk behind this seduction scene as well.[22] While this decorative combination of jewels and enticing language is most closely associated with Aphrodite, Pandora, and Helen, note also that Hephaestus and Athena help to set the scene by providing well-crafted settings and bodily adornments.[23] The poets represent craft as a necessary element in seduction, while the figure of Peitho serves as the conceptual yoke between physical ornamentation and the finely formed words of the agile seducer.

The seduction scene is thus steeped in the kind of physical sensation generally associated with style, the impact of which overwhelms the senses and often precipitates deception (cf. Hes. *Th.* 205; *h.Ven.* 7, 33). This impact is usually visible and tactile, the multiplying of sensory effects signaling the success of the conquest. Just as sweet (*meilichios, glukus*) speech may entice and bewitch, so may sweet (*meilichios, glukus*) desire envelop the senses, leading to a similar kind of distraction (cf. *Il.* 3.446, 14.328; *Th.* 206; *h.Ven.* 2, 45, 143). In Aphrodite's own seduction scene, not only does she decorate her body in elaborate fashion, so that Anchises upon seeing her is struck by the same wonder and desire that she first experienced upon seeing him (*h.Ven.* 57, 84–85, 91). She also deceives him, likening her body to that of a young girl (82) and giving herself a mortal lineage.[24] Entering the bed of a goddess is dangerous, as Anchises knows; he prays that she might have a gracious attitude (εὔφρονα θυμόν, 102) toward him. One may run the risk of being unmanned (cf. *Od.* 10.341) and of being eternally conquered by a dreamy forgetfulness, the half-life of the goddess' consort: compare the Sirens' sweet call and the soft-textured slumber in which Hupnos (persuaded by Hera) envelopes Zeus (ἐγὼ μαλακὸν περὶ κῶμα κάλυψα, *Il.* 14.359). In Sappho (fr. 2 L-P) this *kôma* is what tumbles down (καταίρει) upon those who worship in the precinct of Aphrodite, the gentle lull that attends the goddess' presence.[25] For the lyric poet this lull is part of the general enticement of the precinct and thus of Aphrodite. In *Iliad* 14 it is a place of danger, a stopping of the plot, the wrong end of the story to which Zeus (who drives the war narrative) has been lured by his decorative, guile-minded wife.

Sappho depicts desire as manipulative, if not outright deceptive. In fragment 1 L-P the narrator-lover plays the willing subject of desire,[26] calling upon Aphrodite and recording a teasing conversation that she has had with the goddess. Aphrodite promises to turn events in her favor and to make the object of her desire want her in return. Sappho emphasizes the circularity of desire, and here Aphrodite's role is central; as in the *Iliad*, the goddess promises to arouse in the beloved yearning for the pining lover.[27] Aphrodite thus directs the path of desire, while her assistant Peitho effects the change of heart in the beloved (18–19). Sappho hails her Muse as "Aphrodite of the decorated chair" (ποικιλόθρον')[28] and "guile-weaving" (δολοπλόκε). Such designations combine the visual seduction of intricate adornment like the goddess' *kestos* and the necklaces (ποικίλον, *Il.* 14.215; παμποίκιλοι, *h.Ven.* 88) with the guile-minded qualities of those who do the seducing (δολοφρονέουσα, *Il.* 3.405; cf. Hera, *Il.* 14.197, 300, 329).[29] In fragment 1, Aphrodite serves as the deceitful, decorative manipulator of desire, who deploys *peithô* like the clever brides she cherishes.

The close association of Peitho and Aphrodite reveals that erotic encounters are linked to persuasive situations from early in Greek art and literature and particularly to their dangerously feminized stylistic aspects, such as the decoration of the body that aids seductive speech. Thus corporeal style is sometimes conceived of as an aspect of seduction (e.g., *Il.* 14.166–221) or vice versa (e.g., *Od.* 6.141–210). The association of style with feminine charms and deceit, which figures such as Helen and Pandora embody, helps to delineate a central problem with style: that such decorative elements may distract both ear and eye, overwhelming the listener so that he fails to attend properly to the content of the speech. In Homeric epic the visual significations of the bodies of Helen and Odysseus reveal the intricacies of how visible aspects of style achieve this distraction.

VISIBLE STATURE AND STYLE IN HOMER

Homer depicts Helen and Odysseus as especially associated with activities that distract the eye, including alterations of dress and deportment (Odysseus) and the plying of luminous veils (Helen). Like the careful calibrations of his verbal style, the visible details of Odysseus' impersonations sometimes mirror the self-presentations of his interlocutors. At other times, his speeches paint verbal portraits that gratify his audience, as a means of offsetting his less than heroic appearance. Helen's physical presence in Homer tends to be veiled and gleaming. Her body is obscured by shining fabrics or involved in their rich manufacture, and she both manipulates and is propelled by this association. The two figures are associated with the use of veils and cloaks, gestures that conform to a larger technique of drawing the eye away from another interpretation of the situation, so that their audiences focus less on Helen's culpability, for example, or Odysseus' identity. Their visible deployment of cloaks and veils is thus directly analogous to the verbal deployment of character affects that obscure their true types.

Homer also depicts Helen as literally weaving a richly styled narrative that revolves around her, while he shows Odysseus as figuratively weaving his character in the style to which his audiences are accustomed. If both are figures for the poet, as so many scholars have maintained, they are also proto-oratorical figures, whose abilities center in part on their manipulations of visible stature, which Aristotle would later reluctantly admit constitutes a crucial component of the rhetor's style.[30] Thus the figures of Helen and Odysseus signify more specific aspects of poetic representation and production than has generally been noticed.[31] Their associations with weaving and fabrics link them emblematically to the verbal and visual elements of style that are most effective in the oral context.[32] The Homeric poet's emphasis on the richness, delicacy, and sheen of the materials used by Helen connects her figure to the manner of composition, the play of fabrics paralleling her use of soft and flattering speech.[33]

Odysseus tends instead to describe rich and gleaming materials for purposes of persuasion, but different styles of dress are also strongly bound up with the structuring of his return. Divine females stand ready to clothe him, and often in situations that hinge on his ability to persuade, the quality of his dress affects his verbal style. Odysseus and Helen thus yoke together the realms of literal and figurative weaving in a manner that centers on the visualizing, quasi-tactile manipulation of narrative on the one hand, and the plying of fabrics to control audience reception on the other. Their figures are maneuvered through the plot by goddesses, in a manner that foregrounds the dressing and undressing of bodies. Their corporeal styles are thus linked to plot structure, their figures signifying stylistic choices in both the narrative frames and their own speeches.

THE CHANGEABLE BODY
AND VISUALIZING STYLE: ODYSSEUS

In book 3 of the *Iliad* Priam inquires about the identity of a short, broad-shouldered man, whom he likens to a ram (ἀρνειῷ . . . ἔϊσκω, 3.197). When Helen identifies the man as Odysseus, the Trojan elder Antenor sketches the image that Odysseus presented when he came to address the Trojan assembly. He was a man of downcast and fixed expression (ἴδεσκε κατὰ χθονὸς ὄμματα πήξας) and rigid deportment (σκῆπτρον δ' οὔτ' ὀπίσω οὔτε προπρηνὲς ἐνώμα, / ἀλλ' ἀστεμφὲς ἔχεσκεν) (3.218–219). He *looked like* a stupid man (ἀΐδρεϊ φωτὶ ἐοικώς, 3.219), so that an observer would think him sullen and foolish (φαίης κε ζάκοτόν τέ τιν' ἔμμεναι ἄφρονά τ' αὔτως, 3.220). His speaking style, in sharp contrast, was grand and remarkable. Antenor declares, "But when he sent forth his great voice from his breast, his words seeming like winter snows, then no other man could compete with Odysseus" (ἀλλ' ὅτε δὴ ὄπα τε μεγάλην ἐκ στήθεος εἵη / καὶ ἔπεα νιφάδεσσιν ἐοικότα χειμερίῃσιν, / οὐκ ἂν ἔπειτ' Ὀδυσῆΐ γ' ἐρίσσειε βροτὸς ἄλλος, 3.221–223).

Even though Odysseus is not himself much to look at in the *Iliad*, in his role as henchman of the Achaian leaders, he abuses and physically controls ugly, ill-speaking, low-status types. His stolid bodily *hexis* in the Trojan assembly is thus offset both by his verbal snowstorm and by his adept control of the troops. Like a fleecy ram, he moves unarmed through the ranks (3.195–198), a sure-footed leader whose best defense is his verbal dexterity. Because Odysseus serves such an important authorial function in Homeric epic, the interconnections between his own *hexis* and his reactions to the self-presentations of others are central to understanding what this figure signifies about the visible aspects of style.

In the *Iliad* the counselor Odysseus uses verbal condemnation and physical violence to suppress unruly types such as Thersites in formal assembly. On the spying mission in book 10, he and Diomedes between them handle the ill-favored Trojan Dolon in similar fashion. In his Iliadic role as Agamemnon's diplomat and facilitator, Odysseus thus scorns the lack of physical *charis* that marks these humbler types, especially when they are represented as graceless speakers. The Homeric narrator describes these characters as ugly and demonstrates their rhetorical inferiority by emphasizing Odysseus' control of them in verbal exchanges. In the earlier scene he remarks on the hero's particular revulsion toward his victim, while in book 10 he makes clear the cruel disdain with which Odysseus treats the trembling Trojan.

At *Iliad* 2.220 the narrator declares that Achilles and Odysseus hate the woolly-headed Thersites the most. Odysseus' scornful verbal control of him underlines the detestable profile he is given by the narrator, who carefully details his physical ugliness (2.217–219). Thersites receives public, shaming punishment for his insubordination: Odysseus beats him with the scepter held by the leaders in public assembly and condemns him harshly, threatening to strip the disorderly speaker of his clothes, as if his naked, disfigured body would clearly reveal by visible signs the disfigurement of his words (2.258–268).[34] Odysseus also matches potential violence to his own heroic body with that to Thersites' unheroic one (2.258–264). After roundly denouncing the blame of kings by the common man, he declares that if Thersites continues in this mode, his own head (i.e., Odysseus') will no longer remain on his shoulders if he does not strip Thersites and send him howling back to the ships. Tone for tone and body for body, Odysseus matches and trumps Thersites' inappropriate challenge, finishing off his control of the disruptive man with a blow that brings tears to his eyes (2.265–266). His harsh treatment of Thersites, which joins abusive, controlling words with an abusive and controlling deportment in a public performance of authority, is received with nervous laughter and general approbation (2.270–277).

Odysseus thus turns Thersites' potentially disastrous attack on the vulnerable Agamemnon into an occasion for the derisive rejection of the ugly soldier's ugly speech. He thereby distracts the troops from the accurate content of Thersites' speech by focusing attention on its unsuitable style, which is underscored by the verbal and physical abuse of his unsuitable body. Note, moreover, that this blaming speaker is physically abused by a leader who wields the scepter—the object that identifies the authoritative speaker and blazons his status and diction as praiseworthy within epic. Thus this profoundly appropriate hero attacks the man who is both an abuser and an object of abuse from within the epic perspective. Thersites' *hexis* symbolizes an iambic tradition that challenges the aesthetic mandates of epic poetry and the social hierarchies it supports.[35]

Book 10 of the *Iliad* is an episode that many scholars have thought a later interpolation, in part because it depicts Odysseus as a spy and thief in the night.[36] But as in book 2, Odysseus controls an unattractive and hapless character verbally, while Diomedes abuses him physically. The narrator describes the Trojan spy Dolon as of humble status but rich, ignoble in form (εἶδος . . . κακός, 10.316) but swift-footed. When he is intercepted by Odysseus and Diomedes, he shows himself to be similarly unheroic in temperament by chattering his teeth, growing pale, and bursting into tears (10.374–377). He also offers wealth from his own house, the gesture that sounds the death knell for many terrified Trojan suppliants. Trembling violently at Odysseus' questions, Dolon dithers on and tries to reach Diomedes' chin in supplication. The impatient warrior chops off his head, which rolls in the dust still speaking (10.454–457). Odysseus then strips his head and body of their cap, cloak, and weapons. The scene is a brutally physicalized representation of the weakness and low status attributed to the corporeal style of the iambic type and the violence with which this type is met by epic heroes. Indeed, the heroes literally cut this unheroic speech off in mid-sentence.[37] The type that Odysseus opposes in this scene is not so much the rebellious as the cowardly speaker, whose transparent manner and precise responses (ἀτρεκέως, 10.405, 413, 427) betray both his city and his own weak, unheroic temperament.

If Odysseus' reaction against Thersites and Dolon treats their unbeautiful types as indicative of their disorderly, lower-class behavior, this contrasts importantly with his angry speeches in the *Odyssey*. There Odysseus himself has often to play the role of the lower-class or debased character, whose body has suffered much abuse in the course of his adventures. His confrontations with young noblemen (especially the suitors) also reveal that he is a figure of public abuse in a manner parallel to Thersites in the *Iliad*. But since the *Odyssey* depicts the beggar's *hexis* as a disguise, the ragged Odysseus only embodies *iambos* in this restricted sense. Odysseus responds to insults from Euryalus, the young and graceful Phaeacian athlete (8.166–185), and from Antinous, the most violent of the suitors settled in Odysseus' palace (17.445–465), by calling attention to the gap that may exist between a speaker's noble aspect and his ignoble words. Euryalus suggests that Odysseus does not participate in athletic contests because he is a merchant (i.e., a lower-class type) rather than a warrior, using phrases that clearly highlight his scorn for the older man's apparent status (8.159–164). Odysseus criticizes his rude implications by noting that the handsome man may speak gracelessly (8.174–175). He declares that Euryalus' speech is not appropriate (οὐ . . . κατὰ κόσμον, 8.179). It is disorderly in its lack of suitability to Odysseus' own status as guest and in the insulting conclusions it draws from his weary manner and toughened body (cf. 8.134–137, 153–157).[38] The "disorder" created by Euryalus' insulting style thus arises from the mismatch between visible stature and actual status in two ways. First, his address to the guest reveals the ungenerous connections he has made between Odysseus' stature and status; second, this mistake ironically suggests a gap between his own graceful stature and his rude words.

The young man later apologizes, and among the peaceful Phaeacians no physical violence follows from the encounter. In Odysseus' own halls, in contrast, the handsome but contrary Antinous, who has a reputation for being smart and speaking well (*Od.* 16.419–420), hurls insults and a footstool at the disguised Odysseus. Odysseus has attempted to beg bread from the suitors, approaching Antinous and flattering him by noting his aristocratic bearing (βασιλῆι ἔοικας, 17.416). When Antinous responds harshly, Odysseus remarks that his temperament does not match his noble form (οὐκ ἄρα σοί γ' ἐπὶ εἴδει καὶ φρένες ἦσαν, 17.454), which earns him the blow from the footstool, a piece of furniture that is typically brought out for guests of high status (e.g., 1.131, 10.367). When brandished by the haughty Antinous, the stool further reinforces the contrast between his appearance and his ignoble type, in that he misuses an implement of *xenia* in his arrogant treatment of a humble guest (cf. also Eurymachus, 18.394–397).

Odysseus' association with ideas about physical and verbal grace—about the persuasive qualities of both and the danger of conflating the two—is thus most complicated in the *Odyssey,* where his relationship to the social hierarchies of the Homeric world is itself more ambiguous and changeable. In the *Iliad* Odysseus is positioned in stalwart defense of those who are excellent in social status and physical stature, and the match between pleasing appearance and appropriate speech is countered only by the stocky figure and downcast eyes of Odysseus himself.[39] In the *Odyssey* his own body signifies the possible disjunction between pleasing appearance and fine speech, so that he himself becomes the object of verbal and physical abuse like that with which he controlled Thersites in the *Iliad.* In the classical period, tragedy produced the logical extension of this transformation. Odysseus has become so questionable a character that when Philoctetes describes Thersites' verbal facility in Sophocles' play, Neoptolemus guiltily assumes that he is talking about Odysseus. That is, both Thersites and Odysseus are now associated with the glib audacity that marks the unheroic type.[40]

The *Odyssey* offers the most detailed imagery for assessing what Odysseus' own body signifies about the effects of visible style. The poet uses depictions of the hero's body and its various alterations as visible indices of his persuasive status and of the stylistic calibrations necessary to its augmentation. Extremes of dress or undress (i.e., being elaborately clothed or naked) pose the most consistent threats to this status. The hero himself does once employ to good effect a portrait of himself in fancy dress (to Penelope in book 19), but within the narrative frame, his physical style is most effective when at its most humble and apparently insignificant.

Odysseus' authorial function in the epic suggests that his own use of his image and the Homeric narrator's portraits have a similar status in relation to stylistic effect. At significant junctures, Odysseus himself describes or plays off central features of his visible *hexis.* At other times his body is subject to divine manipulation, and its vulnerabilities parallel his loss of verbal control. Note again that this maneuvering of the hero's body in the *Odyssey* is similar to that of Helen's in the *Iliad*, which I discuss in detail below.

Odysseus' bodily changes are usually of divine instigation. Although he does himself initiate minor instances of disguise, the Homeric depictions tend to emphasize verbal impersonation as his special talent. The hero oversees his oral performances with great finesse, while most often merely attempting to counter or support whatever physical look he finds himself sporting. The figure of Odysseus is thus poised between a passive manipulation of his body by goddesses and his active ability to control discourse by using a flexible verbal style. Although he is repeatedly helped, and occasionally threatened, by the goddesses' care and maneuvering of his body, he manages to adjust his *hexis* to suit whatever situation he encounters, no matter how regrettable his physical appearance may be. Every change in his appearance necessitates some calibration of his self-presentation, some (often slight) alteration of stylistic details, so that his bodily *hexis* as a whole might remain consistent and therefore indicate a recognizable type.

Since, however, Odysseus' disguises are also the visible manifestations of his versatile, circumspect type, changes to his body parallel changes in his agility with the circumspect and strategic response. It is thus worth exploring in some detail what these manipulations of Odysseus' body suggest about the relationship between visible type and rhetorical skill. Three times Odysseus is bathed by goddesses (including the semidivine Helen) and undergoes no greater change than that achieved by cleanliness and a new cloak. However, each bath and change of clothes follow upon or precede scenes in which the hero's body is tested for its vulnerability to physical harm.[41] Helen is the first to bathe and dress Odysseus, as she describes in the tale she tells to the eager Telemachus (*Od.* 4.235–264). She satisfies his craving to hear about the feats of his absent father, but she also casts herself in the role of ministering goddess (one of her many characters; see ch. 2). Only after she has bathed, anointed, and dressed him, and sworn an oath not to reveal him, does he tell her the plans of the Greeks.

The entire episode purports to show off Odysseus' cleverness and warrior strength: for instance, Helen emphasizes the quality of his disguise and the number of Trojans he kills upon leaving. But it really revolves around the hero's contact with Helen and the potential danger to his body, once it is stripped and naked in the bath, that she represents. The oath he insists that Helen swear indicates that as with Calypso and Circe, he is aware of his vulnerability to her powers of perspicuity and perhaps even to her sexual appeal. His body has endured self-inflicted blows before entering Troy, and now he faces helpful but subtly threatening contact with a semi-divine female. He is at his most wary while in his hideous outfit (cf. ὁ δὲ κερδοσύνῃ ἀλέεινεν, 4.251); after his bath and in new clothes, he tells all (πάντα νόον, 4.256). Helen's stripping of his disguise also effectively removes his typically crafty style. Now dressed in the clothes that blazon his identity, he has to fight his way out of Troy rather than cloak his passage in verbal imposture and physical disguise. Thus, at least as Helen tells it, Odysseus divests himself of his signature slyness in her presence and dons the brave visibility typical of Homeric heroes.

Like Helen's threat to Odysseus' body, Circe's is subtle. While obviously sensuous in nature, it interweaves tricks of feeding with those of undressing.[42] Odysseus appears at Circe's door battered by adventure but with his form protected by Hermes' special herb (μῶλυ, 10.305). Circe feeds the hero her own drugs, handing him a specially mixed drink (κυκεών) and tapping him dismissively with her wand (10.316–320). It is only when Odysseus whips out his sword and makes a dash at her that the goddess recognizes him and proposes bed (10.325–335). Odysseus, still suspicious and careful with his words, worries that while naked, Circe might render him "servile and emasculated" (κακὸν καὶ ἀνήνορα, 10.341). He insists that she swear an oath, as Hermes had instructed (10.343–344; cf. 10.299–301).[43] However, once he has climbed into her singularly beautiful bed (περικαλλέος εὐνῆς, 10.347, 480) and been elaborately bathed and dressed by her handmaidens (10.348–370), Odysseus sinks into a sensuous reverie and stays on Circe's island for a year. Hermes' *môlu* may have helped the hero retain his human form and his manly prowess in the goddess' bed, but it did little to protect his sense of direction and thus to further his return.

Calypso presents a more concrete threat to Odysseus' body. Although she complies with Hermes' command to let the hero leave her island, her final bathing and dressing of Odysseus before he leaves nearly finishes him once he is at sea. Calypso is herself a fancy dresser, adorning her body for a trip to the woods in a large, shimmering, and delicately woven cloak, a golden belt, and a veil (5.230–232). When Odysseus has built his raft, she bathes and enwraps him in sweet-smelling clothes (εἵματά τ᾽ ἀμφιέσασα θυώδεα, 5.264), and he sets off. On the eighth day at sea, in sight of Scheria, Odysseus encounters a storm raised by his enemy Poseidon. Wary and wise in his manner of address when slumped on the goddess' shore, once splendidly dressed, he loses his verbal control. Despairing and alone on his raft, he wishes for death (ὡς δὴ ἐγώ γ' ὄφελον θανέειν, 5.308). He goes overboard and almost drowns because of the weight of Calypso's elaborate clothes (εἵματα γάρ ῥ' ἐβάρυνε, τά οἱ πόρε δῖα Καλυψώ, 5.321). He splutters out seawater (στόματος δ' ἐξέπτυσεν ἅλμην / πικρήν, 5.323–324) rather than words; he cannot speak even if he wants to, well dressed for the part though he may be.

The nymph Ino sees him as he sinks and tells him to trade his fancy clothes for her divine scarf (κρήδεμνον . . . ἄμβροτον, 5.346–347). This he uses as a lifejacket, relinquishing it upon reaching Scheria as she had instructed. While the finely wrought clothes of one goddess reduce Odysseus to the language of despair and nearly silence him altogether, the ambrosial veil of another saves him, pulling him toward another island. There he will address the next available female with such well-wrought formality that she will overlook his savage appearance and agree to give him yet one more set of clothes. The Homeric poet thus depicts high-status female figures as manipulating the narrative by their use of clothing. Their various treatments of Odysseus' body immobilize or propel him, inhibiting and aiding his progress by turns.[44]

Divine cosmetics also impede or facilitate Odysseus' progress; only those that transform him into an aging beggar clearly help him on his way. In fact, the changes that make Odysseus uglier tend to precipitate scenes in which he is substantially cared for and nudged closer to his return. These are also the moments when the hero's versatile speaking abilities offset his appearance. In book 6, for instance, the poet carefully details the wild and startling aspect that Odysseus shows to the young girls when he first appears out of the bushes, naked except for a branch, encrusted with brine, and hungry as a lion (6.127–136). The simile that frames Odysseus' contact with the girls has a sexual subtext that heightens the sense of his danger for them: he is bestial and voracious, his eyes burn (6.131), and he is ready to chase his doelike prey anywhere, intending to "mingle" (μίξεσθαι) with them (6.132–133).[45] As he faces them, he debates with himself about whether he should approach the statuesque girl who holds her ground or stand off from her and bridge the gap between their visible statures with a winning speech. He decides that the more formal deportment will bring him more gain (κέρδιον, 6.145), a central (if mercenary) consideration in the plying of *peithô* that suggests the moral ambiguities of the activity.[46]

Thus when he is at his most physically repulsive, Odysseus addresses

Nausicaa with a speech whose style the poet characterizes as "honeyed and cunning" (μειλίχιον καὶ κερδαλέον μῦθον, 6.148). This style appeals to the senses and seeks to get something by a careful flattery. Countering his terrifying appearance with a visualizing and ornamental speech, Odysseus inquires about the girl's status. He suggests that she may be divine and draws attention to her beauty in an elaborate prologue that announces her similarity to Artemis in "form, stature, and bearing" (εἶδός τε μέγεθός τε φυήν τ' ἄγχιστα ἐΐσκω, 6.152). He then declares her family much blessed, describing her as a flourishing shoot (θάλος, 6.157) and predicting the glorious bounty of her wedding day (6.158–159). The filthy man thus deflects the young aristocratic girl's attention from his own dishabille by means of a formal appreciation of her visible qualities and the familial bounty they represent. She is envisioned as a blossoming, richly compensating bride-to-be, so that his speech serves as a flattering mirror of her physical beauty and status. His fulsome comparison of her to a young tree beside Delian Apollo's altar (νέον ἔρνος, 6.162–169) further shifts her focus from his unkempt, bushy profile to her own willowy stature, again achieving with speech the complimentary adornment his nakedness seems to belie.

Odysseus thus persuades Nausicaa to help him when he looks his worst, by means of a visualizing style that offsets his appearance and proves prescient in its suitability. When Nausicaa responds to his supplication, she uses similarly formal, conventional locutions (e.g., 6.188–189, 195–197, 207–208). She also declares that he does not *seem like* a low-born or stupid man (οὔτε κακῷ οὔτ' ἄφρονι φωτί ἔοικας, 6.187), even though he clearly looks like both. He has in effect dressed himself verbally, so that he appears to her now as a respectable type.

After this elevated exchange, Nausicaa gives Odysseus clothes, and he bathes in the river, receiving in the process the sheen of Athena's liquid grace (κάλλεϊ καὶ χάρισι στίλβων, 6.236).[47] In a detailed description that recalls the crafting of Hesiod's Pandora, Odysseus' physical persuasiveness is artificially increased. The process is explicitly compared to the production of glittering objects by a skilled craftsman, whose art is granted by Hephaestus or Athena (6.229–237).[48] His splendidly burnished body pleases Nausicaa, who has a princess' taste for sweetened words and richly adorned bodies.[49] She is so thrilled by his transformation that she announces to her companions that she would like to marry him. "Before," she says, "he seemed *unsuitable*" (lit. "unlike," ἀεικέλιος), "but now he *seems like* the gods" (θεοῖσιν ἔοικε, 6.242–243).

Nausicaa's language underscores Odysseus' central ability: to appear *like* the type that his interlocutor might be prepared to trust, in this case, like the high-status type most similar to herself. Nausicaa is not merely an aristocrat (i.e., not like an unsuitable type); she is the princess of a people who are "dear to the gods" (φίλοι ἀθανάτοισιν, 6.203) and "godlike" (ἀντιθέοισι, 6.241), as she herself declares. Dressed in her brothers' clothes and speaking in the formal style that Nausicaa herself employs, Odysseus manages, with the help of Athena, to appear both visually and verbally like those on whom his fate now depends.

Athena's refashioning of Odysseus before the eyes of Telemachus in book 16 effects a similar mirroring of his interlocutor, but this transformation meets with more resistance. She does not return the hero to his own stature—that of an aging warrior and father. Rather, he appears to Telemachus in a form more like Telemachus' own: tanned, taut, and beardless (ἂψ δὲ μελαγχροιὴς γένετο, γναθμαὶ δὲ τάνυσθεν, / κυάνεαι δ' ἐγένοντο γενειάδες ἀμφὶ γένειον, 16.175–176). Unlike Nausicaa, Telemachus declares that the new Odysseus *is* a god, rather than being *like* one (τις θεός ἐσσι, 16.183), perhaps in part because he has not himself provided the stranger with the new clothes that he inexplicably wears. Odysseus attempts to soften the effect of his divine transformation by using the language of likeness (τί μ' ἀθανάτοισιν ἐΐσκεις, 16.187). But when he declares that he is the boy's father, Telemachus responds that the stranger is some spirit come to charm him (με δαίμων / θέλγει, 16.194–195) with his overly youthful and appealing corporeal style. The son has to be persuaded by the stern and paternal tones of Odysseus' rejoinder that the stranger is not a god but his mortal father (16.202–212).

The interviews in books 19 and 23 between Penelope and Odysseus greatly complicate the stylistic impact effected by a pleasing appearance. The hero is depicted as employing a more layered style of self-presentation than that which he uses to persuade Nausicaa and Telemachus. In book 18 Penelope is herself transformed by Athena in a manner similar to the crafted transformations that augment Odysseus' visible stature in book 23. She appears taller and broader to the eye, has an immortal substance poured over her, and her cheeks are made to look like carved ivory (πριστοῦ ἐλέφαντος, 18.196).[50] In book 19, Penelope enters once again, still looking like a goddess (Ἀρτέμιδι ἰκέλη ἠὲ χρυσέη Ἀφροδίτη, 19.54). Seating herself in a chair inlaid with ivory and silver (δινωτὴν ἐλέφαντι καὶ ἀργύρῳ, 19.56), she responds to the beggar's compliments on her beauty with the same disavowal with which she had earlier rebuffed the suitors (18.251–256, 19.124–129). The beggar uses this encomiastic mode as a means of deflecting her attention from both his hideous guise and what it may mask—her own husband. He offsets his ugliness with a verbal ornamentation of her form that resembles his tactics with Nausicaa, redirecting the queen's focus from his rags to her ornamented stature. Claiming that Penelope's fame spreads widely like that of a wealthy king and emphasizing the sumptuousness of her surroundings (19.108–114), he asks that she not inquire further about his own background, since it is "rather unseemly" (κάκιον) to bewail one's fate "excessively" (lit. "without measure," ἄκριτον, 19.118–120). The beggar's comparison of Penelope to a king (whose reputation sounds like Odysseus' own) draws her attention away from his manifestly unregal appearance; it also obscures the possibility that he himself might occupy such a noble status.

Later in this exchange the clothes with which the beggar sumptuously adorns "Odysseus" effect a similar distraction in a similarly visualizing fashion (19.221–248). When Penelope asks him for evidence that he had seen "Odysseus," as he claimed (19.185), Odysseus gives accurate details of the fine clothes he once wore. Thus the proof of the hero's identity, and evidence of his aristocratic type, are attributed to the "Odysseus" supposedly witnessed by the speaker, who is in fact the hero himself in tattered disguise. Although Penelope modestly relinquishes claim to a beauty crafted by Athena, her bolder husband counters his own unappealing appearance and complements her elevated one with an elaborate description of his former dress, detailing the ornate features of his clothes (19.225–234) and emphasizing that many women admired him (ἦ μὲν πολλαί γ' αὐτὸν ἐθηήσαντο γυναῖκες, 19.235). The beggar thus uses this well-dressed Odysseus as a match for the beautified Penelope who faces him. As with the praise of his wife, praise of himself, although indirect, satisfies both parties: he verbally adorns his body for Penelope's gratification, diverting her attention simultaneously from his beggar's rags and from his identity. Once again, the association of Odysseus' figure with clothing that serves a double ulterior purpose (praise of the hero and proof of identity) parallels the layered quality of his bodily *hexis.*

When in book 23 Penelope faces the same man, now transformed to look more like the "Odysseus" of his story, it is hardly surprising that she should be suspicious of one whose changeable style encompasses both physical and verbal features. Odysseus steps out of the bath lacking the eye-catching sheen with which he appeared to Nausicaa but looking godlike (ἀθανάτοισιν ὁμοῖος, 23.163).[51] His wife is unpersuaded by this divine beauty, viewing his good looks as a kind of clever imitation of the type her husband was. But she contradictorily addresses the stranger intimately as "strange one" (δαιμόνι', 23.173) and declares her memory of Odysseus in a second person address (i.e., "I know very well what sort you were," μάλα δ' εὖ οἶδ' οἷος ἔησθα, 23.175). When disguised as a beggar, Odysseus had described "Odysseus" in the handsome guise she recognized. Now that he stands before her in a similarly handsome guise, the possibility remains that his newly burnished appearance may mask some further deception.

Instead, when she tests him, he offers her the bed. The poet presents this as a more fixed recognition token than clothing, which can be changed very easily, as the hero himself makes all too clear. The divine cosmetics that Athena has used on both Penelope and Odysseus give them the same crafted splendor as the domestic objects that adorn their palace. While in book 18 Penelope's cheeks were described as looking like ivory, Odysseus' bodily crafting is now compared to metalwork (χρυσὸν περιχεύεται ἀργύρῳ, 23.159; cf. 6.232). Together, their ornamented appearances resemble the elaborate inlay that Odysseus himself fashioned on their singular bed (δαιδάλλων χρυσῷ τε καὶ ἀργύρῳ ἠδ' ἐλέφαντι, 23.200).

Thus Athena's crafting of his body in book 23 operates on a figurative level as a visible proof of his identity, in that the hero's bodily ornamentation complements that of his wife in specific relation to their marriage bed. Once Odysseus has provided Penelope with this token of their fixed and ornamented bed, the imagery that links the couple's bodies to each other and to their bed indicates that Odysseus must be her singularly suitable husband. Their corporeal styles match, and together their crafted bodies match the elaborate details of the bed. In a clinching of the plot that boldly asserts this match of signifiers as the right one, the poet triangulates the visible pairing that blazons the couple's like-mindedness (*homophrosunê*) with the fixed image of the bed. The move seeks to insure that likeness and suitability must at last guarantee identity. The techniques the hero had used to deceive finally seem to achieve the reverse: revelation of true type.

THE ELUSIVE BODY AND VISUAL ENTICEMENTS: HELEN

As I argue in chapter 2, Helen in Homeric epic is a formidable speaker, often controlling discourse through a series of rhetorical moves that tend to deflect blame and impede access to her motivations. Her form is likewise a formidable entity. It matches her flattering, indirect speaking style in its bright

but elusive qualities, its tendency to be simultaneously startling and yet re-
mote. The poet does not dwell upon the details of its beauty, although he
does underscore the reaction of others to its startling qualities. In the *Iliad*
Helen's body is more often than not veiled in shining fabrics whose specially luminous effect mark them as divine, and she passes magically unseen
through the streets of Troy. When revealed, her face arrests conversation and
elicits exclamation.

While the high-status objects that Helen plies in the *Odyssey* underscore
her goddess' stature, the *Iliad* provides the visible details most crucial to an
understanding of her figure as emblematic of the subtle, sensuous effects of
style and the dangers of its impact. Her semiotic complexity in the *Iliad* is
reinforced by her bodily *hexis*, her veiled and luminous figure paralleling
the indirect but seductive qualities of her verbal style. The presentation of
Helen's figure thus doubly confounds the audience's perspective: her body
is obscured by divinely wrought veils, and her agency in the events that precipitated the war remains similarly obscure. Moreover, she is sometimes the
shaper of her story and just as often the central object of desire and contention.[52] This is frequently true of female characters, but Helen represents the
paradigm of the double story that might be told about any wife: the prize
whose visible virtues may belie her true type.

Because it embraces this doubling of narratives, Helen's figure incites an
anxious awareness of stylistic effect. It suggests that wives may have at their
command a compendium of styles with which to flatter and manipulate
their husbands (or other men) into submission. Helen's riveting but elusive
appearance and her subtly flattering speaking style both work to convince
the audience which story is the true one and thus which type she really is.
Meanwhile the poet also shows her reacting against such seductions, as the
resistant audience of a visualizing style.

The narrator's depictions of Helen's engagement with other characters
capture her vacillation between viewed object and viewing audience. At
times her eyes pick out other forms in the visual field, and she describes
them; at others she is clearly the viewed object, whose body serves as the
site around which the narrative circles. In the scene at the wall, for instance,
she is first a fearsome center of attention, then asked to contemplate the impressive forms of others. The Trojan elders remark on her beauty—and more
specifically on the expression of her eyes and face—as being somehow responsible for the war: "There can be no righteous anger that the Trojans
and the well-greaved Achaeans have suffered painful events for a very long

time over such a woman: she seems in her look terribly like the immortal goddesses" (οὐ νέμεσις Τρῶας καὶ ἐϋκνήμιδας Ἀχαιοὺς / τοιῇδ' ἀμφὶ γυναικὶ πολὺν χρόνον ἄλγεα πάσχειν· / αἰνῶς ἀθανάτῃσι θεῇς εἰς ὦπα ἔοικεν, Il. 3.156–158). This frighteningly lovely face when viewed stuns the elders with its returning gaze,[53] startling them like a beautiful and terrifying vision. They retreat from verbal attack with a reference to *nemesis*. The goddess Nemesis, who is Helen's mother in the *Cypria*, threatens to surface here as well, even though the elders deny that such just indignation is a correct response to Helen's presence. Their murmurings about her reveal this tension: while they may admire her beauty, they wish her gone, lest she remain a grief for future Trojans (ἀλλὰ καὶ ὣς ποίη περ ἐοῦσ' ἐν νηυσὶ νεέσθω / μηδ' ἡμῖν τεκέεσσί τ' ὀπίσσω πῆμα λίποιτο, Il. 3.159–160).

When she is not speaking in public at the wall, however, Helen is veiled, first to hide her tears for her former husband (3.141–142), then to hide her role as Aphrodite's pawn in the wooing of Paris (3.419–420). Thus in book 3 especially, the Homeric poet suggests two ways of relating Helen's story: Helen's carefully calibrated oral performances, which have their own seductive qualities, and Aphrodite's more voluptuous, image-laden plot manipulation. The poet situates Helen's character as ambiguously caught between these modes, her own deflecting verbal style being offset by Aphrodite's manipulation of her figure as a sensuous match for the ornamental, shining Paris. In these scenes Helen is depicted as attempting to resist the goddess' visualizing, seductive style. Aphrodite's style suits the sensuous effects that Helen's figure emblematizes, even though Homer shows her character struggling to distance herself from its impact. Already in Homer, then, Helen is set up as both the emblem and reluctant audience of this visually enticing style.[54] Aphrodite's narrative maneuvers highlight Helen's connection to the sensuous pleasures of visuality, tying her firmly to shining fabrics and the bodies they veil.

As Linda Clader has emphasized, Helen's figure is a singularly gleaming one, and the materials that make her so seem to be of special manufacture. Even *Argeiê*, the epithet used most often of her in the *Iliad* (nine times), may point to the special sheen she possesses. Clader notes that the epithet is cognate with adjectives meaning "bright" and that since Helen is not represented by Homer as living in Argos, her unique brightness may account for its repeated application to her.[55] Other fabrics associated with high-status female figures in Homer also gleam but only rarely with this special brightness. Compare, for instance, the silver-bright (ἀργύφεον) cloaks of Calypso and Circe (*Od.* 5.230, 10.543). Nor are the items themselves common to other mortal females: only semidivine or divine females wear the *othonê* and the *heanos.*[56]

Early in book 3 Helen's form is described as being "cloaked in garments of shining quality" (ἀργεννῆσι καλυψαμένη ὀθόνῃσιν, *Il.* 3.141), and with these rich and gleaming items she shields her tears for Menelaus as she hurries to the city wall. Aphrodite later uses a similarly bright and gleaming item (κατασχομένη ἑανῷ ἀργῆτι φαεινῷ, *Il.* 3.419) to mask Helen's passage to the bedchamber.[57] Her *heanos* is also referred to as "divinely perfumed" (νεκταρέου ἑανοῦ, *Il.* 3.385) when Aphrodite first grabs it. Compare Hera's ambrosial veil (ἀμβρόσιον ἑανόν, *Il.* 14.178). Helen's presence is thus repeatedly highlighted by veils of a divine type, which call attention to her body while also concealing it from the eye. Sometimes this concealment is complete, as when Aphrodite uses the gleaming *heanos* to hide Helen, which suggests that its sheen may be bright enough to blind. The *Iliad* thus treats Helen's figure as one both singularly visible (i.e., immortally bright) but also difficult to see, her body's veiled and luminous stature repeatedly drawing attention to the startling and elusive qualities of her type.[58]

The poet represents these gleaming veils as impeding the eye for different reasons: the one apparently for purposes of modesty and mourning, the other for deceit and an illicit pleasure. In this later scene Aphrodite literally interrupts the war narrative, manipulating the richly wrought fabrics that signal a sensuous bodily *hexis* and an erotic story line. She makes efficient use of the fancy materials that adorn the bodies of those she loves, effectively tying Helen to Paris by snapping his decorated chin-strap and grabbing her heavenly veil. The goddess' manipulation of fabrics is consonant with her manipulation of narrative, which propels the bodies of Helen and Paris toward sexual satisfaction, the suitable end to this sensuous tale.

As the war-loving Menelaus is dragging off Paris by his helmet, Aphrodite breaks the strap (πολύκεστος ἱμάς)[59] that holds it to his head and saves his soft throat (ἁπαλὴν ὑπὸ δειρήν) (*Il.* 3.371)[60] for the bedroom. She resituates him in the setting more suited to his type, while her actions themselves suggest in exact detail a scene of erotic seizure: she snatches him up (τὸν δ' ἐξήρπαξ'), envelops him in a cloud (ἐκάλυψε δ' ἄρ' ἠέρι πολλῇ), and deposits him in his sweet-smelling, perfumed chambers (κὰδ' δ' εἷσ' ἐν θαλάμῳ εὐώδεϊ κηώεντι, 3.380–382).[61] The goddess then alters her own appearance, cloaking her identity in the guise of an old woolmaker. Sidling up to Helen, she tugs on her veil and tempts her with a description of the beautiful Paris reclining in the bedroom. Aphrodite's portrait of the love object explicitly emphasizes Paris' shimmering appearance (κάλλεϊ τε στίλβων καὶ εἵμασιν, 3.392). Her imagery disturbs Helen's heart (τῇ δ' ἄρα θυμὸν ἐνὶ στήθεσσιν ὄρινε, 3.395), which leads her to recognize Aphrodite by her physical allure and to react against the visually enticing image the goddess deploys. The sparkling quality of Aphrodite's own physical beauty (θεᾶς περικαλλέα δειρὴν / στήθεά θ' ἱμερόεντα καὶ ὄμματα μαρμαίροντα, 3.396–397) matches the sheen of her favorites. Yet the scene positions Helen as a resistant audience to the very appeal that she herself embodies. After bitter protest, she follows the goddess, veiled in the shimmering material (3.419) that protects her body from the critical eyes of the Trojan women.

The entire episode is thus oriented around the shining depictions of Helen, Paris, and Aphrodite. The poet also situates Helen as the viewer of these luminous figures—Aphrodite's and then Paris' in Aphrodite's sensuous description. Helen's appearance is the catalyst for the story; being so closely associated with Aphrodite, she is deeply implicated in its unfolding. But since she serves as the resistant audience to this visual seduction, she is thus the emblematic figure of a sensuous visual style *and* of its threat to morally defensible actions. Helen's reaction against the visual seduction in which she is implicated thereby underscores its central ambiguities, both the pleasures and the dangers of its impact.

In the *Odyssey* Helen's association with the glittering implements of fabric making and with Artemis (who plies the golden distaff) matches her divine stature and her gleaming surroundings.[62] While Helen elaborately weaves her own story in the *Iliad* (3.125–129), in the *Odyssey* fancy spinning implements signal her high status and thus foreshadow the authoritative speaking style she assumes in these scenes. In book 4 she descends from her bedroom accompanied by handmaidens as well as the golden distaff and silver workbasket that were gifts from Egyptian royalty—her own guest-gifts, as the narrator points out, not those obtained by her husband (4.130). Moreover her handmaiden is named Adraste, a name that Clader notes recalls Adrasteia, a cult title of the goddess Nemesis.[63] The scene of her descent in its entirety strongly suggests the entrance of a goddess. Compare also her authoritative style in book 15, where her gift-giving and prophesying similarly underscore her public and semidivine status. There she gives to Telemachus a gown of her own fine weaving as a token of guest-friendship, saying that it is for his wedding. In these scenes Helen plies implements of hosting (the conversation drug *nêpenthê* and the marriage dress) that are somehow profoundly associated with her figure. The items in fact suggest and then eerily suppress the problems that Helen embodies for both the effects of style and the formalities of gift-giving.

When Helen gives Telemachus the robe, she calls it "a memory token from the hands of Helen for the much-desired wedding time" (μνῆμ' Ἑλένης χειρῶν πολυηράτου ἐς γάμου ὥρην, *Od.* 15.126). This is, of course, precisely the ritual whose luxurious trappings and direct transgression she symbolizes. The scene echoes one in *Iliad* 6 where Hecuba chooses a gown that "shines like a star" (ἀστὴρ δ' ὣς ἀπέλαμπεν, *Il.* 6.295) to dedicate to Athena. The poet states explicitly that Paris took these garments from Sidon when he stopped there on his way home with Helen (6.289–292). Thus Hecuba's offering is a precisely matched compensation for Helen's having been brought to Troy with these same rich *peploi*. In this scene Helen's figure surfaces as a reminder of Paris' transgression, as another ruinous object, whose return may not bring about the gods' protection (as the dedication of the gown does not, 6.311).

When Helen gives the gown to Telemachus in *Odyssey* 15, however, the starlike gift (ἀστὴρ δ' ὣς ἀπέλαμπεν, 15.108) is of her own making. She is its author, in effect, and she is depicted as assigning its fitting label.[64] If in the *Iliad* Helen is connected to the rich and shining gowns as the paradigmatic stolen object, now as hostess and high-status bride she hands to Telemachus a gown of similar manufacture but without these negative associations. Helen's double story suggests the possibility of a double perspective and the dependence of any story's good reception on the appropriate style of the teller. But while Helen's status as ruinous object taints Hecuba's gift in *Iliad* 6, in *Odyssey* 15 she maintains such complete control of the exchange that her interlocutors show no memory of that other story, accepting her authoritative version of events without question.

Later Greek writers would regard all versatile and visually impressive styles as suspect and come to doubt the possibility of judging the accuracy of speakers' claims. This was especially true regarding those whose corporeal styles were too obviously molded to suit their audiences—that is, too changeable, elusive, or elaborate in visual details and deportment. Sophocles associates this flexible, often deceptive use of visible character especially with Odysseus, as Euripides does with Helen. Both poets regard the manipulation of type as the most distracting technique a speaker can employ. Aristotle also treats one's visible style of self-presentation as a crucial component in persuasion and worries about its misuse. He is particularly concerned that elaborate delivery might exacerbate the problem, and oratory then becomes even more like a dramatic production, visually deceptive and emotionally distracting.

In Homer these concerns have yet to be fully articulated, and they surface sporadically in responses to richly layered oral performances, when the versatile bodily *hexis* of the speaker suggests a compendium of identities. Homer depicts Helen and Odysseus as singularly adept at the deployment of such versatile, visually seductive types. Even when their personas seem less questionable (as in the *Iliad*), their oral performances reveal their deep connections to anxiety about visual style and the plasticity of character type.

CHAPTER 4

VERBAL
MASQUERADE AND
VISUAL IMPACT
IN TRAGEDY

ἐν γὰρ τραγωιδοποιίαι καὶ ζωγραφίαι ὅστις κα πλεῖστα
ἐξαπατῆι ὅμοια τοῖς ἀληθινοῖς ποιέων, οὗτος ἄριστος.

For in the writing of tragedies and in painting, whoever
deceives the most by making things like to the truth, that
man is the best.

DISSOI LOGOI

The development of the dramatic genres in Athens created an arena in which
oral performers impersonated visible types in a fuller and more extended
fashion than in rhapsodic performances on the one hand, or in sophistic displays on the other. A performer could now appear on stage as Odysseus, in
his costume and mask, and engage in his actions, rather than merely shifting
vocal tone and expression as he moved from speaker to speaker in the recitation of narrative. Both rhapsodic and sophistic performances involved one
elaborately dressed narrator who stirred the audience by his ability to communicate emotions and imagery, but without fully imitating the events related. Such displays did, however, contribute to Athenians' sense of how to
ascertain an individual's type from his visible features, as did painting and
statuary. Aristotle would later remark on this awareness (*Poet.* 1448b15–17)
and connect it to the importance of plot in the dramatic genres (1450a15–32).
Although painting and sculpture lack the linguistic and performative de-

tails on which this discussion centers, fifth-century writers were also clearly aware of and influenced by what these media could capture about character.[1]

The dramatic setting furthers the mimetic illusion by the unique combination of visual details, verbal expression, and physical enactment, thereby broadening the sense in which the audience might be able to witness character as a visible entity. As a mimetic spectacle, however, drama also raises questions about the extent to which the eye may be deceived: Helen becomes "Helen," a man in a mask and an elaborate dress. Whatever type this Helen appears to be on stage, the mimetic effect encourages the audience to query its truth as well as the accuracy of the visible effects of character more generally. The tragic poets, especially Euripides, were clearly aware of and interested in the metatheatrical dimensions in their dramas, as scholars have pointed out.[2] These poets also tend to represent very negatively characters with the most potential for deceiving, distracting, or stunning the audience. Working in a relatively new medium—although one with roots in older civic festivals—the Attic dramatists often highlight artifice and illusion, thereby suggesting the suspect nature of theatrical enactment.

A number of questions arise, then, in the consideration of what effects tragedy as a genre might have had on the perception of character type and typical styles in self-presentation. One question involves this recognition of dramatic enactment as illusion, which thus heightens concerns about the distracting effects of visuality and the difficulty in ascertaining the truth about a character or a situation. Another question concerns whether dramatic effects on the classical Athenian stage actually differed very greatly from the effects of archaic performance, especially that of Homeric recitation.

In fact, it appears that many of the concrete ways we distinguish visibly among types were nearly as absent from tragic representation as they were from earlier poetic performances, whether rhapsodic or choral. For instance, tragic characters seem to have worn costumes of a fairly uniform richness and formality; Euripides is said to have had a penchant for dressing characters in rags, a move toward realism for which he apparently suffered derision.[3] While the gestures and postures of these characters probably offered more clues to a character's status and circumstances, their formal and schematized quality also might have resembled quite closely those used by the rhapsodic impersonator.[4] Many of the visual details that poets from Homer on describe as features of a given character would thus not always have been represented on stage. Those details that were represented might have merely expanded an already entrenched formal vocabulary. Moreover, the language of tragedy uses visualizing imagery similar to that in archaic poetry to indicate how a character ought to be categorized, ranging from details of dress and deportment to figurative analogies for type and bodily *hexis*. Indeed, it appears that in tragic poetry, linguistic imagery still did much of the work of characterization.

For all its similarity to earlier genres, however, dramatic enactment clearly carries a unique semiotic significance.[5] Aristotle emphasizes this difference in the *Poetics,* pointing out that unlike epic, drama shows characters as active, living beings (πϱάττοντας καὶ ἐνεϱγοῦντας τοὺς μιμουμένους, 1448a23–24). The spectacle of different individuals representing different characters must have made their different types much more obvious and concrete. Indeed, with the advent of the dramatic form, the bodily *hexis* of a character could now be more fully enacted, with vocal tone and gesture joining a distinctive appearance to trace in an emphatically visible manner individual status and stature. However formal the dress and deportment of the dramatic character may have been, the audience would nevertheless have witnessed his performance as a particular type, which included such elements unique to dramatic enactment as masks, props, and the actor's disposition on stage in relation to other characters.[6] In addition, comedy exposed audiences to debased and ludicrous bodily *hexeis,* frequently highlighting pointed contrasts among types. The conventional features of comic costumes (e.g., distended bellies, protruding buttocks) proclaimed the denigrated statuses of their wearers, while characters embodying tragic styles often suffered abuse on the comic stage.[7]

In the dignified arena of tragedy, heroic figures were emphatically visible, their easily identifiable types manifesting their particular dilemmas. The elusive figures of Helen and Odysseus stood in more complex relation to the visual schemes of tragedy. They are not the central figures in drama that they are in Homer or even that they seem to be in sophistic set pieces, whose writers may have shared the Homeric rhapsode's fascination with their versatile types. When other classical writers discuss them, they often do so in tones that betray an increasing ambivalence and distrust. Odysseus and Helen remain relatively marginalized in comparison to the growing interest in figures such as Orestes, Oedipus, and Heracles, strongly etched heroes whose stories were perceived as more central to delineating Athens' democratic image.

Except in rare instances, when Odysseus and Helen do appear in the poetry of the classical period, they embody challenges to important Greek values and particularly to Athenian democratic ones. But since they are centrally related to stylistic impact, their challenges are more specialized, focusing attention on the power of the impressive oral performance in situations where group or individual gain and moral concerns conflict. In tragedy these two figures often assume corporeal styles that were perceived as most detrimental to the good kind of *peithô*, as destroying the accurate and "upright" (*orthos*) style that related the story clearly and from the proper moral perspective.[8]

This is the persuasion that Thucydides, for example, presents as both necessary to the democratic process and least attended to by Athenian citizens. In his famous depiction of the Mytilenian debate, the violent and bombastic Cleon berates his fellow participants in the Assembly for behaving "like seated spectators of sophists" (σοφιστῶν θεαταῖς ἐοικότες καθημένοις, 3.38.33–34) rather than deliberating actively like members of a governing body. According to Cleon, the citizens are likely to be led astray by an orator who has been bribed to compose a suitably attractive speech (κέρδει ἐπαιρόμενος τὸ εὐπρεπὲς τοῦ λόγου ἐκπονήσας παράγειν πειράσεται, 3.38.16–17). Athenians, as "spectators of words" (θεαταὶ μὲν τῶν λόγων, 3.38.20), have come to care too much for the competitive thrill of the *agôn,* the speaker's cleverness in presentation, and the novelty of particular arguments. Novelty in particular deceives them (καὶ μετὰ καινότητος μὲν λόγου ἀπατᾶσθαι ἄριστοι, 3.38.24–25). The opposition Cleon constructs here is that between the passive enjoyment of what is essentially a kind of theater (a viewing of words) versus the active participation in and eyewitnessing of deeds.[9] He suggests that the Athenian democratic system encourages this kind of inactivity and overattention to verbal performance in its citizens. The Assembly members are, Cleon says, victims of the pleasure of listening (ἀκοῆς ἡδονῇ ἡσσώμενοι, 3.38.33), whose enjoyment revolves around an attention to style rather than content.

One of the pivotal terms here is *euprepês,* which conjoins the idea of the attractive style with that of suitability, often with the understanding that this is a suspect association. Thucydides employs it fairly frequently, usually in this negative sense. It also turns up in Herodotus and tragedy (especially Euripides), where it may refer positively to a visible *schêma* or *kosmos* and negatively to speaking style.[10] This notion of speciously suitable beauty is clearly important in relation to the figure of Helen. More generally, Cleon's description of this dangerously appealing style points up key features of the kind of speaker to which the Athenian audience is most susceptible: he is likely to fashion for material gain (*kerdos*) a suspiciously handsome or fitting (*euprepês*) speech that misleads (*paragein*) his audience, he may utilize a novel style (*kainotês*) to deceive (*apatasthai*) them, and his clever performance holds them in thrall like spectators (*theatai*) at some dramatic display.

The profile manifestly invokes that of the sophistic rhetor, who famously got paid for his services (i.e., whose opinion could presumably be bought) and whose speaking style might therefore be both specious and misleading. O'Sullivan has pointed out that these sophists performed in festivals where they shared the stage with the dramatic poets. In their elaborate outfits and flamboyant speaking styles, they occupied roles less similar to the politicians than to the rhapsodes, in that they employed Homeric phraseology and impersonated Homeric characters in their speeches.[11] But these redoubtable performers demonstrated techniques that the politicians could use, even though some famous proponents of them clearly considered emotional impact more important than accurate or morally sound arguments.[12]

While the negative depictions of Odysseus and Helen in the dramas of the later fifth century react against this trend, they do not only respond to or contradict the sophists' more positive portrayals of these figures. They also include implicit judgments of sophistic techniques themselves, developing in an increasingly elaborate and detailed manner the associations of Helen and Odysseus with the kind of embellishments and deceptions for which the sophists, with their purple robes and prose, were becoming increasingly famous. In addition, the dramatic depictions echo the analogies drawn in the archaic and classical periods between the female body and a deceptive style.

SUSPECT SUITABILITY AND FACILE LIES
IN CLASSICAL REPRESENTATION

In the second book of his *Histories*, Herodotus discusses the Egyptian kings and attempts to adjudicate in the matter of Helen's double story (2.112–120). He relates the alternative tale that Helen never went to Troy but rather stayed in Egypt under the protection of Proteus. As king at that time, Proteus had insisted that the lying, absconding Paris leave Helen and the other goods he stole from Menelaus in Egypt. Herodotus is convinced that Homer knew of the story that puts Paris on the northern shores of Africa but that he rejected it in favor of the Trojan story because it was "not equally suited to epic poetry" (οὐ γὰρ ὁμοίως ἐς τὴν ἐποποιίην εὐπρεπής, 2.116). Thus the poet's decision to treat the Trojan Helen, according to Herodotus, revolves around the notion of attractive suitability (*euprepês*). As mentioned above, the *euprepês* story—like the beautiful body—may *look* good, but appearances may also be deceiving. The historian thinks that the poet used the Trojan story because he knew it would pleasingly suit his genre, not because he knew it was true. The latter is presumably more of a concern in writing histories.

We might recall that there were versions of the plot predating Herodotus that put Helen in Egypt. Although Herodotus does not mention it, the seventh-century poet Stesichorus had composed a poem in which a copy or image (*eidôlon*) of Helen went to Troy, while the real Helen stayed safely in Egypt.[13] When Socrates regrets his first speech on *erôs* in the *Phaedrus*, he describes how Helen blinded Stesichorus for telling the Trojan story and then restored his sight when he wrote a palinode retracting the tale (243a3–b2). Euripides' *Helen* also follows this version of her tale, exploring the ways in which the doubling of her body impedes access to the true version of events.

In light of this other story, it is tempting to reconsider Homer's depiction of Helen in the *Iliad* as a uniquely bright but elusive presence and to recognize that even there she resembles a luminous phantasm. The tale of the *eidôlon* underscores Helen's relation to and control of the power of sight, insight, and speech, that is, to the connections between seeing and truthtelling.[14] Aeschylus had already echoed this idea of Helen's body double in the first stasimon of the *Agamemnon*. There the chorus bewails the imprints (στίλβοι) of Helen's newly absent form on the marriage bed (411), and her ghost (φάσμα) rules the house (414). The grace of the shapely statues (εὐμόρφων κολοσσῶν . . . χάρις) of her are hateful to the deserted husband, whose eyes grow blank (416–419). Menelaus' gaze is thus impeded by traces of Helen's form—the imprint, the ghost presence, and the statues—whose lifelessness robs the eyes of vision.[15]

By the classical period, then, Helen has become a fabricated item, the emblem of specious or changeable beauty that distracts audiences from the truth about her type. In this she stands for all women, as Pandora does in Hesiod. But Helen's status as a prize that may be a phantasm, and as an enchanting presence that eludes the eye, renders this mutability singularly threatening. The third choral ode in Aeschylus' *Agamemnon* characterizes Helen in Troy as a soft, luxurious, but ultimately monstrous entity, whose being comprises also its opposite: she is the reverie of windless calm (φρόνημα μὲν νηνέμου γαλάνας), the glossy figurine of wealth (ἀκασκαῖον ⟨δ'⟩ ἄγαλμα πλούτου), and the soft shaft of the eyes (μαλθακὸν ὀμμάτων βέλος) (740–742).[16] But as Love's flower, she is also a heart-biter (δηξίθυμον ἔρωτος ἄνθος, 743). Turning on her new community, she makes marriage bitter (δὲ γάμου πικρὰς τελευτάς), and becomes in the end an Erinys who causes brides to weep (νυμφόκλαυτος Ἐρινύς, 745–749).[17] If the figure of Helen evokes the visual and tactile pleasures of the luxury item, she just as quickly brings on a monstrous, deadly terror.

This pivotal quality in her figure, this essential doubleness, links her with a grim censure to the kind of dangerous deception that physical beauty may possess, as a mask that conceals a doggish, hell-bound type. A rich and visually striking performative style may not only be distracting; it may also result in the inverse of the pleasure it affords: danger, even death. The bleaker depictions of such performances insist that susceptible audiences always discover this terrible consequence of pleasure's indulgence. Witness the fates of those who followed the lovely Helen to Troy, those who listened to the sweet-voiced Sirens, and those who believed the dashing Alcibiades' depiction of Sicily.[18]

Helen transforms the style of the song as well. Earlier in the same ode, Aeschylus details how Helen's presence in Troy changed marriage songs into songs of mourning (705–708).[19] The city then learned the dirge, and her husband was renamed:

> μεταμανθάνουσα δ' ὕμνον
> Πριάμου πόλις γεραιὰ
> πολύθρηνον, μέγα που στένει κικλήσκου-
> σα Πάριν τὸν αἰνόλεκτρον.

> The venerable city of Priam,
> learning anew the mourning song,
> groaned greatly, calling Paris
> the dread groom. (709–712)

This transformation within language frames the threatening, inhuman aspects of Helen embodied in the lion cub (717–736) and the alluring gold and beautiful objects that are somehow coextensive with her body (741–743)— as vase paintings of the period also depict.[20] These objects exact their own revenge. After the beautiful Helen has become an Erinys, the poet relates a *logos* about how great wealth may become an insatiable agony (ἀκόρεστον οἰζύν), another transformation of specious pleasure into pain (750–756). Justice, the chorus finally declares, "does not worship the power of wealth stamped falsely by praise" (δύναμιν οὐ σέβουσα πλούτου παράσημον αἴνῳ, 779–780). Helen's value is deceptively high, like the exchange value of gold. Moreover, her substance turns out to be other than the luxurious item that she first appears. Compare the misleading stamp on a counterfeit coin, the *charaktêr* that promises other than it is. The style of speech that adorns its object with laudatory epithets may similarly misrepresent its true quality.[21]

The reputation of Odysseus suffers from a similar association with dissembling types and misleading stories, a denigration of his character that has its roots in earlier classical poetry. In two of his odes, Pindar makes clear what he thinks of the reputation of Odysseus and which aspects of his character should really be highlighted. *Nemean* 7 and 8 treat Odysseus as undeservedly admired and recompensed in contrast to the silent Ajax, who fails to win over the audience of peers in the contest for Achilles' arms. Pindar attributes the misjudgment of the other Achaean leaders to the deceitful misrepresentations of the heroes' characters. He seems to represent the deceit as Homer's, but the portrait he draws of the deceitful character sounds like that of Odysseus; scholars have worried about who was the intended target.[22] Just as the epinician poet's imagery tends to intertwine his own poetic project with that of the victors he praises, so here Homer's and Odysseus' skills merge, as do their audiences. Pindar begins *Nemean* 7 by declaring that "Odysseus' story" (λόγον Ὀδυσσέος) has exceeded his actual suffering because of Homer's sweet style (διὰ τὸν ἁδυεπῆ ... Ὅμηρον, 20–21). But then he adds,

> ἐπεὶ ψεύδεσί οἱ ποτανᾷ ⟨τε⟩ μαχανᾷ
> σεμνὸν ἔπεστί τι· σοφία
>   δὲ κλέπτει παράγοισα μύθοις.

> since majesty somehow settles
> upon his lies and winged contrivance;
> and his cleverness operates secretly,
> leading astray with lofty words. (22–24)

This description more easily suits the reputation of Odysseus than that of Homer. From the ambiguous genitive (λόγον Ὀδυσσέος) to the full-blown description of the storytelling, Pindar's words yoke Homer to his character Odysseus, the man who most of all embodies the lying, contriving robber of judgment whose variegated narrative styles distract (*paragoisa*) his audiences.[23] Farnell tries to explain Pindar's harsh depiction of the poet's style by comparing the passage to *Olympian* 1.30–32. In it, the poet describes grace (*charis*) as fashioning all sweet things (ἅπαντα τεύχει τὰ μείλιχα) and as making the unpersuadable persuasive (ἄπιστον ἐμήσατο πιστόν).[24] While it is true that in *Olympian* 1 the poet seems to take a positive tone when describing the power of the stylistic sweetener *charis*, even here this ability is treated somewhat ambivalently. In fact, the phrase ἄπιστον ἐμήσατο πιστόν anticipates charges that would be made later in the fifth century against the sophists.[25] Moreover, the language of *Nemean* 7 is directly concerned with deceit, and while *Nemean* 8 does import some of the language of seduction, both passages provide a deeply ambivalent depiction of Homer's, and more importantly Odysseus', style.

In *Nemean* 7 Pindar underscores this negative depiction by declaring that most men have a blind heart (τυφλὸν ἦτορ), an ignorance of the truth that led to Ajax's suicide (7.24–26). That is, if the warriors who witnessed the contest between Ajax and Odysseus over Achilles' arms had been more attentive to the truth and less distracted by Odysseus' fine arguments, Homer's own audiences would not have been similarly led astray in their assessments of the two heroes.[26]

Nemean 8 takes up this same argument, enlarging on the conflict between Ajax, the silent and brave type (τιν' ἄγλωσσαν μέν, ἦτορ δ' ἄλκιμον), and Odysseus, the embodiment of shifty falsehood (αἰόλῳ ψεύ- / δει, 8.24–26). While oblivion overwhelms the one, the other wins the prize, as did Odysseus by secret vote (κρυφίαισι . . . ἐν ψάφοις, 27). The lyric poet Corinna depicts a similar scene in an ode about the poetry contest between the mountains Helicon and Cithaeron (fr. 654 *PMG*), which is itself in the tradition of the paradigmatic contest between Homer and Hesiod discussed by ancient commentators.[27] In Corinna's poem the Muse sets up a secret vote (ψᾶφον . . . κρυφίαν, 20–21) among the gods. When Helicon loses, the poet describes the decoration (ἀνεκόσμιον, 27) and delight of the victor Cithaeron as well as the bitter distress of the defeated Helicon.

The fragmentary quality of the remainder of the poem inhibits any understanding of what kind of judgment the poet herself passed on the contest, but Pindar's use of the model of the contest and secret vote clearly demonstrates a link between poetic contests and community decision-making. Once again Pindar completes his version of the episode with a general statement that could apply to the narrative style of both Homer and his authorial figure Odysseus:

> ἐχθρὰ δ' ἄρα πάρφασις ἦν καὶ πάλαι,
> αἱμύλων μύθων ὁμόφοι-
> τος, δολοφραδής, κακοποιὸν ὄνειδος.

> Indeed, enemy beguilement existed also of old,
> a fellow-traveler of flattering stories,
> a guile-deviser, an evil-working disgrace. (*Nem.* 8.33–34)

Recall that in Homer ὀαριστὺς πάρφασις describes the sweet lover's talk that Aphrodite keeps in her charm-filled belt (*Il.* 14.216–217; see ch. 3). The word *parphasis* denotes the kind of persuasion used in the seduction scene, which might include also blandishments. Calypso, for example, mesmerizes Odysseus with such soft and flattering speeches (αἰεὶ δὲ μαλακοῖσι καὶ αἱμυλίοισι λόγοισι / θέλγει, *Od.* 1.56–57). Lies and flattery also characterize the words that Pandora has in her heart (ψεύδεά θ' αἱμυλίους τε λόγους, *WD* 78). For Pindar, this style of speaking is seduction gone bad, transformed into deceitful contrivance that misapplies blame and praise alike. The poet prays that he may never have such a character (ἦθος) and may keep rather to the simple path (κελεύθοις ἁπλόαις) of life (*Nem.* 8.35–36).[28] The criticism of Odysseus is thus concluded by a switch to the voice of the poet, so that the lying hero's blaming, deceitful style becomes an antitype for the epinician poet. As scholars have pointed out, for Pindar, Odysseus plays the role of the slanderer.[29] Since he is the blamer of Ajax, whose bulwark of a body makes him the prototypical athlete, Odysseus' style could not be more misrepresentational, more lying, in fact.

Because Homer champions this lying style and the character type who uses it, some writers in the fifth century were encouraged to associate the techniques of the poet with those of his favorite hero. But the questioning of Homer's veracity in the fifth century is not only a judgment on the poet or poetry in general; it is also an agonistic move, a querying of tradition that promotes another version of events. The stories of poetic contests indicate that this is an old game. It is also central to Pindar's program, insofar as it serves as one way in which he displays his agonistic skills as resembling those of his athletic patrons. More crucial to this discussion, however, is that the merging of Homeric and Odyssean style here effects a link between poet and politician, between the activities of the rhapsode and those of the rhetor. This connection becomes increasingly central to the way fifth-century poets focus on the stylistic techniques of the forceful speakers for whom democratic practice provided so powerful a forum.

RUINOUS TYPES IN ATHENIAN DRAMA

In late fifth-century tragedy, Helen and Odysseus trail negative associations through numerous settings: from the prison camp where the Trojan women are detained to the shores of Lemnos where Philoctetes languishes and even to the halls of Agamemnon in Argos where Orestes hides from angry citizens. In many plays the choral odes detail the threatening traits of these two figures, providing an atmospheric punctuation to particular tragic dilemmas. While Helen shadows the plot as a catalyst of ruin in the odes of Aeschylus' *Agamemnon* and Euripides' *Iphigeneia in Aulis*, Odysseus slips in and out of the early scenes of Sophocles' *Ajax* and Euripides' *Hecuba*, torturing both eponymous characters with the real and imagined dangers of his tongue. Helen also has a consistent presence in the odes of *Hecuba*, so that in this play especially, she and Odysseus together serve as the beginning and the end of Hecuba's pain.

Even when they remain in the background, then, the corporeal styles of Odysseus and Helen arouse anxiety and suggest pain. Their moments on stage tend to be brief and disastrous. Each intervenes as a particular challenge to character integrity and ethical conduct and then departs, leaving behind disgusted or despairing interlocutors. Helen's beauty and love of luxury signal her danger in many of Euripides' plays. *Iphigenia in Aulis, Orestes, Andromache,* and the *Trojan Women* all depict her as visually greedy, her eye distracted by Paris' beauty and Trojan riches. Hecuba's horror of Helen centers on these eyes. Not only does Helen admire beauty in others, but her own appearance and especially her eyes are also disastrously compelling: they ruin those on whom they look (*Tro.* 891–893) and steal happiness (*Hec.* 441–443).

Similarly, when Odysseus arrives onstage in *Hecuba*, his argument with the queen reveals that his speeches mold a specious mask of communal piety, while his stealthy retraction of his beard and hand from Polyxena's suppliant grasp underscores his indirection. In the *Trojan Women* Odysseus' tongue is his most offending body part, and again it is Hecuba who focuses in the most detail on its dangerous qualities:

> μυσαρῷ δολίῳ λέλογχα φωτὶ δουλεύειν,
> πολεμίῳ δίκας, παρανόμῳ δάκει,
> ὅς πάντα τἀκεῖθεν ἐνθάδ(ε στρέφει, τὰ δ')
> ἀντίπαλ' αὖθις ἐκεῖσε διπτύχῳ γλώσσᾳ
> φίλα τὰ πρότερ' ἄφιλα τιθέμενος πάντων.

I have been allotted to serve a tainted, guileful man,
an enemy to justice, a criminal, rabid beast,
who turns everything from there to here
and these back again with his double-folded tongue,
making things formerly beloved unloved by all. (*Tro.* 283–287)

We might note that Hecuba describes the tricks of Odysseus' speaking style in terms that resemble charges leveled at the sophists. Parmentier argues that Hecuba's characterization evokes Odysseus' tactics in his treatment of Palamedes, whose conflict with this infamous liar was depicted in Euripides' play of that name, one of the other plays (with the *Alexander*) in this same trilogy.[30]

This focus on Helen's eyes and Odysseus' tongue can be found also in Aeschylus and Sophocles in different settings. Recall that in the *Agamemnon* the chorus speaks of the "soft arrow of [Helen's] eyes" (μαλθακὸν ὀμμάτων βέλος, 742) as a feature of her destructive nature. Consider as well the ode mentioned above, which lays out the hollow effect the lost sight of her form has on the viewer. The grace of her shapely statues pains her deserted husband, whose eyes grow blank from looking on simulations of her (*Ag.* 416–419). As both viewer and viewed, Helen blinds or stuns those who come into contact with her; her returning gaze is as startling in its effect as her beautiful form. A chorus in Euripides' *Iphigeneia in Aulis* puts the circularity of this effect most succinctly. In direct address to Paris they declare,

> Ἑλένας
> ἐν ἀντωποῖς βλεφάροισιν
> ἔρωτά τ' ἔδωκας, ἔρωτι δ'
> αὐτὸς ἐπτοάθης.

into Helen's returning gaze,
you gave love and by love
were yourself fluttered. (583–586)[31]

Similarly vibrant imagery traces the emotions aroused by Odysseus' sharp tongue in Sophocles' plays. The chorus of Salaminian sailors imagines bitterly Odysseus' whispered report (λόγους ψιθύροις, Aj. 148) of Ajax's downfall as he ranges through the troops, and the delight the teller will give to those who listen (καὶ πᾶς ὁ κλύων / τοῦ λέξαντος χαίρει, 151–152). They warn against the deceiving tales (cf. κλέπτουσι μύθους, 188) and the tongues of those who rave like bacchants (πάντων βακχαζόντων / γλώσσαις, 198–199), both of which Odysseus seems to encourage. When Ajax's vision clears, he moans in horror at the thought of the pleasure (ἡδονῆς) that this "one who sees all and is always the tool of all evil" (πάνθ' ὁρῶν ἁπάντων τ' ἀεὶ / κακῶν ὄργανον) might get from his downfall (379–382). To the suffering hero Odysseus is a wheedler (αἱμυλώτατον, 388) and an irritant (ἄλημα, 381, 389). Although Odysseus does not behave badly in the play, Ajax chafes repeatedly at the thought of the laughter his dilemma will cause. For him, the primary agent of this blaming speech is Odysseus. For Philoctetes, another Sophoclean hero embattled with Odysseus, his tongue "touches all evil speech and mischief" (ἔχοιδα γάρ νιν παντὸς ἂν λόγου κακοῦ / γλώσσῃ θιγόντα καὶ πανουργίας, Phil. 407–408; cf. also ch. 5).

In tragic representation, gender usually determines which faculties point to which stylistic elements. As I discuss in chapter 3, archaic and classical poets regard the female body as the ornamental object of the male gaze, while the authoritative speech act remains primarily the purview of the male hero. Thus a simple pattern would seem to emerge, in which Helen as the most pleasing vision comes to emblematize the startling impact of the visualizing oral style, and Odysseus as the most agile manipulator of character comes to embody the versatile, deceptive techniques of the sophist who performs in this style.[32]

Neither Helen nor Odysseus quite fit this pattern, however. Rather, since both are increasingly associated with aspects of this grand style, their roles tend to overlap: the visually compelling style that Helen embodies also encompasses a spectacular kind of deception, and the disguising style of Odysseus may involve the attractive flattery that cements allegiances. Aphrodite and Odysseus are both intricate-minded (*poikilophrōn*) and deployers of tricks (*doloi*),[33] while Helen may speak with authority, manipulating character effect like Odysseus. That said, in tragedy Helen does more often function as an emblematic figure for the dangers of stylistic impact than an active character, while Odysseus tends to be a backstage manipulator, the agent behind the machinations that threaten the heroic figure.

Of the dramatists, Euripides, especially later in his career, seems to have been most interested in Helen as an ornamental but changeable figure. In the play *Helen,* she is the figure of praise tradition, not responsible for the Trojan war and in fact not even present in Troy; Euripides follows Stesichorus in sending the real Helen to Egypt.[34] There she dresses herself in unwonted mourning, even insisting on cutting her hair, while elsewhere she is said to be reluctant to do so (*Tro.* 1025–1027; *Or.* 128–129). In the *Orestes* Helen is instead an embodiment of blame. The focus for condemnation of all luxury and ornamentation, she signifies the particular threat of decadent beauty to moral action (e.g., 1426–1436, 1467). Such a *habitus* encourages the use of flattery and indirection as an effective costume for wrong-doing, impeding the identification of which type the speaker really is. Compare Aristophanes' *Thesmophoriazusae,* where the dramatist makes a mockery of Euripides' good Helen, using multiple layers of costuming (Mnesilochus playing a woman playing Helen) to indicate the renegade artificiality emblematized by both the figure of Helen and the poets with whom she is associated.

If Helen is infamous in fifth-century drama for her specious ornamentality, Odysseus gains attention especially for his overly flexible and self-serving outlook. This *habitus* is marked by an attention to balance and fair return and thus resembles his strategies in the *Iliad* (cf. ch. 2). For instance, in Euripides' *Hecuba* Odysseus defends the sacrificing of Polyxena by promoting a visible, proportionate recompense that effectively balances the reputation of Achilles with his own reputation (309–320). He thus associates himself not only with the idea of fairness but also with the honor that accrues to the best of the Achaeans. Similarly, when Agamemnon argues with Odysseus over the burial of Ajax in Sophocles' play, Odysseus explains that further vaunting is the equivalent of ill-gotten gains (κέρδεσιν τοῖς μὴ καλοῖς, *Aj.* 1349) and that he (Odysseus) will come to the same end (1365). When Agamemnon questions his self-serving attitude, Odysseus replies, "Whom is it more fitting [εἰκός] that I serve?" (1367).

We might recall that the reference to suitable or reasonable conduct is a common technique in the classical period; but it is also often represented as a sophistic technique and as indicative of the sophistic orator's misleading style. The *Phaedrus* provides the *locus classicus* for this connection: Socrates says that Teisias and his student Gorgias "realized that probabilities [εἰκότα] should be more respected than true things and also made small matters appear great and great small by the force [ῥώμη] of their speech" (267a6–8). The concept is central to Odysseus' significance as an authorial figure in the delineation of ideas about stylistic technique, particularly in relation to the forceful representation of character.[35] *Eikos* arguments address probability, that is, what can be reasonably assumed about a particular type of person in a particular situation.

Thus in fifth-century drama both Helen and Odysseus not only serve as metonyms for certain effects of style but also frequently represent their most suspect authors: the poets and sophists who bring them to life on stage. The two plays from the late fifth century that depict most forcefully the disturbing aspects of these figures—Euripides' *Trojan Women* and Sophocles' *Philoctetes*—show them challenging traditional notions of moral behavior in the style that each promotes. Euripides' *Trojan Women* (415) is the most negative depiction of Helen in any of the extant literature. The production of the play with *Alexander* and *Palamedes* suggests that the trilogy intentionally grouped together the narratives that parallel the threat of Helen's allure in the *Trojan Women*. Thus in this triad of plays Helen and Odysseus (as well as Paris) took the stage together as aspects of the same problem: the dangerous distraction of stylistic effect. Six years later Sophocles' *Philoctetes* reinforced this negative portrait of Odysseus in a more ambiguous setting, where his clearly sophistic style and talent for character impersonation also support an action necessary for the common good.

The *Trojan Women* and *Philoctetes* isolate those aspects of the figures of Helen and Odysseus that most confound judgment and understand them as concerned with style. Responses to their techniques capture their dangerous effects: the chorus warns against Helen's appealing speaking style (λέγει / καλῶς) since she is an "evil-doer" (κακοῦργος, *Tro.* 967–968), while Philoctetes declares that Odysseus makes use of every evil style of speech and all wrong-doing (παντὸς . . . λόγου κακοῦ / . . . καὶ πανουργίας, *Phil.* 408). In each case, the speaker's style is associated with unethical behavior: Helen's by means of a distractingly elegant style (λέγει καλῶς), Odysseus' by means of a craftily profligate one (παντὸς . . . λόγου κακοῦ).

THE ORNAMENTAL BODY:
HELEN IN THE *TROJAN WOMEN*

While there is some consensus that Helen's defense in the *Trojan Women* is loosely based on Gorgias' rhetorical set piece entitled the *Encomium of Helen,* most scholars have foregone any detailed elaboration of the relation between the speeches.[36] Helen's speech in the *Trojan Women* does, however, enact a worldview and style that echo the outlook and tone of Gorgias' *Encomium.* The *agôn* in which Euripides' Helen appears is a pivotal scene; it has been treated to a plethora of responses. A few scholars have chosen to attempt at least partial rehabilitation of Helen's character, arguing that her speech is the desperate expression of a terrified woman or that Euripides in fact gives the captive Helen a calm and ironic defense against the logical but violent Hecuba, who demands blood vengeance.[37] More often, however, Helen's speech has been regarded as weak in argument, superficial in emphasis, and generally inferior to Hecuba's speech in both rhetorical structure and moral outlook.[38] Among these scholars there is, understandably, some puzzlement about how so fundamentally silly an argument as Helen's could in the end win out over Hecuba's reasoned response. Whether they find Helen and her speech a decorative but corrupt form of comic relief[39] or more straightforwardly paradigmatic of corrupt sensibilities,[40] commentators have tended to focus on the content of the speech and to find it deficient.

Helen's well-dressed appearance in the play sets her apart from the Trojan women, and her style of argumentation animates a conception of the world that stands in opposition to Hecuba's ethical mandates. Since Helen's position maintains that mortals are helpless in the face of the overwhelming compulsion that beauty possesses, her argument preempts ethical debate. The stylistic structure of her speech resembles an older narrative form, which tracks the journey of her body across the Aegean, driven by the power of Aphrodite. Since this compulsion is of divine origins, there cannot be any question of right or wrong action: it is the will of the god, the stronger force. Her position echoes the argument regarding the right of the stronger that Gorgias uses in his *Encomium* and that is generally associated with the sophists.[41] From this perspective, Helen can be judged only from a standpoint that accepts a world controlled by force (*bia*), a realm in which ethical choice has no place. While any critic may judge Helen's actions morally, as many have done in following Hecuba's reasoning, the judgment itself does not respond to the vibrant forces that rule the world depicted by Helen, whose corporeal style reproduces the impact of divine desire on the human body.

HELEN'S THREAT TO EYE AND EAR

In the middle of the *Trojan Women*, following an ode that gives ominous and pointed emphasis to the rape of mortal men by gods and goddesses, Menelaus strides onstage (860). He salutes the sun in a sanguine manner, bringing with him a jarring shift in tone from that of the grieving women who have populated the stage until now. With the entrance of Menelaus, the soldiering, violent type that the mournful Trojan women most fear now stands before them. This soldier seems, however, to be on their side. Indeed, Menelaus eagerly announces his intention to kill Helen and commands the servants to "lead her, dragging her out by her hair, deep-dyed with blood-guilt" (κομίζετ' αὐτὴν τῆς μιαιφονωτάτης / κόμης ἐπισπάσαντες, 881–882). In Menelaus' rather limited imagination, his sinning wife will be visibly marked by her error—her hair, which she famously treasures, stained with the blood of the Greeks whose deaths she brought on. Hecuba seems more circumspect about Menelaus' ability to exact this punishment and does not respond directly to his threats of physical violence. Instead she prays that Zeus or whatever force governs events (εἴτ' ἀνάγκη φύσεος εἴτε νοῦς βροτῶν, 886) might manage the situation justly. Menelaus wonders that she offers newfangled prayers to the gods (εὐχὰς ὡς ἐκαίνισας θεῶν, 889), making little of the sophisticated language of her invocation.[42]

When Hecuba responds more directly to Menelaus' claim that he is there to kill Helen, she does so by warning him against the ruin that the mere sight of Helen may bring. She characterizes Helen as an enchantress, describing how she seizes others with her physical beauty, drawing them into a chain reaction of desire and destruction. Helen's body was carried off by Paris for its beauty, and this body in turn captures the eyes of entire leagues of men, carrying off entire cities:

> ὁρᾶν δὲ τήνδε, φεῦγε, μή σ' ἕλη πόθῳ.
> αἱρεῖ γὰρ ἀνδρῶν ὄμματ', ἐξαιρεῖ πόλεις
> πίμπρησιν οἴκους· ὧδ' ἔχει κηλήματα.
> ἐγώ νιν οἶδα καὶ σὺ χοί πεπονθότες.

> Flee seeing her, lest she seize you by desire.
> For she captures the eyes of men, she carries off cities,

and burns houses—such are the spells she possesses.
I know her, as do you and those who have suffered. (891–894)

Looking at Helen, one is seized by her eyes in return.[43] Hecuba locates
Helen's charms, her *kêlêmata*, in her ability to attract with her returning gaze.
Hecuba's vocabulary also implies that her words may have the same effect:
the term *kêlêma* often designates in particular a rhythmic, verbal spellbind-
ing, like the chants (*epôdai*) that encapsulate the magical force of words in
Gorgias' *Encomium*.[44] Hecuba's description treats Helen as the embodiment
of seizure by desire and plays on the affective similarities between capture
by *erôs* and capture by violence. Helen employs the same idea in her speech;
the comparison also parallels the conflation in Gorgias' *Encomium* of physical force with the compulsion of seeing and hearing. Hecuba's emphasis,
however, underscores the moral necessity of resisting such rapture, which
is precisely what Helen will claim is impossible. Helen and Hecuba emerge
in the *agôn* as most opposed regarding the role of human will in the course
of events, but they share an understanding of the power of *erôs*. Neither
denies the ability of a striking appearance and compelling words to overwhelm the will; only Hecuba maintains that resistance to this seduction is
possible. Menelaus' blustering entrance and Hecuba's dour response to his
confidence heightens the tension and expectation surrounding the figure of
Helen. She herself—hurried on by force (896–897) but defiantly well dressed
(1022–1024) and well spoken (966–967)—intensifies the troubling connections already suggested by Hecuba between physical violence and visual
impact.

HELEN'S ENCHANTING PERFORMANCE

Euripides' drama frames the defiant speech of Helen with the cadences
of the mourning Trojan women, in contrast to whom her *hexis* as a whole
seems stunningly anomalous. Her speech questions the perspective that refuses her beautiful form its rightful status as a prized possession and that
seeks to deny its power to attract and overwhelm. In keeping with this attitude, Helen appears on stage dressed in her usual finery. Among the Trojan
women in their drab mourning clothes, her decorative appearance must
have presented quite a study in contrasts for the original audience, as N. A.
Croally has noted.[45] Her visual impact is surely an important aspect of her
role in the play. Although no character remarks on it immediately (until
Hecuba does in her speech, *Tro.* 1021–1023), vase representations set a prece-

dent for this showy, defiant figure, clearly reflecting this same association of Helen with physical adornment. A seventh-century relief pithos depicts Trojan women supplicating Greek men, who are attacking them. Only Helen stands, very elaborately dressed, revealing a shoulder to the stunned Menelaus, who faces her with sword erect.[46] Other versions of this meeting in vase painting portray Helen as similarly well dressed and physically stunning, to the point that in some depictions she causes a pursuing Menelaus to drop his sword.[47] Her adorned and frequently revealing attitudes (i.e., lifting her veil, opening her chiton) resemble bridal deportment; it is this celebratory attitude and image that Helen maintains in most dramatic depictions.[48]

In the *Trojan Women* Helen's speech emphasizes her beauty as a means of distracting Menelaus from a more negative interpretation of her actions. The speech's laudatory treatment of her beautiful form reinforces her decorative appearance on stage and highlights it as significant. Thus the tradition that focuses on Helen's body as dangerously appealing was finally given its spectacular counterpart in Euripides' play, when the elaborately costumed actor playing Helen delivered her blithe and visually compelling speech. In keeping with the growing reaction against the sophists, Euripides depicts the appeal of her figure as signifying the unavoidable but potentially disastrous effects of the impressive oral performance.

Helen's defense uses her body as a stage prop of sorts, at one point even verbally adorning it with a crown of praise. The treatment she is subjected to when initially on stage, however, clearly fails to reflect this celebration of her form. When she first appears on stage, she refers to her forced entrance as an "introduction worthy of fear" (φροίμιον . . . ἄξιον φόβου, 895). Using the technical rhetorical term for the tone-setting prologue of a speech, she characterizes it as brutal in style. She then questions Menelaus about his own sentiments and those of the Greek army regarding her, seeking to determine whether her sentence will likewise be characterized by violence. Her first words thus situate her in relation to this rough corporeal style. Menelaus warns her that she has not been brought out for a precise accounting of events (οὐκ εἰς ἀκριβὲς ἦλθες, 901), using a rather cryptic phrase that echoes contemporary idiom for distinguishing sophistic styles.[49] After telling her, in effect, not to behave like a careful sophist, Menelaus states his intention to kill her, and Helen requests permission to plead in her own defense. Hecuba intervenes and encourages Menelaus to listen to her, if only so that she, Hecuba, may angrily refute her.

The entire exchange is thus underpinned by implicit references to the nature and style of oratorical debate. The opening of Helen's defense focuses on the power of speech (*logos*) and the absence of due process in her treatment. She worries that no matter how elegant her speaking style might be, some preconceived notion of her inimical type may prevent her from being answered properly (ἴσως με, κἂν εὖ κἂν κακῶς δόξω λέγειν / οὐκ ἀνταμείψῃ πολεμίαν ἡγούμενος, 914–915).[50] She suggests, in effect, that if she already looks to Menelaus like the evil-doer the Trojan women have claimed she is, he will react as one might to an armored enemy. Compare what Gorgias says about the sight of the enemy in battle array (πολέμια σώματα . . . ὁπλίσῃ κόσμον χαλκοῦ καὶ σιδήρου): it is so alarming that men flee, "struck" (ἐκπλαγέντες) by the terrible sight (*Hel.* 16). Helen's style might, accordingly, achieve a repelling, negative impact, one opposite to that of the beloved's body. It would be, in fact, opposite to the erotic force to which she will argue that she was herself prey. Consider again Aristotle's claim in the *Rhetoric* that the speech itself ought to convince the audience that one is a certain type, not some preconceived notion of one's status or social disposition.[51] Euripides gives Helen this argument as a means of indicating her awareness of the slander that precedes her and her need to offset it with a winning style.

At the level of invention, Helen's speech seeks to achieve this persuasive victory by deploying her beautiful form as a focus of desire and praise. The speech is structured in an interlocking narrative pattern that mobilizes other figures and organizes them in relation to her. The primary actors thus move in a visual field that has both emblematic and spatial dimensions. This visualizing effect highlights the female form in particular: Paris is chosen to judge the beauty of goddesses (924); Aphrodite offers him Helen because she is struck by Helen's body (929–930); Helen's own beautiful shape may destroy her, when her head should be crowned (935–937); Aphrodite's stature overwhelms Helen (940); Helen's body cannot be hidden (957–958); her body should be treated as a victory prize (962–964). The spatial patterning, in some contrast, focuses on both male and female bodies moving in a geographical field: Paris is born in Troy (920); he judges the goddesses on Mount Ida, where the whole of Europe and Asia is divided for his choosing (924–928); like an inescapable demon, he comes across the Aegean to Helen, with Aphrodite at his side (940–942); Menelaus leaves Helen for Crete (942–943); Helen is seized by the power of Aphrodite and taken to Troy (946–950); Paris goes to the grave (952), but Helen cannot leave Troy for the Argive ships, because her body cannot be moved without being seen (955–957); her body is then seized by Deiphobus and retained in Troy (959–960).

While Helen's speech does not make much use of the alliterative lexicon that dominates Gorgias' *Encomium*, the antithetical and rhythmic style that Euripides gives Helen is similar, as are some of the argumentative tactics.[52] For instance, rhetorical commonplaces punctuate Helen's speech, some of which echo quite closely Gorgias' other extant set piece, *Palamedes' Defense*, as Ruth Scodel has noted.[53] In the *Encomium*, Gorgias begins his praise of Helen by invoking the appropriate praise (κόσμος) for different objects, which results in "praise for those worthy of praise" (ἄξιον ἐπαίνου ἐπαίνῳ, *Hel.* 1). Likewise, in Euripides' play, Helen embarks on the main arguments of her speech with what commentators have recognized as a traditional argument from origins. She pairs the beginning of her speech (πρῶτον) with "the beginning of the evils" (ἀρχὰς . . . τῶν κακῶν), a beginning that itself is matched with Paris' birth (ἔτεκεν . . . τέκουσα, 919–920). The speech-writer Isocrates also makes use of this reflexive style in the opening of the main section of his encomium of Helen (discussed in chapter 5). The similarities among these opening statements suggest that the matching of form or style to content was a typical technique, and perhaps especially used by Gorgias. It seems also to have been considered particularly fitting for *epideixis*, the circular nature of praise encouraging the assertion of this kind of symmetry.[54]

Another Gorgianic echo can be found in the structuring of Helen's speech by means of *tricola* that name and rename a human or divine being, offer possibilities, and enumerate events or characteristics.[55] The speech also ultimately claims that Helen should in fact be treated to an epideictic ornamentation, a reverential handling of her figure that resembles that of Gorgias' *Encomium*. Thus Helen situates the argument from origins as the first in a triad of arguments that incrementally pave the way to the acknowledgment of her divine beauty and her praiseworthy status. The elaborate structuring of this section (919–930) in triads, while something of a rhetorical commonplace, nevertheless gives the impression of an unavoidable visual pattern rather than a sequential (or consequential) progression. The narrative is marked by three arguments about causality, each approximately doubling in length the former. Each stage—Paris' birth, his preservation, and his choice of her as prize—emphasizes with schematic consistency a human response to a divine agenda that failed to prevent Helen's contact with Paris.[56] Each argument also marks the approach of Paris' body to her own: he is born; his infant form (βρέφος)[57] is not destroyed, "bitter image of a firebrand" (δαλοῦ πικρὸν μίμημ', 922) though it is; he chooses the goddess in the beauty contest who offers him Helen's beautiful form (εἶδος, 929).

The triadic structure both has the force of satisfying narrative and is itself echoed by other groups of three (e.g., Paris' three names, the "threefold yoke of three goddesses," τρισσὸν ζεῦγος ὅδε τριῶν θεῶν, 924). This is the kind of stylistic symmetry that Gorgias would have approved. We might also compare here Aristotle's claim in the *Rhetoric* that the compactness and antithetical style (λέξις) of such expressions imitates the syllogism and thus renders them persuasive (*Rhet.* 1401a5–8). Later he asserts that effective style lies in the use of "graspable" numbers or segments to establish its rhythms and *cola* (τοῦτο δέ, ὅτι ἀριθμὸν ἔχει ἡ ἐν περιόδοις λέξις, ὃ πάντων εὐμνημονευτότατον, *Rhet.* 1409b5–6). Thus when Helen depicts a world forged by these triads, her representation of events reflects an essential grouping that is also rhythmically convincing. Paris' three labels, his two proper names framing the vibrant epithet mentioned above (δαλοῦ πικρὸν μίμημ', 922), reiterate this inevitable rhythm.[58] Helen's repeated use of these chiming triads reinforces the sense that those who embody this kind of divine force are beyond praise and blame and thus not answerable to the same laws as others. The technique may also echo Aeschylus' treatment of her figure in the choruses of the *Agamemnon*, where the effect is that of ritual invocation. Finally, this chanting, triadic style recalls Gorgias' comparison of the powers of *logos* to the incantations (*epôdai*) of magic spells.[59]

In the section on the Judgment (924–937), Helen also offers a viewing of her body in three possible scenarios: as the lovely form that "stunned" Aphrodite (ἐκπαγλουμένη, 929), as the beautiful shape that elicits reproach (ὠλόμην ἐγώ / εὐμορφίᾳ πραθεῖσα, 935–936), and as the crowned figure who saved Greece (ἐχρῆν με στέφανον ἐπὶ κάρᾳ λαβεῖν, 937). In a move that parallels Gorgias' claim in the *Encomium* that praise and blame must be properly applied to the proper objects, Helen refutes the charge that she is to blame for the entire chain of events by claiming that her beauty in fact saved Greece from ruin. Since both Hera and Athena offered Paris some form of tyranny over the Greeks (925–928), his choice of her prevented Greece's submission to foreign domination. Effectively addressing all the Greeks, Helen elaborates in another *tricolon* what might have been their fate: they were not conquered by foreigners, nor beaten down in battle, nor ruled by a tyrant (οὐ κρατεῖσθ' ἐκ βαρβάρων, / οὔτ' ἐς δόρυ σταθέντες, οὐ τυραννίδι, 933–

934).[60] She should thus be crowned for her role in Greece's fate, an emblem of praise replacing the marks of blame on the body (κὠνειδίζομαι / ἐξ ὧν ἐχρῆν με στέφανον ἐπὶ κάρα λαβεῖν, 936–937).

Helen, crowned with the salutary power of her beauty, stands next to Paris at the center of the speech, joined to him by Aphrodite. In fact, Aphrodite emerges here as an invincible power whose attendance on Paris renders him also an irresistible force. At this central point in her speech, Helen invokes Paris for the second time by an epithet that captures his destructive relation to the goddess (ὁ τῆσδ' ἀλάστωρ) and by both his names (εἴτ' Ἀλέξανδρον θέλεις / ὀνόματι προσφωνεῖν νιν εἴτε [καὶ Πάριν], 941–942). His presence is thus highlighted by a rhythmic repetition that portrays him as an alarming, inevitable figure. Paris crosses the Aegean with Aphrodite in attendance, the dominant form of the goddess looming over him (ἦλθε οὐχὶ μικρὰν θεὸν ἔχων αὐτοῦ μέτα, 940).[61] Helen claims as well that Menelaus unconscionably left her unprotected precisely at this moment of crisis; he too is an evil presence (ὦ κάκιστε, 943). When she considers her own role in her seizure, she finds Aphrodite hovering there as well. The will of the goddess is stronger even than that of Zeus, and he is her slave (κείνης δὲ δοῦλος ἐστι, 950).[62] The forceful deictic that Helen uses here (κείνης) further underscores the impression of the goddess' looming presence, as τῆσδ' had earlier (941).

When she turns to the death of Paris, Helen remarks that some suspiciously well-fashioned argument (εὐπρεπῆ λόγον, 951) may be brought against her as to why she failed to leave Troy once Paris was gone. Since she goes on to claim that she did in fact attempt to escape, her point seems to be that such a charge, while false and unfair, would *seem* valid if it were suitably expressed. We might remember that Herodotus deems Homer's story about Helen in Troy *euprepês* and indicates its dubious relationship to the truth. In Euripides' *Hecuba*, when the Trojan queen is trying to save her daughter Polyxena from being sacrificed at Achilles' tomb, she declares that Helen should be killed rather than Polyxena, her misleading beauty having brought Achilles to Troy in the first place (266). She calls Helen's form (εἶδος) the "most [speciously] beautiful" one (εὐπρεπεστάτη) and Helen herself a wrong-doer (ἀδικοῦσα, 269–270), both of which make her the most suitable adornment for Achilles' tomb. She thus pairs the image of showy suitability with moral failure, a coupling that Helen repeatedly evokes and that the term *euprepês* usually encompasses. In the *Trojan Women*, Helen's use of the term is more strictly rhetorical, but it nevertheless implies the idea of deceptive beauty with which she is associated and that she thus seeks especially to refute.

To counter the specious claim she fears, Helen employs a tactic that emphasizes the impossibility of tricks. She argues that eyewitnesses would have posed a hindrance to any attempts she might have made to leave Troy. This argument resembles the standard forensic procedure of calling witnesses, as well as Palamedes' claim in Gorgias' speech that guards would have caught him if he had done what Odysseus charged (*Pal.* 10). Helen points out that the Trojan gate wardens would have seen her had she tried to escape by ropes. In fact many eyewitnesses on the ramparts often discovered her, "sneaking away *this* body" (σῶμα κλέπτουσαν τόδε, 958). Her deictic emphasis on her body as it is pictured exposed to eyewitnesses highlights its visual impact. A gesture to her finely dressed figure may well have accompanied the phrase σῶμα . . . τόδε, so that her visible stature on stage could be underscored as reproducing the effect of her very visible presence in Troy. The deixis also suggests that her form is more striking and outstanding than others and thus that it cannot be hidden. In the *Iliad* its special qualities are depicted as poised between magical elusiveness and stunning visibility. In the *Trojan Women* Helen's declaration of her body's hyper-visibility highlights insistently the latter image. In keeping with her adorned beauty and the attention she draws to it, Helen represents her form as necessarily, iconically visible.[63] A repeated focus in her speech in one status or attitude after another (929–930, 935–937, 955–958, 961–963), the image of her beautiful form gives her arguments a visualizing impact that her elaborate appearance on stage reinforces.

Helen further reasons that rather than cloaked and lowered to the ground in a secret bundle, her thrice-captured body should be valued in the same way as victory prizes (νικητηρίων, 963).[64] This section of the speech also moves Helen through three possible scenarios, portraying her body not only as something valuable and difficult to hide but also as the property of another by force and as something akin to prizes won in contests of physical prowess. Its structure thus repeats in slightly different terms the triadic depiction that shifted Helen's body from its status as Aphrodite's prize, to an envisioning of its destruction and again to an image of its crowning (929–937).

The rhythmical, visualizing style of Helen's speech thus reproduces her beauty's effect on those who view it, ultimately arousing deep suspicion in Hecuba and the chorus. It also achieves a softening of resolve in her violent husband, who certainly seems stunned by it, as he is by her ornamental appearance. Helen's emphasis on compulsion, moreover, reiterates at the level of invention the impact of this style, its incremental structure reproducing the incremental forces set in motion by her beauty. As she presents this necessary forward movement, Paris' decision in the Judgment merely continues a chain of events initiated by the overwhelming effects of her visual impact. Utilizing an essentially Iliadic explanation, Helen argues that her form so stunned Aphrodite (Κύπρις . . . ἐκπαγλουμένη, 929) that the goddess deployed it to attract Paris. Helen's beauty thus served the goddess as a visible emblem of love's force. Recall that in the *Iliad* Aphrodite loves Helen and Paris overwhelmingly (ἔκπαγλα, *Il.* 3.415; cf. 5.423).[65] This condition of *ekplêxis* then seems also to strike Helen when Paris arrives with Aphrodite, and she finds herself helpless before him and this divine desire. In Gorgias' *Encomium ekplêxis* renders the viewer incapable of reasoning reaction, and she is overwhelmed by "the necessities of desire" (ἔρωτος ἀνάγκαις, *Hel.* 19; cf. 16). As chapter 5 explains, in the late fifth century this state of stunned admiration commonly characterizes reactions to the grand oral style and particularly to that of Gorgias.[66] In Euripides' speech this startled response carries more direct erotic force and is closely tied to Helen's striking form. In this it echoes the Iliadic association of *ekplêxis* with Aphrodite and *erôs*, but once again its rhetorical use suggests Gorgianic associations between the visual impact of Helen's form and the power of a visualizing oral style.

When Helen finishes speaking, the chorus warns against her persuasive ability, countering her opening statement that her words will probably be to no effect (cf. 914–915). They urge Hecuba to protect her children and country by destroying Helen's persuasive effect (πειθὼ διαφθείρουσα τῆσδ'), "since she speaks eloquently while being an evil-doer" (ἐπεὶ λέγει / καλῶς κακοῦργος οὖσα, 966–967).[67] K. H. Lee (*ad Tro.* 966) compares a fragment from Euripides' *Palamedes,* which maintains a similar suspicion that a fine speaking style may not be matched by the content of the speech: "I would never praise the wisdom of one who speaks finely, but about deeds that are shameful" (ὅστις λέγει μὲν εὖ, τὰ δ' ἔργ' ἐφ' οἷς λέγει αἴσχρ' ἐστί, τούτου τὸ σοφὸν οὐκ αἰνῶ ποτέ, fr. 583 N²). The lines probably refer to Odysseus. Since the *Palamedes* was part of the same trilogy, the comparison between the dangerously persuasive styles of Odysseus and Helen would have been unavoidable.

Like many reactions in tragedy to Odysseus' speaking style, the chorus views Helen's rhetorical agility as dangerous, as the well-spoken defense of an evil-doer. Her combination of verbal dexterity and mischief-making causes the chorus to declare, "This [speech here] is thus a fearsome thing" (δεινόν οὖν τόδε, 968). The deictic τόδε echoes Helen's use of such demonstratives to indicate the formidable presence of Aphrodite. The moment is also reminiscent of the Trojan elders' reactions to Helen in *Iliad* 3. They characterize her as "fearsomely" (αἰνῶς) like the goddesses, using the Ionic equivalent of *deinôs* (*Il.* 3.158). This descriptive is deployed with increasing frequency in fifth- and fourth-century oratory. Speakers make the charge particularly in forensic argumentation, against the opponent who shows himself to be too technically proficient in his style, too premeditated in his approach, and thus too smoothly persuasive in his presentation.[68] The word is also associated with the grand oral style, aspects of which the figures of Helen and Odysseus embody for the sophists (see further in ch. 5).

While some commentators have argued that the chorus is reacting here primarily to the adept arguments of the speech, Helen's style is surely more to be feared, as the chorus suggests by its use of the adverb καλῶς (967). Later they worry that Menelaus will not meet this dangerous situation with the requisite violence, which might ward off from Greece the appearance of feminine weakness (1035; cf. below).[69] Helen's depiction of the effects of her beautiful form suggests that Menelaus should submit to the same compulsion. In Euripides' portrayal, then, Helen's performance reproduces the propulsive force of *erôs* and the stunned reactions it inspires, drawing her audience's attention to the relation between the beautiful image and stylistic effect, precisely the connection that constitutes her particular contribution to archaic and classical ideas about style.

HELEN'S DRESSING DOWN

Hecuba's refutation impugns Helen's stunning appearance and seeks to strip her envisioned form of its ornamental stature. Hecuba also views Helen's elaborate dress, in combination with her depiction of the forces that compelled her, as a performance that speciously covers up immoral acts. In her reply to Helen, she characterizes this as a decorative cloaking of wrong-doing (τὸ σὸν κακὸν κοσμοῦσα, *Tro.* 982). Helen's retelling of her own abduction is represented by Hecuba as blasphemy, as crafted in order to mask her infidelity. Hecuba's phraseology, focusing as it does on decoration and aestheticizing trickery, betrays her fear of Helen's beauty and her emphasis on her startling form in her speech. She thus attempts to counteract Helen's effect by drawing attention to the dubious morals that underlie the visual impact of her oral performance. Initiating a theme that runs throughout her speech, Hecuba emphasizes the cosmetic impropriety of Helen's bodily *hexis*. She also acknowledges the attraction that the beautiful form possesses, but she condemns this type of impact as but one side of a decadent, sensuous attitude. Helen is not only draped in elaborate raiment and verbal finery; she is also too susceptible to the finery of others.

The necessary links forged by the stylistic patterning of Helen's narrative portrays in vibrant form the impossibility of resisting divinely inspired desire, no matter where the god is actually situated. If Aphrodite draws one on, this attraction is the will of the god—necessary, inexorable, irreversible. For the rationalist Hecuba, in contrast, Aphrodite is an internal force. Because Helen's "mind was made Aphrodite when she saw the extraordinary beauty of [Hecuba's] son" (ἦν οὑμὸς υἱὸς κάλλος ἐκπρεπέστατος / ὁ σὸς δ' ἰδών νιν νοῦς ἐποιήθη Κύπρις, 987–988), she is responsible for her actions and thus deserving of blame. One's folly (μῶρα) makes of Aphrodite what pleases one's senses; Hecuba accuses Helen of desire not only for Paris but for his Trojan finery (ὃν εἰσιδοῦσα βαρβάροις ἐσθήμασι / χρυσῷ τε λαμπρὸν ἐξεμαργώθης φρένας, 991–992).[70] Her depiction, like so many of the scenes discussed in previous chapters, emphasizes the role of sight in seduction.

Later in her speech Hecuba returns to the topic of Helen's eye for finery, which now emerges as the central theme of her condemnation. Due to her love of luxury, Helen was loathe to leave her Trojan riches and even appears before her husband dressed like a goddess bent on seduction (κἀπὶ τοῖσδε σὸν δέμας / ἐξῆλθες ἀσκήσασα κἄβλεψας πόσει / τὸν αὐτὸν αἰθέρ', ὦ κατάπτυστον κάρα, 1022–1024).[71] When Helen should be weeping and virtuously disheveled, with shorn hair and a black *peplos* (1025–1027), instead she comes among the Trojan women as finely dressed as ever, flaunting the persuasive impact of her corporeal style. Hecuba wants not only to dismantle the potent effect of such a style but also to destroy the physical form that is its special emblem. Where Helen sought to decorate herself with the crown of martyred beauty, Hecuba judges that Helen's dead body would be the only proper crown for Greece (στεφάνωσον Ἑλλάδ' ἀξίως τήνδε κτανών / σαυτοῦ, 1030–1031). She should be killed as an example to all women, Hecuba concludes, in a brutal reflection of the pervasive negative measure Helen is for the Trojan women.

That Helen emerges victorious in the *agôn* is suggested by the exchange between Hecuba and Menelaus and by the choral ode that follows. This denouement, in keeping with the larger myth, indicates that her first husband cannot resist either her decorative appearance or her visualizing speech. The chorus adds weight to the last of Hecuba's charges by cautioning Menelaus against Helen's allure and counseling him to "remove this charge of effeminacy from Greece" (κἀφελοῦ πρὸς Ἑλλάδος / ψόγον τὸ θῆλύ τ', 1034–1035).[72] Menelaus maintains that he agrees with Hecuba; Helen's claim that Aphrodite drove her actions was wielded, he declares, as a boast (κόμπου χάριν, 1038), a stylistic trick to which he does not intend to fall prey.[73] But then Helen supplicates Menelaus and he relents, denying with a weak joke her danger to him. He claims that he intends to kill her at Argos, but the audience knows how well he carried out that intention. Helen has won.[74] Wielding her compelling image like an adept rhetor, she has herself deployed the same force of divine desire to which she attributed her actions. The play as a whole condemns Helen, but in this episode, Euripides clearly details how her visualizing, sensuous *hexis* could be so persuasive, old-fashioned and weak though her arguments may be.

THE CLOAK OF CHARACTER:
ODYSSEUS AND THE PHILOCTETES PLAYS

When the disguised Odysseus tells his stories to his various interlocutors in the lying scenes of the *Odyssey*, he convinces them that he is a sympathetic type by using a character that both approximates his own and resembles theirs. The lying hero does not simply suit the length and focus of his speech to the visible type that his interlocutor appears to be or that he knows him to be. He also uses his own famous persona as a means of reinforcing the positive reflection of the hearer in the speaker's self-characterization, so that both are allied in their praise of Odysseus. The Homeric poet depicts this kind of versatility, and especially this covert use of persona, as an admirable talent that reveals Odysseus' unique resourcefulness. There is only the merest suggestion that moral trouble might attend his adept deceptions, such as when he cannot stop lying and tells his own father a tale (*Od.* 24.246–279). Antisthenes is said to have regarded Odysseus' chameleon style as an important definition of his famous epithet *polutropos* ("multifaceted"). Aristotle recommended a similar versatility (although with some reservation) under the auspices of "suitability" (τὸ πρέπον), as a means of giving the impression of speaking the truth (*Rhet.* 1408a10–25).

In fifth-century tragedy, Odysseus' speaking style is generally very controlled, well ordered, and to the point, but he uses and teaches tactics that are increasingly associated with mercenary attitudes and sophistic manipulation. In the three dramatic versions of the Philoctetes story, Odysseus aims at a covert manipulation of the viewpoint of others and a ruthless focus on group necessity.[75] The fragments and paraphrases of Aeschylus' and Euripides' treatments, as well as Sophocles' extant play, indicate that these dramatists traced the same basic sequence of events. Odysseus, with or without accomplices, goes to Lemnos to retrieve the bow of Philoctetes, which has become necessary to the Greek victory at Troy. Philoctetes' screaming anguish and foul smell from the bite of a serpent had caused Odysseus to instigate his exile from the Greek camp, so that Odysseus must now find a means of obtaining Philoctetes' compliance without revealing his agency in the plot. The three plays highlight in various ways how speech itself may serve as a disguise; Odysseus projects a character so different from the Odyssean type that its deployment effectively masks the speaker.

Central to understanding the impact of this verbal disguise are the connections outlined in chapter 1 between the *kosmos* of speech and that of appearance. Together these constitute one's bodily *hexis*, making visible the cast of one's character through type markers (e.g., one's verbal habits, allies, and actions) and physical details (e.g., stature, gesture, dress). Odysseus embodies the potential disruption of these connections and the ability of language to disguise identity through the (mis)representation of character. The effects of this stylistic disguise seem to be profound, to alter how one literally sees the speaker.

Bourdieu has emphasized that this kind of "seeing" itself involves misrecognition (*méconnaissance*), in that the details that announce the status of the speaker (including both linguistic style and dress) are inherently misleading and theatrical. Speakers rely on the complicity of the audience in this performance of familiar type. Since these stylistic details have already been invested with social meaning, the authority and trust they inspire have little to do with the particular individual who now makes use of them.[76] The audience thus participates in this misrecognition, drawing conclusions about identity from eyewitness details that merely signal metonymically familiar social categories. Consider again the scepter of the authoritative speaker in Homer, for example; this visual symbol in and of itself functions as a guarantee for the audience of the speaker's public status.

We might compare the misrecognition that occurs in Aeschylus' *Philoc-*

tetes, which caused Dio Chrysostom to offer Philoctetes' long, isolated suffering as an explanation for his failure to recognize Odysseus. The latter seems to be using only bodily *hexis* to hide his identity.[77] In this context the inhabiting of a typical style becomes a palpable disguise, an assumption of character that cloaks one's true identity. This is the kind of forceful impersonation that the sophists practiced when they argued before large audiences in the voices of Homeric characters. Contemporary Athenian audiences both admired such impersonations and treated them with some apprehension, because of the possibilities of deceit and misdirection they imply.

EURIPIDES' *PHILOCTETES*

Euripides' *Philoctetes,* produced in 431, is not extant. The outlines of its plot and character treatments can be gleaned from Dio's synopsis (*Or.* 52) and partial paraphrase (*Or.* 59), as well as from a handful of testimonies from later commentators (frs. 578–590 N²). Nevertheless, it is clear that in this version of the Philoctetes story Odysseus uses the character of Palamedes, whom he had falsely framed for treason, as a mirror of Philoctetes' animosity.[78] In a patent reversal of the allegiances cemented in the *Odyssey* by the praise of Odysseus, here the lying hero, in disguise as a friend of his enemy, capitalizes on the alliance that exists among those who hate Odysseus, so that he may trick another beleaguered man. When the liar reveals his sympathy with Palamedes and his suffering at the hands of "Odysseus," Philoctetes exclaims in ironic apostrophe, "Ah, Odysseus, most devilish of men" (πανουργότατε, *Or.* 59.9), implicitly opposing his wickedly clever machinations to the upstanding style of Palamedes. In Gorgias' *Palamedes,* Odysseus is also maligned implicitly as a *panourgos* type; in both the play and the set piece, the label clearly distinguishes his profligate versatility from the simpler and more visibly virtuous type that his opponent embodies.

Euripides' choice of having Odysseus impersonate a friend of Palamedes may well have signaled more to a contemporary audience than an alliance between two enemies of Odysseus. Palamedes is Odysseus' intimate antitype: both are cultivated men, clever heroes associated with the trappings of civilization, who differ primarily in the types of symbolic expression each represents. Palamedes is famous for his invention of the tools of calculation and record-keeping: weights and measures but also writing and written law. Odysseus operates within the realm of speech; an inventor of startling and manipulative oral techniques, Odysseus contributes to society in a less easily quantifiable and more morally questionable manner.

Nevertheless, both Odysseus and Palamedes seem to represent overly clever sophistic types in late fifth- and fourth-century writing. Odysseus turns up in this guise more frequently, but we should note also that Dionysus calls Euripides a "Palamedes" when he is frustrated by the poet's riddling chatter at the end of Aristophanes' *Frogs* (1451). I suggest in chapter 5 that these two clever heroes came to represent different oratorical styles during this period: Odysseus, the grand oral style of Gorgias; Palamedes, the careful, writerly style of Prodicus and his student Euripides. Aristophanes certainly seems to confirm this connection. Thus when Odysseus assumes the character of a friend of Palamedes in Euripides' play, he is capitalizing not only on Palamedes' alliance with Philoctetes but also on the typical associations of both Odysseus and Palamedes with clever sophistic types. As in the *Odyssey*, where Odysseus assumes disguises by depicting himself as a type similar to his own, here in Euripides he deploys another character adjacent to his type. This time, however, Odysseus' use of Palamedes also calls to mind the slanderous characterization that he foisted on Palamedes. Finally, this disguise may point to similar deceptions fabricated by practitioners of the forceful oral style.

Dio's paraphrase of Euripides' play outlines a depiction of Odysseus that emphasizes the complexity and thoroughness of this stylistic technique.[79] In the debate scene Odysseus apparently argues the Greek cause while still in disguise, so that his viewpoint is voiced by a character whose type is similar but whose outlook is fundamentally opposed to his own, like that of Neoptolemus in Sophocles' *Philoctetes*. Carl Müller has argued that Euripides' use of a traditional narrative (i.e., the Palamedes story) as the context for Odysseus' disguise, instead of the wholesale fabrication of Sophocles' "merchant," inhibits the audience's ability to distinguish the extent of the fiction presented. The play thus reproduces the effect of the liar on his interlocutor.[80] That is, in mirroring the allegiances of the hero by means of a well-known tale, Odysseus throws into question the point at which the fiction ends and the true story begins. This obfuscation is further aided by the similarity in type between Odysseus and Palamedes; the two characters in effect look the same to Philoctetes, although their allegiances are in reality completely at odds.

SOPHOCLES' *PHILOCTETES*

Most scholars have treated Sophocles' depiction of Odysseus in the *Philoctetes* as far harsher than those of other fifth-century writers. It is this play that most encourages the association of Odysseus with the sophists and apparently with their most negative traits. But Sophocles' Odysseus is also the promoter of "normal" and communally efficacious behavior, whose perspective is ultimately supported by the deified Heracles. Many discussions of the play have focused on the moral conflicts that arise between Odysseus' pragmatism on the one hand and the heroic agonies of Philoctetes on the other.[81] Neoptolemus is caught between the two, drawn to Philoctetes by his resemblance to his own proud and resistant father.

My analysis is more concerned with the stylistic techniques that Odysseus promotes and that he encourages others to use. While recent treatments of the *Philoctetes* have highlighted the metatheatrical aspects of the play,[82] none have employed this framework to explore how Odysseus' traditional stylistic technique of mirroring the character of his interlocutor is implemented by Neoptolemus and the sailor disguised as a merchant.[83] Having Neoptolemus and the merchant speak like Odysseus and thus serve as his masks is a Sophoclean innovation that gives the internal plot its sophistic coloring. The drama provides a negative assessment of the character masquerades for which Odysseus was famous. These techniques were also central to the versatile oral styles of sophists such as Gorgias and Hippias.

The Palamedes plays must have provided the other setting for a thorough condemnation of Odysseus' lying style, as Euripides' use of his figure to persuade Philoctetes suggests.[84] In Sophocles' play, however, the figure of Palamedes turns up only as an oblique example of the liar's character fabrications: when Philoctetes throws in Odysseus' face his stratagem of feigned madness and its detection by Palamedes (*Phil.* 1025). Sophocles' tragedy uses the moral compunction of the young Neoptolemus to emphasize the ambiguities of the trickster's *habitus.* Odysseus' central role in the play is that of the plot-deviser who controls the way his victim views the other characters and understands the visible signs of their basic sympathy (e.g., their Greek dress, 223–224). Odysseus' covert and manipulative use of language, especially his speaking through other characters, sharply conflicts with the piercing directness of Philoctetes' mournful style. This contrast has encouraged many readers of the play to reiterate Sophocles' putative condemnation of the deceptive hero. But, again, Odysseus is acting in the interest of the Greek army, and while his frank disregard for Philoctetes' feelings has won him few champions, the character impersonations that he promotes ally him not only with the sophist but also with the dramatist, as some scholars have recently recognized.[85]

Odysseus outlines a plot to Neoptolemus that implements verbal disguise as a means of persuasion. Thus while he speaks only intermittently in the play, he trains others to deploy the misrepresentational techniques that constitute his typical style, as a means of hiding his presence on Lemnos from his victim. I therefore assess this style by considering both the lines spoken by Odysseus' character and those spoken by Neoptolemus and the merchant that make use of his techniques, constructed as they are to forge this same verbal deception. This approach makes it possible to analyze the moments in the play when these impersonations are underway. These scenes capture the machinations of Odysseus' style as fully as do his instructions to Neoptolemus or his violent interruptions in the play's final scenes.[86] The lying hero thus serves as a stage manager who masks his presence by using Neoptolemus and the merchant to trick Philoctetes into relinquishing his bow. Neoptolemus, noble son of Achilles that he strives to show himself to be, ultimately breaks faith with this mercenary attitude, drops his deceptive *hexis,* and sides with Philoctetes. The important moments for this discussion thus occur for the most part early in the play, when Odysseus is training Neoptolemus in his deceptive style and when Neoptolemus and the merchant are engaged in thereby tricking the hero.

Odysseus opens the *Philoctetes* standing on the untrodden shores of Lemnos and explaining why the Greek leaders, at his urging, had transported Philoctetes there. He claims that the wounded man's foul-smelling foot and his wild, ill-omened talk (ἀγρίαις / . . . δυσφημίαις, 9–10) necessitated his removal, since his crying and moaning (βοῶν, στενάζων, 11) made any attempts at ritual practice impossible. Odysseus' description of Philoctetes' cries is enjambed with an abrupt remark on his own speaking style. It is not the right moment for a long narrative, he says (ἀκμὴ γὰρ οὐ μακρῶν λόγων, 12).[87] His aim is that of secrecy, and if Philoctetes gets wind of his presence, he might learn of the strategy (σόφισμα, 14) by which Odysseus means to take the disruptive but now necessary hero back to Troy. Odysseus' presentation of Philoctetes' visible type and subsequent quarantine comprises both a linguistic contrast, characterized by Odysseus as Philoctetes' wild versus his own controlled speech, and the contrasting roles that their corporeal styles imply: the disruptive outcast versus the protector of the community.

Early in the play a reluctant Neoptolemus is trained by Odysseus in the art that the clever hero had perfected in Homer, that of mirroring his interlocutor's type. Odysseus tells the young man that he must "deceive the soul of Philoctetes with speeches" (τὴν Φιλοτήτου σε δεῖ / ψυχὴν ὅπως λόγοισιν ἐκκλέψεις λέγων, 54–55) and encourages him to use his instructor as a figure of abuse.[88] Odysseus suggests that Neoptolemus use the story of the dispute over Achilles' arms (i.e., the Ajax story), casting himself in the role of the angry loser. He tells him to maintain his own identity and to declare, "I am the child of Achilles" ([ἐγώ εἰμ'] Ἀχιλλέως παῖς, 57).[89] He thus actually demonstrates for Neoptolemus how to perform himself in this new guise. Odysseus emphasizes that there will be no deception (τόδ' οὐχὶ κλεπτέον, 57) in regard to the young man's identity; rather, the trick will lie in the representation of his type and allegiances. He then instructs the young man to impugn "Odysseus," speaking of himself in the third person and assuring Neoptolemus that even should he accuse his teacher of the "worst of the worst things" (ἔσχατ' ἐσχάτων κακά, 65), such slander will not harm him (οὐδὲν ἀλγύνει μ', 66).

Like the character Odysseus impersonates in Euripides' *Philoctetes*, Neoptolemus' fictional self-representation depends on the excoriation of the man whose stylistic techniques he employs. Neoptolemus will not himself assume a physical disguise, but in an act of double deception he takes on what is essentially the persona of Ajax (i.e., that of one deprived of Achilles' arms by Odysseus). Like Philoctetes, Ajax suffered at Odysseus' hand; like Neoptolemus, he might be expected to feel that he had a particular right to Achilles' arms. Ajax thus serves implicitly as a fitting (if deeply ironic) mask for Odysseus' plot. Neoptolemus seems genuinely sympathetic to Philoctetes and wary of Odysseus; even his resentment over the arms may not be entirely manufactured for the moment. Neoptolemus' initial function in the play may be to serve as the mouthpiece of Odysseus, but his true type resembles more closely that of Philoctetes. His role is therefore equivalent in tactical terms to that of a disguised Odysseus, while his similarity to Ajax and his own compunction highlight the maneuver as an ethically questionable masquerade.

Odysseus' instruction in how to employ this stylistic theft indicates that he has few qualms about its implementation. His kind of deceit primarily involves a misleading self-performance, which includes impugning or praising the characters of others to forge an allegiance with one's interlocutor. Odysseus describes this activity as "playing the sophist" (σοφισθῆναι, 77) and acknowledges that this speaking style and role are not natural to Neoptolemus (ἔξοιδα, παῖ, φύσει σε μὴ πεφυκότα / τοιαῦτα φωνεῖν μηδὲ τεχνᾶσθαι κακά, 79–80). To "devise evil plots" is the forte of the wicked, unscrupulous (*panourgos*) man (cf. below and in chapter 5). While *technai* in general may be neutral devices for composing a speech or devising a plot, in the *Philoctetes* they signal the morally dubious machinations of the sophist and the liar. Neoptolemus opposes this plan by urging the use of force (βία), confirming that it is not natural to him (ἔφυν) to contrive anything by means of an "evil scheme" (τέχνης . . . κακῆς, 88).[90] The contrast between violence and persuasion turns up in Gorgias' *Encomium of Helen* (6), where the two are considered similar in power and effect. In Sophocles' *Philoctetes,* it eventually becomes clear that Odysseus embodies the violent sophistic type, as do notorious speakers such as Cleon in Thucydides and Callicles in Plato's *Gorgias.* At this juncture in Sophocles' play, however, Odysseus treats violence as clearly distinct from persuasive or deceitful tactics. Indeed, he considers this preference for arms a response that suits Neoptolemus' tender age, noting that the passing years bring with them a recognition of the power of speech over deeds (τὴν γλῶσσαν οὐχὶ τἄργα, 99).[91]

Although Odysseus does acknowledge to Neoptolemus that his own deceptive style does not suit the young man's nature, for him one's "nature" is a constructed thing, relative to one's time of life, experience, and so on. The two men thus have different understandings of what is natural to an individual. Neoptolemus thinks that an unalterable genealogy constitutes his nature, while Odysseus' response implies that for him, nature is really something external and community-developed, something akin to the visible habits that make up Bourdieu's notion of bodily *hexis*.[92] Odysseus' response suggests a deeper difference of perspective between the two, what in fifth-century terms was that between the traditional aristocratic mentality and the outlook of the sophist or democrat.[93] For the one, birth determines type as if by an organic process, while for the other, type may be acquired by training and therefore possibly molded to suit the given situation.

Neoptolemus' second response (102) further indicates Odysseus' understanding of how useful a malleable character can be. When the young man suggests that he use persuasion rather than deceit (in his mind two distinct modes), Odysseus responds that any straightforward attempt at persuasion will fail. Philoctetes, he says, can be taken only by the kind of character impersonation he has described, that is, by a deceitful corporeal style.[94] Odysseus maintains that speaking falsely is not shameful (αἰσχϱόν), as Neoptolemus suggests, if it is aimed at saving a situation (108). This is a pragmatic response to moral apprehension that has been regarded as evidence of Odysseus' brutal temperament.[95] As Neoptolemus begins to capitulate, he indicates his growing understanding of what goes into this disguise, asking what expression he should use when arguing in this bold way (πῶς οὖν βλέπων τις ταῦτα τολμήσει λακεῖν, 110).[96] The question suggests both his lingering distaste for the trick and his awareness that elements such as expression and tone of voice must also reinforce his masquerade.

Although Neoptolemus enters into the deception reluctantly, when the time comes for him to perform, he does well. He adeptly mirrors Philoctetes' character type by echoing his allegiances and the emotional coloring of his tale. Philoctetes has just told his story to Neoptolemus in a passionate and exclamatory style. Neoptolemus' responses suggest that he genuinely sympathizes with the deserted hero; but he also carefully molds his *hexis* to communicate this sympathy. He associates himself and his tale with Philoctetes and his, showing how they have both suffered at the hands of Odysseus and underscoring the similarities of their reactions. Neoptolemus affirms that he is a witness (μάϱτυς, 319) to what Philoctetes says because of his own experience of Odysseus' violence (Ὀδυσσέως βίας, 321; cf. 314).[97] He also picks up on Philoctetes' references to Achilles (260; cf. 344, 347), and emphasizes that the death of his father was the beginning of his own painful experiences.[98] In recounting his sufferings to Neoptolemus, Philoctetes had repeatedly mentioned his illness (νόσος, 258, 266, 281). The young man now allies himself with Philoctetes' pain by using cognate words for pain to describe both the agonies of the wounded man (ἀλγήμαθ', 340) and the grief he himself felt when he learned that Odysseus had received his father's arms (καταλγήσας, 368).[99]

Neoptolemus further echoes Philoctetes' mournful self-reference, declaring the place of his father's tomb "bitter" (πίϰϱον, 355; cf. 254) and thereby suiting the scene to Philoctetes' emotional state, whose proud and isolated disposition resembles his father's.[100] He also declares himself "wretched" (δύσμοϱος, 359), as had Philoctetes (273), and represents his disposition as impulsively emotional: "I burst into tears immediately" (δακϱύσας εὐθύς, 367), he says, and "I was furious immediately" (χολωθεὶς εὐθύς, 374). Philoctetes had already showed himself to be similarly reactive when he used a rhythmic set of anaphoric exclamations to communicate the bitterness of his desertion (ποιᾶν μ' ἀνάστασιν δοκεῖς / ... στῆναι τότε; / ποῖ' ἐκδακρῦσαι, ποῖ' ἀποιμῶξαι κακά, 276–278). Finally, Neoptolemus strikes a note similar to Philoctetes' closing wish for divine vengeance against Odysseus and the Atreidae (οἷς Ὀλύμπιοι θεοὶ / δοῖέν ποτ' αὐτοῖς ἀντίποιν' ἐμοῦ παθεῖν, 315–316). He balances the wounded man's desire for the gods to effect some fair exchange for his pain by declaring that he shares their loyalties (ὁ δ' Ἀτρείδας στυγῶν / ἐμοί θ' ὁμοίως καὶ θεοῖς εἴη φίλος, 389–390). The complexity of Neoptolemus' presentation lies in the layered quality of its rhetorical structure, which highlights an emotional and reactive self-representation that both reflects certain aspects of his own character and resembles closely that of his interlocutor. Compare again the persuasive tactics of the Homeric Odysseus, whose famous lies in the *Odyssey* are carefully molded to combine a character type similar to his own with that of each person he attempts to deceive.

Neoptolemus' speech is thus *poikilos,* as subtly and variously woven as his teacher's lying narratives. It also involves a more elaborately worked impersonation than the *poikilos* style that the "merchant" uses to advance Odysseus' plot.[101] A central aspect of this intricacy lies, again, in how the speakers use the character of Odysseus as a figure of abuse. In the *Odyssey,* when Odysseus refers to "Odysseus" in the lying tales he is always a figure of praise. The liar gains status in association with him, so much so, in fact, that his interlocutors are sometimes suspicious of the hero's fortuitous presence in the liar's narrative.[102] The Philoctetes plays, in sharp contrast, use Odysseus as a figure of abuse: only in allegiance *against* his type can the impersonator gain persuasive status. Neoptolemus underscores Odysseus' baseness at the end of his speech by echoing word for word the abuse of his character that his teacher had encouraged him to use (τοῦ κακίστου κἀκ κακῶν Ὀδυσσέως, Soph. *Phil.* 384; cf. 65). Finally, he indicates his discomfort with his own sharp words by suggesting that "disorderly" leaders are those who have been trained to be base from the speeches of the "teachers" (οἱ δ' ἀκοσμοῦντες βροτῶν / διδασκάλων λόγοισι γίγνονται κακοί, 387–388). His words recall the kinds of bad teaching attributed to those inveterate speechmakers, the sophists. While Neoptolemus thereby guiltily excuses Odysseus to himself, Philoctetes would understand his remark only as further slander of Odysseus' *panourgos* type. Neoptolemus' abusive treatment of Odysseus thus clearly cements his allegiance with the lonely hero, who despises Odysseus' tricky tongue and profligate tendencies (cf. again 407–408; also 440, 448).

In addition to focusing attention on this use of narrative as masquerade, the scene also underscores the influence the visible features of one's *hexis* have on the audience. Neoptolemus' verbal techniques have the same effect as his appearance: his clever layering of true type and fabricated character associations suggests that he really is as he looks—that most welcome ally, a Greek hero who hates Odysseus. From the moment Philoctetes enters and sees the Greeks, their appearance gladdens the lonely hero. Their familiar dress is "most dear" (προσφιλεστάτης, 224) to him, as is the sound of Neoptolemus' voice because he speaks Greek (ὦ φίλτατον φώνημα, 234). Neoptolemus strives to make his character similarly welcome to the isolated Philoctetes by using a style that he finds familiar, including (presumably) the facial expression about which he questioned Odysseus earlier. The type markers Neoptolemus highlights (e.g., the direct emotionalism of the wronged hero, Ajax's narrative, antipathy toward Odysseus) reflect Philoctetes' known character type and the story he tells about himself. Thus Neoptolemus effectively "looks like" Philoctetes and thereby gains his confidence, in a move that corresponds with the happy familiarity of his dress and language.

His self-representation also gives the appearance of eagerness to act in opposition to Odysseus. Philoctetes responds with equal eagerness, saying that he knows that Odysseus has a ready tongue for all kinds of devilish speeches and schemes and that nothing just (δικαίον) can come of his wiles (407–409). His reference to justice contrasts sharply with Odysseus' prediction to Neoptolemus that both will seem just (δίκαιοι) if they put his plot into action (82). Philoctetes instead rejects the notion that the end can justify the means of any action. Moreover, his characterization of Odysseus matches so closely his succinct condemnation of the ill-spoken Thersites (γλώσσῃ δὲ δεινοῦ καὶ σοφοῦ, 440), that Neoptolemus confuses the two.[103] Philoctetes' open condemnation reflects the success of Neoptolemus' disguise. The young man has also warmed to the task; Philoctetes' characterization is merely a more vitriolic response to Neoptolemus' description of his teacher as "that clever wrestler" (σοφὸς παλιστὴς κεῖνος, 431).

After Neoptolemus has established his allegiance with Philoctetes, a sailor disguised as a merchant enters. He carries one step further Neoptolemus' deception of the wounded man and adds a more concrete dimension to Neoptolemus' impersonation. The merchant and Neoptolemus enter into a conversation that encodes issues regarding Philoctetes already discussed by Odysseus and Neoptolemus. The training that Odysseus gave the young man about force, persuasion, and deceit is here reiterated in a manner that cements Neoptolemus' allegiance with the wounded hero. For instance, Neoptolemus asks, in response to the merchant's information that Odysseus has come to take Neoptolemus back to Troy, whether Odysseus' men intend to lead him back by force or persuasion (ὡς ἐκ βίας μ' ἄξοντες ἢ λόγοις πάλιν, 563). The merchant uses the by now familiar phrase to refer to Odysseus' violent type (Ὀδυσσέως βία, 592) and also reiterates Neoptolemus' opposition between force and persuasion when announcing Odysseus' intentions toward Philoctetes (ἢ λόγῳ πείσαντες ἄξειν ἢ πρὸς ἰσχύος κράτος, 593–594; cf. 618–619).

Odysseus earlier warned Neoptolemus that this envoy would speak in an elaborate manner (ποικίλως, 130), that is, like Odysseus himself as well as his trainee. By this point Neoptolemus has already associated Odysseus with *poikilos* settings by beginning his painful tale with a reference to the elaborate outriggings of the ship that brought Odysseus to inform him of his father's death (ἦλθον νηὶ ποικιλοστόλῳ μέτα / δῖός τ' Ὀδυσσεύς, 343–344). Now he helps to facilitate a scene in which the merchant seaman, speaking in *poikilos* fashion, outlines the imminent threat that "Odysseus" poses to his two recently self-proclaimed enemies. Like Neoptolemus, the merchant couches his story in a reactive, abusive style, calling Odysseus "guileful" (δόλιος) and "one who hears [himself called] all sorts of shameful and abusive names" (ὁ πάντ' ἀκούων αἰσχρὰ καὶ λωβήτ' ἔπη, 607–608). Like Neoptolemus, he puts words in the mouth of Odysseus that make the clever hero appear brutal and violent (614–619). The merchant even claims that Odysseus declared he would stake his own head for Philoctetes' return, which recalls the bold threat with which he had menaced Thersites in the *Iliad* (*Phil.* 618–619; cf. *Il.* 2.259). The merchant's *poikilos* references thus match Philoctetes with another of Odysseus' ill-favored enemies. Ignorant of these curious embroideries, Philoctetes again responds with frank disgust, echoing the merchant's abuse by terming Odysseus "a thorough harm" (ἡ πᾶσα βλάβη, 622).[104]

This liar is apparently one of Odysseus' sailors in camouflage, but the same actor would have played both the disguised man and Odysseus. The traveling salesman type is one that the Homeric Odysseus himself uses in some of his lies (*Od.* 14.192–359 and 17.415–444), and with whom he is rudely associated by Euryalus (*Od.* 8.158–164). The type is not a heroic one, but the traveler's exploits are sufficiently similar to Odysseus' actual adventures to make for a useful disguise, although his proximity to the type may itself signal the problematic qualities of the *polutropos* man.[105] While in Homer the guise of the merchant seaman affords Odysseus a relative anonymity invaluable to his aims, in the fifth century, writers with aristocratic allegiances associate this kind of mercenary social status and calculating mobility with sophists and speechwriters (who are paid for their services). The usefulness of these traits to the shifty hero thus serves as a further denigration of his type.

In the *Philoctetes*, the liar's facile deployment of another's character to convince his interlocutor that he is really like him in type, while dutifully undertaken by Neoptolemus, is a skill most suited to the practical man of business, the merchant seaman who shares traits with Odysseus. Like that assumed by Odysseus in the *Odyssey*, the merchant's persona is itself a disguise, so that when he weaves into his speech a character allegiance that mirrors that of his interlocutors, his persuasive technique reduplicates his masked identity. It matters less whether the merchant actually is Odysseus, although this would add a fitting layer of intricacy to the scene. More crucial is his use of Odysseus' speaking style while in physical disguise. The special technique of this masquerading style is clearly linked in its character mimicry to the wholesale appropriation and projection of type that Odysseus perfects in set speeches of the same period. The difference is that in tragic representation, this technique takes on a negative moral cast.

Like Helen in the *Trojan Women*, in the *Philoctetes* Odysseus enjoys a victory that while not directly acknowledged, clearly supports his aim. Although his plot fails, the statesman's goals are reinforced by the decree of Heracles, who orders that Philoctetes and the bow return to Troy. Meanwhile the final exchanges between Odysseus and Philoctetes underscore the clever hero's negative associations with sophistic techniques, which the opening scene had left more implicit. Philoctetes reacts to Odysseus' return at the end of the play by echoing the same abusive label that Odysseus had suggested might be useful in deceiving the wounded man: he calls him "of evil men most evil and over-bold" (ὦ κακῶν κάκιστε καὶ τόλμης πέρα, 984; cf. 65, 88, 110, 384). Odysseus then invokes the persuasive act in a manner that makes it seem like force. He uses a deictic and a verbal adjective to denote emphatic necessity (πειστέον τάδε, 994), and he has Philoctetes physically bound when he threatens suicide.[106] Philoctetes' monologue as prisoner reveals that he blames the entire situation on Odysseus' way of thinking (i.e., his *habitus*, in Bourdieu's terms). This, he says, lacks both health and freedom (ὦ μηδὲν ὑγιὲς μηδ' ἐλεύθερον φρονῶν, 1006), describing in an ironic reversal the mental equivalent of his own physical situation.[107] Odysseus' deceptive techniques, Philoctetes maintains, have shaped the education of Neoptolemus in a manner that encourages cleverness specifically in relation to immoral practices (εὖ προυδίδαξεν ἐν κακοῖς εἶναι σοφόν, 1015).

These are precisely the kind of machinations to which the young man claimed he was a stranger at the outset of the play (cf. 88) and that tend to be attributed to the sophists. Later Philoctetes reinforces this image by calling Odysseus by his Homeric epithet (πολυμηχάνου, 1135) and by emphasizing his role as manufacturer of shameful deceits (αἰσχρὰς ἀπάτας, 1136). His descriptions clearly condemn the stylistic techniques that Odysseus had represented to Neoptolemus as necessary and thus morally neutral. Since the wounded man, now helpless and bound like an entrapped animal, is clearly the sympathetic figure, the audience would witness the visible results of this brutality and understand them as the physical manifestations of the sophist's tactics.

In tragedy the styles that the dramatists depict Helen and Odysseus as embodying reflect concerns about the moral effects of sophistic techniques. Their very different roles in these plays notwithstanding, each figure signifies an aspect of style that threatens good judgment. Helen emblematizes the visual appeal of the flamboyant style, which may distract the audience from moral issues. Odysseus promotes the pleasing familiarity of character impersonation, which involves the misrepresentation of one's true alliances. Both Odysseus and Helen thus incur charges of wrongdoing in tragedy: Helen for speaking in a dangerously attractive style, Odysseus for adopting an ignobly versatile one. The *Trojan Women* and the *Philoctetes* depict the nasty culmination of the negative associations that these figures accumulated in the development of Greek ideas about style.

CHAPTER 5

MANIPULATING
THE SENSES
IN RHETORICAL
SET PIECES

The classical treatments of Helen and Odysseus refract the Athenian political culture of the late fifth century, when a remarkable burst of artistic productivity coincided with a period of political upheaval and external threat from the rival city-state Sparta and its allies. From early in the Peloponnesian war, Athenians had lived more or less continuously in a state of siege, often crowded within the city walls and beset by disease and wartime scarcities. Composing in this climate of ongoing disturbance and faced with potentially devastating challenges to closely held beliefs, Athenian dramatists and prose authors of the period repeatedly indicated their anxiety about democracy's reliance on public display and deliberation. They particularly emphasized citizens' vulnerability to embellishment, deception, and other types of persuasive manipulation effective in the public performances of politicians and professional rhetors. Many of these intellectuals seem to be reacting against one source of influence in particular: the sophistic teachers and speechwriters, whose recent arrival in Athens encouraged among the elite a new level of oratorical versatility. Even as they reveal themselves to be familiar with sophistic ideas, these authors often depict the sophists negatively and argue that the Athenians are especially susceptible to the persuasive techniques they spawned.

In this climate the figures of Helen and Odysseus become repositories for some of the fear and resentment that accompanied the Athenians' exposure to sophistic ideas, particularly the visual impact of embellished performance styles and the appropriative use of character type. Already in the later archaic and early classical periods, portrayals of these figures had often pointed in moralizing fashion to their evasive or dissembling qualities, to Helen's double story and specious allure or Odysseus' deployment of false stories to gain his ends.[1] Reactions to the sophists in the late fifth century share some similarities with earlier writers' connections between the visible adornment of the female body and a visualizing, deceitful style.

The two largest pieces of extant prose from the sophist Gorgias, the *Encomium of Helen* and *Palamedes' Defense*, contain the most interesting positive treatments of these stylistic issues. Both pieces are so-called set speeches, that is, speeches that were written for instruction in how to compose a persuasive speech. They are thus rare examples of a mostly lost tradition of using mythohistorical figures to hone rhetorical technique, and because of this special focus, they make interesting and distinctive use of familiar material. Helen and Odysseus seem to have been common choices for use in this way. There is evidence that other sophists such as Hippias and Antisthenes used these figures in similarly instructive pieces.[2] Helen was presumably a popular subject because she is so difficult to defend (let alone to praise), and Odysseus because he is himself such a famously dissembling and yet persuasive speaker. Since they are directly concerned with demonstrating persuasive technique, these set speeches bring us closer to explicit analyses of stylistic issues. Still lacking is the kind of technical terminology that we find in Aristotle, however. Such language may have been somewhat more in evidence in the *technai* (instruction manuals) from this period, but these are mostly lost.[3]

Gorgias' set pieces suggest instead the sophistic performer's connections to the Homeric rhapsode, even as they also demonstrate an easy familiarity with forensic proofs. While their oral, performative tone affirms and reinvigorates the broad associative categories of stylistic type that are familiar from the earlier literature, their argumentative structures indicate the ways these categories might have been implemented in the Athenian courts and Assembly. Together they encapsulate both Homeric attitude and fifth-century technique. The *Encomium* is particularly reminiscent of a rhapsodic recitation, in which the figure of Helen emerges as the emblem for the oral performer's elaborate style. *Palamedes' Defense* reads more like a typical court appearance and uses the upright figure of Palamedes to throw into sharp relief the deceptive techniques of Odysseus.

These speeches thus point the way toward the development of differentiations among rhetorical styles based on Homeric characters, traces of which can be found in later texts. The figures of Helen and Odysseus are pivotal in developing distinctions among styles in this transitional period. All the writers who use these figures for instruction in character portrayal (*êthopoiia*) and effective argumentation treat them more positively or at least more neutrally than do the dramatists. These rhetorical theorists represent Helen's beauty as emblematic of the visual impact of a flamboyant oral style and ultimately of civic *epideixis*. They treat the figure of Odysseus as signifying the facile alterations of character that constitute another essential aspect of a grand style. Odysseus emblematizes the most extreme tactics in the use of character to persuade, in that his manipulative self-presentations effectively control what the hearer sees.

THE VERSATILE AND EFFEMINATE SOPHISTIC TYPE

Depictions of sophists and Homeric rhapsodes suggest that they shared techniques of oral performance, from their elaborate dress and gestures to their emotive, rhythmical delivery styles, which matched the embellished language of their compositions.[4] Gorgias' style in particular shows strong affinities with the oral poetic tradition. The influence of rhapsodic performance and, by implication, rhapsodic attitudes may well have informed the sophists' relatively positive depictions of Helen and Odysseus, insofar as Homeric tradition tends to celebrate these figures and to suppress the moral ambivalence that they embody. The sophists' appropriation of the rhapsode's role and their reinvention of Homeric characters for use in oratorical debate gained them little respect, however. Their self-adornment and their emotive corporeal styles lent their performances a dramatic cast, while this fusion of dramatic display and oratorical proof aroused the suspicion among their contemporaries that neither the drama nor the proof was to be trusted. Moreover, like rhapsodes, sophistic performers assumed different characters, and might even shift from one impersonation to another in the relaying of a narrative. This visualizing, labile imposture further contributed to the apprehension with which they were received by many members of the educated elite.[5]

The charged political and intellectual climate of the middle to late fifth century thus increased apprehension about the power of grand and emotive styles. Writers show concern that the rhythmic cadences and elaborate imagery of such styles could distract an audience from the accuracy of the speaker's representations, either of his own character or of the situation being addressed. Sometimes such a speaker is described as a type like Thersites in Homer. For instance, in Euripides' *Orestes*, the nameless man who argues for Orestes' death is a bold type (ἰσχύων θράσει) of ambiguous status (Ἀργεῖος οὐκ Ἀργεῖος) with a "doorless" tongue (ἀθυρόγλωσσος, 903–904). This is the type whose sweet style and evil intentions (ἡδὺς τις λόγοις φρονῶν κακῶς) may persuade the masses but promise great ill (κακὸν μέγα) for the polis (907–909).

More often, however, the embodiment of the otiose, distracting style is someone like Alcibiades. Thucydides depicts him as a beautiful aristocrat whose penchant for dressing elaborately matched his love of polishing his public image.[6] His flamboyant, seductive bodily *hexis* effectively announces his decadent attitudes. This dashing oral performer so distracted the Athenian Assembly from a calm assessment of the wisdom of invading Sicily that they followed his urgings blindly and suffered the worst losses of the Peloponnesian war. The illustrious and somewhat dissolute figure that Alcibiades cuts in the writings of Thucydides, Plato, and Xenophon makes him a fitting focus for the kinds of concern aroused by the grand style in oratory.[7] He often seems in these scenes to be the politician's equivalent of Helen, in that both are strongly associated with the visual impact and high-blown style appropriate to the grand oral performance. Both also frequently elicit negative reactions, especially regarding their penchants for elaborate dress. It thus comes as little surprise that Plutarch would later emphasize their similarities in his portrait of Alcibiades.[8]

Like Alcibiades and Helen, the sophists also elicit blame, and for similar reasons. Their contemporaries represent them as a disparate group of foreigners who taught young elite Athenians clever argumentative tactics and dazzling stylistic effects. The dramatists represent the sophists as morally dubious, concerned with pleasing style over integrity or accuracy, and as tending to dissemble or mislead, as being like women, in fact. This effeminization of sophistic rhetoric is most developed in Plato. In the *Gorgias*, Socrates characterizes rhetoric as analogous to cookery and bodily adornment, activities often associated with women. Cosmetics (ἡ κομμωτική) in particular reveal the problem with such activities: they are "evil-doing, deceitful, base, and slavish" (κακοῦργός τε καὶ ἀπαταλὴ καὶ ἀγγενὴς καὶ ἀνελεύθερος, 465b3–4), achieving their effects through a kind of coloration and costuming that only imitates the effects of gymnastics, the activity that achieves true physical beauty. The relegation of rhetoric to the realm of feminine simulation echoes dominant attitudes toward persuasive speech during the late fifth century, as Zeitlin has noted.[9]

Plato represents Gorgias as a not very clever pretender to knowledge and as incapable of explaining what it is that he teaches. This turns out to be the kind of flashy technique that merely makes one *look like* an expert on any topic, rather than actually being one. We might recall that Homer associates the talent for achieving likeness and suitability with Helen and especially Odysseus, and that from early on, this talent was perceived as the central concern of persuasive style. For Plato, however, the teacher of rhetoric is a kind of make-up artist, who indulges in these coy tricks as a means of pleasing and impressing his audience. The connections drawn in this period between women and sophists thus develop in a new, historically specific direction the associations that the archaic poets make between the female body and persuasive style.

The sophists are generally represented as philosophical empiricists, who reacted to the mystical naturalism of Heraclitus and Parmenides. Many of these thinkers adopted a pragmatic, proto-anthropological attitude and espoused a relativism about human customs, laws, and even morals. This eclectic group of teachers and theorists—some of the most prominent of whom were Protagoras, Gorgias, Prodicus, and Hippias—in a loose sense shared attitudes that were, according to earlier scholars, indicative of an "adolescent" stage of philosophical development. W. K. C. Guthrie, for instance, describes the sophists as "ambitious, contentious, breaking out in all directions."[10] This characterization of the sophistic outlook as youthful, a philosophical movement that resembles a rite of passage, implicitly validates the "mature" perspectives of Plato and Aristotle. Gorgias in particular has been treated by scholars as an intellectual lightweight, whose only contributions to rhetorical technique and theory were a handful of overly elaborate stylistic devices.[11] Plato's own mocking portrait of Gorgias and other sophists clearly contributed to this denigration of their roles in the development of Greek thought. Such patronizing depictions have meant that until recently, the sophists were only rarely considered to be proponents of serious and developed theoretical perspectives.[12]

The resistance to treating these figures as serious thinkers may also have arisen from the extent to which they allied their own techniques with those of the poets rather than philosophers, whose intellectual strategies had yet to be fully delineated.[13] Many sophists seem to have positioned themselves in relation to the existing wisdom tradition. Like most classical writers and oral performers, they sought to gain status for their speeches by invoking such hallowed sources as Homer. Sophistic ideas about the suitable representation of character also borrow essential techniques from the poets; this aspect of style is crucial to an effective oral performance, as Aristotle would later note (*Rhet.* 1404b20, 1408a10).[14] Character portrayal was a skill sometimes associated with those writers who exemplify the "middle" (μέσος) or "thin" (ἰσχνός / *tenuis*) style in oratory and, it seems, in poetry as well.[15] The polished precision and mimetic agility that were attributed to speechwriters such as Lysias and perhaps Thrasymachus[16] are also evident in Aristophanes' depiction of Euripides' style in the *Frogs*. O'Sullivan notes that Aristophanes attaches weakness and effeminacy to this kind of polished verbiage, which is reminiscent of the effeminization of the sophists.[17]

But such distinctions are complicated by contradictions among the various characterizations of these writers. For instance, Dionysius says that Thrasymachus is "pure and refined" (καθαρὸς καὶ λεπτός) in his manner of speaking, but also forceful (δεινός) and elegant of expression (στρογγύλως εἰπεῖν, *Is.* 20). This characterization sets him apart from both the restrained style of Lysias or the careful Prodicus and the flamboyant extemporaneous style of Gorgias. Plato lampoons Thrasymachus as the master of a powerful, emotionally stirring style. In the *Phaedrus* Socrates describes his talents for drama and further associates him with Gorgias by representing him as a forceful speaker who spellbinds his audience (267c9–d1).[18] Plato also associates Odysseus with Thrasymachus (*Phdr.* 261c). The *Phaedrus* passage suggests that this characterization of Odysseus' style as grand (μεγαλοπρεπής) was common among fourth-century theorists. Thus it seems that the forceful oral style was emblematized not only by the luxurious visuality associated with Helen's form but also by the rhetorical sleight of hand that is Odysseus' signature tactic.[19] In the earlier period, clearly, when sophists like Gorgias were first impersonating Homeric characters and performing their set speeches on stage, a talent for adept and fluid emotional imposture, as well as a penchant for dazzling figures of speech, could easily have been the prized skills of the same speaker.[20]

HELEN'S BEAUTY AND THE VISUALITY OF PRAISE

Sappho's fragment 16 associates the figure of Helen with a kind of encomiastic speech that emphasizes the persuasive impression of beauty on the eye. The ode has been the focus of much criticism and discussion. While in recent years most scholars have resisted direct moral condemnation of it, many communicate their apprehension by criticizing Sappho's logic. Her use of the beautiful Helen as a convincing proof that what one loves is the most beautiful thing has often been regarded as a clumsy handling of the subject matter.[21] Sappho begins her "proof" with a reference to the pursuer's own outstanding beauty and emphasizes the subjectivity of the particular viewer. This emphasis has been regarded as similar to that of sophistic epistemology.[22] But Sappho's formulation is, as scholars have noted, a standard device in an appeal to authority, in which the one supporting a claim is also praised to lend her—and thereby the speaker's—opinion more weight.[23] The fragment also anticipates the association of the beautiful female form with the physical compulsion achieved by visual effects that Gorgias explores in relation to speech (*logos*).[24]

A few scholars have related the ode specifically to Gorgias' *Encomium of Helen* because of its focus on the persuasive power of sight (*opsis*), and its use of a *recusatio* ("some say *x* . . . but I say *y*") to introduce its focus on desire.[25] These observations help to trace a connection between archaic and classical ideas about persuasion and proof. However, fragment 16 also picks up on an idea about Helen found in nascent form in the *Iliad*: that the movement of her body in the visual field emblematizes the corporeal features of a dazzling style. Moreover, in the *Iliad* as in Sappho's ode, the paradigmatic beauty is propelled into action by looking at beauty. This circularity of effect also underpins Gorgias'—and later Isocrates'—ideas about encomiastic style.

Sappho's choice of Helen to support her claim that the love object is the "most beautiful thing" thus arises from the affirming weight that Helen's beauty possesses to add to the reputation (*kleos*) of other humans.[26] Sappho also suggests that Helen was "led astray" (παράγαγ', 11), probably by Aphrodite, although this section of the poem is fragmentary.[27] Like Cleon's susceptible Athenians, whom the able orator finds it easy to "mislead" (παράγειν) with his pleasing style, Helen may well have been depicted in these lines as similarly tempted by Aphrodite's deployment of the pleasing Paris. Sappho's portrayal would then have echoed the scene in *Iliad* 3 in this way as well and anticipated Helen's speech in Euripides' *Trojan Women*. The link between the visual beauty of the love object and the onrush of sensual response motivates both the poem and its lover-poet. When she describes Anactoria's alluring step and flashing glance, Sappho reinforces the sense that this visual chain reaction is inevitable, an unavoidable physical logic.

The association of the female body with the impact of pleasing visual detail is certainly common in the archaic period. But Sappho further suggests that although physical beauty may lead one astray, this distraction is unavoidable and perhaps divine; we might compare again Euripides' depiction of Helen in the *Trojan Women*. This defense of beauty's impact is also taken up by Gorgias, who relates it to the maddening, quasi-physical compulsion that is achieved by *logos*, and implicitly by his own grand style. Gorgias and Isocrates both seek to cement an analogy between Helen's physical beauty and the visual impressions effected by certain types of language: the embellished oral style in the former case and the ornate elaborations of *epideixis* in the latter. These sophistic writers represent Helen's inherently praiseworthy status as proven by the other praiseworthy types who were drawn toward her; this manifest approval associates her with encomiastic style.

The focus on the reciprocity of praise, and the extent to which its mutually reinforcing ideas circumvent difficult moral questions, eventually somewhat overshadowed the dubious reputations of Helen and Odysseus, at least in their association with epideictic oratory. By the time Aristotle was giving his lectures on rhetoric, they could be treated as worthy of praise because in the tradition, they had been "chosen" deliberately by wise men or women.[28] Helen thus ultimately becomes not merely a decorative object of praise but also one valued by a moral authority, a transformation that blandly avoids her blaming stories and thus the special threat that her beautiful form might pose. For teachers and theorists of rhetoric, Helen does not so much represent, as Odysseus does, the versatile style that uses the most suitable character to persuade. Rather, Gorgias associates her figure with the impact of style on the senses and especially with the vibrant imagery of the grand oral style, which reproduces the effect of beauty on the eye.

GORGIAS AND THE PHYSICALITY OF STYLE

Gorgias' treatment of Helen formulates arguments around her figure as both audience and visual object. In his *Encomium of Helen* he highlights the motivating power of *opsis* that Sappho depicts, but as a teacher of rhetoric, he argues that oral style operates in the same manner as visual impact. Gorgias represents Helen as an object of praise whose famous beauty has its own magnetic power and as the overwhelmed audience of Paris' beauty and seductive power. For Gorgias, Helen is emblematic of the nature of encomiastic speech and ultimately of his own flamboyant oral style. His association of Helen with sophistic epistemology, which, again, some scholars argue is nascent in the Sappho fragment, further cements her connection to ideas about the subjectivity of the viewer, the power of the persuasive image, and what the audience thus sees as the truth about a speaker's character or his topic.[29]

Gorgias begins his praise of Helen by calling attention to which values constitute suitable decoration (κόσμος) for different objects (*Hel.* 1). Attention to suitability may orient stylistic formulation quite generally, but the notion of appropriate adornment is also a Pindaric *topos* and most particular to praise speech. This epinician technique serves to establish the authority of the poet by demonstrating in visualizing terms his grasp of the proper order of things.[30] Gorgias first indicates the type of speech he is delivering by associating it with the ornamental style of praise poetry.[31] Indeed, the opening of the *Encomium* resembles a guide for epideictic composition, in that it matches a set of important entities with their emblematic virtues: "suitable adornment for a city is courage, for a body beauty, for a soul wisdom, for a deed virtue, and for a speech truth" (κόσμος πόλει μὲν εὐανδρία, σώματι δὲ κάλλος, ψυχῇ δὲ σοφία, πράγματι δὲ ἀρετή, λόγῳ δὲ ἀλήθεια, *Hel.* 1).[32] This is followed by a list of objects (ἄνδρα δὲ καὶ γυναῖκα καὶ λόγον καὶ ἔργον καὶ πόλιν καὶ πρᾶγμα) in respect to which proper praise and blame may be assigned. Two of these—the woman and the speech—are set next to each other, and both turn out to have "bodies" to which Gorgias later attributes similar qualities. Thus the conceptual link between the speech's ostensible and actual objects of praise—Helen and *logos*—is first suggested here.

In Gorgias' *Encomium* suitable praise for Helen (as the body of the first line) revolves around her physical excellence. Her form is measured by various standards, and then the attractions of other visibly excellent types to her are highlighted as proof of her praiseworthy status. Gorgias presents her nature (φύσει) and her bloodline (γένει) as the first evidence of this excellence (3); both contributed to her "divine beauty" (τό ἰσόθεος κάλλος), which, Gorgias says, drew others to her (4). Helen's superiority is thus most importantly demonstrated by the power of her single body to attract many other variously excellent bodies (ἑνὶ δὲ σώματι πολλὰ σώματα συνήαγεν ἀνδρῶν, 4). Of these, "some [came] flaunting the enormity of their wealth, some the good name of their ancient nobility, some the fine proportions of their strength, others the power of their glorious wisdom" (ἑνὶ δὲ σώματι πολλὰ σώματα συνήγαγεν ἀνδρῶν ἐπὶ μεγάλοις μέγα φρονούντων, ὧν οἱ μὲν πλούτου μεγέθη, οἱ δὲ εὐγενείας παλαιᾶς εὐδοξίαν, οἱ δὲ ἀλκῆς ἰδίας εὐεξίαν, οἱ δὲ σοφίας ἐπικτήτου δύναμιν ἔσχον, 4).

In his commentary on the speech, Thomas Buchheim has argued that this formulation of physical attraction is Empedoclean in origin.[33] Gorgias was said to have been a pupil of Empedocles (DK 31A1), and his materialist account of *logos* (DK 82B3) does seem to echo Empedocles on perception (DK 31A86, 92). Empedocles argues that all things "are fitted for mixture" (κρῆσιν ἐπαρκέα . . . ἔασιν); having been made like by Aphrodite (ὁμοιωθέντ' Ἀφροδίτῃ), they then love one another (DK 31B17, 4–5). The formulation foreshadows Gorgias' proofs in its embrace of mythical narrative and logical argumentation. Richard Enos also attributes Gorgias' emphasis on the powers of style to Empedocles, whom he credits with serving as a bridge between Homeric inspiration and the rational organization that Aristotle would establish for rhetoric.[34] Aristotle in fact denigrates Empedocles' style, apparently for its dependence on metaphor (*Poet.* 1447b; cf. *Rhet.* 1405a).

Empedocles' elaborate style thus seems to have reflected his ideas about the visualizing and motivating powers of language. This match between form and idea (or style and content) also characterizes Gorgias' *Encomium*, and especially the necessary circularity that he establishes in associating the beautiful Helen with his own elaborate style. Like Sappho, then, Gorgias makes a common move in appealing to authority; like Empedocles, he offers a rhetorical scheme that self-reflexively emphasizes ornamentation and visuality. Helen is affirmed as beautiful by others who are themselves visibly worthy of admiration. Likewise, the elaborate confirmation of her visible excellence is also matched by the sophist's own ornate cadences, so that he might effect a similar impact on his audience.

The logic, in this case, is that of encomiastic style, with a special emphasis on the visual and sensuous aspects of this style. According to Isocrates, the Homeridae relate that Helen made Homer's narrative "charming" (ἐπαφρόδιτον, Isoc. *Hel.* 65). His anecdote suggests that Helen's stylistic effect involves not merely a visually oriented embellishment, which is true of encomiastic style more generally, but also the sensuous attraction associated with those who are preeminently beautiful and themselves susceptible to such beauty. Aphrodite is centrally implicated in the mechanics of this stylistic effect. She initiates the process by which it comes into being, and she dictates the parameters within which it is elaborated. Archaic poetry and classical vase painting treat both Aphrodite and Peitho as super-visors in the fashioning of this kind of visual impact, which indicates that style and persuasion share a connection to the visible and sensuous details of the seduction scene from early on. The more specific point here, however, is that Gorgias does not praise or defend Helen by denying the Trojan story, as others had done. Rather, he demonstrates her praiseworthy (and inno-cent) status by associating her figure with the impact of an embellished and visualizing oral style.

Because of this, the sophist declares that he will avoid discussion of why or how or by whom Helen was taken away to Troy (Gorg. *Hel.* 5). He ex-plains that he will not address the causes and circumstances of Paris' love because such material is generally familiar, and treating what is known makes for conviction (πίστις) but not for pleasure (τέρψις, 5).[35] This expla-nation of the pleasure of speech stands in for the narrating of Helen's and Paris' desire and its consequences. Itself a rhetorical device (paralepsis), the suggestive circumlocution contains an abbreviated argument for the way speech gives pleasure. It also anticipates the more detailed account that will follow (8–14) of the quasi-physical impression that speech makes on the body and its emotions.

Ideas about the pleasure of speech have a long history in Greek poetry and prose. Think of Eumaeus' definition in the *Odyssey* of the bard as one who pleases (τέρπησιν, 17.385), and the teller of *muthoi* as one who charms the heart (θέλγοιτό κέ τοι φίλον ἦτορ, 17.514). For Aristotle, at the other end of this history, pleasure (ἡδονή) operates in persuasive situations as a reassuring affirmation of what is already known.[36] Roland Barthes' idea that the pleasure of narrative suspense lies largely in the realm of the ex-pected but as yet unrevealed perhaps captures more precisely the kind of narrative excitement Gorgias thinks necessary for a successful speech.[37] The audience's reaction to the novel and the beautiful in the speech parallels the anticipatory desire that beautiful bodies arouse in those who see them.

For the pleasure of his audience, then, Gorgias avoids any conventional narration of how Helen went to Troy and what precise role Paris played in that journey. Instead, he offers an explanation of how style operates by de-tailing the types of divine compulsion that might explain the event, and he allows the mortal agents in the events to recede. The possibilities he enu-merates thus stand in for the traditional narrative, suggesting versions of the event that are assigned proper names by Helen in the *Trojan Women*. Gor-gias himself has a fairly concrete sense of the forces that resulted in the rape of Helen: not only does speech (*logos*) have a body, but it approaches personification, eventually emerging as the most forceful character in his narrative. Gorgias' story triangulates persuasive speech with two other possible types of persuasion, broadly defined: persuasion by violence (βία) and by visual impact or desire (ὄψει/ἔρωτι, 6).[38] This grouping is not, according to John Kirby, unusual in early rhetoric and poetics, although the forces rarely occur simultaneously in this triangulated form.[39] Gorgias' understanding of the compelling nature of all four forces (i.e., persuasive speech, violence, visual impact, and desire) sets the stage for the apprehension of the startling powers inherent in the grand oral performance.[40]

Thus speech takes center stage as the force that insures the success of the conquest. Gorgias argues that *logos* itself (not just any particular speech) has physical stature: "Speech is a great lord, who with the smallest and most invisible body accomplishes the most immortal deeds" (λόγος δυνάστης μέγας ἐστίν, ὃς σμικροτάτῳ σώματι καὶ ἀφανεστάτῳ θειότατα ἔργα ἀποτελεῖ, *Hel.* 8).[41] By giving speech a personified, embodied status, Gorgias brings it closer to both physical force and erotic attraction in the effect of its "body" on human perception. The description recalls the power of Helen's body, which attracted so many to vie for its possession (4). This beautiful form is thus implicitly likened to the compelling powers of speech; but its owner is also at its mercy.[42] As in Sappho's ode, Helen's body sets up a chain reaction in respect to attraction. This time, however, a sensually impressive oral style is emphasized as the most powerful vehicle for emotional arousal.

This second section of the speech (8–19) uses Helen's story as an instance of how *logos* effects an impact on human perception analogous to physical force. Helen functions as the reactive audience to the manipulations of speech, but speech as Gorgias describes it is not just any kind. Rather, it is the rhythmic, visualizing oral performance for which he is most famous, and Helen becomes respectively the seduced, deceived, charmed, spellbound, and stricken audience of this especially forceful style of speech. The focus thus shifts from the character of Helen to the nature of speech, even though the "delicate body" of Gorgias' *logos* does also recall the lovely form of Helen. Gorgias thus aligns Helen iconically with the power of a visualizing oral style and also establishes her as representative of all who are susceptible to its impact. This style positions the beautiful form in relation to suitably elaborate vocabulary and cadences, which in turn inspires strong reaction in the audience to its rhythms and imagery. Gorgias uses the impressive and reactive body as the site for the generation of metaphor and as an organizing principle for the discussion of stylistic effect. He describes the nature of persuasive speech in physical terms, in two distinct ways: speech has a body, very powerful yet slight in stature; and speech works its effects on the soul through the body's senses, in a manner that he increasingly likens to physical impact.

While the first half of the *Encomium* called attention to the persuasive attraction of Helen's beauty for those who viewed her, this half is structured by a focus on her physical reactions. Her body's sense perceptions are shown to be so sensitive to the chiming sound and impressive imagery of the grand oral performance that it is impossible to distinguish these reactions from physical compulsion. Moving around Helen's body and matching types of physical perception to aspects of oral style, this section of the *Encomium* renders visible to the mind's eye the palpable impression that a sensual style would make on that body.

Sense of hearing

Much of Gorgias' analysis of the effects of oral style on the audience revolves, inevitably, around the ear. Poetry is the first type of speech to be adduced for its pathetic force, for the way its effect on the ear leads directly to physically registered emotional responses (*Hel.* 9). The emotional reaction of the hearer is closely tied to bodily sensation, as Segal and others have noted.[43] Gorgias indicates how this emotional manipulation comes about, by reference to meter and by his own use of the highblown poetic compounds that Aristotle later found too "chilly" (ψυχρά) for good prose style (*Rhet.* 1405b35).[44] According to Gorgias, however, this poetic style "brings on the hearers the trembling of extreme terror, tear-flooding pity, and grief-loving desire" (τοὺς ἀκούοντας εἰσῆλθε καὶ φρίκη περίφοβος καὶ ἔλεος πολύδακρυς καὶ πόθος φιλοπενθής). Its imagistic expressions can cause its hearers to envision the actions and bodies (πραγμάτων καὶ σωμάτων, 9) of others in good and bad fortune and to react accordingly. Gorgias' rhythmical arrangement of elaborate metaphors reproduces the effects of this oral style by imitating its metrical structure and its highly colored, imagistic language.

In his discussion of "special speech" in oral traditions, Bakker notes that Gorgias' phrasing utilizes rhythms recognizable from poetic genres.[45] Thus when Gorgias defines all poetry as "speech having meter" (τὴν ποίησιν ἅπασαν νομίζω καὶ ὀνομάζω λόγον ἔχοντα μέτρον, 9), he is describing a feature that his own style incorporates. In the meantime, the rhythmic, alliterative manner in which he expresses this idea also demonstrates its force. Bakker goes so far as to argue that Gorgias is more concerned with fashioning a prosey poetic style than a poeticized prose style, precisely because he is interested in this style as "a way in which an orator can use . . . the effects of special speech in performance."[46] In any event, Gorgias' composition clearly embraces stylistic habits of poetry and prose and seeks a combination that serves the special needs of encomiastic performance.

The speech next moves from poetry to the magic spell, which Gorgias declares to be even more effective for this kind of quasi-physical enchantment. He explains, "For epodes infused with divinity through speeches become producers of pleasure and reducers of pain" (αἱ γὰρ ἔνθεοι διὰ λόγων ἐπῳδαὶ ἐπαγωγοὶ ἡδονῆς, ἀπαγωγοὶ λύπης γίνονται, 10). The word *epôdê*, in contrast to *epôdos*, does not refer to the poetic form but rather to the type of charm one recites to heal a wound or cast a spell for or against someone or something.[47] Its rhythmic and binding words achieve physical impact through some special power. Earlier Gorgias had called Helen's beauty "equal to the gods" (ἰσόθεον, 3), and said that speech accomplishes deeds "most godlike" (θειότατα, 8); here the epode is said to be "god-infused" (ἔνθεοι, 10). Thus the beautiful image, the embodied speech, and the enchanting spell all share a divine quality. This quality affords striking images and words forceful, direct access to the mind, so that it perceives these visions and sounds as real objects. Gorgias also likens the effect of metered speech to music, which molds the soul through sound. Here he may be following the music theories of Damon (DK 37B6), as scholars have suggested.[48] Through the conduit of the ear, this speech achieves a "meeting" (συγγινομένη) with the soul and thereby charms, persuades, and even changes it (ἔθελξε καὶ ἔπεισε καὶ μετέστησεν, 10). The power of the rhythmic oral style manages an ordering of elements so compelling, and thereby strikes the senses in so profound a fashion, that one's mind reacts as if physically transformed.

In fact, Gorgias does state elsewhere that *logos* may be an object (DK 82B3), but one fundamentally different in kind from visible or audible objects. Gorgias recognizes that speech operates at one remove in comparison to other objects, since it represents them while itself remaining an external object (see further below). In the *Meno* Socrates associates both Gorgias and Empedocles with the explanation of sense-perception that argues that objects give off "streams" (ἀπορροαί) of matter, which enter the body through the passages that match their different types of impact (76c4–d1). Socrates terms this explanation "theatrical" (τραγική, 76e3), emphasizing its spectacular and tactile qualities.[49] If this theory of sense-perception or one like it does underlie Gorgias' discussion of the nature of *logos* in the *Encomium*, we should not regard the series of analogies between speech and physical impact as analogies from the imperceptible to the perceptible but rather from one type of physical sensation to another. The effects of oral style on the audience are thus not merely comparable to the effects of visual objects on the perceiver. Instead, they come about by essentially the same means: bodily impact.

Sense of touch

Although words do not, for Gorgias, necessarily reflect reality, they are nevertheless perceived by the mind as having a physical shape. Speakers "mold" a false argument (ψευδῆ λόγον πλάσαντες) to persuade an audience, the visceral quality of which combats the slippery (σφαλερά) nature of opinion (δόξα, *Hel.* 11). The speech thus manages to appear true, artificial though its arguments may be.[50] The intimate link between oral style and physical modeling that is established at this point in Gorgias' speech reveals that stylistic elements may have the same violent effect on the body as brute force (βία, 12). Helen's body may have been taken, in effect, by the impression of cadences on her ears and images on her eyes, a sensual aggression whose effect resembles rape. Gorgias' use here of words for physical shaping—and not merely for touching—indicates that he is not primarily interested in the physiology of perception (i.e., the means by which one understands words) but rather in the molding effect on the mind that a vibrant style can have. The plastic imagery that Gorgias uses highlights the importance of the particular form (i.e., style) that the images take, which in turn gives a particular shape to their impress on the mind.

Gorgias then shifts his imagery from comparisons that focus on the body's surfaces (i.e., molding and imprinting) to those that treat its fluid interior. A bad, violent kind of persuasion has the same power as a bad drug. He asserts, "Just as some kinds of drugs take some humors from the body, and some stop illness, others life, so do some speeches sicken hearers, and others delight them" (ὥσπερ γὰρ τῶν φαρμάκων ἄλλους ἄλλα χυμοὺς ἐκ τοῦ σώματος ἐξάγει, καὶ τὰ μὲν νόσου τὰ δὲ βίου παύει, οὕτω καὶ τῶν λόγων οἱ μὲν ἐλύπησαν, οἱ δὲ ἔτερψαν, 14; cf. 17, 19).[51] In this section, Gorgias' use of physical analogies has chemical as well as tactile significance, so that he circles back to the realm of sickness and cure first invoked to describe the power of the epode. Now, however, the forceful style of *logos* takes on a more sinister and ambiguous cast, its effects on the body potentially paralleling either the onrush of pleasure or the creep of disease. This and the following section focus especially on the dangerous aspects of stylistic impact, but the acknowledgment that *peithô* may have negative effects does not seem ultimately to detract from the orator's enthusiastic envisioning of its effects.

Sense of sight

The final and definitive realm in which the *logos* operates, the impact of which the grand oral style especially imitates, is the sense of sight (*opsis*). Now, it must be admitted that in *On Not Being*, Gorgias says that visible objects differ most from *logos*. There are two reasons for this: (1) the object of *logos* refers to the objects of other senses, that is, it functions as a signified (the idea of "lover" as a mental object), rather than a referent (the lover now in one's field of vision); and (2) visible and linguistic objects are grasped by different organs (DK 82B3). In the *Encomium*, however, Gorgias emphasizes analogies among the impact of visual objects, the striking oral style, and physical force, primarily by means of the repetition of the verb *tupeomai*. For Gorgias, the ability of objects in the visual field to impress (ἐτυπώσατο, 13; τυποῦται, 15) the soul parallels the effect of the ornate style he promotes. This parallelism occurs because actual sights and verbal images possess a similar emotive power. We might even go so far as to say that he thereby transforms into a rhetorical technique Sappho's depiction in fragment 16 of physical beauty's stirring effects on its viewers.

The persuasive power of sight and thus of physical beauty is exemplified by Helen, whom Gorgias' speech develops as a trope for the style that uses striking visual patterns. The audience perceives its impact by means of their own reactions to this visualizing style. The description of the way sight affects the soul employs vocabulary that equates it with the way a compelling style achieves its impressions. Both not only "strike" the soul (ἐτυπώσατο, 13; and τυποῦται, 15); but if a visualizing oral style places images before the mind's eye, *opsis* also "inscribes" (ἐνέγραψεν, 17) them in the mind. For Gorgias, then, the power of *logos* lies ultimately in its ability to move an audience by such impressive stylistic effects and thus to achieve persuasion by the impact of imagery on the ear and eye. In the force with which it overwhelms the audience, this impact is akin to the startling vision.

Gorgias is said to have stunned (ἐξέπληξε) Athenian audiences with his elaborate style (DK 82A4), an *ekplêxis* like that which he himself describes as occurring when the eye sees bodies readied for war and alarms the soul, causing the viewers, panic-stricken (ἐκπλαγέντες, *Hel.* 16), to run away. Something of similar force but with pleasurable effect occurs with the sight of a beautiful body. Like a painter's well-crafted image (ἐν σῶμα καὶ σχῆμα τελείως ἀπεργάσωνται, 18) or Paris' form viewed by Helen (σώματι τὸ τῆς Ἑλένης ὄμμα ἡσθέν, 19; cf. εἶδος ἐκπαγλουμένη, Eur. *Tro.* 929), a dazzling style can overwhelm an audience and compel it to make rash or dangerous decisions.[52] Segal explains, "When the aesthetic stimulus is strong enough . . . as in the case of a pleasing vision or moving speech, the passive aesthetic *terpsis* becomes a powerful impulse which diverts the whole course of the psyche. This is the condition of *ekplexis*."[53] Gorgias can give his audience this ambiguous pleasure, stirring them up with his speech the way the bodies he visualizes excite the eye. When words are chosen for their sounds and for the images they call up, and when they are organized so that they possess a lulling, rhythmic cadence, the audience responds as if these words had a physical shape and mobilizing force like Helen's divine body. The power of such words may also use the physical conduits of her body—the ear, the touch, the eye—to imprint her mind with sensual images and thereby effect a near-physical change in her soul.

Helen's body is thus not randomly chosen as a model around which to structure praise speech. Rather, her body, by virtue of its own impact on the eye and its susceptibility to that impact, is treated by Gorgias as *the* structuring device for the way an ornate and visualizing oral style achieves its effects. The implicit suggestion at the outset of the speech is that this style may be especially suited to the encomium, since praise speech functions as a verbal adornment of its object. By the end of Gorgias' speech, however, it becomes clear that he is describing the effects of his own spectacular style, which may be used in contexts of praise or defense—or self-reflexively exercised as an amusement (παίγνιον, 21) for the clever oral performer.

ISOCRATES AND BEAUTY'S RECIPROCITY

Isocrates' speech in praise of Helen reveals how Gorgias' inclusive, nontechnical characterization of the oral style looked to a later writer who emphasized the accurate usage of technical generic categories.[54] Isocrates' *Helen* is a carefully written speech, whose fulsome style nevertheless tends to avoid the heavily alliterative and chiming verbal patterns of Gorgias. While it draws a connection between Helen's beauty and *epideixis* that recalls Gorgias' equations, Isocrates' speech focuses attentively on the kind of reciprocal relationships between praiser and praised on which the genre depends. It may seem a bit perverse to claim that Isocrates is treating Helen's figure as emblematic of epideictic style, since she is so famously an object of blame. But in fact, by focusing on her beauty as her primary attribute, he both circumvents the entire question of her culpability and promotes her as the paradigmatic object of praise, precisely because she is this paradigmatic beauty. Since the perception of physical beauty is centered on visual sensation, like Gorgias he draws a connection between the beauty of Helen and the impact of the ornamental techniques that traditionally characterize encomiastic style.

Isocrates begins his encomium with a contemporary polemic that accuses teachers of rhetoric of choosing trivial subjects for *epideixis* and composing inferior speeches in praise of superior subjects (*Hel.* 1–13). His central argument suggests that epideictic speech is in fact the only type worth engaging in. The negative theses of the Cynics, arguments for the unity of the virtues (1), the overwrought compositions of the older sophists (2), and disputation for its own sake (6) are all shown to be idle occupations. Praise speech, while superior to these for its educational value, is only really effective if one's subject and one's style of presentation are demonstrably excellent (13). Helen is portrayed as a manifestly worthy subject for praise rhetoric, and Isocrates intends to compose a superior speech in praise of her. The circular relationship between the object of praise and effective epideictic style is thus underscored from the outset. Isocrates begins his encomium with a parallel construction that aligns his speech with Helen's birthright: "I shall make the beginning of my speech the beginning of her family" (τὴν μὲν οὖν ἀρχὴν τοῦ λόγου ποιήσομαι τὴν ἀρχὴν τοῦ γένους αὐτῆς, 16).[55]

Like Gorgias, Isocrates emphasizes the body of Helen: in conjunction with that of Heracles, the excellence of these bodies (τὰ σώματ') demonstrates their father's devotion. As proof of Zeus' visible affirmation of Helen in particular, Isocrates maintains that Zeus loved Helen the most, since beauty has the power to bring even strength into subjection.[56] Isocrates then introduces Theseus as the best proof of Helen's excellence and dwells on his manifest virtues (18–38). Theseus' own excellent traits can be seen as parallel to Helen's beauty, because of the public nature of his deeds. The treatment of Theseus is extraordinarily protracted, even though it is merely the first of a series of passages that circumvent a description of Helen's character and focus on the actions of her admirers. Isocrates' technique, which is a fine example of style at the level of invention, avoids any treatment of Helen's stories in favor of an emblematic scheme. Relieved of her disreputable story, Helen becomes merely the beautiful object that admirable men struggle to possess. In these passages she thus signifies instead the nature of praise speech itself. If praise is a response whose decorative imagery reproduces visible excellence, then the most beautiful form should serve not only as the most fitting example of the visual, public nature of communal admiration but more importantly as the emblem of the epideictic speech act.[57]

Theseus serves as the best example of this visible, public praise, but Isocrates (like Hesiod and Gorgias before him) also highlights the competition for Helen's hand in marriage. The paradigmatic, Panhellenic nature of this *agôn* further heightens Helen's status as *the* publicly acclaimed beauty.[58] Here Paris enters into the parade of heroes. A judge of dubious public status, he is nevertheless famous for his own beauty and thus presumably has a special knowledge of its qualities (cf. Hom. *Il.* 3.54–64). When Paris is offered the chance to possess Helen, he cannot choose among the bodies of the goddesses, so overwhelmed is he by the sight of them (τῶν μὲν σωμάτων οὐ δυνηθεὶς λαβεῖν διάγνωσιν ἀλλ' ἡττηθεὶς τῆς τῶν θεῶν ὄψεως, 42). Although Isocrates goes on to argue that Paris' eagerness to marry well determined his choice (43–44), at least initially he suggests that the startling image of these divine bodies compelled Paris to opt for the choice that would give him possession of a body similarly divine—the body acclaimed as the most beautiful in the world. Indeed, in his efforts to prove Paris a worthy admirer of Helen, Isocrates declares that the Trojan prince would have been foolish if he had seen the goddesses contending for beauty and yet disdained beauty himself (εἰ τοὺς θεοὺς εἰδὼς περὶ κάλλους φιλονικοῦντας αὐτός κάλλους κατεφρόνησε, 48).

Each passage in these middle sections aims to demonstrate this kind of reciprocal activity. Theseus, the judge who is visibly great by virtue of the public character of his actions, pursues the love object that he finds most worthy. This pursuit by a lauded hero proves the praiseworthy status of the object (38). All the excellent men of Greece, responding to their shared judgment (γνώμη) of Helen, similarly showed her excellence by their pursuit of her hand, and each expected an increase in his own status as a result of winning this prize (39–41).

Toward the end of the speech, Isocrates reinforces this interlocking set of reciprocal processes by claiming that he is justified in using such highblown language in praise of Helen (τηλικαύταις ὑπερβολαῖς, 54), because she possessed beauty to the greatest extent (κάλλους . . . πλεῖστον μέρος). His style thus takes its cue from her beauty, which turns out to be the single most praiseworthy, precious, and divine quality of all things in existence (ὃ σεμνότερον καὶ τιμιώτατον καὶ θειότατον τῶν ὄντων ἐστίν). The formulation recalls Gorgias' emphasis in the *Encomium* on the extraordinary qualities of both Helen and persuasive style.[59] Isocrates follows his apotheosis of beauty with an argument for its importance as a civic virtue, maintaining that no other virtues are publicly admired without the presence of the outward form (τῆς ἰδέας) to enhance them (54–55). Finally Helen herself, because she surpassed everyone in respect to sight (τὴν ὄψιν), is revealed as equally divine (ἀθανασίας), while her superior status similarly enhances those of her intimates (61–62).

Further associating this divinely beautiful form and the style of its emblematic portrait, Isocrates ultimately emphasizes Helen's effect on the composition of her own narrative. Not only does she affect the sight of those like Stesichorus who write blaming narratives of her (ἐβλασφήμησέ τι περὶ αὐτῆς, 64). She also demands a narrative like Homer's that will inspire the most envy (ζηλωτότερον) and lends that tale the charming, aphrodisiac style (ἐπαφρόδιτον) that made it famous (65). In Isocrates' formulation, Helen thus embodies the visualizing nature of the praise process, actively commands its implementation, and insures that the style in which it is elaborated suits her charming type.

Idea, the word that Isocrates uses when arguing that beauty is the greatest of the virtues, would come to be used in the second century C.E. by the rhetorician Hermogenes to designate speaking style. For Isocrates, it denotes the form by which all other virtues can be seen and understood. Since the beauty of the visible form serves as a medium for the public recognition of less tangible virtues, this beauty represents not only the greatest of the virtues but also a kind of meta-virtue, the best form for all virtuous content. In Isocrates' speech, then, Helen represents this stylization of virtues because she possesses a beautiful form, and this form guarantees her excellence. Any moral questions are effectively circumvented; her visible excellence is an exteriorization of her virtue. Style expresses content in the direct and visualizing manner of epideictic speech.

In the *Evagoras* Isocrates argues that *epideixis* of a measured sort—the praise of a virtuous character without too much exaggeration—is useful for inspiring healthy envy (ζῆλος) in the young (5). He considers character (ἦθος) a positive tool for instruction, in that its suitable depiction might inspire this healthy envy and thus emulation. Encouraging imitation (μίμεσις) by describing praiseworthy character types constitutes a practical use of *êthos* more similar in outlook to Aristotle than to Gorgias. Isocrates seems to follow his teacher in his association of Helen with epideictic style and his affinity for ornate stylistics, which Dionysius of Halicarnassus later likened to "the hodgepodge of applied cosmetics" on a body (τὰ συνερανιζόμενα κόσμοις ἐπιθέτοις, *Isoc.* 3). By treating Helen as a public object of praise, however, his speech circumvents the emotional enchantment that Gorgias emphasizes in relation to her figure. Like Aristotle (*Rhet.* 1363a16–19, 1399a1–3), Isocrates regards Helen as praiseworthy most especially because she was chosen deliberately by an admirable type. She is thereby associated with the publicly affirmed values that civic heroes like Theseus embody. The fourth-century treatment of Helen thus reduces Gorgias' association of her powerful beauty with stylistic impact to a blandly ornamental emblem of civic praise.

ODYSSEUS AND REVERSALS OF VISIBLE TYPE

In contrast to this objectifying use of Helen's beautiful form, the figure of Odysseus serves speechwriters in an authorial capacity. Set pieces in the late fifth century show him to be the prototypical manipulator of character representation, whose changeable type highlights the mutability of style. This changeability is also related to visual effect, but Odysseus' techniques resemble sleights of hand; they confuse the eye rather than offering it pleasurable stimulation. If Helen's beauty comes to stand for the quasi-visible impact of the grand oral style, Odysseus' aptitude for disguise comes to signify the versatile and deceptive aspects of the grand oral style. The clever strategist is depicted as employing his rhetorical tactics to confound his more sympathetic victims: virtuous, upstanding types like Palamedes and Ajax.[60] Among rhetorical writings, the speech that Gorgias gives the wise Palamedes in defense against Odysseus' slander represents the most extended treatment of this type of conflict. Gorgias' student Antisthenes fashions a more abbreviated speech for Ajax in his conflict with Odysseus, as befits the angry hero's terse character type. The characters of Palamedes and Ajax serve in distinct but related ways as material for Odysseus' lying tactics. Antisthenes and Alcidamas, another student of Gorgias, are credited with writing speeches that argue against these two heroes, although the one attributed to Alcidamas is probably only contemporaneous. It is clear

from these pairs of speeches that Odysseus seeks to manipulate his character type and those of his opponents, by appropriating their traits or projecting his own onto them. Elsewhere I have dubbed this maneuver "character
exchange," for lack of a more elegant way of encapsulating what is in fact a
very versatile and carefully calibrated oratorical strategy.[61]

This rhetorical sleight of hand plays on the audience's misrecognition
(*méconnaissance*), which Bourdieu argues is central in the authoritative oral
performance. The tactic seeks to forge positive associations with the features of one's bodily *hexis* and to dispel negative ones, so that the audience "recognizes" the gestures and intonations of the speaker as evidence
of fine character.[62] While this technique may take fairly subtle forms, in oratory it usually reinforces the aggressive relationship between the speakers.
At its harshest it involves the slandering of one's opponent, which Aristotle regards as a standard component of forensic speeches (*Rhet.* 1415a). A
favored tactic among fourth-century orators, it comes to center around the
attribution of traits to one's opponent for which Odysseus is the prototype:
sophistry, versatility, and overpreparedness.[63] The set pieces that dramatize
Odysseus' conflicts with Palamedes and Ajax demonstrate early examples
of this technique, which suggests that he is thought of as its author.

Like Gorgias' *Encomium,* three of the set speeches involving Odysseus
were probably written around 415 and are thus generally contemporaneous
with the tragedies that cast Odysseus in a sophistic, manipulative role. The
style the speeches depict Odysseus as employing centers on precisely the
character manipulation that Plato would denigrate as a crucial technique of
sophistic speechwriters, whose skills depended on their abilities to fashion
their own and others' characters to suit both case and jury. Gorgias' gentler
handling of Odysseus may be attributed to his sophistic perspective, and
those of Antisthenes and "Alcidamas" to Gorgias' influence. But the intellectual environment was more complicated during this period than the familiar Platonic depictions of the disputes between the sophists and Socrates
suggest. Socrates himself is sometimes portrayed as a sophist, and Xenophon depicts Antisthenes as a faithful follower of Socrates.[64] Antisthenes'
appreciation of Odysseus' versatility, which he further indicates in his literary criticism,[65] suggests that our understanding of fifth- and fourth-century
treatments of his figure is too heavily informed by the dramatic portraits
and Plato's opinions. The negative assessments that these writers made
of the techniques associated with Odysseus appear to have been strongly
countered by the work of such theorists as Antisthenes; scholars have long

argued that his influence during the period made him a particular target of Plato.[66]

GORGIAS' *PALAMEDES*

In *Palamedes' Defense,* Odysseus does not speak, of course. It may thus seem slightly forced to claim that one can discern his rhetorical strategies, and especially anything that could be considered his style, from this vantage point. Yet Gorgias' speech throws into sharp relief the type of charges made by Odysseus, as well as the type of man who would make them. The speech revolves largely around issues of character. As such, it seeks to oppose Palamedes' upright, moderate type and his precise, orderly speech to the outrageous tactics and shocking argumentative style of his enemy. As the accuser, Odysseus would have spoken first, which means that his charges and the manner in which they were made should structure the *topoi* of the apology. This use of his character parallels the plotting role he plays in tragedy. Indeed, although Odysseus' false charges may seem to establish the parameters of Palamedes' speech only in some banal sense, he serves as the mythic paradigm for this authorial function.

From Homer on, those who engage with Odysseus more often than not find themselves compelled to respond to his version of events and to the typical style he fabricates for the occasion. Odysseus' presence in Palamedes' speech as a deceiver and a manipulator of perspective conforms to his usual influence on formal discourse. Gorgias' indirect treatment of the lying hero in fact suggests that Odysseus represents certain stylistic techniques that are central to sophistic training, reprehensible though they may appear to critics of the sophists. If some rhetorical theorists show a comparable admiration for Odysseus' techniques, others also associate them with Gorgias' own grand style. One might thus expect that Gorgias' treatment of Odysseus' upstanding opponent would reveal as well tactics particular to both the lying hero and the sophist himself.

Odysseus has accused Palamedes of supplying information to Priam and receiving money in return. In the introduction of Gorgias' speech, intermittently throughout the body of it, and especially in the third section, Palamedes treats the charges as patently false because they give a false portrayal of his type. As is common in the forensic setting, the accuser dictates the character traits that the accused must address in his defense speech; but Palamedes' focus on character effectively overshadows the rest of the defense.[67] In Gorgias' depiction, Palamedes attempts to demonstrate the impossibility and improbability of his being a traitor. A crucial aspect of his defense is his public reputation as a good man, a type who cannot conceive of any way in which his actions would not be visible to all.

Palamedes covers the possibilities of the charges from every angle to demonstrate that he would have needed to have been invisible, inhumanly powerful, and surrounded by accomplices to have carried out the deeds he is accused of. He claims that the details of Odysseus' charges all depend for their proof on others having seen him. This is, however, precisely the challenge that Odysseus embodies. His talent for deception suggests the ease with which the eye can be deceived; and Gorgias was known to have been particularly sensitive to such epistemological quandaries.[68] Palamedes' dependence on eyewitness accounting for his proofs thus begs the very question that Odysseus' figure always brings to the fore: how do we know that what we are seeing conforms with what we think we are seeing? As one who himself managed to steal within the Trojan walls disguised as a slave and into his own house disguised as a beggar, Odysseus' own famously deceptive *hexis* reveals that the eyewitness account is fallible.

Palamedes counterbalances these considerations of what is possible with *eikos* (probability) arguments, which he treats as also dependent on notions of visibility for their proof. He argues that to have committed the acts with which he is charged, he would have needed to be a type opposite to that which he is known to be. Just as anyone should have been able to see Palamedes engaging in the acts that Odysseus charged, so can anyone see his good character through his publicly visible actions. Palamedes' arguments present his bodily *hexis* as transparent, as a clear sign of his virtue. But the epistemological assumptions underlying this connection of probability arguments to the recognition of visible type further indicate the central way in which Gorgias' Palamedes functions as a foil for Odysseus. Gorgias' speech sets up a conflict between the man of common sense and the persuasive storyteller. The one relies on empirical knowledge and eyewitness reporting to determine the facts of the matter, the other on opinion and the deft manipulation of character. *Eikos* arguments form a cornerstone of the latter approach, since notions of probability involve assumptions about social categories and types. As Bourdieu has revealed, such assumptions arise from received notions of character and status; they thrive on opinion and are susceptible to manipulation by authoritative speakers. Moreover, the misrecognition that occurs in the assessment of a speaker's visible character (i.e., *hexis*) corresponds to the tricky nature of probability.

Thus while Gorgias' speech shows Palamedes to be a fitting match for Odysseus, the trust that Palamedes places in eyewitness experience and probabilities based on it ultimately puts him at a disadvantage when confronting Odysseus' elusive type. If it is true that for the sophist Gorgias, all perspectives are crucially affected by opinion and persuasive style, there should be some alliance between the sophist and the lying hero in this regard as well. Recall that Gorgias argues elsewhere that one cannot know anything as generally true. Even the eyewitness account can only be declared true from the subjective viewpoint and can fail as a proof because of the transformative nature of language itself.[69] What little is known about Gorgias' theories of communication suggests that he recognized that all speech is fundamentally molded by style. What one knows cannot be communicated in a transparent form because one must use some manner of expression, some organization and shaping of content. This outlook conforms especially with an understanding of the power of language in its performance, where phraseology, rhythm, and visible attitudes would all shape the audience's reactions. Thus the morally upright figure of Palamedes, who argues in a restrained style that empirical evidence should constitute proof, also indicates by his line of attack the adept manipulation of opinion achieved by his opponent's versatile type and slandering style.

The structure of Gorgias' speech and its grounds for proof follow standard forensic procedure.[70] Palamedes names Odysseus as the accuser and makes a distinction that will dominate the entire speech. Most important for this discussion, it marks the putative character difference between accused and accuser: knowing clearly (σαφῶς ἐπιστάμενος) versus having an opinion (δοξάζων, *Pal.* 3). Although Palamedes initially puts forward these options as potential attitudes of the same man, it soon becomes clear that the former characterizes the speaker's epistemological state and the latter, that of his opponent (5; cf. 22, 24). Palamedes then offers the possibility that Odysseus' accusations may arise from envy (φθόνῳ), falsification (κακοτεχνίᾳ), or criminality (πανουργίᾳ, 3). This, he says, would make his opponent "the worst of men" (κάκιστος ἀνήρ, 3). In any event, he declares, "I know clearly" (σαφῶς οἶδα) that my accuser makes his charges "without clear knowledge" (οὐ σαφῶς εἰδώς, 5). Palamedes uses these distinctions to indicate Odysseus' falsifying, opining style, so that the liar's type of invention may be understood as representative of his character.

Sophocles' *Philoctetes* echoes these associations, suggesting their currency. In that drama, Odysseus recognizes that it goes against Neoptolemus' nature to engage in the devising of plots (τεχνᾶσθαι κακά, 80); later Neoptolemus refers to his natural resistance in similar terms (ἔφυν γὰρ οὐδέν ἐκ τέχνης πράττειν κακῆς, 88). Three times Philoctetes accuses Odysseus and his associates of being the purveyors of *panourgia* (*Phil.* 408, 448, 927; cf. 1357, πανώλει), as does Ajax (*Aj.* 445).[71] We might note also that in the prosecution speech attributed to Alcidamas, Odysseus explicitly claims that *panourgia* is a family trait of Palamedes, which adds to the impression that such charges were commonly associated with the lying Odysseus. In Gorgias' speech Palamedes would thus be attempting to refute a set of negative traits foisted on him by Odysseus, which more often characterized the liar himself.[72]

Like Odysseus beginning his tale to the Phaeacians (*Od.* 9.14), Palamedes debates where he ought to begin. He blames his perplexity on the visible shock (ἔκπληξιν ἐμφανῆ) that Odysseus' accusations have caused (4). This hesitation over the most suitable place to start is a common enough *topos*, but Odysseus' famous use of it in Homer (*Od.* 9.14) is probably its source. Given the sophists' predilection for impersonating the Homeric rhapsodes, Palamedes' deliberation is surely meant to recall the notoriously circumspect storyteller, however ironic or perverse such an echo may seem in this context. *Ekplêxis*, again, is associated with the grand style of oratory; the word captures how the emotionally dramatic and impressive oral performance feels like being struck or startled out of one's usual attitudes.[73] Thus not only does Palamedes utilize the storyteller's preamble, but by blaming his organizational quandary on *ekplêxis*, he also invokes the impact of the oral style with which Odysseus himself is associated.[74] Odysseus shares this verbal flamboyance with Gorgias, who gives Palamedes a comparatively plainspoken style that reflects the Homeric hero's startling techniques like a *camera obscura*.

Ekplêxis and its cognates signal a sensory impression, often visual, like a stunning blow. They describe the startling quality of the love that Aphrodite feels upon seeing her favorites (ἔκπαγλα, *Il.* 3.415, 5.423; ἐκπάγλως, *h.Ven.* 57; ἐκπαγλουμένη, *Tro.* 929), as well as the effect of Gorgias' elaborate style on his audience (ἐξέπληξε, DK 82A4). If by the fifth century the verb and its cognates have come to embrace the effect of this oratorical style and that of visual impact, these are two quasi-physical experiences that Gorgias himself first explicitly linked (ἐκπλαγέντες, *Hel.* 16). In the *Odyssey* Demodocus sings about a dispute (*neikos*) between Odysseus and Achilles, in which the two quarrel "with striking words" (ἐκπάγλοις ἐπέεσσιν, 8.73). By highlighting his stunned reaction to Odysseus' charges, Palamedes suggests that the same effect marked the accusatory style that Odysseus deployed for this courtroom *neikos*. Palamedes presents Odysseus as having fashioned such a shocking, slanderous fiction that he leaves his target in a visible quandary, the state itself reproducing the visually oriented nature of the impact.

In appropriate reaction to this stunning lie, Palamedes declares that he must turn to the truth itself (αὐτῆς τῆς ἀληθείας) and present necessity (τῆς παρούσης ἀνάγκης), since he has "teachers more dangerous than resourceful" (διδασκάλων ἐπικινδυνοτέρων ἢ πορίμωτέρων τυχών, 4). Palamedes' "teachers" are clearly his accuser and the situation he has engineered. In Sophocles' *Philoctetes* Odysseus is also a bad and dangerous teacher. Like the attribution of *panourgia* to Odysseus, the charge of being a bad teacher is a familiar one for him, a denigration of the abilities that he shares with the sophists. Consider again the way Neoptolemus is peremptorily trained by Odysseus to impersonate the character most likely to please his interlocutor. At the end of his deceptive speech to Philoctetes, the young man calls his teacher "the worst of the worst" (τοῦ κακίστου κἀκ κακῶν Ὀδυσσέως, 384). Then, however, he guiltily excuses him by blaming *his* (Odysseus') teachers, declaring that the bad characters of men come from the deforming impact their teachers achieve with speeches (οἱ δ' ἀκοσμοῦντες βροτῶν / διδασκάλων λόγοισι γίγνονται κακοί, 387–388). The lack of a good, improving style (*kosmos*) in such speeches leads to a similar lack in those who listen to them. The teachers thereby disorder (ἀκοσμοῦντες) the characters of their students, so that their own speeches reflect this derangement. This may in turn cause civic disorder if the students are prominent enough citizens, like Odysseus and Neoptolemus. By locating speechmaking as the source of the evil, Neoptolemus points to a charge that was frequently made against the sophists and later popularized by Plato.[75] Philoctetes later reveals the results of such teaching when he declares that Neoptolemus, while not a bad person, has apparently learned shameful conduct from bad men (οὐκ εἶ κακὸς σύ· πρὸς κακῶν δ' ἀνδρῶν μαθὼν / ἔοικας ἥκειν αἰσχρά, 971–972).

Compare the closing statements of Gorgias' speech, where Palamedes offers his inventions as proof that he avoids such shameful and evil deeds (σημεῖον δὲ ποιούμενος ὅτι τῶν αἰσχρῶν καὶ τῶν κακῶν ἔργων ἀπέχομαι, *Pal.* 31). He argues that the reverse of bad training is achieved by someone like him, a civic benefactor (εὐεργέτης, 30, 36) who brings order out of disorder (κεκοσμημένον ἐξ ἀκόσμου, 30). Throughout his speech Palamedes repeatedly reverts to an opposition between civic benefactors and evildoers, and truth and lying—or more specifically, the head-turning fictions and dangerously disordering styles of bad teachers. Gorgias has constructed a character who would condemn the sophist's own type (as a vibrant speaker and influential teacher). Moreover, Palamedes' arguments themselves reveal the striking oratorical skills of his opponent Odysseus, who is clearly a more fitting authorial figure for Gorgias. Gorgias demonstrates his understanding of the subtleties of verbal disguise by using the wise but plain-spoken Palamedes to throw into sharp relief the more circumspect cleverness of Odysseus. Where Palamedes will claim an adherence to the truth and depend on the eyewitness for his proof, Odysseus has apparently fashioned a story that stuns like a beautiful or horrifying image and distorts the mind like bad schooling. The shocking, corrupting style that Palamedes attributes to Odysseus thus itself may distract the jury from apprehending the import of the accused man's visibly upstanding character.

Palamedes has been put in a position where he must prove that he is not an unscrupulous (*panourgos*) type. To do this, he frequently has recourse to arguments from probability (*eikos* arguments), as mentioned above. He states, for example, that it is not probable (οὐκ εἰκός) that someone would betray his country for a little money (9). This claim is soon supported by assertions about his public character. He maintains that he would not have been motivated by a desire for gold, since he has sufficient wealth and wants no more, being a man of moderation. His jurors, Palamedes declares, can count themselves as eyewitnesses to his life: they can see for themselves that he is a moderate type (σύνεστε γάϱ μοι, διὸ σύνιστε ταῦτα, 15).[76] *Eikos* arguments, again, are frequently associated with the sophists, to their detriment.[77] These arguments address what can be reasonably assumed about a certain type of person in a given situation. The concept (if not the term) is as old as Homer, and therefore is particularly associated with Odysseus' stylistic maneuvers, since his use of believable character types depends on this kind of reasonable assumption. Representing oneself as a certain type of person (the portrayal of *êthos*) is crucial to the formulation of *eikos* arguments centered on one's actions, since only by having established oneself as a particular type can one argue what one might be likely to do.

In the *Poetics* (1445a17) Aristotle says that *ekplêxis* can come from the preception of probabilities (τῆς ἐκπλήξεως γιγνομένης δι' εἰκότων), which further associates them with the figure of Odysseus. Odysseus has accused Palamedes of treachery and eluding the eye in a manner more typical of the lying hero. Palamedes responds by emphasizing the necessary visibility of the crimes he is charged with committing, as well as those visible traits that make him an unlikely type to engage in such underhanded tactics. But, once again, his accuser is famous precisely for proving that such visibility might be deceptive. One may be "struck" by the speaker's startling likeness to a particular kind of person, and yet he may be some similar type, or not that type at all. Palamedes' use of probability arguments to combat an opponent like Odysseus thus merely highlights the insecurity of their premises.

Palamedes' assessment of his own character does not, however, depend only on the jury's acquaintance with his visible type. It also makes use of more general notions about the consistency of character. For instance, Palamedes maintains that he is already admired for his wisdom (σοφία), which is "most honored" (ἐντιμότατος, 16). Since, however, he has also been accused of the reverse of traditional wisdom—that is, since Odysseus has implied by his charges that Palamedes has helped enemies and harmed friends—this would seem inconsistent with his visible type.[78] "No one," Palamedes continues, "does evil [πανουργεῖ] wishing to suffer harm" (18; cf. πανουργεῖται, 19). He thereby underscores the self-serving motivations of the *panourgos* man, a characterization he has already argued better suits his opponent. He asks Odysseus to consider what sort of man he must be to charge such things (οἷος ὢν οἷα λέγεις), as a worthless man with a worthless cause (ἀνάξιος ἀναξίῳ) would do (22). Like Philoctetes in Sophocles' drama, Gorgias' Palamedes regards Odysseus as an overbold operator (ὦ πάντων ἀνθρώπων τολμηρότατε, *Pal.* 24; cf. πάντα δὲ / τολμητά, *Phil.* 633–634). Such a man dares to fabricate charges based on opinion rather than truth (δόξῃ πιστεύσας . . . τὴν ἀλήθειαν οὐκ εἰδώς, τολμαῖς ἄνδρα περὶ θανάτου διώκειν, *Pal.* 24). Palamedes' description thus suggests not only how one ought to regard Odysseus' actions but also whether the actions that Odysseus has attributed to him better match Odysseus' own character.

Later in Gorgias' speech Palamedes again criticizes the logic of Odysseus' characterization of him. Odysseus' charges represent, Palamedes argues, an impossibly inconsistent character type, since wisdom and madness cannot coexist in one man: "If you claim that I am crafty [τεχνήεντα], terribly clever [δεινόν], and resourceful [πόριμον]," Palamedes says, "then you are accusing me of wisdom [σοφίαν], but if you say that I betrayed Greece, then you are accusing me of insanity [μανίαν]" (25). Recall that the animosity between the two men was initiated when the clever and resourceful

Odysseus feigned madness and (through Palamedes' own sly exposure of his ruse) revealed his disloyalty to the Greek cause. Thus Odysseus himself had embraced precisely the combination of traits that Palamedes now maintains is impossible. Odysseus' charges once again better suit his own type than that of his victim; and once again, Palamedes' representation of Odysseus' accusations indicates the liar's key tactic of foisting his own famous characteristics onto his opponent.

Palamedes then states that wise men (τοὺς σοφοὺς ἀνδράς) are sensible (φρονίμους) rather than foolish (26); if Odysseus claims that he who is wise lacks understanding, then he is forging a novel argument but not a true one (καινὸς ὁ λόγος, ἀλλ' οὐκ ἀληθής, 26). That is, he is arguing against traditional ideas about character type and using novelty and deceit to distract the jury from this manifest inconsistency. We know from Cleon's speech in Thucydides that the clever, sophistic speaker fashions this kind of novel display to deceive his audience (μετὰ καινότητος μὲν λόγου ἀπατᾶσθαι, 3.38.24–25). It is Odysseus himself who is untrustworthy, as Palamedes has already suggested. "How," he asks, "would it be possible to trust a man who in the same speech says to the same men opposite things concerning the same issues?" (καίτοι πῶς χρὴ ἀνδρὶ τοιούτῳ πιστεύειν ὅστις τὸν αὐτὸν λόγον λέγων πρὸς τοὺς αὐτοὺς ἄνδρας περὶ τῶν αὐτῶν τὰ ἐναντιώτατα λέγει, 25). The phrase "says opposite things" (τὰ ἐναντιώτατα λέγει) brings to mind the most famous charge against the sophists: that they teach their students to argue equally well on both sides of the issue.[79] Moreover, it turns out that Odysseus speaks not only in a falsifying manner but also in an overly clever one (δεινὰ καὶ ψευδῆ, 28). Palamedes thus carefully differentiates between the respectable wise man and the dangerously clever man. In trying to shrug off the association with Odysseus' type that his charges have suggested, Palamedes highlights this image of the prudent, consistent man. He contrasts this type with the changeable cleverness that Odysseus has presented as characterizing him and for which Odysseus himself is famous.

Palamedes' emphasis on the necessary connection between wisdom and prudence is a conjunction that Aristotle regarded as the result of good training. In the *Nicomachean Ethics* he defines cleverness (δεινότητα) as the ability to fix means to ends. If the goal is a good one, this cleverness is praiseworthy; if a bad one, it is consonant with criminality or unscrupulousness (πανουργία). Both prudent or thoughtful men (φρονίμους) and unscrupulous men (πανούργους) may be called clever (δεινούς), since cleverness does not help one distinguish among the moral values of different ends

(1144a23–28). The characterization of one's opponent as *deinos*—that is, fearsomely clever at speechifying—had become a standard strategy in both tragedy and oratory by the late fifth century. The most famous disclaimer regarding this particular type of redoubtable cleverness was made by Socrates in Plato's *Apology* (οὐ δεινὸς λέγειν, *Ap.* 17b1), but the charge also turns up in tragedy (e.g., Eur. *Tro.* 968, fr. 439 N²; Soph. *Phil.* 440, *OT* 545; cf. the discussion in ch. 4).

These uses of the label *deinos* clearly encompass a stylistic attribution, as Palamedes' description of Odysseus' clever words (κατηγορημένον δεινά, *Pal.* 28) seems to, and as later notions of fearsome cleverness certainly do (e.g., Demetr. *Eloc.* 243–286; DH *Comp.* 18). The *deinos* speaker is a forceful, dazzling speaker, the extension of the term thus demarcating the style that reflects this startling and often dangerous cleverness.[80] As mentioned, Plato associates Odysseus with Thrasymachus and Theodorus (*Phdr.* 261c); Theodorus is also called a "speech embroiderer" (λογοδαίδαλον, *Phdr.* 266e4), a title Cicero takes as applying especially to Thrasymachus and Gorgias (*Orat.* 39). Plato further characterizes Thrasymachus as *deinos* and describes his style as emotive and stirring (ὀργίσαι) when he bewails (οἰκτρογόων) old age and poverty or casts verbal spells (ἐπᾴδων κηλεῖν) to calm his audience (*Phdr.* 267c–d). Elsewhere in Plato, Meno says that Gorgias himself declares that making speakers frighteningly clever (δεινούς) is the sole aim of his teaching, in a context that reveals the questionable nature of this goal (*Meno* 95c). In his set speech Gorgias portrays the clever but restrained Palamedes as concerned to dissociate himself from the *deinos* type who is also *panourgos*. This is precisely the combination that in tragedy comprises Odysseus' typical style and moral taint and that Plato thought certain sophists embodied. Palamedes instead associates himself with the clarity and simplicity of the man of visible virtue who trusts his eye and encourages others to do the same.[81]

Gorgias represents Palamedes' manner of speaking as also lucid and relatively plain. This is something of a departure for the sophist. Although the speech is still marked by his alliterative, antithetical style, Gorgias reins in his propensity for elaborate usage to suit Palamedes' straightforward character, as well as the forensic context. Throughout the history of ancient stylistic theory, this opposition between the grand, forceful style and the clear, simple style constitutes the most basic division between types of speech as well as types of speakers.[82] In the set piece attributed to Alcidamas, Odysseus charges Palamedes with a forceful cleverness of speech (τὴν δεινότητα τῶν λόγων, *Od.* 29; cf. 4), thus openly attributing to him a speaking style for which he (Odysseus) is the mythic paradigm. In Gorgias' speech, Palamedes' emphasis on clarity and simplicity seems designed to combat such erroneous attributions. Palamedes presents himself as patently the opposite of the startling, audacious speaker, who stirs up his audience and makes them believe that his opponent resembles his own bold and unscrupulous type.

Palamedes further dissociates himself from Odysseus by offsetting the slanderous label *panourgos* with a strong positive term. As mentioned, he twice claims the formal title of civic "good-deed doer" (εὐεργέτης) for himself (30, 36), emphasizing this distinction by a rehearsal of his inventions and good works. This label famously applies to monster-fighting heroes like Heracles and Theseus, whose efforts protect cities and maintain the borders of the civilized world.[83] As a formal title, εὐεργέτης is very common in fifth-century inscriptions, when the benefactor has done something notable for the public good and usually receives protection for himself, his family, and his property and relief from taxes (e.g., ΕΥΦΕΡΓΕΤΑΝ, Schwyzer 557).[84] Aristotle treats τιμή ("public honor") as a visible sign of this virtuous type (εὐεργετικός, *Rhet.* 1361a28; cf. 1366a38, 1388b12), which accords with the arguments Gorgias gives Palamedes about the visibly virtuous character.

In the final section of his speech, Palamedes turns to the judges (i.e., his fellow warriors), to exhort them one more time as eyewitnesses of his fine and high-minded character. He argues that since he has been accused, it is suitable (εἰκότα) for him to say something true (ἀληθές) about his reputation and to declare these truths before those who know them to be such (τι τῶν ἀληθῶν ἀγαθῶν εἰπεῖν ἐν εἰδόσιν ὑμῖν, 28). These witnesses know that his past life has been free from blame (ἀναμάρτητος, 29) and that his reputation as an inventor serves as further proof of his good character (30–31). All that is needed for the best men to be persuaded of the truth, Palamedes concludes, is the clearest justice (τῷ σαφεστάτῳ δικαίῳ), instruction in the truth (διδάξαντα τἀληθές), and a lack of deceit (οὐκ ἀπατήσαντά με, 33), that is, the kind of lucid, straightforward performance that is the inverse of the distracting, deceitful style that Odysseus represents. Earlier in his speech Palamedes implied that Odysseus was a dangerous teacher (4); we know from Sophocles that such teachers "disorder" character by means of their bad speeches. Palamedes thus presents himself as the kind of leader and instructor who can have the opposite effect on the polis.

In addition, Palamedes once again underscores that his type, unlike Odysseus' elusive one, is emphatically visible: he has invented the things that most benefit human society, which activity serves as a sign (σημεῖον), a visible proof,[85] that he is not the type to commit shameful acts (31). It now emerges that the governing theme of Palamedes' speech has been the connection of his kind of public, upstanding character to the public, concrete quality of eyewitness proof. As mentioned, Palamedes treats arguments from possibility and probability as also depending on the eyewitness account. He supports trust in such validity; Odysseus' elusive type signifies the fundamental challenge to it. Odysseus, as Palamedes has emphasized from the outset of his speech, does not know clearly (σαφῶς εἰδώς, 5) what he accuses. In fact, his character type is revealed by his ability to charge a man with something that he has not seen, as Palamedes later describes (22–24). In Gorgias' speech Palamedes makes Odysseus the embodiment of changeable opinion (δόξα), and himself the emblematic figure of a stable, visible truth (ἀλήθεια). He hopes that this lucid vantage point is shared by his fellow Greek leaders.

The sophist Gorgias, himself famous for his elaborate techniques and his impressive but putatively dangerous effect on students, has created in Palamedes his own antitype. The inventor of measuring techniques, counting devices, and possibly writing, Palamedes resembles more closely the precise and calculating sophist Prodicus. When Aristophanes calls Prodicus' student Euripides a "Palamedes" in the Frogs, he further supports this connection (1451). Prodicus was Gorgias' competitor and disputant, especially over stylistic issues. Gorgias is said to have ridiculed Prodicus for repeating the same carefully written composition on Heracles' ethical choice over and over again (Philostr. DK 82A24; see ch. 1). In Plato, however, Prodicus laughs (ἐγέλασεν) at Gorgias and Teisias for not recognizing that speeches should be of a carefully measured length (Phdr. 267b).[86]

The final arguments of the speech thus reinforce the sense in which Palamedes serves as a metarhetorical foil for Odysseus. Gorgias sets up Palamedes as a type of citizen whose high visibility promotes a dependence on the proof of sight, which in the oral performance of his defense should reinforce the "clarity" of his identity. The sophist who himself questions the validity of such proofs also manages to suggest indirectly that the accused man's dependence on the eyewitness ultimately indicates the epistemological challenge that Odysseus represents to such verification. Gorgias' performance of this speech, with his sophist's elaborate robes and dramatic delivery, would have drawn further attention to the difficulties inherent in "Palamedes'" claims of visible virtue and clear identity. Odysseus' signature techniques surface repeatedly in the strenuous response of his opponent, his bold and distracting accusations revealing the difficulties of offsetting the impact of his style. The story confirms this difficulty, of course, since Palamedes failed in the end to combat such audacious tactics and was put to death.

PS.-ALCIDAMAS' *ODYSSEUS*

The speech entitled *Odysseus on the Betrayal of Palamedes* (*Odysseus kata Palamêdous prodosias*) cannot be attributed or dated with any certainty. Many scholars now doubt that Alcidamas is its author, although a date around the middle of the fourth century is generally accepted.[87] As a companion to Gorgias' speech, it does not really engage in any detailed manner with the earlier and more interesting defense. It does, however, show Odysseus impugning the character of Palamedes by attributing to him (and his father) traits more often associated with Odysseus. The bulk of this rather lopsided speech is taken up with a prolix aside that seeks to prove Palamedes' genetic predisposition for treachery, as well as his excessive material need. These slanderous characterizations make way for the claim that Palamedes did not benefit Greek society in any way. The speech is thus interesting for us precisely because it expends so much energy on character assassination. While one might assume that Odysseus' actual speech would have been better composed, it does show him engaging in the tactics that can only be gleaned second-hand from Gorgias.

In the fashion of fourth-century set speeches (e.g., Isocrates' *Helen* and *Evagoras*), the introduction addresses a contemporary concern, concentrating a blanket attack on those who argue what they think their audiences want to hear in return for more money (1–3). The writer thus pillories types like the sophists and professional orators, with whom Odysseus was particularly associated. In Homer, Odysseus is a famous proponent of this response to the well-paying audience, when he agrees to tell a longer tale after the Phaeacians have offered him more gifts (*Od.* 11.339–353). We may thus recognize that from the outset Odysseus is represented as arguing against his own traditional type.

The introduction concludes with Odysseus claiming that he has had no previous dispute with Palamedes but that the latter is a technically knowledgeable (φιλοσοφός) and rhetorically clever (δεινός) type. Odysseus thus attributes to the accused a character more often associated with himself (*Od.* 4; cf. τὴν δεινότητα τῶν λόγων, 29). Further on, after he has presented the material evidence, he seeks to assure his audience that, although his opponent is a wise type (τοῦ σοφιστοῦ; ὃς φιλοσοφῶν, 12) and thus might seem to have little need of such dealings, he did indeed commit this treacherous act. To achieve conviction, he must prove that Palamedes is really the type to commit treason, by querying the moral tenor of his cleverness. Odysseus thus enters into a long excursus, during which he slanders Palamedes' father by characterizing him as engaged in every form of criminality (πανουργίας τε οὐδεμιᾶς λείπεται, 13) and rounds off the digression by again calling the son a sophist (τὸν σοφιστήν, 21).

Like the *deinos* man, one who is a *sophistês* may be overly clever. From the mid fifth century on, the term is used with the increasingly negative connotation of one who not only possesses a *technê*, a marketable skill or area of expertise, but who also uses it to cheat and deceive.[88] In the *Phaedrus* Socrates asks Phaedrus whether he is familiar with the oratorical training manuals (τεχνὰς . . . περὶ λογῶν) not only by Nestor and Odysseus but also by Palamedes, to which Phaedrus responds, "No, not even Nestor's, unless you mean to set up Gorgias as Nestor, or Thrasymachus and Theodorus as Odysseus" (καὶ ναὶ μὰ Δί' ἔγωγε τῶν Νέστορος, εἰ μὴ Γοργίαν Νέστορά τινα κατασκευάζεις, ἤ τινα Θρασύμαχόν τε καὶ Θεόδωρον Ὀδυσσέα, 261b6–8). Socrates agrees that he may well mean to use the Homeric figures in this way. The context suggests that these heroes, traditionally associated with language invention and use, had come to be treated as types whose characters distinguished oratorical styles[89] and whose invocation signaled particular professional orators or speechwriters. Slobodan Dušanić has argued that Palamedes should be identified with Alcidamas,[90] but he is known especially for a piece that argues against written composition and is treated by Aristotle as sharing Gorgias' grand style.[91] Thus if Palamedes were really meant to call to mind Alcidamas in the *Phaedrus* passage, there would be no real distinction between his style and that of Odysseus, since Odysseus' putative descendant Thrasymachus is teased only slightly later for his supreme handling of the grand style (*Phdr.* 267c). In this later passage, Plato puts forward Prodicus as the figure who differs most strongly from the rest of the sophists in his measured prose.

Given Plato's characterization of Thrasymachus, we might hazard that the *deinos* sophist was the kind of professional extemporaneous speaker particularly good at speaking forcefully on his feet, at character impersonation, and at emotional dramatization. He might also have been explicitly associated with fearsomely clever types such as Odysseus. His opposite would have been the careful, precise Prodicus, whose mythohistorical fore-father may well have been Palamedes. Note that in the *Phaedrus* Odysseus is equated with a negative sophistic type, while Palamedes is saved this indig-nity. At 261d Plato refers to the "Eleatic Palamedes," thus associating him also with Zeno, a thinker whose views Plato seems to have taken seriously and who, like Palamedes, was interested in calculation.[92]

Palamedes' type in Plato seems closer to contemporary thinkers who concerned themselves with precise kinds of measuring, definition, and cal-culation—whether of words or numbers—intellectual activities that Plato also thought worthwhile.[93] By linking Palamedes to the clever sophistic type, then, Ps.-Alcidamas portrays Odysseus as once again foisting onto his opponent the imposing dangerous traits that better suit his own persona.

A few more instances of this projection of character type in Ps.-Alcida-mas' speech further support the idea that it is Odysseus' special technique. These instances also point to characteristics that distinguish the styles of contemporary poets and sophists. After he has completed his long and rather inconclusive history of Palamedes' family background, Odysseus repre-sents Palamedes himself as a deceiver and artful persuader of the young (ἐξαπατῶν τοὺς νέους καὶ παραπείθων, 22). Once again he depicts an *êthos* that far more precisely matches his own character type than that of the ac-cused. His charges also recall the sophists, particularly his kind of sophist: the dangerous teacher and deceiver of young men. Deceit, moreover, is a technique especially associated with the proponents of the grand style; both Aeschylus and Gorgias are most famously its masters.[94] This forceful, emo-tive style involves the pervasive use of metaphors and highblown com-pounds; words are chosen for their impact rather than for their precision. The result is a kind of deceit, a distracting enchantment that stuns the lis-tener so that any concern with accuracy is forgotten.

Similarly, Odysseus charges Palamedes with lying (ψευδόμενος, 23) about his inventions, maintaining that the only things he did discover were measuring tools for hucksters and lowlifes (καπήλοις καὶ ἀγοραίοις ἀν-θρώποις); the game of draughts (πεττούς), which creates strife and abuse among idlers (τοῖς ἀργοῖς τῶν ἀνδρῶν ἔριδας καὶ λοιδορίας); and that of dice-throwing (κύβους), which brings pain and losses for some, as well as derision and disgrace for the losers (τοῖς μὲν ἡττηθεῖσι λύπας καὶ ζημίας, τοῖς δὲ νενικηκόσι καταγέλωτα καὶ ὄνειδος) (27). Odysseus has saved the direct discussion of character for last, but the character he presents as that of his opponent looks far more like the most negative version of his own: a liar, a forceful deceiver of the young, a creator of strife who makes others appear ridiculous by means of his underhanded dealings. His final warning to the jury about the clever (δεινότηια, 29) quality of Palamedes' speech aims to fix in the minds of his listeners a portrait of the *deinos sophistês* that he himself embodies.

ANTISTHENES' *AJAX* AND *ODYSSEUS*

The tradition surrounding the dispute over Achilles' arms depicts Ajax retrieving Achilles' body while Odysseus held off the troops (i.e., defended Ajax). In the *Little Iliad* (scholion on Ar. *Eq.* 1056), this arrangement made a Trojan girl decide that Odysseus deserved the arms, since he was the one who engaged in battle (which only a man could do), while Ajax did the carrying (which any woman could do). This inversion of roles—from defensive to defended, masculine to feminine—seems to signal a turn in Ajax's fortunes. In Sophocles' version of his story, this reversal is suggested by his entrapment in encircling spatial patterns that trace in visible terms his defensive character.[95] Sophocles' relatively gentle depiction of Odysseus in the same play highlights his mobile, flexible type and his emphasis on fair exchange, recalling his dominant traits and speaking style in the *Iliad*. Sophocles did not, however, include the *agôn* between Ajax and Odysseus over the arms, a scene that Pindar had already invested with negative significance, precisely in connection to Odysseus' lying style (cf. the discussion in ch. 4).[96]

In two set speeches attributed to Antisthenes and dated toward the end of the fifth century (ca. 415–410), the author gives Ajax arguments that resemble in general outlook those of Palamedes and shows Odysseus employing a technique similar to that found in the speeches of Gorgias and Ps.-Alcidamas.[97] Antisthenes reveals his admiration of Odysseus' techniques in a more direct fashion than Gorgias, however; and his representation of Odysseus' style better befits the rhetorically adept hero than does the badly structured speech of Ps.-Alcidamas. In Antisthenes' depiction of the terse and angry Ajax, the speaker emphasizes, like Gorgias' Palamedes, the importance of the eyewitness account of what transpired on the battlefield. His arguments border on a blunt rudeness and are less clever than those of Palamedes, as befits the terse man of action.

A notably brief but effective speaker in the embassy scene of *Iliad* 9, Ajax gains a greater concession from Achilles than does Odysseus, for all the latter's genial and well-balanced style. In Antisthenes' depiction, Ajax is no less brutally direct; his phrases tend to be short, with frequent end-stops and simple vocabulary. As a good soldier who belongs on the battlefield rather than in the lawcourt, he highlights the gap between word and deed, abruptly pointing out to the jurors that since they were not present, they do not know what happened, while the issue at hand lies in the deed itself (τὸ δὲ πρᾶγμα ἐγίνετο ἔργῳ, *Aj.* 1; cf. 4). Ajax accuses Odysseus of winning Achilles' arms unfairly and impugns the character of his opponent as a type directly opposite to his own: a wordsmith and stealthy strategist rather than an active and open combatant (5). The angry soldier repeatedly stresses the differences in ethical character between this behind-the-scenes type and the man who deals only in full view of his comrades (3, 5, 6; cf. 8). He thereby accentuates the importance of being able to see a man's character through his actions and achievements, again like Palamedes. Ajax declares that the Trojans would have hidden (ἀπέκρυψαν) Achilles' arms, fearing that Odysseus might obtain them and parade them (ἐπεδείκνυτο) in front of the Achaean army. Such a display would, however, highlight the mismatch between the arms and the man; Ajax also charges that Odysseus intends to sell the arms, being too craven in type to wear them himself. No cowardly man, he says, would use them, knowing that the famous arms would reveal his cowardice (τὴν δειλίαν αὐτοῦ ἐκφαίνει τὰ ὅπλα, 3).

Oppositions between things visible and invisible proliferate in Ajax's speech. He contrasts the Trojan's potential hiding (ἀπέκρυψαν) of Achilles' arms with Odysseus' potential display (ἐπεδείκνυτο) of them, which would in turn reveal (ἐκφαίνει) his character (3). Ajax opposes acting openly (φανερῶς), as he does—a *hexis* that he urges the jury to emulate—to acting in secret (λάθρᾳ), as Odysseus usually does (5; cf. φανερῶς vs. κρύβδην, 8). Finally, he emphasizes the difference between Odysseus' words and the staunch hero's deeds (εἰς τοὺς λόγους, εἰς τὰ ἔργα; λόγῳ . . . ἔργῳ; λόγος πρὸς ἔργον, 7). Ajax sounds themes that reverberate throughout the texts we have considered here: the visibility of character type, Odysseus' eluding of the eye, his use of a deceptive style to achieve this, and the possible gap that his *hexis* suggests between the type one shows to the world and one's true identity.

At the end of his blunt speech, Ajax claims that he alone (μόνος) defended the Achaeans "without walls" (ἄνευ τείχους), while Odysseus was unwilling even to approach the city (9). This adjective marking the solitary fighter parallels the word's prominence in Sophocles' play, where it also suggests the hero's isolating anger (Soph. *Aj.* 29, 47, 349, 461, 467, 511, 796,

1276, 1283). Throughout Antisthenes' speech, Ajax is depicted as striving to set himself apart from Odysseus. This solitary figure shares no elements of typical style with his enemy; he is not "like-mannered" (ὁμοιότροπον), as he notes (Antisth. *Aj.* 5). Ajax's blunt, straightforward style, like his steadfast type, can brook neither physical disguises nor misleading locutions.

Odysseus' speech is a third again as long, and while its vocabulary and rhythm differ only slightly from that of Ajax, an analysis of its style at the level of invention reveals some beautifully executed versions of Odysseus' character reversals. Odysseus opens his speech with a phrase that is structured in such a way as to signal these reversals from the outset, picking up immediately on Ajax's characterization of himself as the sole defense of the Achaeans and as the man who opposes words with deeds. "My speech is not directed at you only," he says to Ajax (Οὐ πρὸς σέ μοι μόνον ὁ λόγος, 1), sandwiching himself (μοι) between his opponent (σέ) and the label he claims (μόνον). Here Odysseus sets himself off from his comrades, pointedly addressing them as a group (ἀλλὰ καὶ πρὸς τοὺς ἄλλους ἅπαντας) and claiming that he has done more for the Greek army than any of them (πλείω γὰρ ἀγαθὰ πεποίηκα τὸ στρατόπεδον ἐγὼ ἢ ὑμεῖς ἅπαντες) (1). He thereby not only situates himself in relation to the claim of being a solitary fighter, he also opens his speech (λόγος) with a boast about his deeds (πλείω . . . πεποίηκα). The strategies that Odysseus then depicts himself as engaging in further separate him from the rest of the army. He repeatedly accentuates the solitary dangers he has risked and highlights his singular type as always vigilant and ready for action, no matter what his attire (1, 2, 7, 8, 9, 10). The word *monos* resurfaces a number of times in these arguments (as does *hen*, "one, alone"). After first separating the label *monos* from Ajax's name in the suggestive manner described, Odysseus reverses its heroic implications in relation to Ajax and then resurrects it in relation to himself. Finally, he firmly affixes the label to the series of his Homeric epithets that he unfurls at the end of his speech.

Odysseus combats Ajax's charge of cowardice (δειλίαν, 6) by questioning the idea that a soldier with a huge shield could really be considered to fight bravely "without a wall." He claims that Ajax is in fact the only man who goes about enwrapped in his own wall (μόνος μὲν οὖν σύ γε ἑπταβόειον περιέρχῃ τεῖχος προβαλλόμενος ἑαυτοῦ, 7). He further declares that the soldier who wears undamaged arms (ὅπλα . . . ἄρρηκτα καὶ ἄτρωτα, 7), as Ajax does, is the most craven (δειλότατον) and most afraid of death (7). The claim directly inverts Ajax's charge that Odysseus is too cowardly to wear Achilles' arms by suggesting that if, as Ajax says, the arms display the man, those of the hulking fence of the Achaeans (ἕρκος Ἀχαιῶν, *Il*. 6.5, 7.11) reveal his own cowardice. While the man of open force is refigured as one who lurks behind his enormous shield, the man of stealth and disguise becomes the true protector of the Achaean army, the guardian (φύλαξ) of the troops (8). Only his own unarmed entrance within the Trojan walls could truly be deemed fighting without walls (ἐγὼ δὲ ἄοπλος . . . εἰς αὐτὰ εἰσέρχομαι τὰ τείχη, 8).

The use of disguise is represented as the noble stratagem of the man prepared for any manner of fighting (ὅντινα ἐθέλει τις τρόπον, 9), his versatility directly opposing the consistency invoked by Ajax. His perpetual readiness even in the dark of night, which for Ajax only marks his craftiness (*Aj*. 3, 6), constitutes, according to Odysseus, the most solid defense of the Achaeans (*Od*. 10). In the end, Ajax is characterized as one of the herd, a man who represents the group (like Odysseus in tragedy). Meanwhile Odysseus rehearses his multifaceted and unique status: much enduring (πολύτλαντα), full of cunning and strategies (πολύμητιν καὶ πολυμήχανον), city-sacker (πτολίπορθον), and finally, sole taker of Troy (μόνον τὴν Τροίαν ἑλόντα, 14). His multiplicity and his singularity are thus triumphantly joined in a parade of epithets that echoes the famous opening of the *Odyssey*.

In Sophocles' *Ajax*, Athena reveals to Odysseus that the maddened hero has been trapped by "nets" of her making (ἕρκη, Soph. *Aj*. 60), using the word that signals the defensive nature of Ajax's own Homeric character (ἕρκος Ἀχαιῶν). Antisthenes' *Odysseus* establishes a similar reversal: Ajax's famous "wall" of a shield (τεῖχος, 7) reveals instead his cowardice. Meanwhile, Odysseus, shielded only by the "armor" of the beggar (τὰ δουλοπρεπῆ ταῦτα ὅπλα, 10), sits within the Trojan walls, the sole defense of the snoring bulwark of the Achaeans.

STYLE AND THE VERSATILE TYPE

From the late fifth century on, the word *tropos* means not only character or disposition but also style.[98] This development points to the increasing theorization of the connections between attitude and stylistic elements, connections captured by Bourdieu's concepts of *habitus* and bodily *hexis*. This confluence can be apprehended visually through one's dress, deportment, meaningful actions, or public achievements, and mentally through visual metaphor. According to Porphyry (scholion on *Od*. 1.1), Antisthenes analyzed Odysseus' most famous epithet *polutropos* as applying equally to his character and his speech; the *polutropos* man had a firm grasp of many *tropoi* (i.e., turns of speech). *Tropos* in Antisthenes' set piece *Odysseus* (9) refers to one's manner of dress and appearance rather than one's speech, but the three meanings of *tropos* that Antisthenes apparently associated with Odysseus—character, speaking style, and manner of dress—in fact constitute the elements central to the liar's fabrication of type. Antisthenes' usage suggests that by the end of the fifth century, Odysseus' mutability of character was understood to extend to his verbal style and that this might in turn be reflected in his changeable dress. Thus his entire bodily *hexis*—from his shifting disguises to his shifting verbal associations—could now be understood to be encapsulated in his signature epithet *polutropos*.

While Antisthenes, most probably like other earlier rhetorical theorists,[99] regarded Odysseus' *polutropos* character in a positive light, Plato's portrait of the sophist Hippias depicts him as attempting to follow the dramatists' wisdom in condemning the versatile type. The *Hippias Minor* contains what is perhaps the most familiar argument for the connection between *polutropia* and Odysseus' corporeal style. The sophist Hippias distinguishes Achilles from Odysseus by opposing their character types as "very simple" (ἁπλούστατος) and "multifaceted" (πολύτροπος, 364e),[100] and seeks to support this differentiation by quoting Achilles on Odysseus' deceptive style in *Iliad* 9.308–313. Hippias' argument is important for its connections between character and style and between *polutropia* and *panourgia*. Socrates inquires whether liars are versatile (πολύτροποι) and deceiving (ἀπατεῶνες) out of stupidity or an evil cunning (ὑπὸ πανουργίας), to which Hippias responds confidently that they are changeable deceivers due to the latter.[101]

Socrates ultimately scuttles Hippias' distinctions by parodying the sophists' analytical techniques, but the dialogue nevertheless provides a useful portrait of conventional thought about the liar's type and specifically about Odysseus' connections to the sophists. Hippias condemns Odysseus, but the joke is (as is usually the case in Plato) on the sophist. Hippias himself serves as a parody of a man whose bodily *hexis* trumpets his overly versatile type. Not only does he know all the *technai*, having made his entire fancy outfit from his engraved ring to his shoes, but he also claims to be capable of writing speeches in many different styles (368b–d).[102] His virtuoso qualities associate him with the *polutropos* type whose abilities run the gamut from costuming to speechwriting. Both portray character in a visible manner and treat it as capable of being altered at will, like a change of dress.

This kind of versatility and the oratorical strategies associated with it may not have been considered unethical in themselves, although the fancily dressed, dramatic, and too facile sophistic speechwriter was certainly regarded with suspicion during the late fifth and early fourth centuries.[103] The manipulations of *êthos* on which I have focused here, of exchanging type with one's opponent or at least dislodging his claims to being a visibly virtuous type, are techniques that became favored in the courts and the Assembly during the fourth century. Demosthenes, for example, often masterfully emphasized his similarity to his audience (e.g., *Against Meidias* 1–8), while Aeschines' *Against Timarchus* is a brilliant example of the kind of suggestive slander that distracts one's audience from one's own reputed type.[104] In the *Rhetoric* Aristotle associates the former technique (i.e., suiting one's character to audience type) with a sense of appropriateness (*prepês, oikeios*, 1408a), an idea whose rhetorical importance may echo Antisthenes' discussion of the *oikeios logos* (frs. 47a, 47b C).[105] For Antisthenes this adjective in its rhetorical application indicates the adaptability with which the *polutropos* man suits his speaking style, and perhaps especially his manner of self-representation, to that of his audience (fr. 51 C). Sly as this technique may be—and Aristotle does say that its employment must be hidden from the audience (*Rhet.* 1404b20)—the technique of character appropriation or projection is somewhat more so. In the *Gorgias* and the *Ion*, for instance, Socrates suggests that rhetors and rhapsodes appropriate the roles of others and mimic their knowledge. For the moral theorist this is a dangerously seductive skill that encourages misguided judgments.

In relation to these two techniques, the fifth-century deployment of *pan*-words to describe the character of Odysseus lies in the moral measure it provides, which distinguishes it from uses of *polu*- words, as in the Homeric *polutropos, polumêtis, polumêchanos*. The two prefixes indicate multiplicity rather than singularity, but *pan*- connotes a profligate inclusivity. Compare again labels commonly affixed to Odysseus during the later period: πανοῦργος, πανώλης, πᾶσα βλαβή, as well as Sophocles' expanded epithet, ὁ πάντ' ἀκούων αἰσχρὰ καὶ λωβῆτ' ἔπη (*Phil.* 607–608). One who will "do everything," or who will take on any character, is not a trustworthy type. As an epithet of Odysseus in the classical period, *panourgos* highlights the unethical versatility that marks the style of the *polutropos* hero.

In the development of rhetorical technique and theory, then, Odysseus comes to signal the troubling aspects of the orator's job, particularly as it overlaps with the rhapsode's in respect to the impersonation of another's character. Indeed, by the fifth century, Odysseus is no longer a figure so much for the poet as for the rhetor, when oratory was developing as the new arena in which the disturbing possibilities of convincing character representation surface. Aristotle worried about the persuasive power of delivery, considering it properly the actor's realm (*Rhet.* 1404a). Like the Homeric bard, the orator was most often both author and performer, a conflation of roles that provides the greatest opportunity for effective character impersonation in the volatile context of the oral performance. Later rhetorical training would come to center on the practice of *êthopoiia:* the invention of speeches to represent suitably the character of the (usually mythic) speaker. In the fraught political climate of the late fifth century, writers associated Odysseus' penchant for disguise with persuasive techniques that make overly clever use of the most manipulative aspects of character representation. This constituted an important development in Greek thinking about style, but it also led to the further denigration of the hero's versatile type.

Helen's figure in the same period came to inspire an equally important elaboration of the nature of oral technique. In Sappho's fragment 16 she exemplifies a proto-rhetorical relationship between the lover and the object of praise, which attributes to the mechanics of *erôs* the same kind of circular relationship that marks the reciprocity of encomiastic invention. As Gorgias' treatment of Helen makes clear, the beautiful form draws toward it those who are themselves excellent in many ways.[106] Her magnetic body is also represented as especially sensitive to the beauty and magnetism of others; this quality has its sensory parallel in an elaborate oral style. Gorgias emphasizes in the *Encomium of Helen* that speech itself has a body, a form or style analogous in its quasi-visible impact to the beautiful body it attracts. This envisioning of *logos* can best be understood in the context of the oral performance, where the elaborate outfit and grand style of Gorgias' own enactment would have similarly startled his audience.

The moral difficulties that the figures of Odysseus and Helen embodied for the poets during the late fifth century were largely avoided by the rhetorical theorists. For these writers, they represent instead types singularly useful in demonstrating stylistic technique and in arguing about the nature of style itself. Odysseus' manipulations of character type and Helen's embodiment of the entrancing *logos* elaborate aspects of the grand style of oratory and thus suggest the potentially dangerous qualities of the dazzling oral performance. The grand style is a deceptive style, and while the grace-ful arcs of its metaphors may please the eye (as it were), they may also cause one to forget oneself and therefore such relatively mundane concerns as accuracy or morality.

The Athenians were themselves susceptible to the startling effects of this style, and its visualizing power continued to sway audiences for centuries to come. For all that Plato and Aristotle criticize the flamboyant strategies of this oral mode, later speechwriters and rhetorical theorists would acknowl-edge the importance of Gorgias and his followers in the development of ideas about style. Because of the tactics it shared with the enchantment of poetry, the grand oral performance emerged as the prototype in relation to which essential stylistic distinctions might be made. This entailed that the visualizing, elaborate style was also frequently regarded with suspicion, even as it was just as frequently defended for its vibrancy and persuasive power. The grand style itself thus has a long history of praise and blame, much like its emblematic figures, Helen and Odysseus.

CONCLUSION

περιεβάλλετο δὲ καὶ ποιητικὰ ὀνόματα ὑπὲρ κόσμου καὶ
σεμνότητος.

[Gorgias] dressed up even poetic words with
ornament and grandeur.

PHILOSTRATUS

Dionysius of Halicarnassus begins his treatise *On Literary Composition* with
an elaborately worded dedication to Rufus Metilius, in which he compares
his literary offering to the embroidered gown that Helen gives the departing
Telemachus in book 15 of the *Odyssey*. With its use of *paronomasia* (assonance)
and the *figura etymologica*, the opening bears some resemblance to the ornate
and chiming style of Gorgias. Although his essay covers the basic components of literary composition, Dionysius is concerned throughout with
the aesthetics of the written word, what he terms the "pleasurable" (*hêdeia*)
qualities of composition. At one point, he compares the process of composition (σύνθεσις) to Athena's molding of Odysseus' appearance (4; citing
Od. 6 and 16). At another, he maintains that the composition of good style
(λέξις) is to the ear what good sculpture and painting are to the eye (10).
Correlations between ear and eye thus surface a number of times in the treatise. At one point taste is included (12), but the primary sense that is used as
an analogy for literary style is sight. Here and in his related essay *Demosthe-*

nes, Dionysius relies on objects of sight, and especially clothed bodies in the visual field, to communicate his sense of what style is and what constitutes its most pleasing and effective forms (cf. also *Comp.* 23; *Dem.* 18, 21, 50).

Dionysius was writing in Rome at the end of the first century B.C.E., during a period when Cicero had already established style as the primary subject matter for the rhetorical theorist (*Orat.* 43–44). Dionysius' larger project is the defense of Atticism, a purity of literary style associated by the Roman intellectual elite with classical Athenian writers.[1] As an antiquarian, he has a learned and somewhat nostalgic respect for the literary composers of archaic and classical Greece. He often cites Homer to demonstrate certain stylistic virtues, and he treats earlier writers as fully cognizant of stylistic differences and of the appropriate match between style and subject matter. Dionysius' references to Helen and Odysseus and his use in his opening address of Gorgianic prose style makes *On Literary Composition* a fitting latter-day point from which to review the material on which this book focuses. More important, the treatise gives explicit expression to associations that were central to earlier conceptions of the role of style in persuasive speaking, especially regarding the interconnections between the visual field and stylistic effects.

The negative reactions of Plato and Aristotle to the ornate oral style and to its foremost proponent Gorgias thus eventually gave way, in the rhetorical if not the philosophical tradition, to a recognition of this style's vibrancy and power. Like Cicero, Dionysius considers the deployment of compelling imagery useful rather than dangerous in persuasive settings. For them, visuality has become merely an important aspect of certain styles, as well as a means of tracing their effects. Both Cicero and Dionysius may regard the so-called Asiatic style as somewhat overly emotive and ornate, but these characteristics no longer indicate the problems with style itself, as they did for Athenian writers of the classical period. Nor do these writers suggest that characters who utilize such grand techniques pose a moral threat to the community. Instead, they harken back to a more archaic attitude toward persuasive speech, one that appreciates the honey-tongued speaker and attempts to characterize what makes his speech so effective.

It is these earlier attitudes and their transformation in the moral climate of the classical period that this discussion has explored. The inclusive understanding of style as revolving around speech in performance—a whole-body experience of language that is bound up in its sensory effects—allows for the recognition of the ways in which early ideas about style developed.

In the absence of any overarching theoretical discussion, I have looked to poets and prose writers for indications of an awareness of this eyewitness experience and have sought to demonstrate that there was in fact wide-spread recognition of stylistic effect.

The figures of Helen and Odysseus uniquely crystallize central notions of style during this earlier period; yet this is clearly only the beginning of a discussion. Other literary figures may well signify other aspects of style in the development of pre-Aristotelian ideas about the topic. Indeed, many of these ideas center not only around particular figures but also around particular body parts, an obvious one being the mouth. The performative perspective captured by the notions of corporeal style and bodily *hexis*, which embrace both the verbal and the visual elements of self-presentation, enriches our understanding of the far-reaching significance of this physicalized conception of language. The recognition that character type has a similarly far-reaching semiotic significance is also central to this approach. Certain "casts" of character trace certain ideas about style in an emblematic, visualizing manner. It is thus not merely that visuality informs early ways of understanding stylistic impact but also that it shapes the very means by which characters like Helen and Odysseus function as metonyms for crucial aspects of that impact.

These figures are thus treated as visually recognizable emblems of the visually oriented, overwhelming, and head-turning effects of style and are aligned with those poets and sophists who implemented its techniques in the most agile fashion. Characters in poetic tradition and the plots that establish their typical behaviors become schemas for the assigning of rhetorical type: if the precise Prodicus is a "Palamedes," the manipulative Thrasymachus is an "Odysseus," and so on. Archaic, and especially Homeric, representation provided the source material for a stylistic taxonomy that remained rooted in narrative and in ideas about visible type. Witness, for example, the durability of *charaktêr* as the stylistic stamp that distinguished one famous orator in Greek tradition from another.

Moreover, the Homeric portrayals of Helen and Odysseus as versatile and profoundly suitable speakers suggest that their types were paradigmatic of precisely these central stylistic concerns. From early on, then, their characters are represented as deploying particularly suitable styles; more important, however, aspects of their figures signify the core aspects of style more generally. This crucial semiotic function contributed to their mixed reception in the classical period. Like the fifth-century depictions of Helen, those of Odysseus range from an ambiguous censure, where the techniques condemned are also those central to poetic composition, to a studied defense, where the techniques admired are also those central to oratorical performance.

Thus the dramatists often show awareness of the dangers of theatrical illusion, while prose writers trained in sophistic technique either promote or react against its spectacular effects. In fourth-century legal cases, speakers made frequent use of their opponent's visible types as a means of impugning their morals. This is itself a technique perfected by the sophists; fourth-century orators also often deride each other as sophists, in implicit recognition of this legacy. The sophists, like Helen and Odysseus, met with suspicion because of their versatile persuasive styles and their luxurious appearances. Like the figures they championed, their types did not conform sufficiently to the conflicted mandates of the consensus-driven democracy.[2] They looked like tyrants, with their elaborate robes and commanding attitudes; their speeches had a tyrannical effect on their audiences. They could alter their visible characters at will and draw their audiences into a nebulous swirl of imagery. Archaic and classical depictions of such speakers indicate a pervasive awareness of the power of their performances and a recognition that submission to their charms (as to those of a beautiful form) may lead to disaster. But these depictions also invigorate an appreciation of style as a lived experience, what Kenneth Burke once called the "dancing of an attitude."[3] This is the understanding of style that I have sought to uncover in Greek literature and that had a profound effect on later rhetorical theory.

NOTES

INTRODUCTION

1. Unless otherwise indicated, all translations are my own.

2. By "visualizing" I mean a verbal style that fosters mental images by means of the depiction of visual details and the use of figurative language. Collins 1991: 1 calls this deployment of envisioning strategies "verbal visuality." This is a useful distinction, since most words that designate such description in common usage only denote the mental picture formed by the reader rather than the writer's written imagery. Cf. Demetrius, for example, who cites Theophrastus as saying that the "beauty" of a word (κάλλος ὀνόματος) is what gives pleasure to the ear or eye (ἐστι τὸ πρὸς τὴν ἀκοὴν ἤ πρὸς τὴν ὄψιν ἡδύ) (*Eloc.* 173). This stylistic visuality takes different forms in Homer as opposed to Gorgias (for example), and within literary depiction may characterize quite different types. It is usually accompanied by a visually striking performance, either that portrayed in fictional settings (e.g., the gleaming garments and riveting face of Helen in the *Iliad*) or that known to be typical of actual performers (e.g., the ornate dress and lavish gestures of the rhapsodes, sophists, or tragic actors). This book focuses primarily on descriptions of the visualizing style of characters in literature, although it includes the scant details of styles in cultural arenas where these are available.

3. See DH *Comp.* 10, 12, 23; also *Dem.* 53, where he highlights the importance of delivery (i.e., the visible use of the body); and cf. Arist. *Rhet.* 1403b–1404a; Demetr. *Eloc.* 14, 27–28; Cic. *Orat.* 36, 54–60; Quint. *Inst. Orat.* 11.1.3; Herm. *Peri Ideiôn* 3.21.

4. Other scholars have noticed this, particularly in regard to the sophists, but not in relation to ideas about style: cf. Enos 1993; Gagarin 1994; Poulakos 1995; Schiappa 1999. Poulakos 1996 differentiates between Plato's and Aristotle's receptions of the sophists.

5. These are the two primary social categories that Bourdieu considers significant; see Bourdieu 1991: 81–89. See Gleason 1995 for the application of Bourdieu's concepts to figures of the Second Sophistic. Gleason emphasizes the training of masculine deportment and offers numerous examples of speakers' visible features. The material I analyze does not always provide as many concrete details as these later texts, in part because the notion of training in some concerted, institutionalized fashion is largely absent. I am, in any case, more concerned with literary representation than with reconstructions of social phenomena, and with how these earlier representational schemas delineate ideas about style without necessarily enumerating many details of the stylistic features themselves. See also Lateiner 1995, for the application of sociological theory to indications of deportment in Homer; and cf. Boegehold 1999 on ancient gesture, although he does not invoke Bourdieu or sociological concepts and is more interested in attempting to reconstruct actual performative deportment.

6. See, e.g., *Catg.* 8b25–9a13; *NE* 1103a26–b25, 1104a11–b3, 1105b19–1106a13. Plato also uses the word (e.g., *Tht.* 153b) to denote bodily habit (cf. also the Hippocratic corpus, e.g., *Alim.* 34, *Mochl.* 41). The word seems to be generally confined to prose, but cf. also Orph. *Arg.* 391.

7. Note that the Latin word *habitus* designates a notion of habitual state similar to *hexis*, and may include visible effects of that state such as appearance and deportment. Elsewhere Bourdieu [1972] 1977 uses the word *ethos* to indicate social habit, emphasizing the connections between the regularized mores of a group and the predictable behavior of the individual (e.g., 77, 94). Cf. the false etymology that originates with Aristotle (ἡ δ' ἠθικὴ ἐξ ἔθους περιγίνεται, *NE* 1103b17).

8. Bourdieu [1980] 1990: 69–70.

9. Bourdieu [1980] 1990: 66–79. That these habits are the result of historical entrenchment of social categories—rather than coming to be in a neutral environment, without a specific history or hierarchized notion of power relations—is essential to understanding the approaches against which Bourdieu is arguing. For Bourdieu, the structural analyses of language initiated by Saussure are undertaken in a vacuum, in which linguistic features are treated as autonymous, affected only by a logic internal to the language that manifests them (Bourdieu 1991: 44–46). This approach thus fails to take account of social context, and therefore of the power relations that shape discourses. The Marxist influence that is evident in Bourdieu's theories further reinforces this notion of attitudes and beliefs as having a history, the visible evidence of which is effectively written on the body. See also Butler 1996.

10. Bourdieu [1980] 1990: 69–70. This conceptual zeugma is essential to the development of ancient Greek ideas about style; see further below and in ch. 1.

11. See, e.g., Foucault 1985: 90, where he quotes Socrates' declaration in the *Republic* that a beautiful character (καλὰ ἤθη) combined with a beautiful form (εἴδει) forge a miraculous harmony (*Rep.* 402d1–4).

12. Foucault 1985: 91, 97.

13. Foucault 1985: 92.

14. A number of other theorists define style in ways that emphasize this more integrated understanding of its parameters: see, e.g., Burke 1957, 1969; Goodman [1975] 1978; B. Lang (ed.) [1974] 1987, esp. the contribution of Meyer.

15. Butler 1990: 139–141. For explicit ancient parallels, compare Cicero's phrase *sermo corporis* (*De orat.* 3.59) and Quintillian's catalog of gestures and general deportment (*Inst. orat.* 11.3), although both of these discussions have to do with physical attitudes as distinguished from verbal style. Elsewhere it is clear that Butler also regards class status and its intersecting power hierarchies as crucially molding one's stylized self-performance (Butler 1996, 1997); in this she also follows Bourdieu and Foucault.

16. Herzfeld 1985: 10, 16.

17. See, e.g., Martin 1989; Gleason 1995; Bassi 1998; Goldhill and Osborne (eds.) 1999; Porter (ed.) 1999. Performance theory has developed through the efforts of theorists from a number of different disciplines, many of whom regard everyday life as "performative" and drama as a particularly elaborate form of such performances: see, e.g., Goffman 1959 (sociology); Turner 1974, Schechner 1985 (anthropology); Wilshire 1982, Garner 1994 (phenomenology); Butler 1990 (gender theory).

18. What I am calling "settings" is roughly equivalent to Bourdieu's notion of "fields" (*champs*) of social practice, although Bourdieu sometimes treats these as if they were only intellectual arenas (e.g., literature, art, religion) rather than also social settings. See Bourdieu [1980] 1990: 113–120.

19. Cf. Bourdieu 1991: 109–113.

20. Burke 1969: 121. The quote is from the chapter entitled "The World of Clothes" in *Sartor Resartus*.

21. *Rhet.* 1405a13–14; see further discussion in ch. 1.

22. E.g., Hdt. 1.107; Aesch. *PV* 11; Antis. *Od.* 9, scholion on *Od.* 1.1 (fr. 51 C); Pl. *Rep.* 398c; Isoc. *Antid.* 45.

23. Goldhill and Osborne (eds.) 1999: 4–5. E.g., Soph. *Phil.* 223; Eur. *Bacch.* 832, *Med.* 1072; Arist. *Poet.* 1447a19.

24. Cf. Foucault 1985. This is also true in contemporary communities, as Bourdieu has argued. In the modern era such categories have tended to be perceived as superficial and restrictive rather than as fundamentally constitutive of human communication.

25. As with the term *charaktêr*, which I discuss in some detail in ch. 1, one of the early uses of *tupos* designated the authentic stamp on a seal or a coin (e.g., Aesch. *Supp.* 282; Eur. *Hipp.* 862; Pl. *Tht.* 192a). But the word also commonly denoted image, pattern, or replica (e.g., Hdt. 2.86, 2.138; Eur. *Phoen.* 1130, *Rh.* 305; Pl. *Rep.* 396e), as well as model, style, type, or general character (Democr. DK 68B228; Pl. *Rep.* 402d, *Tht.* 171e; DH *Pomp.* 4; Herm. *Peri Ideiôn* 2.11). The adjective *tupikos* only comes into use late (Plu. *Mor.* 2.442c; Gal. 7.471). For my purposes it is primarily important that the noun embraces ideas of visibility, similarity, and recognizability.

26. Most scholars think that attention to probability only arose in the mid to late fifth century with the sophists' development of argumentative techniques, and follow Plato (*Phdr.* 267a, 272d–273d) and Aristotle (*Rhet.* 1402a17) in attributing the elaboration of probability arguments to Teisias and/or Corax (cf. Cic. *Brut.* 46–48). But some recognition of likeness and therefore likelihood is evident as early as Homer (see the discussion in ch. 2); cf. G. E. R. Lloyd 1979: 78n. 93. For *eikos* arguments, see, e.g., Gorg. *Pal.* (discussed further in ch. 5); Agathon *TGF* 39f9; Antiph. 1.1.3, 2.4.8, 5.26; Lys. 7.38, 12.27, 24.16; Pl. *Phdr.* 272d–273d; Arist. *Rhet.* 1376a17–23, 1402a17–28 (cf. Kuebler 1944; also Kennedy 1963: 30–31; Salvioni 1985: 6–7, 45–51; Cole 1991: 96–97; Enos 1993: 77–78; Poulakos 1983; Baumhauer 1986: 135–144; Poulakos 1995: 60–63; Gagarin 1994; Schiappa 1999: 36–37; Usher 1999: 3, 24; Hose 2000). The notion of suitability (*to prepon*) is discussed by Aristotle in relation to style (*Rhet.* 1408a) and how to make the details of one's narrative suitable to the character (*êthos*) one describes. This will add to plausibility (*Rhet.* 1417a); cf. Isoc. *Nic.* 32, *Evag.* 5–8 and further discussion in ch. 1. See Pohlenz 1933; Baumhauer 1986: 162–164.

27. The verb *prepô* originally designates the impression of something as conspicuous or clearly seen (e.g., Hom. *Il.* 12.104, *Od.* 8.172; Hes. *Th.* 92). *Eikos* is from *eoika* ("seem likely"), as is the related *eikôn*, the word for likeness or image (e.g., Sim. 122.81 *PG*; Hdt. 2.130, 7.69; Aesch. *Th.* 559; Eur. *Hel.* 77, *Med.* 1162).

28. I should note that there have not been very many studies dedicated to ancient Greek conceptions of style alone (but see Salvioni 1985; O'Sullivan 1992; Dover 1997). Moreover, many older studies do not address how ancient Greek writers thought about style, but in-

stead describe their various stylistic techniques (see, e.g., Norden 1958; Delauny 1959; Carrière 1967).

29. See books on ancient literary criticism (e.g., Grube 1965; Harriot 1969; Russell 1981) and on the rise of rhetoric (e.g., Blass 1877; Volkmann 1963; Kennedy 1963, 1994; J. Martin 1974; Baumhauer 1986; Cole 1991; Enos 1993; Poulakos 1995; Schiappa 1999).

30. The curiously circular nature of such a thesis has not prevented contention over the earliest possible dating for words isolated as technical terminology, as has occurred exhaustively with the term *rhetorikê*. Schiappa 1999: 14–29 contains the most recent rehearsal of this debate; cf. Cole 1991: 98–99; O'Sullivan 1992: 87; Walker 2000: 34–41. Gagarin 1994: 48–49 argues briefly but persuasively that technical discussions of rhetoric were going on well before Plato; cf. also Usher 1999: 1–6.

31. This is also true of books on literary criticism: cf. Harriot 1969, who makes a similar argument for her focus on material before Plato; cf. Russell 1981; Too 1999. See also Karp 1977.

32. See esp. Baumhauer: 166–179; also Cole 1991: 122; Poulakos 1995: 45.

33. Enos 1993: 60.

34. O'Sullivan 1992; cf. also Salvioni 1985, although he focuses primarily on fourth-century material.

35. Scholars have recognized this: e.g., R. P. Martin 1989; Cole 1991; Kennedy 1963; Kennedy 1994. Salvioni 1985: 20–29 notes this in particular relation to style.

36. Usher 1999: 2–3 argues that although most scholars think that these handbooks only contained speeches, the inclusion of some analysis is likely.

37. The information about Polus comes from Suidas (see the fragments in Radermacher 1951: B.xiv); that about Antisthenes from Diogenes Laertius (6.15). Diogenes gives the title for Antisthenes' treatise as *Peri Lexeôs ê Peri Charaktêrôn*; see further discussion in chs. 1 and 5.

38. See also Enos 1993: 87–90. Cf. Jones 1962 on character in Aristotle's *Poetics*. Again, by "performative" I mean that one's character was apprehended by the witnessing of public behavior and actions. In a culture so centered around civic ritual (including the dramatic festivals, processional occasions, oratorical displays), one performed the role of good citizen by visibly engaging in civic practice in the right manner; see further below.

39. Cf. Baumhauer 1986; Enos 1993; Gagarin 1994; Usher 1999.

40. Cole 1991: 122; I should note that Cole's main argument is that no awareness of rhetoric as a concept existed before Plato.

41. Cf. Cole 1991: 122. Aristotle does separate written style (*lexis graphikê*) from the "contentious" style (*lexis agonistikê*) that deliberative speeches best illustrate (*Rhet.* 1413b–1414a); but his discussion makes clear that this distinction between written and deliberative techniques is really focused on written composition. Gagarin 1999, following a trend in oral theory to look beyond epic poetry for evidence of oral technique, has pointed to the manifest orality of oratory, and has outlined some stylistic differences between speeches that he thinks were composed for performance and those that were composed to be read. O'Sullivan's 1996 argument that the sophists were often associated with books (and thus with the written word) would seem to contradict this. But he also admits that only certain sophists (i.e., Protagoras and Prodicus) were so associated and that Gorgias—the sophist most important to my discussion—manifestly was not. Their styles were also distinguished along similar

lines, Protagoras and Prodicus being concerned with exactitude (*orthoepeia*), Gorgias with timeliness (*kairos*) (O'Sullivan 1996: 121–122).

42. We might note that *hupokrisis* does not cause Dionysius such concern (e.g., *Dem.* 53).

43. E.g., Thuc. *Hist.* 2.65, 3.38, 6.15; Soph. *Phil.* 407–409; Eur. *Hec.* 130–135, *Or.* 889–894, 902–906, *Tro.* 282–287, 966–968.

44. Cf. Ober 1998: 106, 112–113, 140–141.

45. Cf. Gill 1996, who critiques how post-Romantic notions of personhood and individuality have influenced classical scholars. He proposes an understanding of ancient ideas about personality that takes into account more fully individuals' participation in normative values and behaviors.

46. The phrase is from Rehm 1992: 3.

47. Halliwell 1990 has emphasized that a visual stylization marks the treatment of character in Greek literary tradition. Although it is particularly notable in praise speech, he argues that the focus on public action most strongly affects the assessment of individual worth in general. Cf. also Goldhill 1998.

48. Dover 1997: 3; cf. Todorov 1971, who distinguishes among three intersecting components—the verbal (concrete sentences), the syntactic (interrelation of parts of the text), and the semantic (universal themes evoked)—while still maintaining that style may itself intersect in different ways with each category. Barthes [1969] 1986 argues that style operates at every level of expression, due to what he calls "the *layered* quality of discourse" (99).

49. Cf. Enos 1993: 85–87, who maintains that for the sophists, style *is* the argument.

50. I am thus not primarily concerned with elucidating the ideas of Plato, Aristotle, or other later theorists who discuss the topic of style. I address some of their analyses only to show that their accounts may be better understood as a response to earlier ideas about style and character type and how these accounts in turn affected subsequent discussions.

51. Herzfeld 1985: 10 argues that all self-performances involve individual deviations from familiar categories of type; but the literary characters that I am interested in violate these categories and thus challenge the notion of identity as a stable, "natural" state of being.

52. From early on, style is often conceived as a kind of fancy dress. Adjectives such as *poikilos* show a connection between visual elaboration and the variegated mind of someone like Odysseus. In fifth-century tragedy, *poikilos* became a negative and suspect term that pointed to a tyrannical kind of decoration, whether of speech or appearance. See further in ch. 1.

53. Pindar, a staunch supporter of aristocratic ideology, declares, "The wise man knows many things in his blood; the vulgar are taught" (σοφὸς ὁ πολλὰ εἰδὼς φυᾶι· / μαθόντες δὲ λάβροι, *Ol.* 2.86–87).

54. Regarding the evil cunning of wise women, cf. Eur. *Hipp.* 642 (τὸ γὰρ κακοῦργον μᾶλλον ἐτίκτει Κύπρις ἐν ταῖς σοφαῖσιν); and *Andr.* 936–937 (κἀγὼ κλύουσα τούσδε Σειρήνων λόγους / σοφῶν πανούργων ποικίλων λαλημάτων / ἐξηνεμώθην μωρίᾳ).

55. Cf. Soph. *Ant.* 1046 regarding clever types (δεινοὶ) who speak well (καλῶς). These sentiments are particularly pervasive in Euripides: cf. Eur. *Phoen.* 526–527, *Hec.* 256–258 on Odysseus; similarly destructive traits are attributed to Helen's eyes: *Hec.* 441–443, *Tro.* 891–894, *Or.* 1383–1387. Regarding what North 1981 has termed "unscrupulous eloquence" more generally, *Hipp.* 486–489, *Bacch.* 270–271, *Hec.* 1187–1191; and compare the way unbridled women's speech is described: *Tro.* 651–653, *Hipp.* 642–648, *Andr.* 930–938. Aristophanes has

much to say on the *lalia* of female (or too carefully crafted and therefore effeminate) speech (e.g., *Ran.* 91, 815, 841, 943, 1069, 1071, 1160, 1492; *Eccl.* 120; *Ach.* 716; *Eq.* 1381). The conflation of female speech and that of the too-polished poet or orator is important in this period for distinguishing both styles and moral types. I discuss these themes in greater detail in chs. 4 and 5.

56. For Helen, see esp. Clader 1976; also Ghali-Kahil 1955; Atchity 1978; Skutsch 1987; Suzuki 1989; Austin 1994. The bibliography on the history of Odysseus' figure is extensive, but Stanford 1954 is still the definitive study of the history of the Odysseus type. For other analyses more focused on the connections between his figure and the use of language, see Austin 1975; Pucci 1987; Peradotto 1990; Ford 1992; Segal 1994; Olson 1995.

57. Barthes [1970] 1974: 67–68.

58. A metonym operates as an index of a larger event or situation (e.g., smoke for fire) and connects contiguous elements (i.e., part for a whole), as opposed to the symbol, which forges connections by means of formal likeness. The idea of the emblem is important for its suggestion of visuality. See Pierce 1931–1958; also Elam 1980: 28 for this usage in relation to drama.

59. Both comedy and tragedy show an awareness of the metatheatrical, as numerous scholars have discussed. While Aristophanes' plays provide important background material for the issues on which my analysis focuses, tragedy is where the anxiety about these characters and the dangers of stylistic effect really comes into focus. See further in ch. 4.

CHAPTER 1

1. Russell 1981: 130–131; e.g., Demetr. *Eloc.* 36; DH *Dem.* 9 (τῷ Δημοσθενικῷ χαρακτῆρι); DH *Lys.* 11 (χαρακτὴρ λέξεως).

2. Compare Pl. *Ap.* 17d and *Lg.* 816d, where *lexis* appears to mean something like "speech type," rather than designating specifically the aspect of speaking that has to do with word choice and arrangement (versus argument).

3. Russell 1981: 128.

4. Salvioni 1985: 6–7; he also emphasizes the importance of character to ideas about style.

5. Muecke 1982: 51. But cf. Prodicus' story about Heracles, discussed below; and Plato's Ion, who decorates both his body (τὸ σῶμα κεκοσμῆσθαι) and Homer (κεκόσμηκα τὸν Ὅμερων) (*Ion* 530b5–d8).

6. O'Sullivan 1992.

7. Prier 1989; cf. also Vernant [1986] 1989, [1986] 1991; Benediktson 2000; Zeitlin forthcoming.

8. E.g., *eidos*: Arist. [*Rh. Al.*] 1441b9, Isoc. 13.17, 15.74; *idea*: Arist. *Poet.* 1449b8, 1450b34, [*Rh. Al.*] 1425a9, Isoc. 2.48, Herm. *Ideai*, where it designates a particular quality of style (e.g., σαφήνεια ἰδέα). Cf. also Syr. *In Herm.* for its use as a distinctive style of an author (e.g., here even the phrase Πλατωνικὴ ἰδέα [1.112] means "style" rather than "form"). Dionysius and Cicero use *charaktêr* to designate a similar notion of individual style; see n. 1 above and further discussion below.

9. Prier 1989: 18.

10. Migne, *PG* 122.81. I would also note that poetic usage often maintains or reinvigo-

rates the visualizing associations that delineate character. For example, even a verb like *herpô*, which literally means "creep" but came commonly to mean "move" in fifth-century dramatic usage, regains its visualizing force in a play like Sophocles' *Philoctetes*, where it so clearly points to the hero's physical debility. Cf. Worman 2000.

11. Cf. Cartledge, Millet, and von Reden (eds.) 1998.

12. See Burke 1969: 55–59 on the concept of identification in rhetorical practice.

13. E.g., *Il.* 2.213–214, 5.759, 8.12; cf. *h.Merc.* 255; Solon 13.11 W².

14. The verbs ἀμφιπεριστέφεται and στέφει associate the type of speech Odysseus is describing with praise poetry; cf. Theog. 1259–1262 and the language of Pindar below. On the phrases *kata kosmon* and *moiran* and their relation to truth claims, see Adkins 1972 and the discussions in ch. 2.

15. In keeping with his attention to such mismatches, Odysseus later praises the blind and decrepit Demodicus for singing κατὰ κόσμον about the Trojan war (8.489). Note also that Alcinous praises Odysseus' narrative of his adventures as having a formal coherence (μορφὴ ἐπέων, 11.367), a phrase that similarly highlights visible shape.

16. For both incidents, see further in ch. 2.

17. This latter use of *kosmos* to denote the form given to words seems to be retained by the Presocratic philosophers. Parmenides' poem on the order of the universe relates the narrative of an unnamed goddess, who declares that her words concerning mortal opinions have a "deceitful ordering" (κόσμον . . . ἐπέων ἀπατηλόν, fr. 8.52). The atomist Democritus is said to have claimed for Homer a god-given, natural ability to fashion an "order out of all kinds of words" (ἐπέων κόσμον . . . παντοίων, fr. 21 DK; cf. Solon fr. 1 W²).

18. Gagarin 1994: 51 also notes this use of likeness and probability in the hymn.

19. Hesiod uses *kosmos* almost exclusively to refer to the adornment of Pandora (*Th.* 570, 587; *WD* 72, 76), a highly artificial fabrication that emphasizes her impact on those who view her. See further in ch. 3.

20. Elsewhere (*Ol.* 8.13) Pindar's "gleaming decoration" (λιπαρὸν κόσμον) for the victor Callimachus recalls Theognis 947–948, where decorating the city is also invoked: πατρίδα κοσμήσω, λιπαρήν πόλιν, οὔτ' ἐπὶ δήμωι / τρέψας οὔτ' ἀδίκοις ἀνδράσι πειθόμενος. See Kurke 1991: 163–194 regarding *megaloprepeia* and "adorning the city" in Pindar. See ch. 4 for further discussion of Pindar on praise and blame.

21. Cf., e.g., R. P. Martin 1989: 111–113 on ἀκριτόμυθε (*Il.* 2.246); Nagy 1979: 40 and n. 2, 82n., and 134 on οὐ παρὰ μοῖραν (*Od.* 14.509).

22. Cf. *Ion* 834, *Med.* 576, *Andr.* 956; *Hippolytus* shows a more concrete vision of what kind of deceptive decoration women encourage. In the words of the bitter hero, "[Her husband] delights in adding adornment to his idol, a noble thing to a base one" (γέγηθε κόσμον προστιθεὶς ἀγάλματι / καλὸν κακίστω, 631–632).

23. For the relevance of this play to the connections drawn in drama between ideas about style and Helen, see ch. 4.

24. For a less explicit juxtaposition of skillful speaking and just (or unjust) actions, compare the chorus' remark to Jason after he has defended himself against Medea's charges: "Jason, you arranged your arguments well . . . but you seem in having betrayed your wife not to act justly" (εὖ μὲν τούσδ' ἐκόσμησας λόγους . . . δοκεῖς προδοὺς σὴν ἄλοχον οὐ δίκαια δρᾶν, *Med.* 576–578). Cf. also Odysseus in Euripides' *Hecuba* and *Troades* and the discussions

in ch. 4. Homer mostly uses *kosmos* in the positive sense: Odysseus, as mentioned, remarks that Demodocus sings very appropriately (λίην . . . κατὰ κόσμον, *Od.* 8.489). But even in Homer *kosmos* can have the sense of deceptive contrivance, as Odysseus' usage shows only a few lines later, when he says to Demodocus, "Sing about the strategem of the wooden horse" (ἵππου κόσμον ἄεισον / δουρατέου, 492).

25. Coulter 1964; Woodruff 1999.

26. On this type of generic appropriation in Plato, see Nightingale 1995.

27. Note that Aristotle uses Theodorus as an example of someone who successfully hides his projection of a type that suits his audience (*Rhet.* 1404b18–23). That is, he molds (πλάζω) a character appropriate to his subject and his audience without seeming to do so.

28. E.g., *Gorg.* 493c6, d2, 494a1, 504a1–d1, 506e1–e7; cf. also *Phdr.* 239d1–d2, 245a4, 246c2, 247a1, 256b2, and *Prot.* 315b6, 320d5–e1, 322c3, 347d7. But cf. the defendant Palamedes, who claims that he is a μέγας εὐεργέτης of Greece, who makes life "well-ordered" (κεκοσμη-μένον) (Gorg. *Pal.* 30). Plato's uses of *kosmos* in a similar sense most frequently in the *Gorg.* suggest that the epideictic orator ignores this kind of moral orderliness. In the *Menexenus kosmos* is used primarily in its rhetorical sense (fitting decoration), since Socrates is reciting a funeral oration (which he attributes to Pericles' learned mistress Aspasia): 236d7 and e2 (twice in the first two sentences of the speech), 237c3, 237c4, 239c1, 246a3, 248c5. In the *Hippias Minor* and the *Ion*, variants of *kosmos* are used to contrast literal adornment (esp. dress) negatively with what is truly beautiful (*kalos*) in the *Hippias Minor*, and with real knowledge in the *Ion*. See further discussion below and in ch. 5.

29. This application of the term is not as innovative as it may seem, however; the same character type is also defended by the speechwriter Lysias (e.g., 1.26, 7.41, 19.16, 21.19). See Lateiner 1982 on Lysias' usage.

30. Arist. *Rhet.* 1408a14, *Pol.* 1457b2; Isoc. 9.9; DH *Dem.* 25 (in relation to Gorgias' "theatrical" style), *Dem.* 52 (in relation to delivery), *Comp.* 3.

31. See further discussion below.

32. Cf. Dover 1997: 97n. 2, where he notes that although Aristotle may use *kosmos* to mean "the design apparent in the interrelation of the parts of the whole," elsewhere his usage suggests that the word signifies a kind of embellishment, and that particular types of words (such as obsolete or foreign terms [*glôttai*]) may achieve it.

33. On Thersites, see further in chs. 2 and 3.

34. Plut. *Mor.* 348c.

35. On the appearance of the sophist, see further in ch. 5.

36. Aristotle is considered by most commentators to use *êthos* as a positive term only, embracing positive qualities such as beneficence; but cf., e.g., *Rhet.* 1417a21–35, where it is clear that *êthos* must also cover negative traits (Cope 1877: 192–193 notes this). The authoritative study of *êthos* is still that of Süss 1910; see also Wisse 1989; Pelling (ed.) 1990; Gill 1996; Scotti 1996.

37. See below, n. 57; also the discussion in ch. 4.

38. Theognis also likens the *êthos* to the mobile, many-limbed qualities of the octopus (215–216).

39. Cf. Solon 13.39–40 W².

40. Cf. the nightingale in Hesiod's *Theogony;* she is called "singer" (ἀοιδόν), and her throat (i.e., whence the voice comes) is "variegated" (ποικιλόδειρον, *WD* 203-208). If we follow Pucci 1977: 62 in understanding the nightingale as a figure for the poet, the bird's variegated throat could similarly be read as a visualizing metaphor for the poet's multifaceted style.

41. See Worman 1999b, 2001b.

42. But cf. *Ol.* 6.87, where ποικίλον ὕμνον is not negative.

43. Cf. also Eur. *Or.* 823, where the word is coupled with impiety (ἀσέβεια ποικίλα), and *Phoen.* 469-470, where the "simple tale of truth" (ἁπλοῦς ὁ μῦθος τῆς ἀληθείας) is opposed to the intricate interpretation (ποικίλων ἑρμηνευμάτων) that is superfluous to the just cause. In Sophocles the outcast Oedipus accuses Creon of managing to extract some fancy trick from every just claim (κἀπὸ παντὸς ἂν φέρων / λόγου δικαίου μηχάνημα ποίκιλον, *OC* 762).

44. Particularly relevant to this discussion are the descriptions of the disguised style that Odysseus encourages, and the characterization of female domestic speech as that of "elaborate babblers" (cf. above and n. 43). In the *Rhetoric* Aristotle opposes the λόγος that is ἁπλούστερος to that which is ποικίλος (1416b25); cf. again Eur. *Phoen.* 469-472, where Polyneices represents the unjust speech as needing some "clever drug" (φαρμάκων . . . σοφῶν).

45. E.g., in Sophocles' *Ajax,* the dead hero is characterized by the chorus as "intractable" (δυστράπελος, 914)—the opposite of which (εὐτράπελος) would presumably describe the flexible Odysseus, as it does the Athenian character in Pericles' Funeral Oration (Thuc. 2.41). See Worman 2001b and further discussion in ch. 4.

46. Gill 1990: 6-7; cf. Gill 1984: 153 and Gill 1996: 21-22. Goldhill 1990: 102 makes a similar point, though with a different focus.

47. Russell 1990: 199.

48. E.g., Eur. *El.* 362-363, 384-385, *Med.* 103; but cf. Soph. *Trach.* 308-309; Eur. *Ion* 239-240, where *phusis* may also extend to visible traits. See further in ch. 4.

49. There are many passages in tragedy that show more ambiguous usage, however: see, e.g., Soph. *Aj.* 594-595; Eur. *Supp.* 902-908.

50. χ. γλώσσης, Hdt. 1.57, 1.142, χ. τοῦ προσώπου, 1.116; cf. Soph. fr. 176 Radt, Ar. *Pax* 220.

51. *Med.* 519, *Hec.* 379, *HF* 659; cf. *El.* 368-369. A Lesbian inscription typical of the early fourth century that legislates against the dilution of gold shows a similar concern that a gap may open up between the actual worth of the material and the stamp that should mark it as genuine (*IG* XII.ii.1; Schwyzer 1923: 619). Compare Theognis' κίβδηλον ἐπίκλοπον ἦθος (965), cited above, and similarly 119-120: χρυσοῦ κιβδήλοιο καὶ ἀργύρου ἀνσχετὸς ἄτη / Κύρνε, καὶ ἐξευρεῖν ῥάιδιον ἀνδρὶ σοφῶι. Coinage provides the poets with a rich source of metaphor from the sixth century on (see Kurke 1991, 1999).

52. Cf. the discussion in Worman 1999b.

53. Cf. Phld. *Rh.* 2.137S.; Arr. *Epict. Diss.* 3.22.80; DH *Dem.* 9. Cicero translates the word as *forma* (*Orat.* 36), that is, as if it meant something closer to *idea.* He uses *forma* also of types of speech (e.g., epideictic), which further supports this connection with *idea;* cf. *Orat.* 134.

54. On Aristotle's treatment of *êthos,* see Dale [1959] 1969; Jones 1962; Salvioni 1985; Baumhauer 1986; Halliwell 1990; Fortenbaugh 1996.

55. Cf. Cic. *Orat.* 71 on *decorum.*

56. We might note that this is a technique at which Odysseus in particular excells and which falls under Dover's category of style at the level of invention (Dover 1997: 3). See further in ch. 5.

57. Schütrumpf 1970 has analyzed Aristotle's treatment of *êthos* in the *Poetics* at length, differentiating between a broad and a narrow sense of the word and concluding that the latter, which excludes thought (*dianoia*), is at use in the *Poetics*. This largely follows the opinions of Dale [1959] 1969 and Else 1957. Held 1985 argues that *êthos* does include *dianoia* in the sense of intellectual habits (*hexeis*) and that its range in the *Poetics* is similar to that in the *Ethics*: "the sum total of [a person's] moral qualities, good and bad" (280). Both Schütrumpf and Held agree that *êthos* in the *Rhetoric* delineates the broadest range of all, in part because one's attitudes toward the gods would also be useful for character proof.

58. See also Halliwell's 1990 discussion of the passage.

59. Note that Plato also uses this correlation between physical stature and character type in his mythological excurses. Socrates' description of the two horses of the soul in the *Phaedrus* follows this schema: the noble horse is white and has a fine form and sound judgment (εἶδος ὀρθός . . . σωφροσύνη), while the ignoble horse is black and has a crooked shape and prideful behavior (σκολιός . . . ὕβρις, 253d4–e5). Cf. also Pl. *Rep.* 402d1–4.

60. Nightingale 1995: 1–12.

61. The defense of this connection parallels that which Isocrates attempts to forge between the role of the *philosophos* man and the public practices of the democracy; see Nightingale 1995: 26–40.

62. See Halliwell's 1990 discussion of this encomium; also Benediktson 2000: 35–36.

63. O'Sullivan 1992: esp. 130–139.

64. E.g., *Ran.* 826–829; cf. 91, 815, 841, 943, 1069, 1071, 1160, 1492. The characterizations (ironically enough) apply especially to Euripides, Socrates, and the sophists (and therefore to young men, their putative students) and became associated with the ἰσχνός χαρακτήρ (Cic. *Orat.* 62–64; DH *Dem.* 2).

65. Aristotle called Alcidamas' own compositional style *psuchros* ("chilly," like Gorgias': *Rhet.* 1405b35, 1406b12). How Alcidamas and others (esp. Isocrates) distinguish among these different styles, and how these distinctions intersect with their ideas about speaking versus writing, is a complex issue; but see O'Sullivan 1992: 59, 113–115.

66. These are reactions that Gorgias had attributed to the spoken word, conceived of as itself having physical weight and impact (*Hel.* 8 and *passim*). Recall also that Gorgias likens the power of oratory (esp. epideictic) to poetry, but for him the similarity has less to do with the fine polish of these types of expression than with their incantatory power.

67. Cf. Aristotle, who quotes Alcidamas' description of the *Odyssey* as an example of an overblown metaphor: καλὸν ἀνθρωπίνου βίου κάτοπτρον (*Rhet.* 1406b12). In his treatise, however, Alcidamas seems suspicious of this kind of visual effect and of the suggestive images to which it gives rise.

68. Süss 1910: 34ff. makes a detailed comparison among these two texts and Isocrates' *Against the Sophists*. As a whole, the debate over speech versus writing in the *Phaedrus* (and in *Ep.* 7) is beyond the scope of this book; the bibliography is long and runs the gamut from the detailed analysis (e.g., Ferrari 1987) to the infamous poststructuralist reading (Derrida 1981: 63–171). Gill 1992 points out that although in both the *Phaedrus* and the *Ep.* 7 Plato re-

jects writing as a fitting medium for philosophical insight, he is not really defining a type of understanding independent of verbal or visual representation. The *Ep.* 7 in particular makes clear that "names and speeches and sights and physical sensations [ὀνόματα καὶ λόγοι ὄψεις τε καὶ αἰσθήσεις]" all contribute to philosophical understanding (φρόνησις, 344b4–7). This insight "flashes out [ἐξέλαμψε]" like a beacon, another traditional metaphor that highlights both light and vision. Plato does, however, regard writing as more concretely analogous to visual effect, for obvious reasons (cf. *Cra.* 424b–425a). See also Halliwell 2000 on the importance of painting in the formation of Plato's thinking about visuality and representation (*mimêsis*).

69. In a characteristic move, Plato chooses the strongly visual adjective so familiar in fifth- and fourth-century usage for the description of both speaking style and character type (e.g., Dem. 29.1; Isoc. 5.27, 12.4, 12.246; see Halliwell 2000 and the discussion above). Plato himself uses ποικίλος fairly frequently but almost always in a purely figurative sense (e.g., *Cra.* 393d, 417e; *Tht.* 146d; *Soph.* 223c, 226a, 234b; *Phlb.* 12c, 53e). An exception interesting for the metaphorical link between speech and appearance is *Ion* 535d, where the rhapsode's ornamental speaking style is matched by the fancy clothes with which he adorns himself (κεκοσμημένος ἐσθῆτι ποικίλῃ). Cf. also *Gorg.* 513a ff., 513c1.

70. Note Antisthenes also uses ἁρμόδιος; cf. Plato's παναρμονίους.

71. Gill 1992: 160. In a similar move, Plato fashions a different meaning for the word *philosophos*, reserving it for those who write and declaim with the requisite knowledge and the appropriate respect for the truth (*Phdr.* 278d4–5); see Nightingale 1995: 14–21.

72. Halliwell 1988: 127 notes that Plato uses the cognate ἐπιχρωννύσθαι for suntan, as a metaphor for shallow learning (*Ep.* 7.340d7).

CHAPTER 2

1. Bakker 1997: 18–19 notes this problem; cf. Griffin 1980: xiv; Thalmann 1984: xx, e.g. There has been a move in recent years away from M. Parry's 1971 and Lord's 1960 focus on the formulaic assessment of Homeric semantics, while most still accept their claims concerning the fundamental orality of the texts and the nature of its composition: cf. Edwards 1997 for a useful overview. Austin 1975 was an early advocate of regarding the Homeric use of formulae as meaningful and the Homeric poet as not merely governed by tradition; cf. Nagy 1979. For the argument that tradition itself fosters meaningful usage and flexibility, see J. M. Foley 1999.

2. Bakker 1997: 55 says, "Epic speech is presented as a verbalization of things *seen*"; cf. Calame 1986: 41–42.

3. See Bakker's explanation of how this works, especially in relation to sequential units (1997: 56–57, 67–69).

4. Plato's *Ion* gives a full (if caricaturish) description of rhapsodic style, which includes emotive delivery and character impersonation (cf. the red-figure amphora in the British Museum [E 270A], which depicts a rhapsode performing). See also Kirk 1962; Felson [1994] 1997: 137–138; Boegehold 1999: 37. On rhapsodic techniques and audience experience more generally, see Havelock 1963 (ch. 9); Thalmann 1984 (ch. 4); Calame 1986: 35–41; Nagy 1990a: 40–47; Nagy 1990b: 20–28; Nagy 1996: 80–86.

5. De Jong 1987; cf. de Jong 1991. A general introduction to narratological theory can be found in Bal 1985; see also Bal 1984, which explores the semiotic implications of the narratologist's claim that all discourse is subjective.

6. R. P. Martin 1989; Lateiner 1995.

7. Bakker 1993, 1997, 1999.

8. I thus am somewhat wary of, for example, R. P. Martin's (1989) tendency to handle the Iliadic warriors as if they were anthropological types rather than literary constructs. His argument that the Homeric awareness of stylistic types is primarily a cultural rather than a poetic process (96) may underestimate the literariness of the material. Contrast Barthes' (1974) definition of the literary character as "a product of [semiological] combinations" (67).

9. Cf. Bourdieu 1991: 86, who highlights the mouth in this way: "The most frequent articulatory position is an element in an *overall way of using the mouth* (in talking but also in eating, drinking, laughing, etc.) and therefore a component of the bodily hexis." Bourdieu calls this an " 'articulatory style,' a life-style 'made flesh,' " which affects pronunciation as one aspect among many of the mouth's stylistic habits.

10. See Solmsen 1954; Detienne [1967] 1996: 69–88; Pucci 1977: 16–27; Pucci [1979] 1998.

11. *Meilichios* words are particularly persuasive in circumstances where some kind of emotional attachment (actual or potential) can be leaned upon. Cf. Nestor's advice regarding how to persuade Achilles: "But still even now let us consider how we might persuade him, soothing him with gentle gifts and honey-sweet words" (ἀλλ' ἔτι καὶ νῦν / φραζώμεθα ὥς κέν μιν ἀρεσσάμενοι πεπίθωμεν / δώροισίν τ' ἀγανοῖσιν ἔπεσσι τε μειλιχίοισι, *Il.* 9.111–113).

12. Again, cf. Nestor, *Il.* 9.93–94, where the poet emphasizes his especially thoughtful, if dated, speech: "First of all the old man Nestor began to weave a plot for them, whose counsel seemed best in earlier times" (τοῖς ὁ γέρων πάμπρωτος ὑφαίνειν ἤρχετο μῆτιν / Νέστωρ, οὗ καὶ πρόσθεν ἀρίστη φαίνετο βουλή).

13. Cf. *Il.* 5.127–128 (clear-sighted), 252–254 (brave, stalwart), 815–816 (clear-sighted), 6.214 (honeyed), 9.50–54 (best in counsel), 10.169 (appropriate), 10.227 (persuasive), 14.133 (persuasive). R. P. Martin 1989: 124–125 argues that Diomedes is still rather clumsy in his use of speech formalities, but he is often praised precisely for his speaking skills, as the passages quoted above show.

14. Cf. Nagy 1979: 40 and 132–135.

15. E.g., Hom. *Od.* 14.127–132, 362–365, 395–397, 508–517; 17.415–418, 559–560; Hes. *Th.* 26; Hipp. frs. 26, 128 W².

16. A. Parry 1964; R. P. Martin 1989; Mackie 1995; Worman 2001a.

17. Cf. Collins 1991: 4–5.

18. See, e.g., Redfield 1975: 122; Edwards 1987: 195–196; Suzuki 1989; Austin 1994; Graver 1995.

19. See esp. Pucci [1979] 1998, who associates the Muses' ability with the Sirens, Circe, and Helen; also Atchity 1978: 82–99; Monsacré 1984: 119–121; Crane 1988: 42; Suzuki 1989: 69; Wohl 1993: 33–34; Doherty 1995b; Doherty 1995a: 135–138. For broader discussions, see Clader 1976; Bergren 1983; Austin 1975; Austin 1994; Felson [1994] 1997.

20. E.g., the lamenting of family ties, the dilation on the effect the death will have on

one's life. See Alexiou 1974; Holst-Warhaft 1992. Andromache's voice is so consistent that she repeats nearly the same set of fears and regrets three out of the four times she speaks (*Il.* 6.407–439, 22.450–459, 24.725–745).

21. See esp. Clader 1976: 10–12.

22. *Il.* 3.171, 3.427, 6.343, 24.777; *Od.* 4.234. See R. P. Martin 1989.

23. Helen uses this same label of herself in the *Odyssey* (κυνώπιδος, 4.145). Cf. the characterization of Aphrodite in *Od.* 8, who (dog-faced) devours her husband's energy and wealth alike. Hephaestus mentions not only his pain (ἀκάχημα) but also the bride-price that goes with this daughter of Zeus, who is beautiful but not "heart-restraining" (ἀλλά σφωε δόλος καὶ δεσμὸς ἐρύξει / εἰς ὅ κέ μοι μάλα πάντα πατὴρ ἀποδῷσιν ἔεδνα / ὅσσα οἱ ἐγγυάλιξα κυνώπιδος εἵνεκα κούρης / οὕνεκά οἱ καλὴ θηγάτηρ ἀτὰρ οὐκ ἐχέθυμος, 8.314–320). See Graver 1995: 51.

24. In the *Odyssey* Odysseus often utters the phrase (four times in the *Od.* and once in the *Il.*). Like Odysseus in the *Odyssey*, Helen uses it more frequently than other speakers in the *Iliad*, five times in all. Cf. Odysseus' famous exclamation (ὡς δὴ ἐγώ γ' ὄφελον θανέειν καὶ πότμον ἐπισπεῖν, 5.308), discussed further below, as well as a similar usage with the Phaiacians as audience (ὡς δὴ μὴ ὄφελον νικᾶν τοιῷδ' ἐπ' ἀέθλῳ, 11.547).

25. Helen's response suggests a connection between pleasure and death, a pairing with which some scholars have argued her figure is strongly associated. See Vernant [1986] 1991: 102, who argues that *erôs* and *thanatos* are strongly linked in the Greek imaginary, and calls Helen a "fatal beauty"; cf. Vermeule 1979; Monsacré 1984: 131–133. Helen makes a similar declaration in her mourning speech over the body of Hector in book 24 but without the suggestion of pleasure (ὤφελον ὀλέσθαι, 764).

26. Cf. *Il.* 11.380–381 (Paris taunts Diomedes: ὡς ὄφελόν τοι / νείατον ἐς κενεῶνα βαλὼν ἐκ θυμὸν ἑλέσθαι); *Il.* 14.84–85 (Odysseus curses Agamemnon: αἴθ' ὤφελλες ἀεικελίου στρατοῦ ἄλλου / σημαίνειν); *Il.* 24.253–254 (Priam curses his living children: αἴθ' ἅμα πάντες / Ἕκτορος ὠφέλετ' ἀντὶ . . . πεφάσθαι); *Od.* 2.183–184 (Eurymachos taunts the old seer Halitherses: ὡς καὶ σὺ καταφθίσθαι . . . ὤφελες); *Od.* 18.401 (the suitors taunt the beggar Odysseus: αἴθ' ὤφελλ' . . . ὀλέσθαι).

27. Boedecker 1974.

28. See R. P. Martin 1989: 111–113 on this understanding of the epithet ἀκριτόμυθε, which Odysseus uses of Thersites (*Il.* 2.246; cf. Iris on the μῦθοι . . . ἄκριτοι of Priam, *Il.* 2.796).

29. Friedrich 1978: 46–47. On the extreme proximity between the figures of Aphrodite and Helen, see Boedecker 1974: 48, 54–55, 61 (e.g., both are snatched from the χορός when raped [*h.Ven.* 117–118; Plut. *Thes.* 31.2] and both transgress the marriage bond [*Od.* 8.266–366]). For this scene in particular, note that Aphrodite makes reference to the dance floor (χορός, *Il.* 3.394) that Paris has just left. Clader 1976: 74 notes that in later tradition Helen is referred to as the daughter and the sister of Aphrodite (respectively, Ptolemaeus in Phot., *Bibl.* 149 A f Bekker; first-century B.C.E. Egyptian inscription, *SEG* 8.500). See also Suter 1987.

30. Helen's use of dog epithets, for instance, is a common flyting tactic (Graver 1995: 49), although her turning of them against herself is anomalous. On the typical contexts of flyting in epic, see Parks 1990. Parks does not think that flyting patterns are often transferred to amorous or familial conflicts, but he does admit the similarity between these and warrior

disputes (12–13). Parks does not, however, treat speech patterns in any great detail, nor does he consider nondueling verbal exchanges. On the abuse of Paris in particular, see Suter 1993.

31. Scholars have attempted to attribute Helen's shift of direction and ultimate acquiescence to her weakness and attraction to Paris (e.g., Hooker 1979; Edwards 1987: 195–196). Kirk 1985: 327 regards the entire speech as "bitterly sarcastic and hostile," although he admits that it is difficult to determine what Helen is actually feeling, noting cautiously, "There is a certain kind of residual ambiguity about which it is unwise to be too dogmatic in this kind of literary *genre*." Cf. also Atchity 1978: 84, who attributes Helen's passivity to her function as an "anti-exemplum."

32. Cf. Hector's disparaging reference to Paris' "gifts of Aphrodite" (δῶρ' Ἀφροδίτης, 3.54) and Paris' own affirmation of the same (δῶρ' ἐρατὰ . . . χρυσέης Ἀφροδίτης, 3.64). See Monsacré 1984: 46–50.

33. We might include Penelope in this group: although she does not use *ophelon* phrases as frequently, she engages in a number of delicate exchanges about her reputation with her disguised husband, and she is represented as undergoing a kind of journey in book 23 during her reunion with him.

34. Mackie 1995: 118–119 remarks that Helen's phrases seem carefully chosen to suit Hector's outlook.

35. See Pucci [1979] 1998: 204; R. P. Martin 1989: 102, 105; Dickson 1995: 38.

36. See Graver 1995, who makes more explicit what Clader's 1976 data seem to suggest.

37. Cf. Clader 1976: 17–18, 46–47; Graver 1995.

38. Helen wishes for a type of end that Vernant [1986] 1991: 102–103 has related to erotic seizure by a god. Penelope makes a similar despairing wish to be borne away by a gust of wind (*Od.* 20.61–65). See also Johnston 1994, who details the strong connection between procreation and destruction that divinities like the Erinyes embody; this is the dark side of the *kourotrophos* identified with Artemis (and possibly Helen), as Clader 1976: 75–78 has discussed. If Helen represents in narrative terms the other route that Penelope could have chosen (as Katz 1991, Felson [1994] 1997, and others have argued), she may also be connected on a symbolic level to the fate of women in marriage and childbirth (Penelope included).

39. See Graver 1995.

40. When alive, Hector seeks to cheer his weeping wife with grim praise for himself (*Il.* 6.460–461); see above regarding Helen's fear of ill-repute, which is a hero's fear rather than a hero's wife's fear.

41. Holst-Warhaft 1992: 112–113.

42. The only other time φρίσσω occurs in the *Iliad* is when Paris describes the effect of Diomedes' *aristeia* on the Trojans, after the former has wounded the latter (11.383). In both places it suggests that those who induce these shudders in others have some ominous quality to them.

43. Cf. Clader 1976: 18–20, who compares ὀκρυοέσσης (6.344) and στυγερήν (lit. "Styx-like," 3.404), words that Helen uses of herself. Cf. the awareness of the *nemesis* that attends the presence of Helen (οὐ νέμεσις, 3.156; νεμεσσητόν, 3.410; οὐ . . . χόλῳ οὐδὲ νεμέσσι / ἥμην ἐν θαλάμῳ, 6.335–336; ὃς ἤδη νέμεσίν τε καὶ αἴσχεα πόλλ' ἀνθρώπων, 6.351).

44. Note that Helen's question, "Should I lie or should I speak the truth?" (ψεύσομαι, ἦ

ἔτυμον ἐρέω, *Od.* 4.140), recalls the power that the Muses possess. Cf. Hes. *Th.* 27; Homer's Muses "know all things" (ἴστε τε πάντα, *Il.* 2.485), which implies both truth and lies. Wohl 1993: 33–34 notes this connection and thinks that Helen represents "pure female creative power." In this scene, however, Helen functions as both Muse and poet, an authoritative rhetorician whose gender features are mostly indeterminate.

45. Cf. *Od.* 5.177–179, 5.263–264, 10.342–344, 358–365. Cf. Olson 1989 on Helen's use of Odysseus to bolster her status.

46. Regarding the effects of these goddesses on Odysseus' bodily *hexis*, see further in ch. 3.

47. Cf. Agamemnon to Nestor: ναὶ δὴ ταῦτά γε πάντα, γέρον, κατὰ μοῖραν ἔειπες, *Il.* 1.286). Remember that Odysseus calls the beautiful Euryalus' words οὐ κατὰ κόσμον (*Od.* 8.179) but praises Demodocus as singing κατὰ κόσμον about the Trojan war (*Od.* 8.489). Cf. *Od.* 14.363, 14.509; *Il. Parv.* (scholion on Ar. *Eq.*, fr. 2 Allen 1056). See Adkins 1972 and ch. 1.

48. Nagy 1979: 40 and n. 2, 82n., 134; cf. *huper moron* and *huper aisan*, related phrases that denote the opposite, that is, a hubristic inattention to fitting measure or, in Nagy's terms, an excess that is anathema to epic.

49. Cf. *Il.* 2.484–759. (Catalogue of Ships) and see Ford 1992: 72–74 (*Il.* 2.488 = *Od.* 4.240). On this collapse of roles by Hesiod, see Lardinois 1995: 201. Helen's use of the phrase makes it sound as if she might be able to tell all, while the poet emphasizes his incapability (*Il.* 2.489–490).

50. Cf. *Il.* 3.420: ἦρχε δὲ δαίμων (Aphrodite leading Helen to Paris).

51. The poet calls this feat a θαῦμα, and his praise of the Delian maidens is covert praise for himself, just as Helen's narrative seduction suggests the poet's own. See Nagy 1990a: 56–57, who discusses this as the process of "connecting like with like."

52. Zeitlin 1982; Bergren 1983; Loraux 1989.

53. See, e.g., Austin 1975: 187–189. He "corrects" his reading in his later analysis of the same scene (1994: 81–82); cf. also Felson 1997: 133–134.

54. Lynn-George 1988: 33.

55. See Clader 1976: 63–64, 69, 72–78; Skutsch 1987: 189, 190–191.

56. Cf. Odysseus' label for Thersites (ἀκριτόμυθε, 2.246) and further discussion below.

57. R. P. Martin 1989: 110–113. The description of Thersites is unformulaic in the extreme, as Stanley 1993: 55 has also noted. Thus the phrase that the narrator uses to describe his character's words (*epea akosma*) is reflected in the narrator's lack of conventional diction, while the character's own speech is in fact rhetorically facile. Note also that Thersites' speech is referred to by the same phrase used for Nestor's (*ligus agorêtês*: 1.248, 2.246). Cf. Adkins 1972: 15–16; Thalmann 1988: 17–21; Rose 1988: 19; Seibel 1995: 396–397.

58. Kirk 1985: 140; cf. also Whitman 1958: 161 and the critiques of Rose 1988 and Thalmann 1988.

59. Cf. the quarrel among the gods at the marriage feast of Peleus and Thetis that opens the *Cypria* (fr. 1 Allen), the possible failure of Agamemnon to invite Achilles to a feast of the Achaeans (Chrestomathia 23–24, p. 104 Allen), and the quarrel among Oedipus and his sons over the fair apportionment of meat (*Thebais*, fr. 3 Allen). See Saïd 1979; Schmitt-Pantel 1992.

60. Nagy 1979: 42–58 thinks that the *Iliad* shows an awareness of this *neikos* tradition if not

of the *Odyssey* itself; his book contains a series of discussions on the relationship between the *dais* and the *neikos*. See Nimis 1987: 23–42 on the importance of the meal for social harmony. Lohmann 1970: 233 notes the careful balance of the speech and its orderly ring composition.

61. Lohmann 1970: 233 describes this arrangement in more abstract terms: "Die gleiche dialektische Differenzierung besteht auch zwischen beiden Komponenten des Aussenringes: Die Hilfe aus der Sicht der Bedrängten (I) und des Helfenden (III)."

62. Cf. Redfield 1975: 15–16; Mueller 1984: 44–47; Lynn-George 1988: 86–92.

63. Lohmann 1970: 232–236; Kennedy 1980: 12. Lohmann regards Odysseus' role as that of the official speaker and likens his speech to a school exercise in internal composition (232–233). While the characterization is somewhat trivializing, this was the fate of many speeches from Homer in antiquity.

64. A. Parry 1964. R. P. Martin 1989 reviews the debate Parry initiated (152–159) and points out in the course of a detailed examination that Achilles' language is unusual in a restricted sense, that is, in a manner that still operates within Homeric norms (171–179). See also Gill 1996: 136–148, who emphasizes that Achilles' speech criticizes the failure of the leaders to adhere to shared values governing social interaction.

65. Cf. R. P. Martin 1989: 120, who considers Odysseus to be especially interested in the workings of speech itself.

66. The same proverb is uttered to Eumaeus by Odysseus in disguise; see below. Plato discusses it as obviously directed at Odysseus (*Hp. Mi.* 364e–365b). See Stanford 1954: 18 for the ancient commentators who take the proverb as directed at Odysseus.

67. Edwards 1991: 254 refers to this as the attention to "the meal schedule and the protocol of handing over compensation" that marks the "good subordinate officer." He also criticizes Page 1959: 314 for his joking comments about "luncheon [stealing] the limelight" (253), but his own comments suggest that Odysseus' attempts to reestablish army concord and appropriate hierarchies among warriors are merely the actions of an obedient henchman. Pucci 1987: 169 argues that "this confrontation between the man of *gastêr* and the man of *thumos*" is an important contrast between the *Odyssey* and the *Iliad*, which serves as an intertextual "response" of the former to the latter.

68. E.g., θυμός (19.164, 178, 229), φρήν (19.169, 174, 178), ἦτορ (19.169), γαστήρ (19.225), γυῖα (19.165, 169), χρώς (19.233), νέκυς (19.225), an attention to the body and the practicalities of living that characterizes the "man of *gastêr*" (cf. Hes. WD; Hipponax). Stanford 1954: 68–70 notes that Odysseus was later characterized as a glutton (due in part to these scenes in the *Iliad*) and remarks on the connections made between this attention to the belly and sophistic argumentation in such satires as Athenaeus' *Deipnosophists*. But he does not himself relate Odysseus' attention to food and its division to Odysseus' characteristic style, which he considers "strictly functional" (71). Cf. Arnould 1989; Crotty 1994: 130–159; Worman forthcoming.

69. Cf. *Il.* 9.225–227: δαιτὸς μὲν ἐΐσης οὐκ ἐπιδευεῖς / ἠμὲν ἐνὶ κλισίῃ Ἀγαμέμνονος Ἀτρεΐδαο / ἠδὲ καὶ ἐνθάδε νῦν. Edwards 1991: 255 comments on the ring composition that marks Odysseus' argumentation in book 19.

70. Lohmann 1970: 66 notes the gnomic quality of Odysseus' speech, articulating the central maxim here as "Ein guter Soldat muß auch gut essen." Lohmann does not, however, ex-

pand the use of gnomic utterances to include style differentiations; for him, they are merely suited to the pragmatism of Odysseus' outlook.

71. This is an argument much narrower in scope than the idea that the *Odyssey* is in some sense "about language," which has been much discussed in recent years. Austin 1975: 180 notes "a yawning chasm in critical discussion of the *Odyssey* caused by the simple failure to recognize that the *Odyssey* is a poem about words, about the use of language." This is itself more specific than declaring the poem to be "about brains," as Heatherington 1976 does. Austin does not develop fully the overlap of the poem's and its hero's strategies, but his awareness of it is evident. Cf. Pucci 1987; R. P. Martin 1989; Peradotto 1990; Ford 1992; Felson [1994] 1997; Segal 1994; Olson 1995.

72. While there is obviously a big distinction between the tone taken toward the Odysseus figure by the Homeric poet and that by classical poets, note that in *Od.* 14 Eumaeus is against lies that harm (here by raising hopes impossible to fulfill, 14.122–125). He does, however, accept as harmless the pragmatic use of stories and does not condemn Odysseus for his verbal disguises after his identity is revealed. Moreover, the beggar's use of Odysseus in the story of the cloak amuses Eumaeus in its clever pragmatism (14.508–509). See, e.g., Pratt 1993: 55–94 and the discussion below.

73. For the details of this similarity without reference to these strategies as stylistic ploys, see Walcot 1977; Haft 1984; and Emlyn-Jones 1986.

74. Odysseus' use of Crete has been attributed traditionally to mainland Greek culture's fascination with the island, plus the Cretan reputation for being agile sailors and raiders. See Càssola 1975: 74n.; Hoekstra 1974: 179. Peradotto 1990: 109–110, 120 notes the most obvious association with Cretans, which is that they are liars. Peradotto does not explain very precisely why he thinks Odysseus' use of Crete is meaningful, but he seems to imply that it constitutes a purposeful encoding of a clue to the nature of Odysseus' tale, i.e., that it is false. Haft 1984: 291n. 9 cites the literature of the debate on how the Cretans got their reputation for lying, but her classical citations show that the *Homeric Hymn to Demeter* is the only early text that emphasizes this aspect of Crete.

75. The fictional Odysseus' ambush, with its vocabulary of secrecy (οὐδέ τις ἡμέας / ἀνθρώπων ἐνόησε, λάθον δέ ἑ θυμὸν ἀπούρας, *Od.* 13.269–270), functions as an encoded indication of the speaker's own facility for deceit and plotting. See Haft 1984: 298 regarding Odysseus' and Meriones' excellence in ambush as aspects of their characters in the tradition.

76. Trahman 1952: 35 regards this as indicating that in this lie he is "cautious and noncommittal," as opposed to those he tells to Eumaeus and Penelope, where he is more fulsome in his description of his background.

77. The scholiasts noted regarding line 214 that the husk metaphor (καλάμην) added a rustic quality to Odysseus' speech. Aristotle (*Rhet.* 1410b14–15) approves the aptness of the metaphor and treats it as a stock reference to old age. The style seems also to borrow from travel or information gathering tales, e.g., the line with which Odysseus begins the tale told to Eumaeus echoes that of Eidothea to Menelaus (τοιγὰρ ἐγώ τοι ταῦτα μάλ' ἀτρεκέως ἀγορεύσω, *Od.* 14.192; cf. 4.383, 399; also *Il.* 10.405, 413, 427). And cf. Shipp 1972: 340 on the "Hesiodic style reflections" that characterize Eumaeus' own speech.

78. Cloaks have this symbolic significance in relation to both Odysseus and Helen; cf. further discussion in ch. 3.

79. Haft 1984: 293–294 notes the similarity of presentation between the Meriones passage in the Catalog of Ships (*Il.* 2.645–652) and Odysseus' praise of Crete here. The speech type that dominates in the catalog is formal praise, in both diction and tone.

80. Peradotto 1990: 109–110 takes the use of Idomeneus to be particularly meaningful here, apparently as a means of implying the veracity of the disguised Odysseus' eyewitness account.

81. Note the care taken to defend against detection of falsehood by repeatedly pairing "Aethon" with his more famous brother Idomeneus (19.181, 184, 190). The strategy fends off surprise at his lack of renown by emphasizing his youth and his happenstance entertainment of Odysseus. See Haft 1984: 296–299, following Shewan 1911: 169 and Clay 1983: 100. Odysseus seems to have "chosen" the Meriones persona as one likely to be familiar to his audiences (and therefore persuasive) but not specifically identifiable (and therefore safe as a disguise).

82. Cf. de Romilly 1974 and H. Parry 1992 on the magical implications of *thelgein*.

83. This technique is a good example of "style at the level of invention." Aristotle recognizes this use of character as one of the "artful" (ἔντεκνοι) proofs (*Rhet.* 1355b–1356a).

84. See Pl. *Ap.* 17a; Arist. *Rhet.* 1355b; also Demosth 18, 19, 35. See further discussion in ch. 5.

85. E.g., Gorg. *Hel.*; Thuc. 3.38; Eur. *Hec.* 131–132, *IA* 526. Halliwell 1997: 122 notes that in Thucydides, Cleon employs a quasi-Gorgianic style when inveighing against the Athenian connoiseurship of speeches.

CHAPTER 3

1. Vernant [1986] 1989: 28; also Monsacré 1984: 51–54. Cf. Goldhill 1998: 105–106.

2. MacLachlan 1993: 52; see 37n. 33 for Mycenean evidence associating *charis* and metallic shine. See also Prier 1989: 22, who notes that light in archaic Greek is the property that differentiates between "seeming" and "appearing," the latter identifying the emanation from the object. See also H. P. Foley 1998.

3. Zeitlin 1995a: 176.

4. E.g., Aphrodite (*Il.* 5.331, 425, *h.Ven.* 58–59), Hera (*Il.* 14.170–186), Helen (*Il.* 3.382, 385), and Paris (*Il.* 3.45, 371), Dionysus (Eur. *Bacch.* 453–459) for softness and perfume (and see discussion below); e.g., Odysseus (esp. *Od.* 6.137 and 13.435) for encrustedness and stench, Menelaus (*Od.* 4.441–442) and Philoctetes (Soph. *Phil.* 875–876) for stench, Orestes (Eur. *Or.* 220) for encrustedness. Lateiner 1995: 107 remarks, "Every culture has olfactory boundaries as well as touch boundaries, beyond which we register trespass."

5. E.g., Helen, *Il.* 3.141, 419–420; Aphrodite, *Il.* 3.64, 396–397, *Od.* 8.364–366, *h.Ven.* 1, 60–65, 85–90; Paris, *Il.* 3.392, 6.318–322, Eur. *Tro.* 987–992.

6. E.g., Helen, *Il.* 3.156–158, Eur. *Hec.* 441–443, *Or.* 1383–1387, *Tro.* 891–894; Aphrodite, *Il.* 3.396–397; cf. Anactoria in Sapph. fr. 16. These examples are discussed in greater detail below and in ch. 4.

7. That said, such distinctions may also be complicated by differences in status and gen-

eral *habitus*. In Homer a devious goddess like Hera unquestionably exerts her will on situations far more forcefully than do tender, pretty types like Paris. It is not only that their statuses are distinct as goddess and mortal but also that their significant features are: Hera's figure is more emphatically marked by a combative, bellicose affect, while Paris' manifests more passive, domestic affiliations. Paris seems to have earned his own blame tradition for being so clearly against the heroic male type (Suter 1993). Both he and Hera are roundly condemned by numerous characters in Homer. But it is more Paris' strong connections to the bedroom and the scene of seduction that earn him this abuse than (e.g.) his status as a bowman who thus does not engage in the more manly hand-to-hand combat. Note that Odysseus is also a bowman, and so are Heracles and Philoctetes, hardly effeminate types (cf. Eur. *HF* 157–161, 188–203).

8. Stehle 1997: 237–239 calls the poem a "compendium of topoi" and regards it as evidence of the threat women posed to the cohesion of the symposium.

9. The tone resembles that of Hes. *WD*, but Hesiod does not remark on the physical attributes of good and bad wives, regarding them all as pains in the lives of men. He lingers only over the body of Pandora in this way, while the links between the sexuality of women and the draining heat of the dog star suggest the connections between female character and bestiality that Semonides sets out in more emphatic terms (*WD* 582–588; cf. also Alcaeus fr. 347 L-P).

10. The Indo-European root *lôb*- is frequently associated with both physical and verbal disgrace; cf., e.g., *Od.* 20.285–300 and Nagy 1979: 261. Loraux 1993: 102–106 analyzes the way the figure of the bee woman conflates the categories of praise and blame (cf. Helen).

11. *Od.* 11.152, 11.628, 12.161, 12.434, 14.468, 14.503, 17.464, 21.426, 22.226; see Zeitlin 1995b: 29–30.

12. Buxton 1982: 31.

13. Like the bride, Helen's status as a decorative object traded among men is complicated by her ability to speak. Scholars of gender in Greek literature are fond of highlighting the problem that female characters pose as producers of signs (since they are themselves signs of a sort traded among male agents). They often cite Lévi-Strauss' famous formulation of this conundrum: "For words do not speak, while women do; as producers of signs, women can never be reduced to the status of symbols or tokens" (Lévi-Strauss 1963: 61). See, e.g., Bergren 1983; DuBois [1984] 1995; Suzuki 1989; Joplin 1991; Katz 1991; Wohl 1998.

14. See Calame 1977: 345–349 on Helen as leader of young girls' choruses and her relation to marriage; also Lardinois 2001. Cf. Stehle's (1997: 78–79) illuminating discussion on the passivity of the "acceptable" female body and its praise as part of public ritual.

15. See Mauss 1925 for the original formulation of this conundrum in early cultures. I address only what can be gleaned from archaic representation, but the cultural parallels are intriguing.

16. Cf. Calypso's soft and wheedling style (αἰεὶ δὲ μαλακοῖσι καὶ αἱμυλίοισι λόγοισι / θέλγει, *Od.* 1.56–57).

17. Loraux 1993; Saintillan 1995; Vernant 1995; Zeitlin 1995b.

18. See Loraux 1989: 241–243 on these connections.

19. This is a textual crux, as Solmsen (ed.) 1970 emphasizes; Verdenius 1984 ignores it. On Peitho, see Buxton 1982: 29–48.

20. A fifth-century amphoriskos typical of this type depicts a thoughtful Helen seated on Aphrodite's lap; Peitho stands behind, holding a jewelry box (pyxis). Jewelry boxes or flowers are the typical implements of Peitho in these scenes: see Ghali-Kahil 1955: 42, 71–89, pls. 42–45, 48, 56–62; Shapiro 1993: 192–194 and pl. 129, and cf. 203, pl. 1). On other vases Helen's clothing often seems to be particularly revealing or fancy. Although Hedreen 1996: 157–161, 168–169 argues that Helen's dress may not demonstrate her physical appeal, he agrees with Ghali-Kahil that the inclusion of Aphrodite, Eros, and/or Peitho in the scenes does indicate Helen's effect on her husband.

21. In Gorgias' defense of Helen (discussed in ch. 5), *erôs, peithô,* and *bia* are not simply abstractions but could be read as designating divine forces. Gorgias' lexicon—like that of other fifth-century writers on rhetoric, ethics, and epistemology—should not be categorized as strictly philosophical; such generic distinctions initiate with Aristotle. Rather, especially in the *Encomium,* Gorgias' style straddles what later tradition considered different genres, while his speech discusses peithô in inclusive terms. One could argue, moreover, that the iconographic lexicon of the period indicates the extent to which late fifth-century writers might not conceive of such figures as Peitho and Eros, who are so often depicted on fifth-century vases, as purely abstract forces. See Shapiro 1993: 110–124, 186–207; also Caskey and Beazley 1931–1963: 32–39; Buxton 1982: 49.

22. See Pepe 1967: 32 and Detienne [1967] 1996: 80–81 on ὀαριστὺς πάρφασις. Cf. the presence of Peitho in the abduction and return of Helen in vase depiction: Ghali-Kahil 1955: 55, 56, 57, 225–229, 252–256 and pls. 8.2–3, 11, 13, 23–35; Caskey and Beazley 1931–1963: 1.32–39; Shapiro 1993: 186–207.

23. On the role of these two figures in the crafting of Odysseus' appearance, see further below.

24. Recall that Aphrodite is "guile-minded" (δολοφρονέουσα) in Homer.

25. Cf. also Horace *Epod.* 14, where the soft forgetfulness of Amor ("deus") prevents the lover-poet from writing iambics for his patron:

> Mollis inertia cur tantam diffuderit imis
>   oblivionem sensibus,
> pocula Lethaeos ut si ducentia somnos
>   arente fauce traxerim,
> candide Maecenas, occidis saepe rogando.
>   deus, deus nam me vetat
> inceptos olim, promissum carmen, iambos
>   ad umbilicum adducere.

> You kill me often, glorious Maecenas,
> by asking why a gentle lassitude has spread
> such oblivion to my deepest senses,
> as if I had drunk down my dry throat
> cups bringing on the forgetful slumbers.
> For a god, a god prevents me
> from leading the iambs once begun,
> the promised song, to the margin.

The poem suggests that desire even affects one's ability to speak (or write) in a particular style (or genre).

26. Helen seems often to assume this position in lyric: cf. Sapph. fr. 16 L-P; Alc. frs. 111, 134 L-P.

27. It has been suggested that the lacuna in fr. 16.12–14 contained a reference to Aphrodite, particularly in relation to her role in Helen's abduction (e.g., Kirkwood 1979: 108; Burnett 1983: 228; Gentili [1985] 1988: 87 and n. 82). But even so, fr. 1 centers the maneuvering of the lover on the agency of Aphrodite as fr. 16 does not and like many lyric poems, explicitly designates Peitho as the agent who effects the change of heart in the reluctant beloved (τίνα δηὖτε πείθω / ‡ ἄψ σ' ἄγην ‡ ἐς σὰν φιλότατα, 18–19). Cf. Alcaeus fr. 134 L-P: πεῖθ' ἔρωι θῦμο (regarding Helen); Ibycus 288 PMG: Κύπρις / ἅ τ' ἀγανοβλέφαρος Πει-/ θώ (regarding one Euryalus).

28. Or "of the variegated mind," ποικιλόφρον; L-P iii codd. M, R, U, D, K; see Winkler 1990: 167.

29. Cf. Theog. 221–226 for a more austere application of these terms, but one that maintains the connection between mental intricacy and plot-weaving:

ὅστις τοι δοκέει τὸν πλησίον ἴδμεναι οὐδέν,
ἀλλ' αὐτὸς μοῦνος ποικίλα δήνε' ἔχειν,
κεῖνός γ' ἄφρων ἐστί, νόου βεβλαμμένος ἐσθλοῦ·
ἴσως γὰρ πάντες ποικίλ' ἐπιστάμεθα·
ἀλλ' ὁ μὲν οὐκ ἐθέλει κακοκερδείησιν ἕπεσθαι,
τῶι δὲ δολοπλοκίαι μᾶλλον ἄπιστοι ἅδον.

Whoever thinks that his neighbor knows nothing,
but that he himself alone has complex thoughts,
that man is a fool, distracted from right thinking.
For perhaps we all understand complex things;
but one man does not wish to pursue base desires,
while to another false guile-weaving gives more pleasure.

Elsewhere, the poet refers to Aphrodite as δολοπλόκε (1386), further supporting the analogies argued for here: even in the passage from 221–226, δολοπλοκίαι would have this additional resonance.

30. Cf. Rhet. 1356a13.

31. On Helen, cf. Clader 1976: 6–11; Atchity 1978; Zeitlin 1982; Bergren 1983; Kennedy 1986. On Helen and Odysseus separately, cf. Austin 1975: 127–128. On Odysseus, cf. Austin 1975; Pucci 1987, 1998: 131–178; Segal 1994; Rose 1992: 92–140.

32. On the relation between weaving and cunning, see Detienne and Vernant 1978. On specifically Greek imagery, see Stanford [1936] 1972: 130; for the Indo-European background, see Snyder 1981. Scheid and Svenbro 1996 provide a full-length study of weaving imagery. Menelaus' and Odysseus' speechifying (as a paradigmatic example in Homer) is described by Antenor as weaving muthoi in an embassy to the Trojans (μύθους καὶ μήδεα ὕφαινον, Il. 3.212); cf. Il. 6.187, 7.324; Od. 4.677–678, 5.356–357, 9.422–423, 13.303–304, 13.386. See also Pucci 1987; R. P. Martin 1989: 95–96; Nagy 1996: 64–65n. 93.

33. On women and weaving, see Austin 1975; Bergren 1979–1980; Joplin 1991; Katz 1991; Scheid and Svenbro 1996.

34. Cf. Rose 1988: 17–18 on Thersites' physical type. The threatened removal of Thersites' clothes underscores how his already offensive appearance exacerbates the negative effect of his disorderly verbal conduct. The narrator also highlights his words as unpersuasive, since they are literally out of place (*akosmos*) within the hierarchy of the Achaean assembly. This treatment of the puny but clever challengers of heroes repeatedly turns up in modern popular drama: e.g., in a past season of the television show *NYPD Blue*, the handsome, heroic Detective Simone responded to the devious locutions of a small, hunch-shouldered, bespectacled, balding informant by striking him and threatening him with being stripped and sent running through the streets of New York.

35. See Nagy 1979: 259–262.

36. It thus seems more similar to the later tradition that denigrates Odysseus (but cf. Hainsworth 1993: 151).

37. Dolon's body is thus also treated in an iambic manner. Bakhtin 1984: 195, 347–352 has emphasized that satiric writers describe the body in piecemeal fashion, with its most disreputable parts emphasized especially when the body is beaten, abused, denied, or threatened with a dismemberment that reiterates the representational scheme.

38. Cf. Walsh 1984: 7: "One man is physically undistinguished, but his words have *morphê*; another, godlike in appearance, speaks without grace (*kharis*)." Walsh argues that the Homeric notion of *kosmos* is that of fit between the ordering of the poet's song and that of the world (9), which is pleasing and which is to be distinguished from "a selective, pointed truth, which seems inevitably disturbing" (20). He urges further that poetry inspires belief by its enchanting style, unlike the pointed story, which—because it taps into the listener's experience—gives that listener the tools by which to judge the story's veracity. Such distinctions are problematic and ultimately disintegrate under inspection of individual episodes. Eumaeus, for instance, is charmed by Odysseus' fabricated life story, which is clearly pointed and shaped to appeal to the listener's experience.

39. R. P. Martin 1989: 96 regards Odysseus' uncommanding posture and way of holding the staff as "an unconventional strategy for capturing his audience." This positive framing of the hero's stance does not, however, account sufficiently for why the poet highlights the contrast between his deportment and his speaking style. Stanley 1993: 64 comments that the scepter is a reminder of previous deception (*Il.* 2.199) and notes but does not analyze the contrast between Odysseus' "unprepossessing looks" and his "magnificent rhetoric."

40. Soph. *Phil.* 440–442; Philoctetes refers to a man "redoubtable and clever in speech" (γλώσσῃ δὲ δεινοῦ καὶ σοφοῦ, 440). Further parallels tie the figures of Odysseus and Thersites together. For instance, Odysseus describes his herald Eurybates as round-shouldered, dark-skinned, and wooly-haired (γυρὸς ἐν ὤμοισιν, μελανόχροος, οὐλοκάρηνος, *Od.* 19.246); but he is also like Odysseus in character (οἱ φρεσὶν ἄρτια, 19.248). Moreover, the blows with which Odysseus threatens the abusive Thersites in the *Iliad* (πεπλήγων . . . ἀεικέσσιν πληγῇσιν, 2.264) parallel the striking rhetorical effect emblematized by Odysseus' figure in fifth-century literature (e.g., ἔμπληκτοι, Soph. *Aj.* 1358; ἔκπληξιν, Gorg. *Pal.* 4; see the discussion in ch. 5). Note also that although Alcibiades likens Socrates to a satyr,

he also credits him with inducing *ekplêxis* in his listeners (ἐκπεπληγμένοι, Pl. *Symp.* 215d5). Alcibiades' description thus suggests a pairing of unheroic aspect with striking speech that resembles that embodied by Odysseus.

41. *Od.* 4.252–253, 5.264, 10.360–367. Vernant [1986] 1991: 102–110 considers Helen, Circe, the Sirens, and Calypso as all personifying a deadly desire, likening them to the Kêres. Cf. Vermeule 1979: 69.

42. Circe and Helen also share the handling of *pharmaka* and the accompanying ability to distract, manipulate, and deceive others (*Od.* 4.220, 10.235). Both thereby offer their guests a forgetfulness that suits an atmosphere of sustained pleasure seeking. Helen's ambiguous drug has the palliative effect that Circe's entire domestic atmosphere seems to offer. Although Circe's drug would seem to be one of ill effect (κακά, λύγρ': 10.213, 236), Odysseus' men weep when they are returned to their human forms, raising a γόος that fills Circe's house and upsets even her (10.398; see Suzuki 1989: 66–67). This weeping scene has traditionally been interpreted as one of joyful relief, but the scene seems deliberately ambiguous. Crane 1988: 31 notes the similarity of this transformation to that between this world and Hades. Helen and Circe also share powers of prophecy and insight, so that their male advisees Odysseus and Telemachus hold similarly subordinate positions in relation to their divine types (10.487–495, 503–540 and 15.172–178); cf. also Nagler 1996.

43. The cluster of vocabulary surrounding the scenes involving threatening goddesses suggests not only aestheticizing references to garments and bodies (*ambrosios, poikilos*) but also the charm (*thelxis*) that accompanies such seductions. Compare *Od.* 10.318 (*thelxis, perikallês*), Hera's preparation for seduction at *Il.* 14.161–186 (*thelxis, ambrosios, poikilos*), and Aphrodite's seduction of Anchises in the *h.Ven.* 61–90 (*ambrosios, poikilos*).

44. Cf. Block 1985: 10–11, who notes this patterning of divine females clothing Odysseus but does not relate it to narrative structure. See also Bassi 1998: 118–133, who argues that such manipulations render the hero's body "theatrical."

45. The verb has sexual connotations (e.g., μίγη φιλότητι καί εὐνῆ, *Od.* 5.126). Nausicaa uses a form of it twice (ἐπιμίσγεται, 6.205, 241) to underscore the singularity of Odysseus' coming into contact with the Phaeacians.

46. *Kerdos* may be a neutral consideration in persuasive situations or carry negative connotations (see esp. Hes. *WD*). Cf. the related κερδαλέον, which gain-seeking quality Athena later allies with "deceptive" (ἐπίκλοπος) tendencies in her teasing characterization of Odysseus (*Od.* 13.291).

47. When Aphrodite describes Paris to titillate Helen, she gives him this same glistening look (κάλλεῖ τε στίλβων καὶ εἵμασιν, *Il.* 3.392).

48. Regarding this polishing of Odysseus, Clay 1983: 168 comments on the likening of the crafted objects of gods to those of men.

49. See Shipp 1972: 327, who considers the passage "distinguished by meaningless alliteration." But it is precisely this type of feature (i.e., alliteration) to which the term *meilichios* (6.143, 146, 148) most likely refers, the pleasant quality arising more from *how* one says something than from *what* one says. The unremarkable diction of Odysseus' speech is appropriately formal, familiar and thus unthreatening in content, and sweetly chiming, as a means of counteracting the frightening savagery of the naked, salty man.

50. Odysseus: μείζονά τ' εἰσιδέειν καὶ πάσσονα (*Od.* 6.230, 23.157); Penelope: καί μιν μακροτέρην καὶ πάσσονα θῆκεν ἰδέσθαι (18.195); Odysseus: χάρις (6.235, 23.162); Penelope: κάλλει . . . ἀμβροσίῳ (18.192–193).

51. *Od.* 23.156–163. This is the only difference between the passages: cf. κάλλει καὶ χάρισι στίλβων (6.237).

52. H. P. Foley 2001 has analyzed the relevance of Aristotle's notion of *prohairesis* and his assumptions about women's capacity for moral choice to Penelope's decision to await the return of Odysseus. My point here is that the very identification of agency is obscure in Helen's case, as Penelope herself indicates (23.222). On Helen's ambiguity in a deconstructive sense—i.e., as a "figure of difference"—see Suzuki 1989.

53. Prier 1989: 76 notes that the word ὤψ designates the expression of the eyes seen in the act of looking. Regarding the deadly power of Helen's eyes, cf. Eur. *Hec.* 441–443, *Or.* 1383–1387; and see Zeitlin [1991] 1995: 201–202 (and cf. 186). See also Austin 1994: 80–82 on Helen's "fateful gaze" and her powers of detection.

54. In the *Iliad* Helen's rejection of her own passion and her desire for death connect her to more chaste female characters like Penelope. See Clader 1976; cf. Penelope's invocation of Artemis and wish for death (*Od.* 20.61–65), which echo Helen's in *Il.* 6.

55. Clader 1976: 56–60. Cf. Nagler 1974: 44–60 on the significance of the *krêdemnon* in Homer.

56. The *othonê* turns up in two other places in Homer: on the attendants of Ariadne on Achilles' shield (*Il.* 18.595) and in the hands of the godlike Phaeacian women (*Od.* 7.107). Besides Helen, only Hera and Artemis wear the *heanos* (*Il.* 14.178, 21.507), the adjectival form of which means "fine." Thus the substantive designates a "fine cloth," which seems to be used as a veil by these goddesses.

57. Recall that elsewhere the narrator describes Helen's own handiwork as fine or rich (δίπλακα πορφυρέην, 3.126; περικλυτὰ ἔργα, 6.324; cf. *Od.* 15.105–108). Theocritus emphasizes her talent as a weaver (*Id.* 22), which suggests that this was an important aspect of her traditional character.

58. Later poets seem to have reversed the Homeric tradition of cloaking Helen's body or at least suggested that she used her uncovered body to avert Menelaus' wrath. The iconographic evidence may well parallel this change from the representation of her body as fully cloaked (and often veiled) to partially or fully naked. The influence of poetic on iconographic images of Helen (or vice versa) has been much disputed, and scholars cannot even agree on whether certain images do record Helen—or Aphrodite—uncovering Helen's body and to what extent. Ghali-Kahil's 1955 study of the iconographic and literary treatment of Helen is still the most exhaustive treatment of the visual evidence to date; regarding the pursuit scenes, see Kahil 1988: 539–545. Two fifth-century texts record Menelaus' reaction to Helen's form: both Aristophanes' *Lysistrata* (155–156) and Euripides' *Andromache* (629–630) depict her naked body as literally disarming, since her stunned husband drops his sword at the sight of her breasts. Scholiasts on both texts attribute this tradition to Ibycus; that on the *Lysistrata* also credits Lesches' *Little Iliad* (see Davies, ed. 1988: 58 no. 19; 1991: 289 no. 296). Some scholars have thought that certain visual representations that predate the plays might record a similar scene, but cf. Hedreen 1996, who has argued that none of the images thought to show the revealing of Helen's body actually do so. However tenuous the relationship be-

tween text and image may be, it does seem clear that there is a tradition in which Helen's appearance has this disarming effect. Later images of Helen's toilette and her meeting with Paris show her partly or fully nude: Ghali-Kahil 1955: pls. 21, 23, 28.3, 29.4, 38.3, 42.1; see also Shapiro 1993: pls. 29, 59. Note that Euripides has Helen claim that her body *cannot* be hidden (*Tro.* 958; see further discussion in ch. 4).

59. The magic belt that contains Aphrodite's love charms in the *Dios apatê* is also called a κεστὸς ἱμάς (*Il.* 14.214–215); see Faraone 1990.

60. Aphrodite's own throat is described elsewhere as soft (ἁπαλῇ δειρῇ, *h.Ven.* 88); see below regarding Helen's recognition of her "very lovely throat" (περικαλλέα δειρήν, 3.396). Cf. also the body of Briseis (another object of desire and contention) at *Il.* 19.285: στήθεά τ' ἠδ' ἁπαλὴν δειρήν.

61. ἁρπάζω is the verb commonly used in such scenes (cf. Paris' own seizure of Helen, 3.443); καλύπτω also tends to indicate being saved for the love scene and/or enveloped in desire itself (*Il.* 3.442, 14.343). Helen's bedrooms are also perfumed (with incense): *Il.* 3.382 (θαλάμῳ εὐώδεϊ; *Od.* 4.121 (θαλάμοιο θυώδεος). Aphrodite's Cyprus is similarly sweet smelling in *h.Ven.* (θυώδεα / εὐώδεα Κύπρον, 58, 66), as is her altar (βωμός τε θυώδης, 59).

62. Clader 1976: 57 points out that the poet depicts the palace in Sparta as shining like the sun (e.g., *Od.* 4.42, 73) and generally gleaming with rich metals.

63. Clader 1976: 62. Clader also connects both Nemesis and Helen to Artemis as goddesses of vegetation. Note that in the *Odyssey* passage, Helen is likened to Artemis, a common comparison for aristocratic women (cf. Nausicaa and Penelope, e.g.). But here the comparison may serve as a link between Helen and a goddess similar to her: both have a golden distaff (29); both may be *kourotrophoi* (Clader 1976: 75–78).

64. Note that Helen uses the word μνῆμα, which designates some sort of ritual marker, such as a monument or tombstone, something often inscribed, which is analogous to the public, authoritative labeling of the gown that Helen effects with her speech.

CHAPTER 4

1. The interaction between writing and the visual arts has been much discussed in recent years; see, e.g., Calame 1986; Goldhill and Osborne (eds.) 1994; Benediktson 2000; Rutter and Sparkes (eds.) 2000; Steiner 2001; Zeitlin forthcoming. For the ways in which the visible details of staging intersect with written imagery in dramatic mimesis, see (e.g.) H. P. Foley 1980; Wiles 1991; Worman 1999b, 2001b.

2. Zeitlin 1980, 1990; Segal 1982; cf. Falkner 1998; Lada-Richards 1998; Ringer 1998.

3. Ar. *Ach.* 407–89, *Ran.* 1063. The sources for tragic costumes in general are troublingly late: e.g., Athen. 1.21d; Philostr. *V.A.* 6.11. See the discussion of Pickard-Cambridge 1968: 177–180; also Rehm 1992: 66–67; Csapo and Slater 1995: 256–257; Bassi 1998: 14–15.

4. Cf. ch. 2, n. 4.

5. On the semiotics of theater, see Ubersfeld 1977; Elam 1980.

6. Masks and props of various sorts were also used in earlier ritual, of course, but the theatrical setting develops this kind of enactment into full-blown spectacle centered on character and plot.

7. E.g., Agathon and Euripides in Ar. *Thesm.*; Dionysus in Ar. *Ran.* On the comic body type, see H. P. Foley 2000.

8. Cf. Gorg. *Hel.* 2; Pl. *Phdr.* 2.73a10; Arist. *Rhet.* 1378a11.

9. See Ober 1989: 59; Poulakos 1995: 44–45.

10. E.g., Hdt. 1.60, 2.37, 2.47, 3.72; Aesch. *Pers.* 833; Eur. *Hec.* 269, *Or.* 1145, *Tro.* 951, *Rhes.* 841.

11. The sophists wore the purple robes of the rhapsodes (Aelian *VH* 12.32); cf. Pl. *Hp. Mi.* 363c and O'Sullivan 1992: 66–67.

12. Gorgias is the most obvious example; in this he is followed by Alcidamas (cf. *Soph.* 3, 22, 34).

13. We know about this version from Eur. *Hel.*; Pl. *Phdr.* 243a3–b2; and a Hellenistic commentary (*POxy.* 2506, fr. 26, col. 1). On Stesichorus and Helen's relationship to the construction of an authoritative tradition see Bassi 1993; and cf. Nagy 1990a: 419–423. Austin 1994 provides an exhaustive treatment of this version of Helen's story.

14. See Zeitlin forthcoming.

15. MacLachlan 1993: 66 explains, "At the departure of one of the love partners, the *charis* that is connected with this love-flash of the eyes disappears." See also Fletcher 1999.

16. Praise speech is the language of *agalmata*, as Pindar and the choral odes in tragedy often make clear (e.g., *Nem.* 3.21, 8.27; Eur. *HF* 358, 425), but praise of Helen is difficult to sustain.

17. Denniston and Page 1957 are adamant that neither the lion cub nor the Erinys should be identified with Helen; but both clearly illuminate aspects of her traditional character (cf. Barlow 1971: 4–6). Even the troublesome epithet νυμφόκλαυτος, which as a -τος adjective means literally "wept for by brides," may also suggest the reverse: a bride who makes others weep.

18. See ch. 5 for further discussion of Alcibiades.

19. As Zeus' revenge for past wrongs, cf. Pandora.

20. See ch. 3.

21. In Euripides' *Hippolytus* the chaste protagonist finds women deceptively valuable: "O Zeus, why did you make women—a counterfeit evil for men [κίβδηλον ἀνθρώποις κακόν]—dwell in the light of the sun?" (616–617). Hippolytus' assessment sets women in relation to a system of exchange that has no essential value (no use value); the coin's exchange value depends on its appearing to conform to accepted standards of weight and measure, guaranteed by official imprimatur. The underlying suggestion is that public standards for the assessment of worth may be mistaken and that in the case of women they are paradigmatically so. On Helen and currency, see Wohl 1998: 228n. 2.

22. See Carey 1981: 144–146; Most 1985: 148–156; Pratt 1993: 128.

23. Note that this is the effect that Aphrodite has on her favorites; cf. Sapph. fr. 16 and discussion in ch. 5. For the idea contained in κλέπτουσι ... μύθοις, cf. Soph. *Aj.* 188, *Phil.* 55, and discussion below.

24. Farnell [1932] 1965: 291. Pratt 1993: 124 argues that the passage is in fact "praise of poetry's persuasive power" (following Gerber 1982: 59–60).

25. Cf. also Hecuba's charge against Odysseus in the *Trojan Women*, which makes him sound like a sophist (283–287); see further below.

26. These arguments had their own tradition in the epic cycles and later in fifth-century poetry and rhetoric (Arct. *Aeth.; Il. Parv.;* Aesch. fr. 175 N²; Antisth. *Aj.*). See further discussion in ch. 5.

27. *Certamen,* fr. Allen.

28. Note, again, that in the *Rhetoric* Aristotle opposes the λόγος that is ἁπλούστερος to that which is ποικίλος (1416b25), but without condemnation of the latter; cf. Eur. *Phoen.* 469–470 for a more critical view: ἁπλοῦς ὁ μῦθος τῆς ἀληθείας ἔφυ, / κοὐ ποικίλων δεῖ τἄνδιχ' ἑρμηνευμάτων.

29. Nagy 1979: 224–227; Pratt 1993: 121, 128. A similar tradition seems to have developed in the fifth century around Palamedes (e.g., Pl. *Ap.* 41b; Xen. *Ap.* 26).

30. Parmentier 1948: 6–9, 40; Scodel 1980. Cf. Ar. *Thesm.* 528–530: ὑπὸ λίθῳ γὰρ / παντί που χρὴ / μὴ δάκη ῥήτωρ ἀθρεῖν.

31. In this same play Agamemnon describes this love exchange in similarly elegant terms (ἐρῶν ἐρῶσαν, 75). Helen is the one with the fluttered heart in the Lesbian poets, most famously Sappho, fr. 16, but cf. also Alcaeus fr. 283 L-P.

32. Cf. Saïd 1985 on the relationship between sophistic ideas and the figure of Prometheus in Aesch. *PV.* For further discussion of the features of the grand sophistic style, see ch. 5.

33. E.g., Aphrodite: *Il.* 3.405 (δολοφρονέουσα); Sapph. fr. 1.1 (ποικιλόφρον, Neuberger-Donath ms.); Sapph. fr. 1.2 (δολοπλόκε); Sim. 43 (δολόμητις); Eur. *Andr.* 289 (δολίοις . . . λόγοις), *IA* 1300 (δολιόφρων), *Hel.* 238 (δόλιος). Odysseus: *Il.* 11.482 (ποικιλομήτης); *Od.* 3.163, 7.168, 13.293, 22.115, 202, 281 (ποικιλομήτης); Eur. *Hec.* 131 (ποικιλόφρων); Eur. *Rhes.* 894 (δόλιος); Eur. *Tro.* 282 (δολίῳ); Soph. *Phil.* 608 (δόλιος), cf. 100–134, where Odysseus' favored technique is persuasion by guile (δόλῳ, 101).

34. While the reference to Helen's story in Plato's *Phaedrus* is encouraging for its insertion into a speech about desire, especially in a dialogue about good and bad *peithô,* Socrates' invocation of her is not developed further. Nor is there any development of these ideas in the fragments of Stesichorus; and Euripides in his play does not focus on how the figure of Helen forges connections between vision and persuasive speech so much as between vision and reality, effectively circumventing the problems that persuasive style raises regarding the relation between the way things appear and the way they are. There is, however, much to say about how Helen and her *eidôlon* relate to seeing double, the doubling of narrative, and the metatheatrical aspects of her figure; many scholars have addressed these topics: see, e.g., Woodbury 1967; Zeitlin 1982; Bergren 1983; Walsh 1984; Bassi 1993; Austin 1994; Zeitlin forthcoming.

35. Stanford 1963 [1981] notes this connection (*ad Aj.* 1367).

36. Most commentators consider the composition of Gorgias' speech to be slightly earlier than that of the *Trojan Women*—around 416. For a review of the dating debate, see DK 1952: 288n. 1; Buchheim 1989: 160n. 2. Gregory 1991: 158 thinks that Gorgias' influence can be seen throughout the play, but she makes only superficial use of the Gorgianic material. Scodel 1980: 90n. 26, 99, 144 similarly avoids any detailed comparison of the two speeches, although she asserts that Euripides used Gorgias as a source not only for Helen's speech in the *Trojan Women* but also for Palamedes' in the *Palamedes.* Goldhill 1986: 237 agrees. See also Croally 1994: 137–145, who notes that Helen is adept at using rhetorical commonplaces (which is not

in itself particular to Helen in Greek tragedy) and that at least three of her arguments are Gorgianic in their attribution of blame (divine will, physical force, erotic attraction). Only Lloyd 1992: 100–101 to my knowledge rejects any correlation between the two speeches, arguing that there is little precise correspondence of *topoi* in the speeches and that the subject matter was common fodder for set pieces of the period.

37. Lloyd 1984; Vellacott 1975: 136–148.

38. So Kitto 1950: 213; Lee 1976; Scodel 1980; and Gellie 1986. Ebener 1954 thinks Hecuba is also reduced in stature in this episode.

39. Gellie 1986.

40. E.g., Paley 1872; Lee 1976; Scodel 1980; Gregory 1991.

41. Cf. the argument that Callicles takes up in Plato's *Gorgias,* and note that Helen and Callicles are both dashing and seductive speakers. Gorgias and Plato are not, however, treating the issue of the will of the stronger in the same manner: Gorgias merely notes that it is natural (πέφυκε, *Hel.* 3), while Plato's Callicles seeks to demonstrate that this is how it ought to be: "Nature herself declares that it is right that the better man have more than the lesser, and the more powerful more than the less powerful" (φύσις αὐτὴ ἀποφαίνει αὐτό, ὅτι δίκαιόν ἐστι τὸν ἀμείνω τοῦ χείρονος πλέον ἔχειν καὶ τὸν δυνατώτερον τοῦ ἀδυνατωτέρου, *Gorg.* 483c8–d2; cf. Thrasymachus in *Rep.* 341a, 343c). Scodel 1980: 98 proposes that Helen's invocation of such late fifth-century theories as the right of the stronger gives currency to her otherwise tenuous claim that Aphrodite was to blame for her behavior.

42. Cf. Theoclymenus and Menelaus in *Hel.* and Menelaus in *IA,* for this character type: dependent on *bia,* slow-thinking, especially in contrast to the female characters. Biehl 1989: 320 refers to Menelaus' entrance as "Tragikomik."

43. Regarding the deadly power of Helen's eyes, cf. *Hec.* 441–443, *Or.* 1383–1387, *IA* 583–586. Recall also that in Homer, Helen's appearance at the Trojan wall suggests that she is like Medusa, whose gaze is overwhelming (*Il.* 3.156–158); cf. Hecuba's baleful wish for the sight of Helen, which is followed by a claim that Helen's beautiful eyes steal happiness from others (Ἑλένην ἴδοιμι· διὰ καλῶν γὰρ ὀμμάττων / αἴσχιστα Τροίαν εἷλε τὴν εὐδαίμονα, *Hec.* 442–443). On Helen as a kind of fiery-eyed avenger in the *Hec.* (ἀλάστωρ, 687) see Zeitlin 1991: 201–202; cf. 186. Clader 1976: 16–23 argues convincingly that there are traces of the dread Helen inspires in Homer also (e.g., κυνὸς κακομηχάνου ὀκρυοέσσης [6.344], στυγερήν [3.404], and πεφρίκασιν [24.775], all metaphors associated with fear and death that Helen uses to describe her effect on others). Cf. also Eur. *Hel.* 926.

44. See further in ch. 5. The meanings of κήλημα, κήλησις, ἐπῳδή, and ἐπῳδός all overlap. For example, the process of κήλησις involves ἐπῳδαί in Pl. *Euthd.* 289e–290a; Gorgias uses both ἐπῳδή and ἐπῳδός to describe the rhythmic enchantment of *logos* (*Hel.* 9). Paley 1872 compares Aesch. *Ag.* 689–690, where Aeschylus gives Helen's name the famous etymology of catastrophe: ἕλεναυς, ἕλανδρος, ἑλέπτολις.

45. Croally 1994: 136, 145; see also Lee 1976: 225, 241; Burnett 1977: 294–295. Lloyd 1984: 305 disagrees.

46. This is Kahil's reading of the figure (Kahil [= Ghali-Kahil] 1988: 538, no. 225). On the striking quality of the image, see Burnett 1977: 292–293n. 4.

47. Ghali-Kahil 1955: 42, 71–89; pls. 42–45, 48, 56–62. Hedreen 1996: 157–161, 168–169 argues that Helen's clothing is not necessarily revealing, but he agrees with Kahil that the

typical inclusion of Aphrodite, Eros, and/or Peitho in the scenes indicates Helen's effect on her husband.

48. Again, only in Euripides' anomalous play *Helen* is the heroine prepared to cut her hair and put on mourning clothes for purposes of deceit (*Hel.* 1053-1054). Remember also that in the *Or.*, Electra calls attention to Helen's reluctance to cut her hair (128-130).

49. This kind of exactitude (ἀκρίβεια) was said to mark the precise, writerly styles of Prodicus and Euripides. See O'Sullivan 1992: 14-22.

50. Schiassi 1953: 161 thinks εὖ λέγειν refers to content rather than style; Parmentier 1948: 65 also translates the phrase "*mes raisons.*" But clearly the phrase refers to *how* the speech is structured, as the adverbial εὖ κἂν κακῶς indicates (and cf. the aforementioned phrase of the chorus: λέγει καλῶς, 967-968).

51. Cf. the discussion in ch. 1.

52. One can, however, isolate similarities of expression here and there: e.g., the alliteration in 917-918 (ἀντιθεῖσ' ἀμείψομαι . . . αἰτιάματα), the parisosis in 941-942 (ὁ τῆσδ' ἀλάστωρ, εἴτ' Ἀλέξανδρον θέλεις . . . εἴτε καὶ Πάριν), or the homoioteleuton of 946-947 (φρονοῦσα . . . προδοῦσα). Bers 1994: 178 (and n. 11) notes that the literal transference of rhetorical figures to verse is rare.

53. Scodel 1980: 53-100.

54. On the circularity of praise speech, see further in ch. 5.

55. E.g., ἧς τοὺς ἀκούοντας εἰσῆλθε καὶ φρίκη περίφοβος καὶ ἔλεος πολύδακρυς καὶ πόθος φιλοπενθής (*Hel.* 9.22-23; cf. 6.1-2, 7.10-11, 9.28).

56. Apollodorus tells the story of Hecuba's dream of the firebrand, which warned her about the threat her new son posed to the safety of Troy (3.12.5). Lloyd 1992: 102 argues that "the existence of . . . parallels [in Euripides' plays] suggests that Helen's argument [that Hecuba and Priam were originally responsible for the chain of events] has some substance" and that Euripides was himself very interested in the causal sequence that led to the Trojan war. That is, Helen's use of the argument is not merely an ironic extension of a rhetorical commonplace but rather serves as a legitimate means to question the attribution of blame.

57. The word βρέφος refers to the physical body of the newly born human or animal, and is cognate with ἔμβρυον (embryo, cf. Lat. *mortuus*).

58. Helen repeats this triangulation halfway through her speech (ὁ τῆσδ' ἀλάστωρ, εἴτ' Ἀλέξανδρον . . . εἴτε καὶ Πάριν). Cf. Alcman, fr. 73 (40 D): Δύσπαρις, αἰνόπαρις, κακὸν Ἑλλάδι βωτιανείρᾳ; and, again, Aeschylus' triadic play on Helen's name in the *Ag.* (689-690). Suter 1993 has argued that the names Ἀλέξανδρος and Πάρις divide praise and blame traditions respectively between them, which would suggest that in Helen's speech Paris' double tradition (which should recall her own) flanks an epithet that marks him as the kind of fiery force that she is herself often described as embodying.

59. Cf. Havelock 1963: 145-164, who argues that the physical experience of rhythms in ancient Greek poetic performance constituted the central means by which the poetic perspective was inculcated and effectively lived. Bourdieu [1980] 1990: 73 cites this idea as an example of the body's involvement in the learning of cultural habits and beliefs.

60. Lloyd 1992: 101 notes Helen's similarity to Palamedes in Gorgias' speech: they both must speak first, although they are the defendants (he also compares the Plataeans in Thuc. 3.53.2, and Socrates in Pl. *Ap.* 18b1-d7). I would add that Helen also echoes Palamedes' mode

of argumentation in more specific ways: here, when she exhorts her larger audience to consider what she has done for them (cf. *Pal.* 28); when she uses an argument from eyewitness accounting to deny the possibility of her escape (*Tro.* 955–958; cf. *Pal.* 7, 9); and when she uses connective sentences such as τὸν ἐνθέν' ὡς ἔχει σκέψαι λόγον (931; cf. *Pal.* 13: σκέψασθε κοινῇ καὶ τόδε). The speech in the *Trojan Women* thus incorporates both deeper stylistic patternings from Gorgias' *Encomium of Helen* and more superficial strategic elements from *Palamedes' Defense*. As mentioned above, Scodel 1980 thinks that both of Gorgias' speeches, as well as his philosophical treatises *On Not Being* (*Peri tou mê ontos*) and *On Nature* (*Peri phuseos*), were known to Euripides and influenced his presentation of these arguments.

61. Cf. vase depictions of the marriage of Paris and Helen (cited above and in ch. 3), where Aphrodite, Eros, and/or Peitho are in attendance.

62. At *Od.* 4.261 Helen, in her speech to her drugged audience, presents the will of Aphrodite as regrettably irresistible.

63. Suggesting an emerging attitude toward the depiction of those figures most closely associated with *erôs*, the *Trojan Women*, like Gorgias' *Encomium*, emphasizes Helen's body while continuing to question her agency in her seduction. The references in Aristophanes (*Lys.* 155–156) and Euripides (*Andr.* 629–630) to Helen partially revealing her body stand in contrast to the earlier vase depictions, which show her fully covered. In the visual arts depictions of Helen changed radically later on: she is sometimes shown partially nude after the fifth century (Hedreen 1996: 160); cf. the figure of Aphrodite.

64. The wording is somewhat ambiguous: τὰ δ' οἴκοθεν κεῖν' ἀντὶ νικητηρίων / πικρῶς ἐδούλευσ'. Ought Helen to be treated as or herself receive the victory prizes? Lee (1976) takes it as the former, Scodel (1980) as the latter. Since the verb δουλεύω marks the state of being a slave, the more obvious parallel would be the argument that she should be treated like a victory prize, which in any case accords much better with Homeric tradition. The line would thus read: "In the affairs of the household I was, bitterly, a slave, instead of [being treated like] victory prizes are." The image recalls the tapestry of the battles being fought over her that she weaves in book 3 of the *Iliad*, as well as the repeated treatment there of her as a disputed prize akin to other household valuables. Compare also Helen's use of her body as property in her supplication speech in Euripides' *Helen*.

65. On *ekplêxis*, see also ch. 5.

66. DK 82A4, Gorg. *Hel.* 16, *Pal.* 4; cf. O'Sullivan 1992: 21 and n. 104.

67. Croally 1994: 145 thinks that the chorus' invocation of *peithô* here in fact constitutes a pun on Hecuba's warning to Menelaus about Helen's ability to seize "by desire" (πόθῳ, 891).

68. The implication there as here is that of the danger of learned contrivance in persuasive speech (Demosth. 35.40–43, 39.14; Isae. 10.1; Lyc. 1.20); see Ober 1989: 166–174 on the suspicions aroused by the perception that a speaker is too well prepared. For Aristotle, κατασκευάζειν seems to denote the "preparation" of the judge by the use of character commendation and appeals to his emotions (*Rhet.* 1377b20–78a5). In Plato's *Gorgias* (509–510), preparation (παρασκευή) is discussed as a technique (τέχνη) for wrongdoing. Cf. also Plato's *Apology*, where Socrates denies his capacity for clever speech (*deinos legein*) while uttering well-balanced, elaborate, and rhythmically effective phrases; see North 1988.

69. Cf. Andromache's claim to her mother that she does not participate in the "polished talk" (κομψὰ ... ἔπη) of the women's quarters (651–652). Note also that Schiassi 1953: 167 and

Lee 1976: 234–235 see this as a reference to both facile speech and specious argumentation ("rovinosi discorsi"). Parmentier 1948 compares *Gorgias* 453a regarding *peithô*.

70. Helen's desire for Trojan riches (cf. *Tro.* 991–997) is a common charge of the Greeks against her, according to the anomalous Helen in *Helen* (294–296). Cf. also Euripides' *Cretans*, where Pasiphae (attempting to explain her passion for the bull) details in terms similar to Hecuba's the kind of well-dressed beauty that would normally have tempted her (Eur. *Cret.* fr. 472e N²). Foreigners, and particularly those from the East, often betray such decadent tastes in Greek literature; cf. also the *lampros* style of Alcibiades in Thucydides, and the discussion in cf. 5.

71. Cf. Hera's finery in the deception of Zeus (ἀμφὶ δ' ἄρ' ἀμβρόσιον ἑανὸν ἔσαθ', ὅν οἱ Ἀθήνη / ἔξυσ' ἀσκήσασα, τίθει δ' ἐνὶ δαίδαλα πολλά, *Il.* 14.178–179). Euripides' *Electra* also reveals the negative force that *askeô* may have when Electra scornfully describes her mother's tending of her beauty (ξανθὸν κατόπτρῳ πλόκαμον ἐξήσκεις κόμης, 1071).

72. Editors have argued over how to take πρὸς Ἑλλάδος in this context. Lee 1976 (*ad Tro.* 1033) takes it—more awkwardly, but perhaps with better support—as "remove (from yourself) this charge of effeminacy from Greece" (following Paley 1872: 272). Diggle 1981: 68–69 thinks that ψόγον τὸ θῆλυ should be taken more closely with πρὸς Ἑλλάδος, so that the blame would be that which the female sex has accrued from the example of Helen. This reading necessitates emendation, however (removal of the τ').

73. Cf. Eur. *Cyc.* 317, where Polyphemus connects such "bluster" (κόμποι) to a decorative style (λόγων εὐμορφία), both of which are meant to characterize Odysseus' arguments.

74. Croally 1994: 159 agrees. Although he argues that the outcome of the *agôn* is ambiguous at the textual level, he does admit that Helen alone has achieved an improvement of her prospects.

75. This is in contrast to Homer, whose few references to Philoctetes do not give Odysseus any special role in his abandonment on Lemnos; nor does the evidence from other parts of the epic cycle contain any indication that such was his role (Jouan 1966: 313–314).

76. Bourdieu 1991: 111–116.

77. Dio Chrys. *Or.* 59.5–6; see Olson 1991: 271–272. Compare again the alterations of bodily *hexis* that Tom Ripley employs when deceiving his interlocutors in Highsmith's novel.

78. Compare here Sinon in *Aeneid* 2, who also employs Odysseus as a figure of abuse to trick the Trojans into bringing the horse within their city walls.

79. Dio's synopsis and paraphrase also relate a use of the figure of Athena that parallels her role not only in the *Odyssey* but also in Sophocles' *Ajax*. In that play Athena makes Odysseus invisible to Ajax; in Euripides' *Philoctetes* she makes his identity effectively invisible to Philoctetes.

80. Müller 1990: 209; cf. Müller 2000: 56–59. Müller offers a reconstruction of the exchange in which Odysseus claims to be a friend of the condemned man, refining the structure of the early episode that has been extracted from Dio's paraphrase of the first part of the play.

81. See, e.g., Podlecki 1966; Segal 1981; Blundell 1989; Rose 1992. Podlecki 1966: 244 refers to Odysseus as "an unprincipled man of action" who is attempting to "corrupt" Neoptolemus. Müller 1990 argues that Odysseus' craft is thrown into sharp relief by his use of Palamedes in Euripides' play, which turns up as an "amoralischen Utilitarismus" in Sophocles' play.

82. E.g., Falkner 1998; Lada-Richards 1998; Ringer 1998.

83. Cf. Worman 1999a.

84. See Szarmach 1974b, 1975.

85. E.g., Falkner 1998; Ringer 1998.

86. Cf., e.g., Podlecki 1966 and Segal 1981: 333–340.

87. Cf. Neoptolemus, τοὖργον οὐ μακρὰν λέγεις, 26. Socrates criticizes the rhetor's *makros logos* in Plato's *Gorgias* (e.g., 461d–462a) and *Protagoras* (e.g., 334c–335a).

88. Cf. Aesch. *Cho.* 854; Eur. fr. 39 N² attributes such deception to a glib style (εὐτρόχοισι στόμασι τἀληθέστατα κλέπτουσιν). See also Aristotle on the natural, fluid style that best conceals (κλέπτεται) artifice (*Rhet.* 1404b24); he regards Euripides as its inventor. Aristotle explains later that this deception of the hearer (κλέπτεται ὁ ἀκροατής) is achieved by attention to propriety (τὸ δὲ πρέπον) (1408a–b). I return to this topic in ch. 5.

89. Webster 1963 remarks, "Odysseus knows that Neoptolemus naturally acts directly by physical force, but this has to be a victory of words (hence the repeated λόγοισι, λέγων, etc.) over a mind, ψυχήν (here already in the Platonic opposition to σῶμα . . .)" (*ad Phil.* 72). Viansino 1963, regarding the process by which Odysseus instructs Neoptolemus in deceit, compares Euripides' use of a character allied in his hatred of Odysseus (*ad Phil.* 56).

90. Blundell 1988 thinks that the development of Neoptolemus' self-knowledge underlies this scene, although she does not refer to the *nomos-phusis* debate evident in both tragedy and sophistic writings (see, e.g., Guthrie 1971; Kerferd 1981).

91. Cf. Aristotle's categories of age in *Rhetoric* 2.14 and references in 3.2 regarding styles suitable to particular character types and ages.

92. Cf. Aristotle's idea that habituation (ἔθος) becomes character (ἦθος) (*NE* 1103b17) and that habit itself is "like nature" (τῇ φύσει ἔοικεν, *NE* 1152a30; cf. *Rhet.* 1370a6–7). Viansino 1963: 25 conflates nature and character. Recall that *phusis* is often treated this way in tragedy, that is, like character, as something revealed by one's visible personality (e.g., Soph. *Trach.* 308–309; Eur. *Ion* 239–240).

93. Whitman 1951: 179–180 recognizes these distinctions as a context for the *Philoctetes.* See also Guthrie 1971: 152–155, who cites Antiphon's fragmentary comments on equality, the gist of which is that it is essentially barbaric to differentiate between elites and commons, or even between barbarian and Greek (DK 78B44). The archaizing tendencies in this period align the aristocratic viewpoint with that of a heroic militarism. The sophists were generally associated with more democratic (if still elite) attitudes, especially toward the end of the fifth century and into the fourth. See Rose's 1992: 311 discussion regarding who associated with individual sophists; he concludes that they were generally connected with "what we might call the liberal wing of the ruling class." Cf. Ober 1989: 172–173.

94. Cf. Kamerbeek 1980: 41; also Nauck 1886: 32, who qualifies the relationship between deceit and persuasion: "Zu dem δόλος bildet das πειθώ einen Gegensatz, sofern es den Begriff des gütlichen Verfahrens und der durch die Macht der Rede, also durch Vernunftgründe gewonnenen Zustimmung enthält." Cf., e.g., Gorgias, DK 82B3.

95. E.g., Segal 1981; Blundell 1989; Rose 1992. Viansino compares Soph. fr. 325 N²: καλὸν μὲν οὖν οὔκ ἔστι τὸ ψευδῆ λέγειν.

96. Viansino 1963 (*ad Phil.* 110) provides other citations of a similar usage of both ὄμμα and βλέπων; Webster 1963 understands the persuasive expression to mean the ability to look one's interlocutor in the eyes. Note also Neoptolemus' use of τολμήσει when posing

this question to Odysseus, whose brazenness both Philoctetes and Palamedes emphasize. Whitman 1951 notes that it is a quality typically applied to Odysseus; but in the mouths of these archaic heroes it sounds like a term of abuse, denoting the unheroic shamelessness of the pragmatic politician.

97. Note that Neoptolemus' reference to Odysseus' use of force takes the form of a legal charge.

98. When referring to his father, Neoptolemus echoes the verb that Philoctetes employs to describe the effects of his wound (ἀγρίᾳ νόσῳ καταφθίνοντα, 265–266; κατέφθιτο, 346).

99. Cf. Odysseus' imperviousness to the pain of verbal abuse (οὐδὲν ἀλγύνεῖ μ', 66).

100. Webster notes this (ad Phil. 355).

101. Recall that poikilos is used of Odysseus' quality of mind and speaking manner in archaic poetry, tragedy, and rhetorical theory (see chs. 1 and 5).

102. Eumaeus and Penelope (i.e., Odysseus' intimates) suspect this use of the hero, Eumaeus warning the disguised Odysseus against this technique before he has even told his lying tale (Od. 14.122–32; cf. 14.361–365, 19.215–217).

103. Nagy 1979: 260–261 notes that the name Thersites has the root thersi-, which is cognate with tharsos ("boldness"). He compares the passage in the Odyssey where Antinous calls the beggar Odysseus tharsaleos, arguing that this is the boldness of the blame poet. In the Philoctetes Odysseus is frequently associated with a kind of boldness that is unheroic: a scheming, verbally dextrous kind of daring that marks the actions of the low-status but clever man.

104. Note that βλάπτω can have the connotation "deceive" when it refers to mental harm; the word thus suits Odysseus precisely.

105. Segal 1981: 304–305 thinks that Sophocles' association of Odysseus with sea-trading activities emphasizes the "humane and civilized spirit" embodied by Philoctetes to the detriment of the "manipulative and self-seeking" tactics of the merchant seaman. The class loyalties that Segal's language implies may well underlie Sophocles' depiction. My concern, however, is to demonstrate how this type is deployed by Odysseus, the comforting familiarity of which leads to reassurance and thus persuasion.

106. See Schein 1999 on the importance of these verbal adjectives in the play.

107. Cf. Pl. Gorg. 465b2–c2, where Socrates declares that cosmetics (which he likens to sophistic argument and rhetoric) are "ignoble and illiberal" (ἀγεννὴς καὶ ἀνελεύθερος).

CHAPTER 5

1. Cf. the discussion in ch. 4.

2. Cf., e.g., Plato's Hippias Minor; Antisthenes' extant Odysseus, as well as On Helen and Penelope, a piece known only by its title (DL 6.17); Ps.-Alcidamas' Odysseus; and Isocrates' Helen.

3. Cf. Pl. Phdr. 261b. The evidence is collected in Radermacher 1951. See also Kennedy 1963: 54–61; Schiappa 1999: 45–47.

4. Pl. Ion 530b; cf. Arist. Rhet. 1403b21–24, 1404a20–26. See O'Sullivan 1992: 66–67; the arguments of Enos 1993: 10–22 and Poulakos 1995: 39–46 also support this comparison.

5. See Collins 1991: 4–5 on the different visual experiences of the audience in witness-

ing the diegetic versus the mimetic performance. On referential or "mimetic" gestures, cf. Edmunds 1996, 24–25; Wiles 1997, 16–18. Aristotle (*Poet.* 1459b22–29) distinguishes between the singular frame of mimesis on stage (μιμεῖσθαι . . . τὸ ἐπὶ τῆς σκηνῆς καὶ τῶν ὑποκριτῶν μέρος μόνον) versus the multiple frames possible in epic narrative (διὰ τὸ διήγησιν εἶναι ἔστι πολλὰ μέρη ἅμα ποιεῖν περαινόμενα).

6. E.g., ἰδίᾳ ἐλλαμπρύνεσθαι; λαμπρύνομαι; λαμπρότητι (Thuc. 6.12.2, 6.16.3, 6.16.5). Cf. the dressing up of Demos in Ar. *Eq.* (ἀρχαίῳ σχήματι λαμπρός, 1331); also Pl. *Hp. Mi.* 368d7 regarding the versatile sophist's illustrious type (λαμπρότατος). See Geddes 1987: 307 on the *lampros* style of dress as older and aristocratic.

7. Cf. Pl. *Symp.* 212d–223a, *Alc. I* 103–105; Xen. *Mem.* 2.12–47; also Plut. *Alc.* 1.26, 16.25. See O'Sullivan 1992: 107–130 on the *genus grande* in Aristophanes (and elsewhere); and Gribble 1999 on the portraits of Alcibiades. Cf. also de Romilly 1995.

8. Plut. *Alc.* 23. Gribble 1999: 37 points out that Alcibiades was a favorite subject in later declamation. See also his remarks on Alcibiades' beauty and love of luxury in Hellenistic depiction (39–40).

9. Zeitlin 1990: 92–99; also Jarratt 1991: 65.

10. Guthrie 1971: 49; cf. Joël 1921: 674, who christened this energy "Rausch der Jugend"; also Zeller 1922: 1432; Jaeger 1939–45: 288; Untersteiner 1952. Cf. McKirahan 1994.

11. See the discussion of Enos 1993: 72–73. Kerferd 1981: ch. 2 has argued that while the sophists enjoyed some influence in intellectual circles, they were marginalized in Athenian society more generally.

12. O'Sullivan 1996: 124–125 has emphasized how this treatment of the sophists even shaped the presentation of the evidence. The death of Socrates is traditionally used as the cut-off point for dating the sophistic movement, which means that important sophists like Alcidamas are excluded in the Diels-Kranz collection, the basic source book for sophistic fragments. See also Enos 1993; Ford 1993; Schiappa 1999.

13. Cf. O'Sullivan 1992: 66–67.

14. Character representation is a troubled topic in the *Rhetoric*. Aristotle seems to deal with it in book 2.12–17, where he establishes types of character according to age, social status, etc. But this is an aspect of character representation distinct from *êthos*, when it is defined as encompassing positive moral traits (as it is earlier in 2.1). Cf. discussions in ch. 1 and the conclusion.

15. Gorgias makes a similar connection between epideictic rhetoric and poetry (*Hel.* 9), but the polemics involved in this association are more evident in the writings of Plato (*Phdr.*), Isocrates (*Evag., Antid.*), Aristotle (*Rhet.* 3), and Alcidamas (*Peri Soph.*).

16. Dionysius of Halicarnassus says that Theophrastus considered Thrasymachus the inventor of the "mixed" (μικτή) style; Dionysius himself seems to treat this information with some hesitation (εἰ δὴ πηγή τις ἦν ὄντως τῆς μεσότητος, DH *Dem.* 3; cf. Baiter and Sauppe 1967). This may have been a misunderstanding on Dionysius' part; cf. O'Sullivan 1992: 5, 114n. 49. Elsewhere, Thrasymachus is represented as a bold and emotional speaker; see further below.

17. E.g., *Ran.* 826–829 (ἔνθεν δὴ στοματουργὸς ἐπῶν βασανίστρια λίσπη / γλῶσσ', ἀνελισσομένη φθονερούς κινοῦσα χαλινούς, / ῥήματα δαιομένη καταλεπτολογήσει).

O'Sullivan (1992, 131n. 165) contrasts στοματουργός with γηγενεῖ φυσήματι in the preceding line, which describes Aeschylus' words. The distinction is that of crafted versus natural, Euripides' style being too fussy and finely wrought. O'Sullivan notes that there may also be some connotation of sexual passivity in the focus on the mouth (131n. 165 and 147); and he shows that στοματουργός is associated with στωμυλία and λαλιά (Ran. 91, 815, 841, 943, 1069, 1071, 1160, 1492), both of which apply especially to Euripides, Socrates, the sophists, and therefore to young men (i.e., their putative students) (131–133). λαλιά characterizes the speech of both women and certain sophists (e.g., Prodicus; see below n. 20), and this style became associated with the ἰσχνὸς χαρακτήρ (Cic. Orat. 62–64, DH Dem. 2). Hesychius glosses κομψεία—a term that means something like "well-dressed elegance" and that is also associated with the ἰσχνὸς χαρακτήρ—as ποικίλη λαλιά, a fastidious, richly ornamental chatter (cf. also ch. 1 on ποικίλος). For distinguishing the styles of the poets as masculine or feminine, see Muecke 1982; O'Sullivan 1992: 145–150 adduces more evidence for her claims. Cf. also McClure 1999 regarding gendered speaking styles in drama. Salvioni 1985 (esp. ch. 4) emphasizes the "physiology" of stylistic distinctions during this period.

18. On this connection to magic, see de Romilly 1974, H. Parry 1992, and Hesk 1999; cf. below regarding Gorgias' own ideas about magic and the powers of logos. Cf. also Thrasymachus' violent type in Rep. 1.

19. Cf. Ar. Ran. 909–910; Gorg. Hel. 11; and DK 82B23.

20. O'Sullivan 1992: 19–20 points out that distinctions need to be made among the sophists' styles as they are among the styles of the poets. Thus if Aeschylus can be said to embody the grand style, as he does in Aristophanes, so can Gorgias. This cannot be said of Prodicus, in contrast, who was reputedly a teacher of Euripides and who seems to have influenced his refined, hair-splitting style. Cf. also Schiappa 1999: 85–113, who studies the features of Gorgias' style in detail, including ancient assessments of it as "grand" and highly metaphorical.

21. E.g., Page 1955: 56. West 1970: 318 regards the poem as "a pragmatically sympathetic evaluation," which he deems "typically feminine." Both Page and West are less inclined to see any sort of logic underlying Sappho's use of Helen than are later scholars. Dane 1981: 192, while attempting to show that the poem is aesthetically successful, nevertheless concludes that it does not aim at more profound coherence. Earlier commentators considered the fragment a condemnation of Helen's choice and thus of her character: e.g., Merkelbach 1957 reads fr. 16 as iambos of sorts; Wilamowitz 1914, Theander 1934, and Bowra 1935 as proof of the waywardness of the female heart. But the archaic judgment of Helen had not, in fact, been nearly as harsh as it would become in the classical period. In Homer only Helen directly chastises Helen; Hesiod also tells a story that averts blame from Helen (frs. 196–204 M-W). Cf. the scholion on Eur. Or. 249, in which Stesichorus deems Tyndareus responsible for his daughters' inconstancy, since in forgetting to sacrifice to Aphrodite he brought the anger of the goddess upon them.

22. Race 1989–1990; Pelliccia 1992. Burnett 1983: 282 remarks on what she terms Sappho's "too-philosophical priamel" and notes the already prevalent recourse among archaic poets to a progression "towards analytic language." DuBois [1984] 1995: 98–115 similarly regards Sappho's poem as "protophilosophical," representing a move toward more abstract notions of value.

23. Most 1981; Pelliccia 1992: 67 and n. 10 notes the repetition of this device in Gorgias' *Encomium*, where the suitors who admire Helen are admired (4).

24. On Sappho's focus on the gaze, see Stehle 1990; on the body, H. P. Foley 1998; on *erôs* and persuasion, Segal 1974. DuBois [1984] 1995: 102–103 emphasizes the propulsion inherent in Sappho's connections between Helen as the most beautiful human and her pursuit of the "most beautiful thing" (τὸ κάλλιστον). See also Gentili 1988: 86 on the paradigmatic character of Helen as lover. Cf. Barkhuizen and Els 1983.

25. Race 1989–1990; Pelliccia 1992.

26. See also Isocrates' *Helen*.

27. Kirkwood (1979: 108) emphasizes Aphrodite's possible role.

28. *Rhet.* 1363a16–19: καὶ ὁ τῶν φρονίμων τις ἢ τῶν ἀγαθῶν ἀνδρῶν ἢ γυναικῶν προέκρινεν, οἷον Ὀδυσσέα Ἀθηνᾶ καὶ Ἑλένην Θησεὺς καὶ Ἀλέξανδρον αἱ θεαὶ καὶ Ἀχιλλέα Ὅμηρος. καὶ ὅλως τὰ προαιρετά (cf. 1399a1–3). Helen becomes a worthy object of praise because her value is confirmed by the *proairesis* of an Athenian hero. In Aristotle *proairesis* comprises both intellectual and impulsive inclinations, signals voluntary action, and is more especially concerned with moral choice (*NE* 1113a10–12). Cf. Cope 1877: 113–114.

29. Cf. Diogenes Laertius, who quotes the statement that became the most famous Protagorean dictum: "A human being is the measure of all things" (πάντων χρημάτων μέτρον ἄνθρωπος: DK 80B1). He credits Protagoras with the development of the technique of speaking on both sides of an issue (DK 80A1), of which the anonymous so-called *Dissoi Logoi* (DK 90) is the largest extant example. Gorgias appears to have developed most fully the conclusions to be drawn from these statements regarding the power of *logos* to influence opinion, in both the *Hel.* and the text quoted by Sextus Empiricus (*Pros. Log.* 65–87) called *On Not Being* (DK 82B3). Cf. again Pl. *Phdr.* 267a6–8; and see Enos 1976; Porter 1993.

30. E.g., Pind. *Ol.* 1, 2, 13. Cf. also Isocrates' *Evag.* 5–11 regarding the socially normative power of praise genres.

31. Isocrates' charge that Gorgias composed a defense (ἀπολογία) rather than an encomium does not necessarily entail that Gorgias was unaware of this type of formal distinction, although scholars have often assumed that the fluid, interconnected style of the *Encomium* signals a primitive attitude toward genre definition (e.g., Cole 1991; Schiappa 1996, 1999: 117–120).

32. The notion that truth might be an "adornment" of speech rather than its foundation seems to relegate it to the status of any other rhetorical device. Bergren 1983: 85 has noted that Gorgias' later statement that "false speech" (ψευδῆ λόγον) is ultimately persuasive (*Hel.* 11) contradicts this introductory claim. She suggests that he may be signaling Helen's "uncontrollability," her association with the "ungovernable rhetoricity of language." Gorgias' statements treat both truth and falsehood as affecting the "shape" of the speech (i.e., truth is a decoration [κόσμος] of speech, speakers "mold" [πλάσαντες] falsehood). This suggests that for Gorgias, style is not merely a superficial addendum to speech but rather affects its structure at all levels. See Enos 1993; Porter 1995.

33. Buchheim 1989: 162n. 10.

34. Enos 1993: 60.

35. This is the first aspect of what Segal 1965 termed the "psychology of the *logos.*"

36. In the *Rhetoric* Aristotle argues that the most persuasive mode makes use of the familiar but then takes the hearers a step beyond what they already know and agree with (1395b–1396a). This effectively comes down to telling people what they want to hear, or at least making people think that one is doing so.

37. Barthes 1974: 10–11, 40–41, 47–48. Barthes says, "Confronting it, the New is bliss (Freud: 'In the adult, novelty always constitutes the condition for orgasm')" (41). Thucydides' Cleon associates such novelty and pleasures with the sophists (cf. ch. 4).

38. Immisch 1927: ὄψει; Buchheim 1989: ἔρωτι (an emendation). Since I am arguing that *erôs* and *opsis* are intimately related, their confluence here is confirming rather than troubling.

39. Kirby 1990 investigates separately the relations of *peithô* to *bia*, *peithô* to *erôs*, and *erôs* to *bia*, and discusses *bia* as a "psychosocial" phenomenon, in conjunction with *erôs* and *peithô*.

40. Kirby 1990: 225 thinks that *peithô*, *bia*, and *erôs* are subsumed by Gorgias under the will of the gods—incorrectly, it seems to me. Casertano 1986 regards *erôs* as the primary force that binds together the elements Gorgias presents as similar in capacity.

41. The sophist Alcidamas in a treatise entitled *On the Sophists* (*Peri sophistôn*, 28) compares a *logos* to the living body, while Plato in the *Phaedrus* (264c) states that a speech should be constructed like one. Aristotle describes the same form of measure for the composition of a tragic plot in the *Poetics* (7), with greater emphasis on the beauty of suitable proportion in both the body and the written work.

42. Walsh 1984: 82, 101 relates the "quasi-physical influence" of words to Euripides' *eidôlon* in the *Helen*, regarding the latter as "fit[ting] nicely into a gap left by Gorgianic psychology, which can find nothing in the phenomenal world that possesses the immediacy of speech." Buchheim 1989: 164n. 19 relates Helen's ability to attract many bodies with her one body to the ability of speech to do the same, and suggests that Gorgias is formulating a comparison to the way visual arts affect the viewer.

43. Segal 1965: 104 emphasizes that Gorgias treats psychological processes as if they had a "quasi-physical reality," while de Romilly 1974: 16 argues that Gorgias' references to magic are purely figurative. H. Parry 1992: 151–152 has pointed out that de Romilly's reasoning from philological evidence does not hold up: Gorgias' use of *technê* to refer to the magic of words is paralleled by uses of the same term to denote Medea's skill (Eur. *Med.* 402) and Jason's devices in defeating the bull (Pind. *Pyth.* 4.249). Although Parry admits that the argument for a figurative reading could be sustained on other grounds, he regards Gorgias as having some remnant of a literalist attitude toward the powers of speech. See also Havelock 1963: 145–164; Walsh 1984: 83–84; Mourelatos 1987.

44. Aristotle cites both Gorgias and Alcidamas as indulging in these poetic compounds (ἐν τοῖς διπλοῖς ὀνόμασιν, *Rhet.* 1405b35).

45. Bakker 1997: 143–144, following Norden 1958. Cf. Segal 1965: 120.

46. Bakker 1997: 143n. 42. Cf. Schiappa 1996: 76–78.

47. Cf. Hom. *Od.* 19.457; Pind. *Pyth.* 4.384; Soph. *Aj.* 582; Hdt. 1.132, regarding the Magi.

48. Segal 1965: 127, and 141–142n. 41, 150–151nn. 103–105 for bibliography; also Walsh 1984: 83–84.

49. This materialist account is opposed by Socrates to an explanation that considers the

telos of a given phenomenon, which for Socrates is the correct way to approach the matter. But the adjective τραγική is surely not accidental; Socrates is no friend of the theater (cf. *Gorg.* 502b, e.g.).

50. Cf. Odysseus' activities in Sophocles' *Ajax* (τοιούσδε λόγους ψιθύρους πλάσσων, 148); also Arist. *Rhet.* 1404b18–20. See Walsh 1984: 82–83.

51. Cf. Helen's role in *Od.* 4: she accompanies her speech with a *pharmakon* that removes painful emotions. Cf. Croally 1994: 32nn. 55 and 56, regarding the association of rhetoric with medicine elsewhere in the tradition.

52. We might note that *ekplêxis* is a signature effect of tragedy, in Aristotle's conception (*Poet.* 1454a4, 1455a17). Cf. again Aphrodite's reactions to Helen (ἔκπαγλα φίλησα, *Il.* 3.415) and Paris (ἔκπαγλα φίλησε, *Il.* 5.423); the *Tro.* passage is discussed in ch. 4. See also Benediktson 2000: 32 on Gorgias and the visual arts.

53. Segal 1965: 126.

54. See Kennedy 1963: 174–203 for an analysis of Isocrates and the development of epideixis in the fourth century.

55. Kennedy 1958 has argued (against Arist. *Rhet.* 1414b27–29) that Isocrates' proemium is thematically connected to Helen because both are central to the Panhellenic flavor of the piece; cf. also Guardini 1987: 336. Heilbrunn 1977 disagrees. But these scholars do not analyze the purposeful circularity of the argument, which ties the proemium to the narrative by making Helen's birth parallel the beginning of his praise, a move effected by a stylistic trick (anaphora). Cf. Eur. *Tro.* 919–920.

56. Recall that Helen makes this same argument at *Tro.* 948–950 (τὴν θεὸν κόλαζε καὶ Διὸς κρείσσων γενοῦ, / ὃς τῶν μὲν ἄλλων δαιμόνων ἔχει κράτος, / κείνης δὲ δοῦλός ἐστι). Isocrates in fact makes an argument identical to Helen's later in his speech (59–60).

57. Cf. the admiration of the beautiful female form in choral poetry, and see Calame 1977; Stehle 1997.

58. Cf. Hes. *Ehoiae* (fr. 204 M-W). Hesiod states explicitly that Idomeneus (the "viewer") did not send a proxy because he wanted to see Helen's beauty for himself, rather than merely hearing the *muthos* of her, which was already Panhellenic (ὃς] ἤδη πᾶσαν ἐπὶ [χθ]όνα δῖαν ἵκαν[εν, 56–63).

59. Again, Gorgias says that Helen's beauty is "equal to the gods" (ἰσόθεον, *Hel.* 3), speech accomplishes deeds "most godlike" (θειότατα, 8), and the stylized form of the epode is "god-infused" (ἔνθεοι, 8).

60. Cf. also Philoctetes' similar role in tragedy, discussed in ch. 4.

61. Worman 1999a.

62. An excellent example of this maneuver can be found in a famous dispute between the fourth-century orators Demosthenes and Aeschines. In his speech *On the Crown* (18.251–255), Demosthenes mocks Aeschines' aping of Solon's restrained gestures (his visible *hexis*) as a failure to borrow what is really valuable from the statesman: his quality of mind (τὴν ψυχὴν . . . καὶ τὴν διάνοιαν, 253; i.e., his *habitus*). He then suggests that Aeschines really extends his hand not as a solemn accompaniment to his portentious speaking style, but with the palm up—for the taking of bribes (255).

63. Cf. Ober 1989: 170–177; Hesk 1999: 208–211.

64. *Mem.* 2.5.1–4, 3.11.17. The evidence for the scope of Antisthenes' work and perspective is mostly late and therefore of questionable accuracy; see Guthrie 1971: 304–311; Rankin 1986. The fragments and testimonia have been collected by Caizzi 1966 (-C); they represent the shockingly paltry remains of a very prolific author (cf. DL 6.1–19).

65. Cf. ch. 1 and below.

66. See, e.g., Caizzi 1964; Guthrie 1975: 310; Kahn 1996: 122–124.

67. But see Tordesillas 1990, for a discussion of the scope of Palamedes' speech.

68. Cf. Gorgias' treatise *On Not Being* and further discussion below.

69. Cf. Thucydides' (1.22) remark concerning the difficulties of writing history based on eyewitness accounts: eyewitnesses always give different versions of events due to imperfect memory or partiality. On Gorgias, see Buchheim's 1989 comment, discussed in greater detail below: truth can only come of the particular situation witnessed but cannot be communicated through speech. Buchheim seems to be extracting from *On Not Being*. See also Kerferd 1981; Verdenius 1981.

70. In fact, the speech employs the usual order of the speeches of Lysias, the speechwriter most adept at *êthopoiia*: (1) factual evidence, (2) probability, and (3) character proof.

71. Cf. also Dem. 19.98, where he deems the flamboyant and voluble Aeschines *panourgos*.

72. I discuss Ps.-Alcidamas' speech in more detail below.

73. Cf. O'Sullivan 1992: 21 and n. 104; Segal 1965: 126; also the discussion above.

74. Cf. Kennedy 1963.

75. Cf. Socrates in Plato: e.g., *Gorg.* 493c6 in particular, but also *Phdr.* 239d1 and *Prot.* 315b6.

76. Buchheim 1989: 178n. 22 argues that this emphasis on the eyewitness proof is indicative of an acceptance on Gorgias' part of a truth specific to a situation, which cannot, however, be communicated through speech. He compares Bertrand Russell's contrast between "knowledge by acquaintance" and "knowledge by description" and stresses the centrality of this distinction to the speech. This is precisely the problem that Gorgias would have with a belief in the definitive proof of eyewitness accounting. For him, the fact of the matter can only be established *in the context of* the particular situation witnessed, but this witnessing cannot be proven true through its conveyance in words. Cf. also Woodruff 1999.

77. Stanford [1963] 1981 notes the connection of *eikos* arguments with the sophists (*ad Aj.* 1367); see also the discussion in the Introduction.

78. In Odysseus' speech by Ps.-Alcidamas, the accuser does directly charge Palamedes with the reverse of this heroic dictum; see further below.

79. Cf., e.g., Arist. *Rhet.* 1407a, 1410a–b.

80. Cf. O'Sullivan 1992: 12–13; cf. North 1988.

81. Note again Palamedes' reiteration of *saphês* in his introduction (3, 5; cf. 33), as well as his reiteration throughout of related terms like *phaneros* and *dêlos* (1, 8, 10, 11, 12, 19, 24, 31, 35, 36). The final repetition of *phanera* in 36 echoes that of *saphôs* in 5. And cf. Aristoph. *Ran.* 927, 1122; Arist. *Rhet.* 1406a33, 1406b6–8.

82. Again, O'Sullivan 1992 regards it as the predominant and overarching distinction in stylistic type from the late fifth century on and structures his book around its elucidation.

83. This is Heracles' title (Eur. *HF* 877, 1252, 1309); and cf. Philoctetes, who claims that

Heracles gave him his famous bow for his good deeds (εὐεργετῶν, *Phil.* 670). In Isocrates' *Helen* this civic good deed doing gains Theseus his laudable status (*Hel.* 25, 37).

84. For example, one inscription awards the title to a man who procured the return of stolen gold and silver to Delphi: *IG* IX.ii.257; cf. Böckh 1828: I. 1562–1567, 1693. This is, of course, an institutionalized and familiar honorific.

85. Cf. Arist. *Rhet.* 1357a–b.

86. Pfeiffer 1968: 30 notes that in a fragment of Aristophanes (fr. 506 K-A) Prodicus is equated with a book; and O'Sullivan 1992: 19 argues that the distinction in Plato is meant to be understood as that between, extemporaneous speaking (Gorgias) and written speeches (Prodicus).

87. Avezzù 1982. The commentary includes an exhaustive bibliography for both the *Odysseus* and *Peri tôn sophistôn*, the latter of which has received the most attention (see below). Also in Blass 1871.

88. See Nightingale 1995: 14–21 on the use of the word *philosophos* during this period. Cf. also the less censorious use of *philosophos* in Isoc. 1.40 12.1; Pl. *Symp.* 182e.

89. Cf. Vlastos 1975.

90. Dušanić 1992.

91. Cf. Arist. *Rhet.* 1404a26, 1404b4, 1406a32.

92. Cf. Dušanić 1992: 352; see also Vlastos 1975: 131–161.

93. It must be admitted that Plato lampooned Prodicus' hair-splitting kind of analysis (cf. *Prot.* 337a, e.g.), but this does not seriously affect the idea that Palamedes is closer to his type.

94. Cf. Aristoph. *Ran.* 907–913 regarding Aeschylus' style; and compare Gorgias' characterization of rhetoric (*Hel.* 11) and the illusion of theater (DK 82B23).

95. See Worman 2001b.

96. Arctinus had treated the scene earlier in his *Aethiopis* (cf. frr. in Munroe and Allen); Aeschylus' treatment is almost entirely lost, which prohibits any definitive understanding of his depiction of Odysseus (cf. fr. 175 Radt).

97. See Caizzi 1966 for an introduction and a bibliography. Much of the scholarship on Antisthenes has focused on his philosophy of language and his connection to Socrates rather than on his literary criticism (e.g., Höistad 1948). For a more general introduction that also argues for his sophistic connections, see Rankin 1986.

98. E.g., Pl. *Rep.* 398c, 400d, 424c; Isoc. *Antid.* 45; Phld. *Mus.* p. 9K.

99. Detienne 1967: 55.

100. Recall that Aristotle (*Rhet.* 1416b25) opposes the ἁπλούστερος λόγος to that which is ποικίλος.

101.   ΣΩ. Πολύτροποι δ' εἰσὶ καὶ ἀπατεῶνες ὑπὸ ἠλιθιότητος
         καὶ ἀφροσύνης, ἢ ὑπὸ πανουργίας καὶ φρονήσεώς τινος;
         ΙΠ. Ὑπὸ πανουργίας πάντων μάλιστα καὶ φρονήσεως. (365e2–5)

102. The rhapsode Ion is similarly fancily dressed in Plato's dialogue of that name—a match for his embellished speaking style (*Ion* 530b–d).

103. As is suggested (e.g.) at *Phdr.* 257c; cf. Dem. 19.246–248 (regarding both logographers and sophists more generally). See Ober 1989: 172, 175; Ford 1993.

104. Cf. also Dem. 18.10–11, 19.121–127. The pairs of speeches that frame the ongoing con-

test between Demosthenes and Aeschines repeatedly show this kind of character exchange (e.g., Aeschin. and Dem. 19; Aeschin. 3; Dem. 18). Again, see Ober 1989: 171–177; Hesk 1999: 208–211.

105. On the philosophical ramifications of Antisthenes' *oikeios logos,* see Brancacci 1990; a less technical discussion can be found in Rankin 1986.

106. Cf. also Hes. *Helenae proci* (frs. 196–204 M-W).

CONCLUSION

1. See Cic. *De Or.* 3.43 and *Orat.* 23–32, 75–78, 97–99 for analyses of Greek oratory and expositions of Attic versus Asianic styles.

2. This included, apparently, Alcibiades, whose figure in tradition shares features with both Helen and Odysseus. E.g., Lys. 14 and 15; Ps.-Andoc. 4; Isoc. 16 are extant, but there may well have been more. See Gribble 1999: 118; 198, 209; cf. 27, 202, and 269–270.

3. Burke 1957: 9.

Adkins, A. W. H. 1972. "Truth, ΚΟΣΜΟΣ, and ΑΡΕΤΗ in the Homeric Poems." *CQ* 22: 5–18.

Alexiou, M. 1974. *The Ritual Lament in Greek Tradition.* Cambridge.

Arnould, D. 1989. "Le chauve et le glouton chez Homère: Remarques sur le personnage d' Ulysse." *REG* 102: 510–514.

Atchity, K. J. 1978. *Homer's Iliad: The Shield of Memory.* Carbondale, IL.

Austin, N. 1975. *Archery at the Dark of the Moon: Poetic Problems in Homer's* Odyssey. Berkeley.

———. 1994. *Helen of Troy and Her Shameless Phantom.* Ithaca.

Avezzù, G. 1982. *Alcidamante: Orazioni e frammenti.* Rome.

Baiter, G., and H. Sauppe (eds.). 1967. *Oratores Attici.* Hildescheim.

Bakhtin, M. 1984. *Rabelais and His World,* tr. H. Iswolsky. Bloomington.

Bakker, E. 1993. "Discourse and Performance: Involvement, Visualization and 'Presence' in Homeric Poetry." *CA* 12: 1–29.

———. 1997. *Poetry in Speech: Orality and Homeric Discourse.* Ithaca.

———. 1999. "Homeric ΟΥΤΟΣ and the Poetics of Deixis." *CP* 94.1: 1–19.

Bal, M. 1984. "The Rhetoric of Subjectivity." *Poetics Today* 5.2: 337–376.

———. 1985. *Narratology: Introduction to the Theory of Narrative.* Toronto.

Barkhuizen, J. H., and G. H. Els. 1983. "On Sappho, Fr. 16 (L. P.)." *Acta Classica* 15: 23–32.

Barlow, S. 1971. *The Imagery of Euripides.* Bristol.

———. 1986. *Euripides: Trojan Women.* Warminster.

Barthes, R. [1969] 1986. "Style and Its Image." In *The Rustle of Language,* tr. R. Howard. New York.

———. [1970] 1974. *S/Z,* tr. R. Miller. New York.

Bassi, K. 1993. "Helen and the Discourse of Denial in Stesichorus' Palinode." *Arethusa* 26: 51–75.

———. 1998. *Acting Like Men: Gender, Drama, and Nostalgia in Ancient Greece.* Ann Arbor.

Baumhauer, O. A. 1986. *Die sophistische Rhetorik: Eine Theorie Sprachlicher Kommunikation.* Stuttgart.

Benediktson, D. T. 2000. *Literature and the Visual Arts in Ancient Greece and Rome.* Norman, OK.

Bergren, A. L. T. 1979–1980. "Helen's Web: Time and Tableau in the *Iliad*," *Helios* 7.1: 19–34.

———. 1983. "Language and the Female in Early Greek Thought." *Arethusa* 16: 69–95.

Bers, V. 1994. "Tragedy and Rhetoric." In *Persuasion: Greek Rhetoric in Action,* ed. I. Worthington. New York. 176–195.

Biehl, W. 1989. *Euripides Troades.* Heidelberg.

Blass, F. 1871. *Antiphontis orationes et fragmenta adiunctis Gorgiae Antisthenis Alcidamantis declamationibus.* Leipzig.

Blass, F. 1877. *Die attische Beredsamkeit,* vol. 1. Leipzig.

Block, E. 1985. "Clothing Makes the Man: A Pattern in the *Odyssey.*" *TAPA* 115: 1–11.

Blundell, M. W. 1988. "The Phusis of Neoptolemus in Sophocles' *Philoctetes.*" *G&R* 35.2: 137–148.

————. 1989. *Helping Friends and Harming Enemies: A Study in Sophocles and Greek Ethics.* Berkeley.

Böckh, A. 1828. *Corpus inscriptionum graecarum.* Berlin.

Boedecker, D. 1974. *Aphrodite's Entry into Greek Epic.* Leiden.

Boegehold, A. L. 1999. *When a Gesture Was Expected: A Selection of Examples from Archaic and Classical Literature.* Princeton.

Bourdieu, P. [1972] 1977. *Outline of a Theory of Practice,* tr. R. Nice. Cambridge.

————. [1980] 1990. *The Logic of Practice,* tr. R. Nice. Stanford.

————. 1991. *Language and Symbolic Power,* tr. G. Raymond and M. Adamson. Cambridge, MA.

Bowra, C. M. 1935. "Zu Alcaeus und Sappho." *Hermes* 70: 238–241.

Brancacci, A. 1990. Oikeios logos: *La filosofia del linguaggio di Antistene.* Rome.

Buchheim, T. 1989. *Gorgias: Reden, Fragmente und Testimonien.* Hamburg.

Burke, K. 1957. *On Symbols and Society.* Chicago.

————. 1969. *A Rhetoric of Motives.* Berkeley.

Burnett, A. P. 1977. "*Trojan Women* and the Ganymede Ode." *YCS* 25: 291–316.

————. 1983. *Three Archaic Poets: Archilochus, Alcaeus, Sappho.* Cambridge, MA.

Butler, J. 1990. *Gender Trouble: Feminism and the Subversion of Identity.* London.

————. 1996. "Performativity's Social Magic." In *The Social and Political Body,* ed. T. R. Schatzki and W. Natter. New York. 29–47.

————. 1997. *The Psychic Life of Power: Theories in Subjection.* Stanford.

Buxton, G. A. 1982. *Persuasion in Greek Tragedy.* Cambridge.

Caizzi, F. D. 1964. "Antistene." *Stud. Urb.* 38: 48–99.

————. 1966. *Antisthenis Fragmenta.* Milan.

Calame, C. 1977. *Les chœurs de jeunes filles en Grèce archaïque,* vol. 1. Rome.

————. 1986. *Le récit en Grèce ancienne: Enonciations et representations de poetes.* Paris.

Carey, C. A. 1981. *A Commentary on Five Odes of Pindar.* New York.

Carrière, J. 1967. *Stylistique grecque.* Paris.

Cartledge, P., P. Millet, and S. von Reden (eds.). 1998. *Kosmos: Essays in Order, Conflict, and Community in Classical Athens.* Cambridge.

Casertano, G. 1986. "L'amour entre *Logos* et *Pathos.*" In *Positions de la sophistique,* ed. B. Cassin. Paris. 211–220.

Caskey, L. D., and J. D. Beazley. 1931–1963. *Attic Vase Paintings in the Museum of Fine Arts, Boston.* Boston.

Càssola, F. 1975. *Inni Omerici.* Milan.

Clader, L. L. 1976. *Helen: The Evolution from Divine to Heroic in Greek Epic Tradition.* Leiden.

Classen, C. J. 1981. "Aristotle's Picture of the Sophists." In *The Sophists and Their Legacy,* ed. G. B. Kerferd. *Hermes Einzelschriften* 44: 7–24.

Clay, J. S. 1983. *The Wrath of Athena: Gods and Men in the* Odyssey. Princeton.

Cole, T. 1991. *The Origins of Rhetoric in Ancient Greece.* Baltimore.

Collard, C. 1975. "Formal Debates in Euripides' Dramas." *G&R* 22: 58–71.

Collins, C. 1991. *The Poetics of the Mind's Eye: Literature and the Psychology of Imagination.* University Park, PA.

Cope, E. M. 1877. *Aristotle: Rhetoric,* 3 vols. Cambridge.

Coulter, J. A. 1964. "The Relation of the *Apology of Socrates* and Plato's Critique of Gorgianic Rhetoric." *HSCP* 68: 269–303.

Crane, G. 1988. *Calypso: Backgrounds and Conventions of the* Odyssey. Beiträge zur klassischen Philologie, 191. Frankfurt am Main.

Croally, N. A. 1994. *Euripidean Polemic: The* Trojan Women *and the Function of Tragedy.* Cambridge.

Crotty, K. 1994. *The Poetics of Supplication: Homer's* Iliad *and* Odyssey. Ithaca.

Csapo, E., and W. J. Slater. 1995. *The Context of Athenian Drama.* Ann Arbor.

Cyrino, M. S. 1995. *In Pandora's Jar: Lovesickness in Early Greek Poetry.* Lanham, MD.

Dale, A. M. 1954. *Euripides Alcestis.* Oxford.

———. [1959] 1969. "Ethos and Dianoia: 'Character' and 'Thought' in Aristotle's *Poetics.*" In *Collected Papers.* Cambridge (orig. *Australasian Universities Modern Language Association* 11: 3–16).

Dane, J. A. 1981. "Sappho Fr. 16: An Analysis," *Eos* 49: 185–192.

Davies, M., ed. 1988. *Epicorum Graecorum Fragmenta.* Göttingen.

———. 1991. *Poetarum Melicorum Graecorum Fragmenta* 1: *Alcman, Stesichorus, Ibycus.* Oxford.

de Jong, I. 1987. *Narrators and Focalizers: The Presentation of the Story in the* Iliad. Amsterdam.

———. 1991. "Narratology and Oral Poetry: The Case of Homer." *Poetics Today* 12.3: 403–423.

Delauny, M. 1959. *Le plan rhétorique dans l'éloquence grecque d'Homère à Démosthène.* Brussels.

Denniston, J. D., and D. L. Page. 1957. *Aeschylus Agamemnon.* Oxford.

de Romilly, J. 1974. *Magic and Rhetoric in Ancient Greece.* Cambridge, MA.

———. 1995. *Alcibiade, ou les dangers de l'ambition.* Paris.

Derrida, J. 1981. *Dissemination,* tr. B. Johnson. Chicago.

Detienne, M. [1967] 1996. *The Masters of Truth in Archaic Greece.* New York.

Detienne, M., and J.-P. Vernant. 1978. *Cunning Intelligence in Greek Culture and Society.* Atlantic Highlands, NJ.

Dickson, K. 1995. *Nestor: Poetic Memory in Greek Epic.* New York.

Diels, H., and W. Kranz. 1966–67. *Die Fragmente der Vorsokratiker,* 12th ed. Berlin.

Diggle, J. 1981. *Studies on the Text of Euripides.* Oxford.

Doherty, L. 1995a. *Siren Songs: Gender, Audiences, and Narrators in the* Odyssey. Ann Arbor.

———. 1995b. "Sirens, Muses, and Female Narrators in the *Odyssey.*" In *The Distaff Side,* ed. B. Cohen. Oxford. 81–92.

Dover, K. 1997. *The Evolution of Greek Prose Style.* Oxford.

DuBois, P. [1984] 1995. *Sappho Is Burning.* Chicago.

Duchemin, J. 1968. *L'agon dans le tragédie grecque.* Paris.

Dušanić, S. 1992. "Alcidamas of Elaea in Plato's *Phaedrus.*" *CQ* 42: 347–357.

Easterling, P. (ed.). 1997. *The Cambridge Companion to Greek Tragedy.* Cambridge.

Ebener, D. 1954. "Die Helenaszene der Troerinnen." *Wissenschaft Zeitschrift Helle-Wittenberg* 3: 691–722.

Edmunds, L. 1996. *Theatrical Space and Historical Place in Sophocles'* Oedipus at Colonus. Lanham, MD.

Edwards, M. 1987. *Homer: Poet of the* Iliad. Baltimore.

———. 1991. *The Iliad: A Commentary,* vol. V: books 17–20. Cambridge.

———. 1997. "Homeric Style and 'Oral Poetics.' " In *A New Companion to Homer,* ed. I. Morris and B. Powell. Leiden. 261–283.

Elam, K. 1980. *The Semiotics of Theatre and Drama.* London.

Else, G. F. 1957. *Aristotle's* Poetics: The Argument. Cambridge, MA.

Emlyn-Jones, C. 1986. "True and Lying Tales in the *Odyssey." G&R* 33.1: 1–10.

Enos, R. L. 1976. "The Epistemology of Gorgias' Rhetoric: A Re-examination." *Southern Speech Communication Journal* 42: 35–51.

———. 1993. *Greek Rhetoric Before Aristotle.* Prospect Heights, IL.

Falkner, T. M. 1998. "Containing Tragedy: Rhetoric and Self-Representation in Sophocles' *Philoctetes. CA* 17.1: 25–58.

Faraone, C. 1990. "Aphrodite's ΚΕΣΤΟΣ and Apples for Atalanta: Aphrodisiaca in Early Greek Myth and Ritual." *Phoenix* 44.3: 219–243.

Farnell, L. J. [1932] 1965. *A Critical Commentary to the Works of Pindar.* Amsterdam (orig. London).

Felson, N. [1994] 1997. *Regarding Penelope: From Character to Poetics.* Norman, OK (orig. Princeton).

Ferrari, G. 1987. *Listening to the Cicadas: A Study of Plato's* Phaedrus. Cambridge.

Fletcher, J. 1999. "Exchanging Glances: Vision and Representation in Aeschylus' *Agamemnon." Helios* 26.1: 11–34.

Foley, H. P. 1980. "The Masque of Dionysus." *TAPA* 110: 107–133.

———. 1998. " 'The Mother of the Argument': Eros and the Body in Sappho and Plato's *Phaedrus."* In *Parchments of Gender: Deciphering the Bodies of Antiquity,* ed. M. Wyke. Oxford. 39–70.

———. 2000. "The Comic Body in Greek Art and Drama." In *Not the Classical Ideal: Athens and the Construction of the Other in Greek Art,* ed. B. Cohen. Leiden. 275–311.

———. 2001. *Female Acts in Greek Tragedy.* Princeton.

Foley, J. M. 1999. *Homer's Traditional Art.* University Park, PA.

Ford, A. L. 1992. *Homer: Poet of the Past.* Ithaca.

———. 1993. "Platonic Insults: 'Sophistic.' " *Common Knowledge* 1: 33–47.

Fortenbaugh, W. W. 1996. "Aristotle's Accounts of Persuasion Through Character." In *Theory, Text, Context: Issues in Greek Rhetoric and Oratory,* ed. C. L. Johnstone, 147–168. Albany.

Foucault, M. 1985. *The History of Sexuality,* vol. 2, *The Use of Pleasure,* tr. R. Hurley. New York.

Fraenkel, E. 1950. *Aeschylus Agamemnon,* vol. 2. Oxford.

Friedrich, P. 1978. *The Meaning of Aphrodite.* Chicago.

Gagarin, M. 1994. "Probability and Persuasion: Plato and Early Greek Rhetoric." In *Persuasion: Greek Rhetoric in Action,* ed. I. Worthington. New York. 46–68.

———. 1999. "The Orality of Greek Oratory." In *Signs of Orality: The Oral Tradition and Its Influence in the Greek and Roman World,* ed. E. A. Mackay. Leiden. 163–180.

Garner, S. B. 1994. *Bodied Spaces: Phenomenology and Performance in Contemporary Drama.* Ithaca.

Geddes, A. G. 1987. "Rags and Riches: The Costume of Athenian Men in the Fifth Century." *CQ* 37.2: 307–331.

Gellie, G. 1986. "Helen in the *Trojan Women*." In *Studies in T. B. L. Webster's Honor,* ed. J. Betts, J. Hooker, and J. Green. Oxford. 114–121.

Gentili, B. 1988. *Poetry and Its Public in Ancient Greece: From Homer to the Fifth Century,* tr. A. T. Cole. Baltimore.

Gerber, D. E. 1982. *Pindar's* Olympian One, *A Commentary. Phoenix* Suppl. 15. Toronto.

Ghali-Kahil, L. 1955. *Les enlèvements et le retour d'Hélène.* Ecole Française d'Athènes 10.

Gill, C. 1984. "The *Êthos-Pathos* Distinction in Rhetorical and Literary Criticism." *CQ* 34: 146–166.

———. 1990. "The Character-Personality Distinction." In Pelling, 1–31.

———. 1992. "Dogmatic Dialogue in *Phaedrus* 276–7?" In *Understanding the* Phaedrus: *Proceedings of the II Symposium Platonicum,* ed. L. Rossetti. St. Augustine. 156–172.

———. 1996. *Personality in Greek Epic, Tragedy, and Philosophy: The Self in Dialogue.* Oxford.

Gleason, M. 1995. *Making Men: Sophists and Self-Representation in Ancient Rome.* Princeton.

Goffman, E. 1959. *The Presentation of the Self in Everyday Life.* Garden City, NY.

Goldhill, S. 1986. *Reading Greek Tragedy.* Cambridge.

———. 1990. "Character and Action, Representation and Reading: Greek Tragedy and Its Critics." In Pelling, 100–127.

———. 1998. "The Seductions of the Gaze: Socrates and his Girlfriends." In Cartledge, Millet, and von Reden, 105–125.

Goldhill, S., and R. Osborne (eds.). 1994. *Art and Text in Ancient Greek Culture.* Cambridge.

———. 1999. *Performance Culture and Athenian Democracy.* Oxford.

Goodman, N. [1975] 1978. "The Status of Style." In *Ways of Worldmaking,* 23–40 (orig. in *Critical Inquiry* I: 799–811). Indianapolis.

Graver, M. 1995. "Dog-Helen and Homeric Insult." *CA* 14.1: 41–61.

Gregory, J. 1991. *Euripides and the Instruction of the Athenians.* Ann Arbor.

Gribble, D. 1999. *Alcibiades and Athens: A Study in Literary Presentation.* Oxford.

Griffin, J. 1980. *Homer on Life and Death.* Oxford.

Grube, G. M. A. 1965. *Greek and Roman Critics.* London.

Guardini, M. L. 1987. *Il mito di Elena: Testi di Euripide e Isocrate.* Treviso.

Guthrie, W. K. C. 1971. *The Sophists.* Cambridge.

Haft, A. J. 1984. "Odysseus, Idomeneus and Meriones: The Cretan Lies of *Odyssey* 13–19." *CJ* 79.4: 289–306.

Hainsworth, B. 1993. *The Iliad: A Commentary,* vol. 3. Cambridge.

Halliwell, S. 1988. *Plato Gorgias.* Warminster.

———. 1990. "Traditional Greek Conceptions of Character." In Pelling, 32–59.

———. 1997. "Between Public and Private: Tragedy and Athenian Experience of Rhetoric." In *Greek Tragedy and the Historian,* ed. C. Pelling. Oxford. 121–141.

———. 2000. "Plato and Painting." In *Word and Image in Ancient Greece,* ed. K. Rutter and B. A. Sparkes. Edinburgh. 99–116.

Harriot, R. 1969. *Poetry and Criticism before Plato.* London.

Havelock, E. A. 1963. *Preface to Plato.* Cambridge, MA.

Heatherington, M. E. 1976. "Chaos, Order, and Cunning in the *Odyssey.*" *SPh* 73.3: 225–238.

Hedreen, G. 1996. "Image, Text and Story in the Recovery of Helen." *CA* 15.1: 152–192.

Heilbrunn, G. 1977. "The Composition of Isocrates' *Helen.*" *TAPA* 107: 147–159.

Held, G. F. 1985. "The Meaning of ῬΗΘΟΣ in the *Poetics.*" *Hermes* 113: 280–293.

Herzfeld, M. 1985. *The Poetics of Manhood: Contest and Identity in a Cretan Mountain Village.* Princeton.

Hesk, J. 1999. "The Rhetoric of Anti-Rhetoric in Athenian Oratory." In Goldhill and Osborne, 201–230.

Hoekstra, A. 1974. *Homer Odyssey.* Oxford.

Höistad, R. 1948. *Cynic Hero and Cynic King.* Uppsala.

Holst-Warhaft, G. 1992. *Dangerous Voices: Women's Lament in Greek Literature.* New York.

Hooker, J. T. 1979. *Iliad III.* Bristol.

Hose, M. 2000. "Wahrscheinlich ist gerade dies, daß Menschen viel Unwahrscheinliches geschieht: Über das *eikos* in der attischen Tragödie." In *Skenika: Beiträge zum antiken Theater und seiner Rezeption,* ed. S. Godde and T. Heinze. Darmstadt. 17–30.

Huebeck, A., and A. Hoekstra. 1989. *The Odyssey: A Commentary,* vol. 2. Oxford.

Immisch, O. (ed.). 1927. *Gorgias Fragmente.* Berlin.

Jaeger, W. 1939–1945. *Paideia: The Ideals of Greek Culture.* Oxford.

Jarratt, S. C. 1991. *Rereading the Sophists: Classical Rhetoric Refigured.* Carbondale, IL.

Joël, K. 1921. *Geschichte der antiken Philosophie,* Band I. Tübingen.

Johnston, S. I. 1994. "Penelope and the Erinyes: *Odyssey* 20. 61–82." *Helios* 21.2: 137–159.

Jones, J. 1962. *On Aristotle and Greek Tragedy.* Oxford.

Joplin, P. K. 1991. "The Voice of the Shuttle Is Ours." *Rape and Representation,* ed. L. A. Higgins and B. R. Silver. New York. 35–64.

Jouan, F. 1966. *Euripide et les légendes des chants cypriens.* Paris.

Kahil, L. 1988. "Hélène." *LIMC* 4: 538–550.

Kahn, C. 1996. *Plato and the Socratic Dialogue: The Philosophical Use of a Literary Form.* Cambridge.

Kamerbeek, J. C. 1980. *The Plays of Sophocles,* pt. IV *Philoctetes.* Leiden.

Karp, A. J. 1977. "Homeric Origins of Ancient Rhetoric." *Arethusa* 10.2: 237–258.

Katz, M. A. 1991. *Penelope's Renown: Meaning and Indeterminacy in the "Odyssey,"* Princeton.

Kennedy, G. A. 1958. "Isocrates' Encomium of Helen: A Panhellenic Document." *TAPA* 89: 77–83.

———. 1963. *The Art of Persuasion in Greece.* Princeton.

———. 1986. "Helen's Web Unraveled." *Arethusa* 19: 5–14.

———. 1994. *A New History of Classical Rhetoric.* Princeton.

Kerferd, G. B. 1981. *The Sophistic Movement.* Cambridge.

Kirby, J. 1990. "The 'Great Triangle' in Early Greek Rhetoric and Poetics." *Rhetorica* 8.3: 213–228.

Kirk, G. S. 1962. *The Songs of Homer.* Cambridge.

———. 1985. *The Iliad: A Commentary,* vols. 1 and 2: 1–4, 5–8. Cambridge.

Kirkwood, G. 1979. *Early Greek Monody: The History of a Poetic Type.* Ithaca.

Kitto, G. 1950. *Greek Tragedy.* London.

Kuebler, C. 1944. *The Argument from Probability in Early Attic Oratory.* Chicago.

Kurke, L. 1991. *The Traffic in Praise: Pindar and the Poetics of Social Economy.* Ithaca.

———. 1999. *Coins, Bodies, Games, and Gold: The Politics of Meaning in Archaic Greece.* Princeton.

Lada-Richards, I. 1998. "Staging the *Ephebeia:* Theatrical Role-Playing and Ritual Transition in Sophocles' *Philoctetes.*" *Ramus* 27.1: 1–26.

Lang, B. (ed.). [1979] 1987. "Postface." In *The Concept of Style.* Ithaca. 13–17.

Lardinois, A. 1995. "Wisdom in Context: The Use of Gnomic Utterances in Archaic Greek Poetry." Diss. Princeton.

———. 2001. "Keening Sappho: Female Speech Genres in Sappho's Poetry." In *Making Silence Speak: Women's Voices in Greek Literature and Society,* ed. A. Lardinois and L. McClure. Princeton. 75–92.

Lateiner, D. 1982. "The Man Who Does Not Meddle in Politics." *CW* 76.1: 1–12.

———. 1995. *Sardonic Smile: Nonverbal Behavior in Homeric Epic.* Ann Arbor.

Lee, K. H. 1976. *Euripides Troades.* London.

Legrand, P. (ed.). 1927. *Bucoliques grecs.* Paris.

Lévi-Strauss, C. 1963. *Structural Anthropology,* tr. C. Jacobson and B. Grundfest Schoepf. New York.

Lloyd, G. E. R. 1979. *Magic, Reason and Experience: Studies in the Origins and Developments of Greek Science.* London.

Lloyd, M. 1984. "The Helen Scene in Euripides' *Troades.*" *CQ* 34: 303–313.

———. 1992. *The Agon in Euripides.* Oxford.

Lobel, E., and D. Page. 1955. *Poetarum Lesbiorum Fragmenta.* Oxford.

Lohmann, D. 1970. *Die Komposition der Reden in der Ilias.* Berlin.

Loraux, N. 1989. *Les expériences de Tirésias: Le féminin et l'homme grec.* Paris.

———. 1993. *Children of Athena: Athenian Ideas about Citizenship and the Division between the Sexes.* Princeton.

Lord, A. 1960. *The Singer of Tales.* Cambridge, MA.

Lynn-George, M. 1988. Epos: *Word, Narrative, and the Iliad.* Atlantic Highlands, NJ.

Mackie, H. 1995. *Talking Trojan: Speech and Community in the Iliad.* Lanham, MD.

MacLachlan, B. 1993. *The Age of Grace: Charis in Early Greek Poetry.* Princeton.

Martin, J. 1974. *Antike Rhetorik: Technik und Methode (Handb. der Altertumswiss. II 3).* Munich.

Martin, R. P. 1989. *The Language of Heroes: Speech and Performance in the Iliad.* Ithaca.

Mauss, M. 1925. *Essai sur le don, forme archaïque de l'échange.* Paris.

McClure, L. 1999. *Spoken Like a Woman: Speech and Gender in Athenian Drama.* Princeton.

McKirahan, R. D. 1994. *Philosophy before Socrates.* Cambridge.

Merkelbach, R. 1957. "Sappho und Ihr Kreis." *Philologus* 101: 1–29.

Meyer, L. 1987. "Toward a Theory of Style." In Lang, 21–71.

Monsacré, H. 1984. *Les larmes d'Achille: Les héros, la femme, et la souffrance dans la poesie d'Homère.* Paris.

Most, G. W. 1981. "Sappho FR. 16.6–7 L-P." *CQ* 31: 11–17.

————. 1985. *The Measures of Praise: Structure and Function in Pindar's Second Pythian and Seventh Nemean Odes*. Göttingen.

Mourelatos, A. P. 1987. "Gorgias and the Function of Language." *Philosophical Topics* 15: 135–171.

Muecke, F. 1982. "A Portrait of the Artist as a Young Woman." *CQ* 32: 41–55.

Mueller, M. 1984. *The Iliad*. London.

Müller, C. W. 1990. "Der Palamedesmythos im 'Philoktet' des Euripides." *RhM* 133.3–4: 195–209.

————. 2000. *Euripides Philoktet*. Berlin.

Munroe, D. B., and T. W. Allen. 1912–1920. *Homeri Opera I–V*. Oxford.

Murray, 1904. *Euripidis Fabulae II*. Oxford.

Nagler, M. N. 1974. *Spontaneity and Tradition: A Study of Oral Art in Homer*. Berkeley.

————. 1996. "Dread Goddess Revisited." In *Reading the* Odyssey: *Selected Interpretive Essays*, ed. S. Schein. Princeton. 141–161.

Nagy, G. 1979. *The Best of the Achaeans*. Baltimore.

————. 1990a. *Greek Mythology and Poetics*. Ithaca.

————. 1990b. *Pindar's Homer: The Lyric Possession of an Epic Past*. Baltimore.

————. 1996. *Poetry as Performance: Homer and Beyond*. Cambridge.

Nauck, A. 1886. *Sophocles*. Berlin.

Nightingale, A. W. 1995. *Genres in Dialogue: Plato and the Construct of Philosophy*. Cambridge.

Nimis, S. A. 1987. *Narrative Semiotics in the Epic Tradition*. Bloomington.

Norden, E. 1958. *Die Antike Kunstprosa*, vol. 1. Darmstadt.

North, H. F. 1981. "*Inutilis Sibi, Perniciosus Patriae*: A Platonic Argument against Sophistic Rhetoric." *ICS* 6.2: 242–271.

————. 1988. "Socrates *Deinos Legein*." In *Language and the Tragic Hero*, ed. P. Pucci. Atlanta. 121–130.

Ober, J. 1989. *Mass and Elite in Democratic Athens: Rhetoric, Ideology, and the Power of the People*. Princeton.

————. 1998. *Political Dissent in Democratic Athens: Intellectual Critics of Popular Rule*. Princeton.

Olson, S. D. 1989. "The Stories of Helen and Menelaus (*Odyssey* 4.240–89) and the Return of Odysseus." *AJP* 110: 387–394.

————. 1991. "Politics and the Lost Euripidean *Philoctetes*." *Hesperia* 60: 269–283.

————. 1995. *Blood and Iron: Stories and Storytelling in the* Odyssey. Leiden.

O'Sullivan, N. 1992. *Alcidamas, Aristophanes, and Early Greek Stylistic Theory*. Hermes Einzel- schriften 60. Stuttgart.

————. 1996. "Written and Spoken in the First Sophistic." In *Voice into Text: Orality and Literacy in Ancient Greece*, ed. I. Worthington. Leiden. 115–127.

Page, D. L. 1938. *Euripides Medea*. Oxford.

————. 1955. *Sappho and Alcaeus: An Introduction to Archaic Lesbian Poetry*. Oxford.

————. 1959. *History and the Homeric Iliad*. Berkeley.

Paley, F. A. 1872. *Euripides*, 2nd ed., vol. 1. London.

Parks, W. 1990. *Verbal Dueling in Heroic Narrative*. Princeton.

Parmentier, L. 1948. *Les Troyennes*. Paris.

Parry, A. 1964. "The Language of Achilles." In *Language and the Background of Homer*, ed. G. S. Kirk. Cambridge. 49–54.

Parry, H. 1992. *Thelxis: Magic and Imagination in Greek Myth and Poetry*. London.

Parry, M. 1971. *The Making of Homeric Verse: The Collected Papers of Milman Parry*. Oxford.

Pearson, A. C. 1963. *The Fragments of Sophocles*, vol. 1. Amsterdam.

Pelliccia, H. 1992. "Sappho 16, Gorgias' *Helen*, and the Preface to Herodotus' *Histories*." *YCS* 29: 63–84.

Pelling, C. (ed.). 1990. *Characterization and Individuality in Greek Literature*. Oxford.

Pepe, G. M. 1967. "Studies in Peitho." Diss. Princeton.

Peradotto, J. 1990. *Man in the Middle Voice: Name and Narration in the* Odyssey. Princeton.

Pfeiffer, R. 1968. *History of Classical Scholarship from the Beginnings to the End of the Hellenistic Age*. Oxford.

Pickard-Cambridge, A. W. 1968. *The Dramatic Festivals of Athens*, 2nd ed., rev. J. Gould and D. M. Lewis. Oxford.

Pierce, C. S. 1931–1958. *Collected Papers*. Cambridge, MA.

Podlecki, A. J. 1966. "The Power of the Word in Sophocles' *Philoctetes*." *GRBS* 7: 233–250.

Pohlenz, M. 1933. "τὸ πρέπον: ein Beitrag zur Geschichte des griechischen Geistes." *Nachrichten von der königlichen Gesellschaft der Wissenschaft zu Göttingen, Philologische-historische Klasse.* 53–92.

Porter, J. 1993. "Helen's Not Being: Gorgias and the 'Autonomy' of Logos." *CA* 13.2: 267–299.

———. (ed.) 1999. *Constructions of the Classical Body*. Ann Arbor.

Poulakos, J. 1983. "Gorgias' *Encomium to Helen* and the Defense of Rhetoric." *Rhetorica* I: 11–116.

———. 1995. *Sophistical Rhetoric in Classical Greece*. Columbia, SC.

———. 1996. "Extending and Correcting the Rhetorical Tradition: Aristotle's Perception of the Sophists." In *Theory, Text, Context: Issues in Greek Rhetoric and Oratory*, ed. C. L. Johnstone. Albany. 45–64.

Pratt, L. 1993. *Lying and Poetry from Homer to Pindar: Falsehood and Deception in Archaic Greek Poetics*. Ann Arbor.

Prier, R. A. 1989. *Thauma Idesthai: The Phenomenology of Sight and Appearance in Archaic Greek*. Tallahassee.

Pucci, P. [1979] 1998. "The Song of the Sirens." In *The Song of the Sirens: Essays on Homer*. Lanham, MD. 1–8.

———. 1987. *Odysseus Polutropos: Intertextual Readings in the* Odyssey *and the* Iliad. Ithaca.

Race, W. H. 1989–1990. "Sappho, Fr. 16 L-P. and Alkaios, Fr. 42 L-P.: Romantic and Classical Strains in Lesbian Lyric." *CJ* 85: 16–33.

Radermacher, L. 1951. *Artium scriptores*. Wein.

Rankin, H. D. 1986. *Antisthenes Sokratikos*. Amsterdam.

Redfield, J. A. 1975. *Nature and Culture in the* Iliad: *The Tragedy of Hector*. Chicago.

Rehm, R. 1992. *Greek Tragic Theatre*. London.

Ringer, M. 1998. *Electra and the Empty Urn: Metatheater and Role-Playing in Sophocles*. Chapel Hill.

Rose, P. 1988. "Thersites and the Plural Voices of Homer." *Arethusa* 21.1: 5–25.

————. 1992. *Sons of the Gods, Children of Earth.* Ithaca.

Russell, D. A. 1981. *Criticism in Antiquity.* New York.

————. 1990. "Êthos in Oratory and Rhetoric." In Pelling, 197–212.

Rutter, N. K., and B. A. Sparkes. 2000. *Word and Image in Ancient Greece.* Edinburgh.

Saïd, S. 1979. "Les crimes des prétendants, la maison d'Ulysse et les festins de l'Odyssée." *Etudes de littérature ancienne.* Paris. 9–49.

————. 1985. *Sophiste et tyran, ou, le problème du Promethée enchaine.* Paris.

Saintillan, D. 1996. "De festin à l'échange: Les grâces de Pandore." In *Les métiers du mythe: Hésiode et ses vérités,* ed. F. Blaise, P. Judet de la Combe, and P. Rousseau. Paris. 316–348.

Salvioni, L. 1985. *Persuasione e grandezza: Il dibatto antico intorno alla retorica e l'origine delle classificazioni stilistiche.* Verona.

Schechner, R. 1985. *Between Theater and Anthropology.* Philadelphia.

Scheid, J., and J. Svenbro. 1996. *The Craft of Zeus: Myths of Weaving and Fabric,* tr. C. Volk. Cambridge, MA.

Schein, S. 1999. "Verbal Adjectives in Sophocles: Necessity and Morality." *CP* 93.4: 293–307.

Schiappa, E. 1996. "Toward a Predisciplinary Analysis of Gorgias' *Helen.*" In *Theory, Text, Context: Issues in Greek Rhetoric and Oratory,* ed. C. L. Johnstone. Albany. 65–86.

————. 1999. *The Beginnings of Rhetorical Theory in Classical Greece.* New Haven.

Schiassi, G. 1953. *Euripides Troades.* Florence.

Schmitt-Pantel, P. 1992. *La cité au banquet: Histoire des repas publics dans les cités grecques.* Rome.

Schütrumpf, E. 1970. *Die Bedeutung des Wortes ἦθος in der Poetik des Aristoteles. Zetemata 49.* Munich.

Schwartz, E. 1877. *Scolia in Euripidem,* vol. 1. Berlin.

Schwyzer, E. 1923. *Dialectorum graecarum exempla epigraphica.* Leipzig.

Scodel, R. 1980. *The Trojan Trilogy of Euripides. Hypermestra 60.* Göttingen.

Scotti, F. P. 1996. *Ethos e consenso. Nella teoria e nella practica dell' oratoria greca e latina.* Bologna.

Segal, C. P. 1965. "Gorgias and the Psychology of the *Logos.*" *HSCP* 66: 99–155.

————. 1974. "Eros and Incantation: Sappho and Oral Poetry." *Arethusa* 7: 139–160.

————. 1981. *Tragedy and Civilization: An Interpretation of Sophocles.* Cambridge, MA.

————. 1982. *Dionysian Poetics and Euripides' Bacchae.* Princeton.

————. 1994. *Singers, Heroes, and Gods in the* Odyssey. Ithaca.

Seibel, A. 1995. "Widerstreit und Ergänzung: Thersites und Odysseus als rivalisierende Demagogen in der *Ilias* (B 190–264)." *Hermes* 123.4: 385–397.

Shapiro, H. A. 1993. *Personifications in Greek Art: The Representation of Abstract Concepts 600–400 B.C.* Kilchberg and Zurich.

Shewan, A. 1911. *The Lay of Dolon.* London.

Shipp, G. P. 1972. *Studies in the Language of Homer.* Cambridge.

Skutsch, O. 1987. "Helen, Her Name and Nature." *JHS* 107: 188–193.

Snell, B. 1937. *Euripides Alexandros.* Hermes Einzelschriften V. Stuttgart.

Snyder, J. 1981. "The Web of Song: Weaving Imagery in Homer and the Lyric Poets." *CJ* 76.3 (February–March): 193–196.

Solmsen, F. 1954. "The Gift of Speech in Homer and Hesiod." *TAPA* 85: 1–15.

———. (ed.) 1970. *Hesiodi Theogonia Opera et Dies Scutum.* Oxford.

Stanford, W. B. [1936] 1972. *Greek Metaphor.* New York (orig. Oxford).

———. 1950. "Studies in the Characterization of Ulysses—III: The Lies of Odysseus." *Hermathena* 75: 35–48.

———. 1954. *The Ulysses Theme: A Study of the Adaptability of a Traditional Hero.* Oxford.

———. [1963] 1981. *Sophocles Ajax.* Bristol.

Stanley, K. 1993. *The Shield of Homer: Narrative Structure in the* Iliad. Princeton.

Stehle, E. 1990. "Sappho's Gaze: Fantasies of a Goddess and a Young Man." *Differences* 2.1: 88–1125.

———. 1997. *Performance and Gender in Ancient Greece: Nondramatic Poetry in Its Setting.* Princeton.

Steiner, D. 2000. *Images in Mind: Statues in Archaic and Classical Greek Literature and Thought.* Princeton.

Stevens, P. T. 1971. *Euripides Andromache.* Oxford.

Stinton, T. C. W. 1965. *Euripides and the Judgement of Paris.* London.

Süss, W. 1910. *Ethos: Studien zur älteren griechischen Rhetorik.* Leipzig.

Suter, A. 1993. "Paris and Dionysos: *Iambos* in the *Iliad.*" *Arethusa* 26: 1–18.

Suzuki, M. 1989. *Metamorphoses of Helen.* Ithaca.

Szarmach, M. 1974a. "Le mythe de Palamède avant la tragédie grecque." *Eos* 62: 35–47.

———. 1974b. "Les tragédies d'Eschyle et de Sophocle sur Palamède." *Eos* 62: 193–204.

———. 1975. "Le 'Palamède' d'Euripide." *Eos* 63: 49–71.

Thalmann, W. G. 1984. *Conventions of Form and Thought in Early Greek Epic Poetry.* Baltimore.

———. 1988. "Thersites: Comedy, Scapegoats, and Heroic Ideology in the *Iliad. TAPA* 118: 1–28.

Theander, C. 1934. "Studia Sapphica." *Eranos* 32: 57–85.

Todorov, T. 1971. "The Place of Style in the Structure of the Text." In *Literary Style: A Symposium,* ed. S. Chatman. Oxford. 29–39.

Too, Y.-L. 1995. *The Rhetoric of Identity in Isocrates.* Cambridge.

———. 1999. *The Idea of Ancient Literary Criticism.* Oxford.

Tordesillas, A. 1990. "Palamède contra toutes raisons." In *La naissance de la raison en Grèce,* ed. J. F. Mattéi. Paris. 241–255.

Trahman, C. R. 1952. "Odysseus' Lies." *Phoenix* 6.2: 31–43.

Turner, V. 1974. *Dramas, Fields, Metaphors.* Ithaca.

Ubersfeld, A. 1977. *Lire le théâtre.* Paris.

Untersteiner, M. 1952. *The Sophists,* trans. K. Freeman. Oxford.

Usher, S. 1999. *Greek Oratory: Tradition and Originality.* Oxford.

Vellacott, P. 1975. *Ironic Drama: A Study of Euripides' Method and Meaning.* New York.

Verdenius, W. J. 1981. "Gorgias' Doctrine of Deception." In *The Sophists and Their Legacy,* ed. G. B. Kerferd. *Hermes Einzelschriften* 44. Stuttgart. 116–128.

———. 1984. *Hesiod: Works and Days.* Leiden.

Vermeule, E. 1979. *Aspects of Death in Early Greek Art and Poetry.* Berkeley.

Vernant, J.-P. [1986] 1991. *Mortals and Immortals.* Princeton.

———. [1986] 1989. "Dim Body, Dazzling Body." In *Fragments for a History of the Human Body,* vol. 1, tr. A. Wilson. New York.

———. 1996. "Les semblances de Pandora." In *Les métiers du mythe: Hésiode et ses vérités,* ed. F. Blaise, P. Judet de la Combe, and P. Rousseau. Paris. 381–392.

Viansino, G. 1963. *Sofocle Filottete.* Torino.

Vlastos, G. 1975. "Plato's Testimony Concerning Zeno of Elea." *JHS* 95: 136–162.

Voigt, E.-M. 1971. *Sappho et Alcaeus: Fragmenta.* Amsterdam.

Volkmann, R. 1963. *Die Rhetorik der Griechen und Römer in Systematischer Übersicht.* Hildescheim.

Walcot, P. 1977. "Odysseus and the Art of Lying." *Anc. Soc.* 8–9: 1–19.

Walker, J. 2000. *Rhetoric and Poetics in Antiquity.* Oxford.

Walsh, G. B. 1984. *The Varieties of Enchantment.* Chapel Hill.

Webster, T. B. L. 1963. *Sophocles: Philoctetes.* Cambridge.

West, M. L. 1970. "Burning Sappho." *Maia* 22: 307–330.

Whitman, C. H. 1951. *Sophocles: A Study of Heroic Humanism.* Cambridge, MA.

———. 1958. *Homer and the Heroic Tradition.* Cambridge, MA.

Wilamowitz, U. von. 1914. "Neue Lesbische Lyrik (Oxyrynchus Papyri X)." *NJb* 33: 225–247.

Wiles, D. 1991. *The Masks of Menander: Sign and Meaning in Greek and Roman Performance.* Cambridge.

———. 1997. *Tragedy in Athens: Performance Space and Theatrical Meaning.* Oxford.

Wilshire, B. 1982. *Role-Playing and Identity: The Limits of Theater as Metaphor.* Bloomington.

Winkler, J. J. 1990. *Constraints of Desire: The Anthropology of Sex and Gender in Ancient Greece.* New York.

Wisse, J. 1989. Ethos *and* Pathos *from Aristotle to Cicero.* Amsterdam.

Wohl, V. J. 1993. "Standing by the Stathmos: The Creation of Sexual Ideology in the *Odyssey.*" *Arethusa* 26: 19–50.

———. 1998. *Intimate Commerce: Exchange, Gender, and Subjectivity in Greek Tragedy.* Austin.

Woodbury, L. 1967. "Helen and the Palinode." *Phoenix* 2: 157–176.

Woodruff, P. 1999. "Rhetoric and Relativism: Protagoras and Gorgias." In *The Cambridge Companion to Early Greek Philosophy,* ed. A. A. Long. Cambridge. 290–310.

Worman, N. 1999a. "Odysseus *Panourgos:* The Liar's Style in Oratory and Tragedy." *Helios* 26.1: 35–68.

———. 1999b. "The Ties That Bind: Transformations of Costume and Connection in Euripides' *Heracles.*" *Ramus* 28.2: 89–107.

———. 2000. "Infection in the Sentence: The Discourse of Disease in Sophocles' *Philoctetes.*" *Arethusa* 33.1: 1–36.

———. 2001a. "This Voice Which Is Not One: Helen's Verbal Guises in Homeric Epic." In *Making Silence Speak: Women's Voices in Greek Literature and Society,* ed. A. Lardinois and L. McClure. 19–37. Princeton.

———. 2001b. "The *Herkos Achaiôn* Transformed: Character Type and Spatial Meaning in the *Ajax.*" *CP* 96.3: 228–252.

———. 2002. "Odysseus, Ingestive Rhetoric, and Euripides' *Cyclops.*" *Helios* 29.2: 1–25.

Zeitlin, F. I. 1980. "The Closet of Masks: Role-Playing and Myth-Making in the *Orestes* of Euripides." *Ramus* 9: 51–77.

———. 1982. "Travesties of Gender and Genre in Aristophanes' *Thesmophoriazousae*." In *Reflections of Women in Antiquity*, ed. H. P. Foley. London. 169–217. (1995b: 375–316.)

———. 1990. "Playing the Other: Theater, Theatricality, and the Feminine in Greek Drama." In *Nothing to Do with Dionysus? Athenian Drama in Its Social Context*, ed. J. J. Winkler and F. I. Zeitlin. Princeton. 63–96. (1995b: 341–374.)

———. 1991. "Euripides' *Hekabe* and the Somatics of Dionysiac Drama," *Ramus* 20: 53–94. (1995b: 172–216.)

———. 1995b. *Playing the Other: Gender and Society in Classical Greek Literature*. Chicago.

———. Forthcoming. *Vision, Figuration, and Image from Theater to Romance*. Berkeley.

Zeller, E. 1922. *Die Philosophie der Griechen*. Leipzig.

Achilles, 208n. 11, 211n. 59; arms of, 115–
116, 185; language of, 51, 71, 72, 212n. 64;
Odysseus and, 65, 67–73, 91, 188, 189
Adkins, A. W. H., 203n. 14, 211n. 47, 211n. 57
Adraste, 105
Adrasteia, 105
Aeneas, 51
Aeschines, 234n. 62, 235n. 71, 236–237n. 104;
Against Timarchus, 190
Aeschylus: *Agamemnon,* 31, 32, 113–115, 118,
119, 129, 224n. 44, 225n. 58; on Ajax,
236n. 96; oral style and, 37, 129, 230–
231n. 17, 231n. 20; *Persians,* 32; *Philoctetes,*
136–137
Agamemnon, 31, 48, 66–73, 118, 121, 209n. 26,
211n. 47, 211n. 59, 223n. 31
Agathon, 18, 222n. 7
agôn, 123, 125, 134
Ajax: in Antisthenes, 185–188; in *Iliad,* 48; in
Pindar, 115–118; in Sophocles, 120, 121, 136,
174, 227n. 79; visible type and, 169–170
akritomuthe, 66–67, 227n. 70; cf. *akrita,* 50,
akriton, 100
Alcibiades, 114, 152, 218n. 40, 218–219n. 40,
222n. 18, 227n. 70, 230n. 7, 230n. 8, 237n. 2
Alcidamas, 18, 230n. 12; *Odysseus on the Betrayal of Palamedes,* 169, 170, 174, 182–85,
229n. 2, 235n. 72, 235n. 78; *On the Sophists,*
37–38, 222n. 12, 230n. 15, 233n. 41; style of,
206n. 65, 206n. 67, 233n. 44
Alexiou, M., 208n. 20
ambrosios, 219n. 43
Anchises, 23, 88
Andromache, 46, 48, 54, 208–209n. 20, 226n. 69
Antenor, 90–91, 217n. 32
Antinous, 93–94, 229n. 103
Antiphon, 228n. 93
Antisthenes, 235n. 64, 236n. 97, 237n. 105; *Ajax,*
33, 185–187; *Odysseus,* 33, 135, 169, 170, 187–
189, 229n. 2; *On Helen and Penelope,* 229n. 2;
On Style or on Types, 33; oral style and, 8, 33,
169, 170; set speeches and, 150–151; visible
type and, 38

apatasthai, 112
Aphrodite, 209n. 29, 210n. 32, 211n. 50,
217n. 27, 219n. 47, 220n. 58, 221n. 60,
221n. 61, 222n. 23, 224n. 41, 226n. 62,
226n. 63, 231n. 21, 232n. 27; blaming speech
and, 49–52; character of, 120, 209n. 23,
216n. 24, 217n. 29, 223n. 33; *ekplêxis* and,
129, 132, 174, 226n. 65, 234n. 52; *Encomium
of Helen* and, 158–159; in *Hymn to Aphrodite,* 23, 88, 219n. 43; in *Iliad,* 47, 49–52,
103–105, 214n. 4, 214n. 5, 214n. 6; love
charms of, 87–88, 117, 221n. 59; in *Odyssey,*
61, 214n. 5; Peitho and, 87, 89, 159, 215–
216n. 20, 224–225n. 47, 226n. 61; in Sappho,
88–89, 155, 217n. 27; in *Trojan Women,* 123,
127, 129–130, 132–135; visual seduction
and, 87–89
Apollo, 23, 98
Apollodorus, 225n. 56
Archilochus, 85
Arctinus, 236n. 96
aretê, 13
Aretê, 35–36
Argeiê, 103
Ariadne, 220n. 56
Aristophanes, 230n. 7; *Frogs,* 19, 138, 154, 181;
oral style and, 18–19, 37; *Thesmophoriazusae,*
18, 121; written style and, 37, 154, 181
Aristotle: on Alcidamas, 183, 206n. 65,
206n. 67; on *êthos,* 33–35, 169, 198n. 7,
204n. 36, 205n. 54, 206n. 57, 228n. 92,
230n. 14; on *kosmos,* 27–28, 204n. 32; *Nicomachean Ethics,* 178; oral style and, 2–3,
8–10, 18–19, 37, 127, 154, 158–159, 170, 194,
205n. 44; on persuasive style, 7, 129, 135,
159, 191, 200–201n. 41, 201n. 50, 204n. 27,
213n. 77, 214n. 83, 223n. 28, 226n. 68,
228n. 88, 228n. 91, 230n. 15, 233n. 36; on
probability, 176–177, 199n. 26; on *prohairesis,* 220n. 52, 232n. 28; *Poetics,* 27–28, 34–35,
110, 176, 200n. 38; *Rhetoric,* 7–9, 17–18,
27–28, 33–35, 127, 129, 190, 223n. 28; on
suitability, 34, 199n. 26; on tragedy, 229–

230n. 5, 233n. 41, 234n. 52; visible type, 27–28, 90, 107, 108–109, 110, 180
Arnould, D., 212n. 68
Artemis, 98, 105, 210n. 38, 220n. 56, 221n. 63
Astyanax, 54
Atchity, K. J., 202n. 56, 208n. 19, 210n. 31, 217n. 31
Athena, 62, 73, 78, 87–88, 98–101, 106, 129, 219n. 46, 227n. 79
Athenaeus, 212n. 68
audience: reaction of, to oral style, 108–112, 161–163; vulnerability of, to deception, 136–137, 149–150, 165, 189–190
Austin, N., 202n. 56, 207n. 1, 208n. 18, 208n. 19, 211n. 53, 213n. 71, 217n. 31, 218n. 33, 220n. 53, 222n. 13, 223n. 34
Avezzù, G., 236n. 87

Baiter, G., 230n. 16
Bakhtin, M., 218n. 37
Bakker, E., 41, 42, 161–162, 207n. 1, 207n. 2, 207n. 3, 208n. 7, 233n. 45, 233n. 46
Bal, M., 208n. 5
Barkhuizen, J. H., 232n. 24
Barlow, S., 222n. 17
Barthes, R., 14, 159, 201n. 48, 202n. 57, 208n. 8, 233n. 37
basileus, 66
Bassi, K., 198n. 17, 219n. 44, 221n. 3, 222n. 13, 223n. 34
Baumhauer, O. A., 199n. 26, 200n. 29, 200n. 32, 200n. 39, 205n. 54
Beazley, J. D., 216n. 21, 216n. 22
Benediktson, D. T., 202n. 7, 206n. 62, 221n. 1, 234n. 52
Bergren, A. L. T., 208n. 19, 211n. 52, 215n. 13, 217n. 31, 218n. 33, 223n. 34, 232n. 32
Bers, V., 225n. 52
bia, 123, 216n. 21, 224n. 42
Biehl, W., 224n. 42
blaming speech, 47–52, 53–55
Blass, F., 236n. 87
Block, E., 219n. 44
Blundell, M. W., 227n. 81, 228n. 90, 228n. 95
Böckh, A., 236n. 84
bodily hexis. See hexis
Boedecker, D., 209n. 27, 209n. 29
Boegehold, A. L., 197n. 5, 207n. 4
Bourdieu, P., 3–4, 5, 6–7, 12, 20, 21, 32, 39, 43–44, 136, 142, 170, 172, 188, 197n. 5, 198n. 7, 198n. 8, 198n. 9, 198n. 10, 198n. 15, 199n. 18, 199n. 19, 199n. 24, 208n. 9, 225n. 59, 227n. 76

Bowra, C. M., 231n. 21
Brancacci, A., 237n. 105
Briseis, 73, 221n. 60
Buchheim, T., 158, 223n. 36, 232n. 33, 233n. 38, 233n. 42, 235n. 69, 235n. 76
Burke, K., 5, 196, 198n. 14, 199n. 20, 203n. 12, 237n. 3
Burnett, A. P., 217n. 27, 224n. 45, 224n. 46, 231n. 22
Butler, J., 4, 12, 21, 198n. 9, 198n. 15, 198n. 17
Buxton, G. A., 86, 215n. 12, 215n. 19, 216n. 21

Caizzi, F. D., 235n. 64, 235n. 66, 236n. 97
Calame, C., 207n. 2, 207n. 4, 215n. 14, 221n. 1, 234n. 57
Callicles, 142, 224n. 41
Callimachus, 203n. 20
Calypso, 58, 62, 95–97, 103–104, 117, 215n. 16, 219n. 41
Carey, C. A., 222n. 22
Carlyle, Thomas, 5
Carrière, J., 199–200n. 28
Cartledge, P., 203n. 11
Casertano, G., 233n. 40
Caskey, L. D., 216n. 21, 216n. 22
Càssola, F., 213n. 74
cast of character, 1, 6, 13, 21, 136, 195. See also visible type
character impersonation: Helen's, 65; Neoptolemus', 144, 145; Odysseus', 89, 95, 122, 140, 142–143, 148, 190; of rhapsodes, 42, 46, 207n. 4; of sophists, 13, 151, 183
character type, 4–5, 10–12, 17–20, 201n. 47, 201n. 50, 204n. 29; body and, 82–84; clothing and, 88–90, 100–101, 104–106, 121; in drama, 108–111; êthos and, 29–32, 228n. 91; in Homeric poetry, 41–43; performative aspects of, 200n. 38; sophists and, 149–151; visual details of, 30–37, 206n. 59, 207n. 69. See also charaktêr; hexis; visible type
charaktêr, 8, 17–18, 29, 32–33, 195, 199n. 25, 202n. 8
charassô, 17
charis, 83, 91, 116; cf. kharis, 218n. 38
Cicero, 2–3, 26, 179, 194, 198n. 15, 202n. 8
Circe, 58, 62, 95–96, 104, 208n. 19, 219n. 41, 219n. 42
Cithaeron, 116
Clader, L. L., 103, 105, 202n. 56, 208n. 19, 209n. 21, 209n. 29, 210n. 36, 210n. 37, 210n. 38, 210n. 43, 211n. 55, 217n. 31, 220n. 54, 220n. 55, 221n. 62, 221n. 63, 224n. 43

Clay, J. S., 214n. 81, 219n. 48
Cleon, 111–112, 142, 178, 214n. 85
clothing: deception and, 88–90, 100–101, 104–
    106, 121; seduction and, 86–88; visible type
    and, 97–101
coinage as metaphor, 205n. 51
Cole, T., 9, 199n. 26, 200n. 29, 200n. 30, 200n. 32,
    200n. 35, 200n. 40, 200n. 41, 232n. 31
Collins, C., 197n. 2, 208n. 17, 229n. 5
Cope, E. M., 204n. 36, 232n. 28
Corax, 18, 199n. 26
Corinna, 116
corporeal style, 82, 89, 90, 106, 111, 118, 126,
    195; Butler's concept of, 4, 21; Helen's, 124,
    134; of iambic type, 93; Odysseus', 24, 99,
    101, 141, 143, 134, 189; sophists', 151. See
    also hexis; visible type
Coulter, J. A., 204n. 25
Crane, G., 208n. 19, 219n. 42
Creon, 205n. 43
Creusa, 6, 31
Croally, N. A., 125, 223n. 36, 224n. 45, 226n. 67,
    227n. 74, 234n. 51
Crotty, K., 212n. 68
Csapo, E., 221n. 3
Cypria, 103

Dale, A. M., 205n. 54, 206n. 57
Dane, J. A., 231n. 21
Darius, 32
Davies, M., 220n. 58
deception: audience susceptibility to, 136–137,
    149–150, 165, 189–190; clothing and, 89–90,
    100–101, 104–106, 121; Helen as emblem
    of, 14, 101–104, 113–115, 120–121; Odysseus
    as emblem of, 14, 115–118, 181–182; oral
    style and, 135–137, 139–148, 169–170, 188–
    192; typical style and, 12–14, 58–59; visible
    type and, 58–59, 86–89, 106–107. See also
    méconnaissance
decoration: female body and, 89, 203n. 22;
    Helen and, 133; kosmos and, 21, 24, 25, 37,
    116, 157, 203n. 20, 204n. 28, 232n. 32; poikilos
    style and, 31, 201n. 52
deinos, 179, 183, 185, 226n. 68; cf. deinôs, 133,
    deinotês, 185
deixis, 42, 130, 131, 133, 147
De Jong, I., 42, 208n. 5
Delauney, M., 199–200n. 28
delivery, 8–10, 27–28, 34–35, 42, 63, 70, 151, 181,
    190–191, 197n. 3, 198n. 15, 204n. 30, 207n. 4
Demetrius, 2–3, 27, 197n. 2

Demodocus, 46, 211n. 47
Demos, 230n. 6
Demosthenes, 234n. 62, 236–237n. 104; Against
    Meidias, 190
Denniston, 222n. 17
deportment, 1–4, 6–8, 10, 13, 17, 18, 35–36,
    38, 82, 106, 188, 197n. 5, 198n. 7, 198n. 15,
    218n. 39; drama and, 110; êthos and, 29–
    30, 34, Helen's, 47, 126; in Homer, 41, 43;
    kosmos and, 21, 27; Odysseus', 66, 75, 79, 89,
    91, 92, 97
De Romilly, J., 214n. 82, 230n. 7, 231n. 18,
    233n. 43
Derrida, J., 206n. 68
Detienne, M., 208n. 10, 216n. 22, 217n. 32,
    236n. 99
Dickson, K., 210n. 35
Diggle, J., 227n. 72
Dio Chrysostom, 137–138
Diogenes Laertius, 33, 232n. 29
Diomedes, 46, 91–92, 208n. 13, 209n. 26,
    210n. 42
Dionysius of Halicarnassus, 2–3, 27, 154, 169,
    201n. 42, 202n. 8, 230n. 16; Demosthenes,
    193–194; On Literary Composition, 193–194
Dionysus, 138, 214n. 4, 222n. 7
Doherty, L., 208n. 19
doloi, 120–121; cf. 117–118, 119, 146, 216n. 24,
    217n. 29, 223n. 33
Dolon, 91–93, 218n. 37
Dover, K., 10, 199n. 28, 201n. 48, 204n. 32,
    206n. 56
dramatic enactment, 108–112
DuBois, P., 215n. 13, 231n. 22, 232n. 24
Dusanic, S., 183, 236n. 90, 236n. 92

Ebener, D., 224n. 38
Edmunds, L., 229–230n. 5
Edwards, M., 207n. 1, 208n. 18, 210n. 31,
    212n. 67, 212n. 69
eidôlon, 113, 223n. 34, 233n. 42
eidos, 20, 202n. 8; cf. idea
eikos, 6, 18, 121–122, 172, 176–177, 199n. 26,
    199n. 27, 235n. 77; cf. 23, 57–58, 98–99,
    203n. 18; cf. eoikota, 56, 62, eikôn, 199n. 27
ekplêxis, 127, 129, 132, 164–165, 174–175, 218–
    219n. 40, 226n. 65, 234n. 52
Elam, K., 202n. 58, 221n. 5
Els, G. H., 232n. 24
Else, G. F., 206n. 57
emblems: bodily hexis and, 18, 21, 23–24, 60,
    73; fabrics/weaving and, 89–90, 103–106;

Helen as, 43; of deception, 101–105, 113–115, 120–121; of grand style, 14, 15, 148, 150–151, 154, 155–157, 166–169, 192; of visual impact, 55, 127, 129–132, 134; of suitability, 47, 60; metonymic, 14, 122, 195, 202n. 58; Odysseus as, 43; of deception, 115–120, 148, 169, 181–182; of grand style, 14, 150–151, 154, 192; of suitability, 73–74, 79–80; Palamedes as, 181–182; Pandora as, 86; style and, 11, 195; visible type and, 5, 83

Emlyn-Jones, C., 213n. 73

Empedocles, 158, 162

empedos, 85; cf. 215n. 11

encomiastic speech, 76, 79, 100, 156, 158, 162

Enos, R., 8, 158–159, 197n. 4, 199n. 26, 200n. 29, 200n. 33, 200n. 38, 200n. 39, 201n. 49, 229n. 4, 230n. 11, 230n. 12, 232n. 29, 232n. 32, 232n. 34

epideictic speech, 128, 151, 156, 157, 166–169, 204n. 28, 205n. 53, 206n. 66, 230n. 15, 234n. 54. *See also* encomiastic speech; praise speech

epieikês, 18

epôdê, 162; cf. *epôdai*, 125, 129, *epôdos*, 162

Erinys, 114–115, 222n. 17; cf. Erinyes, 210n. 38

Eros (god), 226n. 61

erôs, 125, 209n. 25, 216n. 21, 226n. 63, 232n. 24, 233n. 38

êthopoiia, 150–151, 235n. 70

êthos, 14, 29–30, 32, 33–35, 39, 169, 176, 184, 190, 198n. 7, 199n. 26, 204n. 36, 204n. 38, 205n. 54, 206n. 57, 230n. 14

Eumaeus, 22, 23, 75–78, 80, 159, 213n. 72, 213n. 76, 218n. 38, 229n. 102

euprepês, 111–112, 130

Euripides: *Alexander*, 122; *Andromache*, 25, 118; *charaktêr* in, 32; *Electra*, 25; *Hecuba*, 31, 118–119, 121, 130; *Helen*, 25, 113, 121, 223n. 34, 225n. 48; *Heracles*, 32; *Hippolytus*, 203n. 22, 222n. 21; *Ion*, 6; *Iphigenia in Aulis*, 31, 118–119; *Iphigeneia in Taurus*, 25; *kosmos* in, 24–25, 26; *Medea*, 31; oral style and, 132, 133, 135; *Orestes*, 118, 121, 152, 225n. 48; *Palamedes*, 122, 132, 223n. 36; *Philoctetes*, 136, 137–138, 227n. 79; *poikilos* in, 31; style of, 9, 37, 154, 181, 222n. 7, 228n. 88, 230–231n. 17, 231n. 20; *Trojan Women*, 6, 118–119, 122–135, 147–148, 155, 156, 159–160, 222n. 25, 223n. 36, 225–226n. 60, 226n. 63; visible type and, 6, 31, 106–107, 109, 111

Euryalus, 22, 28, 93, 146, 211n. 47

Eurybates, 218n. 40

Eurymachos, 209n. 26

Evagoras, 36

fabric as emblem, 89–90, 103–106

Falkner, T. M., 221n. 2, 227n. 82, 228n. 85

Faraone, C., 221n. 59

Farnell, L. J., 222n. 24

Felson, N., 207n. 4, 208n. 19, 210n. 38, 211n. 53, 213n. 71

feminine adornment, 86–89

Ferrari, G. 206n. 68

Fletcher, J., 222n. 15

Foley, H. P., 214n. 2, 220n. 52, 221n. 1, 222n. 7, 232n. 24

Foley, J. M., 207n. 1

Ford, A. L., 202n. 56, 211n. 49, 213n. 71, 230n. 12, 236n. 103

Fortenbaugh, W. W., 205n. 54

Foucault, M., 4, 12, 198n. 11, 198n. 12, 198n. 13, 198n. 15, 199n. 24

Friedrich, P., 209n. 29

Gagarin, M., 197n. 4, 199n. 26, 200n. 30, 200n. 39, 200n. 41, 203n. 18

Garner, S. B., 198n. 17

Geddes, A. G., 230n. 6

Gellie, G., 224n. 38, 224n. 39

gender stereotypes, 83–85, 215n. 9, 215n. 13

Gentilli, B., 217n. 27, 232n. 24

Gerber, D. E., 222n. 24

gesture: bodily *hexis* and, 136, 170, 198n. 15, 234n. 62; in drama, 34–35, 109–110, 131, 229–230n. 5; in Homer, 43–44, 89; of sophists/rhapsodes, 29, 151, 197n. 2; visible type and, 2, 10, 27, 29, 197n. 5

Ghali-Kahil, L., 202n. 56, 215–216n. 20, 216n. 22, 220–221n. 58, 224n. 46, 224n. 47

Gill, C., 32, 201n. 45, 204n. 36, 205n. 46, 206n. 68, 207n. 71, 212n. 64

Gleason, M., 197n. 5, 198n. 17

glukeros, 45; cf. *glukus*, 88

Goffman, E., 198n. 17

Goldhill, S., 6, 198n. 17, 199n. 23, 201n. 47, 205n. 46, 214n. 1, 221n. 1, 223n. 36

Goodman, N., 198n. 14

Gorgias: *Encomium of Helen*, 24, 123, 125, 128–132, 142, 150, 155, 156–161, 163, 164, 168, 170, 191, 223n. 36, 232n. 31; grand oral style and, 8, 24, 26, 27, 37, 139, 151, 154, 169, 183–184, 194, 231n. 20, 233n. 44, 236n. 86; *kosmos* in, 24, 26, 27–29, 157; *On Not Being*, 164, 235n. 68, 235n. 69; *Palamedes' Defense*, 26,

128, 137, 150, 170–182, 223n. 36; on *peithô*,
155, 159–160, 233n. 40, 233n. 43, 234n. 59;
praise speech and, 155, 156–161, 165–169;
on sensory impact, 127, 161–165; sophistic
style and, 122, 153, 170, 222n. 12
grand oral style, 18–19; deception and, 113–
118, 120–121, 169–170, 181–182; development of, 8, 194–195; emblematized by
Helen and Odysseus, 120, 138, 151, 155,
169, 183–184, 191–192; and *ekplêxis*, 37–39,
132–133, 164–165, 174; and *kosmos*, 24–29;
sophists and, 151–154; and visual impact,
160–161, 164–165. *See also* oral style
Graver, M., 208n. 18, 209n. 23, 209n. 30,
210n. 36, 210n. 37, 210n. 39
Gregory, J., 223n. 36, 224n. 40
Gribble, D., 230n. 7, 230n. 8, 237n. 2
Griffin, J., 207n. 1
Grube, G. M. A., 200n. 29
Guardini, M. L., 234n. 55
Guthrie, W. K. C., 228n. 90, 228n. 93, 230n. 10,
235n. 64, 235n. 66

habitus: Bourdieu's concept of, 3, 5, 39, 188,
198n. 7; gender and, 214–215n. 7; Helen's,
48, 121; Odysseus', 74–75, 121, 139, 147;
Solon's, 234n. 62
Haft, A. J., 213n. 73, 213n. 74, 213n. 75, 214n. 79,
214n. 81
Hainsworth, B., 218n. 36
Halitherses, 209n. 26
Halliwell, S., 201n. 47, 205n. 54, 206n. 58,
206n. 62, 206–207n. 68, 207n. 69, 207n. 72,
214n. 85
Harriot, R., 200n. 29, 200n. 31
Havelock, E. A., 207n. 4, 225n. 59, 233n. 43
heanos, 104, 220n. 56
Heatherington, M. E., 213n. 71
Hector, 47, 50–52, 53–55, 69, 210n. 34, 210n. 40
Hecuba, 106, 118–119, 123–126, 132, 133–
135, 222n. 25, 224n. 38, 225n. 56, 226n. 67,
227n. 70
Hedreen, G., 215–216n. 20, 220n. 58, 224n. 47,
226n. 63
Heilbrunn, G., 234n. 55
Held, G. F., 206n. 57
Helen
—in *Agamemnon*, 113–115, 119, 129, 225n. 58
—agency of, 102–103, 220n. 52
—and Aphrodite, 87–88, 209n. 29; in *Iliad*, 49–
51, 61–62, 103–105, 211n. 50; in *Odyssey*,
226n. 62; in Sappho, 217n. 27; in *Trojan*

Women, 127, 129–130, 131–132, 134–135; in
vase paintings, 87, 158–159, 215–216n. 20,
220–221n. 58, 224–225n. 47, 226n. 61
—arguments, details of, 223n. 36, 225n. 56,
225n. 58, 225–226n. 60, 227n. 74, 234n. 56
—authoritative tradition and, 222n. 13
—beauty of, 102–103, 118, 130, 132, 133, 154–
156, 157–158, 165–169, 234n. 58, 234n. 59
—blaming speech and, 47–52, 53–55, 215n. 10
—bodily *hexis* and, 47, 49, 58, 60, 102, 104, 125,
134, 135
—body of: blinding, 103–104, 113; as emblem
of *logos*, 157, 160–165, 233n. 42; ornamental, 123, 133, 226n. 64; veiled, 89, 102–103;
well-dressed, 125–126, 131, 134
—as bridal figure, 86–87, 126, 215n. 13, 215n. 14
—cloaking of, 89–90, 102–104, 131, 214n. 78,
220–221n. 58
—clothing/adornment of, 86–87, 89–90, 102,
104, 134, 220n. 55, 220n. 56, 224–225n. 47
—clothing, deception, and, 89–90, 104–106
—currency and, 115, 222n. 21
—decorative object, status as, 126, 133, 215n. 13
—desire and, 50, 87, 102, 124–125, 127, 132,
134–135, 155, 159–160, 210n. 31, 217n. 26,
219n. 41, 220n. 54, 221n. 61, 223n. 31,
223n. 34, 226n. 67
—dog epithets, use of, 49, 53, 63, 209n. 23,
209n. 30
—dramatic enactment and, 110–112
—*ekplêxis* and, 127, 129, 132, 164–165, 234n. 52
—as emblem of deception, 101–104, 113–115,
120–121
—as emblem of grand style, 14, 15, 148, 150–
151, 154, 155–157, 166–169, 191–192
—as Erinys, 114–115, 222n. 17; cf. 210n. 38
—eyes of, 102–103, 118–119, 124–125, 220n. 53,
224n. 43
—fabrics/weaving and, 90, 104–106, 220n. 56,
220n. 57, 221n. 64, 227n. 70
—as goddess of vegetation, 221n. 63
—hair of, 121, 124, 134, 225n. 48
—in *Hecuba*, 118, 130, 224n. 43
—in Herodotus, 112–113, 130
—history of type, 202n. 56, 208n. 19, 217n. 31
—ill-repute of, 47–48, 53–55, 64–65, 129–130,
132–135, 210n. 40, 227n. 72, 231n. 21; cf.
kleos (below)
—in *Iphigeneia in Aulis*, 118–119
—*kêlêmata* and, 125, 224n. 44
—*kleos* and, 47–49, 54–55, 155
—*kosmos* and, 22–24, 59–60, 87, 157

—as leader of young girls' choruses, 215n. 14
—Muses and, 47, 57, 61–64, 210–211n. 44
—nemesis and, 53, 103, 210n. 43
—Odysseus, use of, 57–59, 210n. 45
—*ophelon* phrases, use of, 49, 54; cf. 209n. 24
—in *Phaedrus*, 113, 223n. 34
—*pharmaka* and, 56, 105–106, 219n. 42, 234n. 51
—pleasure and death, connection to, 209n. 25
—praise speech and, 154–159, 164–169, 222n. 16, 232n. 23, 232n. 28, 234n. 55
—return of, 216n. 22
—rhapsodes and, 62, 65, 110, 150, 151
—seizure of, 220n. 61
—sophists and, 122, 148, 150, 151–153, 195–196, 237n. 2
—style and, 43–46, 203n. 23; abusive, 49–54; authoritative, 48–49, 56–65, 75, 105–106, 211n. 49; deceptive, 120–122; honey-sweet, 45, 52; ornamental, 121–122, 125–126, 131–132; seductive, 45–46, 211n. 51, 224n. 41; suitable, 56, 59–60, 62, 64–65, 113, 153, 210n. 34; versatile, 13–14; visualizing, 3, 14, 21–23, 101–103, 120, 131–132, 135, 158–159, 160–161, 164–165, 168, 192, 195–196, 197n. 2
—as subject of set speeches, 150–151, 216n. 21
—visible type of, 84–85, 101–103, 123–131, 133–135, 154–159
—visual seduction and, 86–89, 232n. 24
Helicon, 116
Hephaestus, 85, 87–88, 98, 209n. 23
Hera, 87–88, 104, 129, 219n. 43, 220n. 56, 227n. 71
Heracles, 35–36, 110, 139, 166, 180, 202n. 5, 214–215n. 7, 235–236n. 83
Heraclitus, 153
Hermes, 23, 29, 30, 96
Hermione, 25, 27, 31
Hermogenes, 35, 168
Herodotus: *charaktêr* in, 32; *euprepês* in, 111, 130; *Histories*, 111–113
Herzfeld, M., 4, 198n. 16, 201n. 51
Hesiod, 116; *êthos* in, 29; Helen in, 167, 231n. 21, 234n. 58; *kosmos* in, 87, 203n. 19; oral style and, 45–46; Pandora in, 23, 87; visible type and, 83, 85, 98, 113; *Works and Days*, 87; *Theogony*, 87, 88
Hesk, J., 231n. 18, 234n. 63, 236–237n. 104
Hesychius, 231n. 17
hexis, 18, 21, 35, 39, 43–44, 82–83, 107, 110, 136, 195, 198n. 6, 227n. 77
—Achilles', 73
—Aeschines', 234n. 62

—Ajax's, 186
—Alcibiades', 152
—Bourdieu's concept of, 3–4, 6–7, 20, 21, 39, 170, 188, 197n. 5, 198n. 7, 208n. 9
—Helen's, 125, 135; bodily, 102, 104, 134; verbal, 47, 49, 58, 60
—Neoptolemus', 140, 143, 145
—Odysseus', 172, 186, 188; bodily, 91, 93–95, 100, 142, 211n. 46; verbal, 66, 71, 73, 75, 79, 80, 137, 211n. 46
—Palamedes', 172
—Thersites', 66, 92
—*See also* corporeal style; visible type
Hippias, 139, 150, 153, 189
Hipponax, 46, 212n. 68
Hoekstra, A., 213n. 74
Höistad, R., 236n. 97
Holst-Warhaft, G., 208n. 20, 210n. 41
Homer
—body in, 83–85, 89–90
—clothing and deception in, 89–90
—deceptive style in, 144, 146–147
—*êthos* in, 29
—gender representation and, 47, 84, 214n. 7
—on Helen and Odysseus: as antitypes, 19; distracting qualities of, 89–90; indirection of, 52; suitability of, 73–74, 195
—*Iliad*: Helen in, 47–55, 101–105; Odysseus in, 65–74, 90–93
—*kosmos* in, 22–23, 28, 203–204n. 24
—in later tradition, 202n. 5, 203n. 17; on Helen, 112–113, 130, 168; on Odysseus, 115–118, 174, 182, 189
—literary discourse and, 43, 208n. 8
—*Odyssey*, 213n. 71; Helen in, 56–65, 105–106; Odysseus in, 74–81, 93–101
—oral performance and, 42–43
—orality and, 207n. 1
—*poikilos* in, 30, 219n. 43
—probability and, 199n. 26
—on speakers' styles, 8, 45–46
—visible type, 43, 83, 107, 136, 197n. 5
—visualizing style of, 41–42, 197n. 2
Homeric hymns: *Hymn to Aphrodite*, 23–24, 88; *Hymn to Delian Apollo*, 62; *Hymn to Hermes*, 23
honeyed speech, 45, 52, 98; cf. *meilichios*
Hooker, J. T., 210n. 31
Horace, 216n. 25
Hose, M., 199n. 26
huphainô, 45
hupokrisis, 9, 201n. 42. *See also* delivery

iambos, 93
Ibycus, 220n. 58
idea, 35, 120, 168, 202n. 8, 205n. 53
Idomeneus, 48, 79, 234n. 58; Odysseus' use of, 214n. 80, 214n. 81
Immisch, O., 233n. 38
Ino, 97
Ion (in Euripides), 6
Ion (in Plato), 202n. 5, 236n. 102
Iris, 209n. 28
Isocrates: *Demonicus,* 38–39; *Evagoras,* 36–37, 39, 168–169, 182; grand oral style and, 38; *Helen,* 158, 165–169, 182, 229n. 2; *kosmos* in, 38–39; *Nicocles,* 39; ornate style of, 38, 165, 169, 234n. 55; *Philippus,* 38; praise speech and, 158–159, 165–169, 230n. 15, 234n. 54; on style, 9, 18, 128, 155, 206–207n. 68; visible type in, 36–37, 38–39, 206n. 61

Jaeger, W., 230n. 10
Jarratt, S. C., 230n. 9
Jason, 203n. 24, 233n. 43
Joël, K., 230n. 10
Johnston, S. I., 210n. 38
Jones, J., 200n. 38, 205n. 54
Joplin, P. K., 215n. 13, 218n. 33
Jouan, F., 227n. 75

Kahil, 220n. 58
Kahn, C., 235n. 66
kainotês, 112
Kakia, 35–36
Kamerbeek, J. C., 228n. 94
Karp, A. J., 200n. 31
Katz, M. A., 210n. 38, 215n. 13, 218n. 33
kêlêmata, 125, 224n. 44
Kennedy, G. A., 199n. 26, 200n. 29, 200n. 35, 212n. 63, 217n. 31, 229n. 3, 234n. 54, 234n. 55, 235n. 74
kerdos, 112, 219n. 46
Kerferd, G. B., 228n. 90, 230n. 11, 235n. 69
Kirby, J., 160, 233n. 39, 233n. 40
Kirk, G. S., 67, 207n. 4, 210n. 31, 211n. 8
Kirkwood, G., 217n. 27, 232n. 27
Kitto, G., 224n. 38
kleos, 47–49, 54–55
kosmos, 6, 14, 21–29, 33, 38–39, 87, 111, 136, 175, 203n. 17, 203n. 19, 203–204n. 24, 204n. 28, 204n. 32, 218n. 38; cf. *kosmeô, kosmios,* 21, 26; *akosmos,* 66–67, 218n. 34; cf. 175; *huper aisan,* 211n. 48; *huper moron,* 211n. 48; *kata aisan,* 59–60; *kata kosmon,* 21, 22, 59,

203n. 14, 211n. 47; *kata moiran,* 22, 59–60, 203n. 14; cf. 80; *ou para moiran,* 22–23; cf. 78, 80; *para kairon,* 24; *para moiran,* 24. *See also* suitable and unsuitable style; visible type
Kuebler, C., 199n. 26
Kurke, L., 203n. 20, 205n. 51
Kurnos, 29–30

Lada-Richards, I., 221n. 2, 227n. 82
lalia, 202n. 55
lampros, 230n. 6
Lang, B., 198n. 14
Lardinois, A., 211n. 49, 215n. 14
Lateiner, D., 42, 197n. 5, 204n. 69, 208n. 6, 214n. 4
Lee, K. H., 224n. 38, 224n. 40, 224n. 45, 226n. 64, 226–227n. 69, 227n. 72
Lemnos, 227n. 75
Lévi-Strauss, C., 215n. 13
lexis, 9, 17–18, 28, 33, 202n. 2; *agonistikê,* 200n. 41; *graphikê,* 200n. 41. *See also* oral style; written style
Lloyd, G. E. R., 199n. 26, 223–224n. 36, 224n. 37, 224n. 45, 225n. 56, 225n. 60
Lobel, E., 217n. 28
logographer, 37–38, 236n. 103
logos, 115, 127, 129, 155, 157, 158, 160, 162–164, 191, 224n. 44, 228n. 87, 231n. 18, 232n. 29, 232n. 35, 233n. 41; cf. *oikeios logos,* 190, 237n. 105
Lohmann, D., 211–212n. 60, 212n. 61, 212n. 63, 212n. 70
Loraux, N., 211n. 52, 215n. 10, 215n. 17, 215n. 18
Lord, A., 207n. 1
Lynn-George, M., 64, 211n. 54, 212n. 62
Lysias, 38, 154, 235n. 70

Mackie, 208n. 16, 210n. 34
MacLachlan, B., 214n. 2, 222n. 15
malakos, 45, 52
Martin, J., 198n. 17, 200n. 29
Martin, R. P., 42, 67, 200n. 35, 203n. 21, 208n. 6, 208n. 8, 208n. 13, 208n. 16, 209n. 22, 209n. 28, 210n. 35, 211n. 57, 212n. 64, 212n. 65, 213n. 71, 217n. 32, 218n. 39
Mauss, M., 215n. 15
McClure, L., 230–231n. 17
McKirahan, R. D., 230n. 10
méconnaissance, 136–137, 170; cf. 172
Medea, 203n. 24, 233n. 43
Medusa, 224n. 43
Meilichios, 45, 52, 88, 208n. 11, 219n. 49

Menelaus: in *Agamemnon,* 113; in Herodotus, 112; in *Iliad,* 48, 51, 104; in *Odyssey,* 23, 56–57; speaking style of, 59–64, 75, 217n. 32; in *Trojan Women,* 124–127, 130, 133, 224n. 42, 226n. 67; in vase painting, 220n. 58

Meno, 179

Merkelbach, R., 231n. 21

Metilius, Rufus, 193

metonymic emblems, 14, 122, 195

Meyer, L., 198n. 14

middle oral style, 37, 154

Millet, P., 203n. 11

Mnesilochus, 121

Moira, 73

monos, 186–187

Monsacré, H., 208n. 19, 209n. 25, 210n. 32, 214n. 1

moral character. *See êthos*

mores, 35

Most, G. W., 222n. 22, 232n. 23

Mourelatos, 233n. 43

mouth, 44–45, 208n. 9

Muecke, F., 18, 202n. 5, 230–231n. 17

Mueller, M., 212n. 62

Müller, C. W., 138, 227n. 80, 227n. 81

Muses, 45–46, 57, 61, 62, 63, 64, 208n. 19

muthos, 66, 76, 234n. 58; cf. *muthoi,* 48–49

Nagler, M. N., 219n. 42, 220n. 55

Nagy, G., 60, 203n. 21, 207n. 1, 207n. 4, 208n. 14, 211n. 48, 211n. 51, 211n. 60, 215n. 10, 217n. 32, 218n. 35, 222n. 13, 223n. 29, 229n. 103

narratological theory, 42, 208n. 5

Nauck, A., 228n. 94

Nausicaa, 98–100

neikos, 67, 211–212n. 60

nemesis, 53, 103, 210n. 43

Nemesis (goddess), 103, 105, 221n. 63

Neoptolemus, 31, 94, 138, 139–148, 173–175, 227n. 81, 228n. 87, 228n. 89, 228n. 90, 228–229n. 96, 229n. 97, 229n. 98

nêpenthê, 106

Nestor, 75, 183, 208n. 11, 208n. 12, 211n. 47

Nightingale, A. W., 36, 204n. 26, 206n. 60, 206n. 61, 207n. 71, 236n. 88

Nimis, S. A., 211–212n. 60

Norden, E., 199–200n. 28, 233n. 45

North, H. F., 201n.55, 226n. 68, 235n. 80

Ober, J., 201n. 44, 222n. 9, 226n. 68, 228n. 93, 234n. 63, 236n. 103, 236–237n. 104

Odysseus
—abuse of, 22, 93–94, 227n. 78, 229n. 99
—in *Ajax* (Sophocles'), 118, 120, 185, 188, 234n. 50
—Athena and, 76–78, 98–99, 101, 219n. 46, 227n. 79
—bodily *hexis* and, 66, 71, 73, 75, 79, 80, 91, 93–95, 100, 137, 142, 172, 186, 188, 211n. 46
—body of, 90–91; crafted, 98, 101, 216n. 23, 219n. 48, 220n. 50; debased, 58, 93–94, 97, 214n. 4; vulnerable, 95–97
—character and, appropriation, 135–137, 139–148, 213n. 72, 214n. 80, 214n. 81; exchange, 169–170, 171–188
—cloaks and, 78–79, 214n. 78
—clothing, deception, and, 89–90, 99–101
—clothing of, 90, 98, 100–101
—Crete, use of, 76–78, 79, 213n. 74, 213n. 79—denigration of, in later tradition, 115, 136, 139, 148, 218n. 36, 227n. 81
—deportment of, 66, 85, 89, 218n. 39, 228–229n. 96
—in dramatic enactment, 110–112
—*eikos* arguments and, 121–122, 172, 176–177, 199n. 26, 235n. 77; cf. 23, 57–58, 98–99, 203n. 18
—*ekplêxis* and, 174–175, 218–219n. 40
—as emblem: of deception, 115–120, 169, 181–182; of grand style, 14, 150–151, 154, 192
—*êthos* and, 30–31, 176, 184, 190
—*gastêr* and, 212n. 67, 212n. 68, 212n. 70
—gender representation and, 84–85, 214–215n. 7
—goddesses and, 90, 95–99, 210n. 46
—in *Hecuba,* 31, 118–119, 121
—Helen's use of, 57–59, 210n. 45, 223n. 33
—history of type, 202n. 56, 217n. 31
—in *Iphigeneia in Aulis,* 31
—*kosmos* and, 22–24, 25, 136, 175, 203n. 15, 203–204n. 24, 211n. 47, 218n. 38
—as merchant type, 146–147, 229n. 105
—*ophelon* phrases, use of, 49; cf. 209n. 24, 209n. 26
—as *panourgos* type, 137, 142, 144, 173–176, 178–180, 189–190
—in Pindar, 115–117
—as *poikilos* type, 30, 31, 205n. 44, 229n. 101
—praise speech and, 203n. 14
—rhapsodes and, 110, 150, 151
—sophists and, 122, 142, 148, 150, 151–153, 170, 184, 195–196, 237n. 2

—style and, 43–44, 206n. 56; authoritative, 61, 66–67, 75; deceitful, 115–118, 120–122, 212n. 66, 213n. 75, 219n. 46, 229n. 104, 234n. 50; *deinos*, 132–133, 178–179, 183–185, 201–202n. 55, 203n. 24, 222n. 25; fair-sharing, 65, 67–71, 72–74; grand, 38, 138, 191–192; honey-sweet, 45–46, 52, 98; mirroring, 75–81, 218n. 38; ornamental, 101, 201n. 52, 227n. 73; slanderous, 171–172, 182; suitable, 22, 58–59, 65–74, 153, 156, 211n. 47, 213n. 77, 219n. 49; versatile, 6, 13–14, 74–75, 80–81, 82, 84, 135, 170, 188–192; visualizing, 3, 14, 21–23, 98, 100, 120, 195–196
—subject of set speeches, 150–151
—Thersites and, 66–67, 90–91, 209n. 28, 210n. 56, 218n. 40, 229n. 103
—in *Trojan Women*, 119
—as unscrupulous type, 142, 180, 229n. 103, 229n. 97, 235n. 78; cf. *panourgos* type (above)
—visible type of, 75–81, 84–85, 90–101
—weaving and, 90, 217n. 32
Oedipus, 110, 205n. 43, 211n. 59
Olson, S. D., 202n. 56, 211n. 45, 213n. 71, 227n. 77
ophelon, 49, 54; cf. 209n. 24, 209n. 26
opsis, 155, 164–165, 233n. 38
oral style, 2–3
—archaic images of, 44–46
—audience reaction to, 108–112, 161–163
—authoritative, 48–49, 66–67, 75, 105–106, 120, 170
—blaming, 47–52, 53–55
—character type and, 32–35: appropriation of, 135–137, 139–148; exchange of, 169–188
—development of, 7–10
—in dramatic enactment, 108–112
—extemporaneous, 37–38
—grand, middle, and plain, 18–19, 37, 154
—ornamental, 21–29, 121–122, 157, 193–194
—praise speech and, 155, 156–159, 164–169
—rhythmic, 129–130, 162–163
—seductive, 52–53, 86–89, 98
—senses and, 161–165
—sophistic, 149–154, 170, 196
—suitable and unsuitable, 59–60, 70–71, 93–94, 121–122
—thin/writerly style, versus, 37, 154
—versatility and, 188–192
—visible type and, 8–10, 41–44, 90–101, 123–135
—visualizing, 2–3, 14, 21–23, 41–44, 120, 127,

131–132, 135, 154–156, 158–159, 160–161, 164–165, 168, 191–192, 195–196, 197n. 2
—*See also* Grand oral style; Lexis
Orestes, 110, 118, 214n. 4
ornamental style, 21–29, 157, 193–194; Helen, 121–122, 125–126, 131–132; Odysseus and Penelope, 101
Osborne, R., 198n. 17, 199n. 23, 221n. 1
O'Sullivan, N., 8, 18, 112, 154, 199n. 28, 200n. 30, 200n. 34, 200–201n. 41, 202n. 6, 206n. 63, 206n. 65, 222n. 9, 222n. 11, 225n. 49, 226n. 66, 229n. 4, 230n. 7, 230n. 12, 230n. 13, 230n. 16, 230–231n. 17, 231n. 20, 235n. 73, 235n. 80, 235n. 82, 236n. 86
othonê, 104, 220n. 56

Page, D. L., 212n. 67, 222n. 17, 231n. 21
Palamedes: in Alcidamas, 182–185, 235n. 78, 236n. 93; in Gorgias, 169, 171–182, 223n. 36, 225–226n. 60, 235n. 81; tragedy and, 137–138, 139, 228–229n. 96
Paley, F. A., 224n. 40, 224n. 44, 227n. 72
Pandora: adornment of, 86–88, 98, 203n. 19; as bane, 85, 113, 222n. 19; character of, 29, 117, 215n. 9
panourgos, 137, 142, 144, 173–176, 178–180, 189–190; cf. *panourgia*, 174
paragein, 112; cf. *paragoisa*, 116
Paris: abuse of, 49–54, 209n. 30; attraction of, 210n. 31, 210n. 32, 214n. 4, 214n. 5, 214n. 7; desire and, 122, 134, 159; in *Encomium of Helen*, 159, 165; in *Helen* (Isocrates), 167; in Herodotus, 112–113; in *Iliad*, 49–54; in *Trojan Women*, 127–134; in vase depictions, 220–221n. 58, 226n. 61; visual impact and, 103–105, 127–130, 132, 164–165, 167, 209n. 29, 219n. 47
Parks, W., 209n. 30
Parmenides, 153
Parmentier, L., 223n. 30, 225n. 50, 226–227n. 69
parphasis, 117; 87–88, 216n. 22
Parry, A., 46, 70, 208n. 16, 212n. 64
Parry, H., 214n. 82, 231n. 18, 233n. 43
Parry, M., 207n. 1
Pasiphae, 227n. 70
pathos, 70
Patroclus, 71
Peisistratus, 63
Peitho (goddess), 86, 87, 89, 215–216n. 20, 216n. 21, 217n. 27, 226n. 61
peithô, 86, 89, 97, 111, 159, 164, 215n. 21, 216n. 21, 223n. 34, 226n. 67, 226–227n. 69, 233n. 39, 233n. 40

Peleus, 211n. 59
Pelliccia, H., 231n. 22, 232n. 23, 232n. 25
Pelling, C., 204n. 36
Penelope: agency of, 220n. 52; as audience of deceitful speech, 80, 213n. 76, 229n. 102; as audience of encomiastic speech, 75–76, 79; Helen and, 62, 210n. 38, 220n. 54; *kleos* and, 47, 210n. 33; visual impact and, 99–101, 220n. 50
Pepe, G. M., 216n. 22
peplos, 134; cf. *peploi*, 106
Peradotto, J., 202n. 56, 213n. 71, 213n. 74, 214n. 80
persuasive techniques: deceit and, 146–147, 149–151, 191; development of, 7–9; in oral settings, imagery of, 44–46; ornamentation and, in writing, 36–37; seduction and, 52–53; suitability and, 70–71; visual impact and, 86–89, 153, 154–156, 159–161, 191
Pfeiffer, R., 236n. 86
phaneros, 235n. 81
pharmaka, 56, 105–106, 219n. 42, 234n. 51; cf. *pharmakon*, 56
Philoctetes: as bowman, 214–215n. 7; as civic benefactor, 235–236n. 83; Lemnos and, 118, 136, 140, 227n. 75; on Odysseus, 25, 137–138, 174–175, 177, 228–229n. 96; in *Philoctetes* (Aeschylus), 136–137; in *Philoctetes* (Euripides), 137–138; in *Philoctetes* (Sophocles), 139–148; speaking styles and, 94, 120, 136, 139–148, 218–219n. 40; wound of, 136, 214n. 4, 229n. 98
philosophos, 206n. 61, 207n. 71, 236n. 88; cf. 182–183
phusis, 29, 32, 205n. 48, 228n. 92; cf. 141–142
Pickard-Cambridge, A. W., 221n. 3
Pierce, C. S., 202n. 58
Pindar: *kosmos* in, 24, 26; *Nemean* 7 and 8, 115–117; *Olympian* 1, 116; on Odysseus, 115–118; *poikilos* in, 30–31; visibility of character and, 37
Plato: *Apology*, 25, 179, 226n. 68; *Gorgias*, 9, 39, 142, 152, 190, 224n. 41, 226n. 68, 228n. 87; *Hippias Minor*, 189, 212n. 66, 229n. 2; *Ion*, 190, 202n. 5, 207n. 4, 236n. 102; on *kosmos*, 25–26, 204n. 28; *Meno*, 162; oral style and, 9, 19, 25–26, 37–38, 194, 201n. 50, 206–207n. 68, 207n. 69; *Phaedrus*, 26, 37, 38, 113, 122, 154, 183–184, 206n. 59, 223n. 34, 230n. 15, 233n. 29; *philosophos* and, 182–183, 207n. 71, 236n. 88; on probability, 122, 199n. 26; *Protagoras*, 228n. 87; *Republic*, 39; on sophistic style, 142, 152–153, 154, 170–

171, 175, 183–184, 236n. 93; visible type and, 36, 38, 39, 206n. 59, 236n. 102
Podlecki, A. J., 227n. 81, 228n. 86
Pohlenz, M., 199n. 26
poikilos, 30–31, 144, 201n. 52, 205n. 43, 217n. 29, 219n. 43, 223n. 28, 229n. 101; cf. *poiklia*, 38, *poikilophrôn*, 120
Polus, 8
polutropos, 135, 188–190; cf. *polumêchanos*, 77, 190, *polumêtis*, 190, *polutropia*, 189
Polyphemus, 227n. 73
Polyxena, 118–119, 121, 130
Porphyry, 188
Porter, J., 198n. 17, 232n. 29, 232n. 32
Poseidon, 96
Poulakos, J., 197n. 4, 199n. 26, 200n. 29, 200n. 32, 222n. 9, 229n. 4
praise speech, 154–159, 164–169. *See also* encomiastic speech; epideictic speech
Pratt, L., 213n. 72, 222n. 22, 222n. 24, 223n. 29
prepôn, 6, 199n. 27; cf. *prepês*, 190. *See also* suitable and unsuitable style
Priam, 47–48, 49, 90, 171, 209n. 26, 225n. 56
Prier, R. A., 20, 202n. 7, 202n. 9, 214n. 2, 220n. 53
probability, 6, 18, 56, 62, 121–122, 172, 176–177, 199n. 26, 199n. 27, 235n. 77; cf. 23, 57–58, 98–99, 203n. 18. *See also eikos*
Prodicus, 35, 36, 138, 153, 154, 181, 195, 200–201n. 41, 202n. 5, 225n. 49, 231n. 20, 236n. 86, 236n. 93
Prometheus, 30, 223n. 32
Protagoras, 153, 200–201n. 41
Proteus, 112
Pucci, P., 202n. 56, 205n. 40, 208n. 10, 208n. 19, 210n. 35, 212n. 67, 213n. 71, 217n. 31, 217n. 32

Quintilian, 35, 198n. 15

Race, W. H., 231n. 22, 232n. 25
Radermacher, L., 200n. 37, 229n. 3
Rankin, H. D., 235n. 64, 236n. 97, 237n. 105
recusatio, 155
Redfield, J. A., 208n. 18, 212n. 62
Rehm, R., 201n. 46, 221n. 3
rhapsodic style, 42, 62, 65, 110, 150, 151, 207n. 4
rhetorical theory: character impersonation and, 169–172, 181–188; development of, 2–3, 7–10, 17–19, 149–154, 188–192, 200n. 29, 200n. 30, 200n. 40; *êthos* and, 33–35; techniques of, in archaic poetry, 44, 49, 56, 58–60, 65–67, 70–71, 91–92, 101–102;

techniques of, in tragedy, 123, 126–127, 128–131, 141–145, 223–224n. 36, 225n. 56, 229n. 101; visual effects and, 20, 24, 25–28, 35–40, 86–89, 154–156, 164–169, 229n. 107

Ringer, M., 221n. 2, 227n. 82, 228n. 85

Rose, P., 211n. 57, 211n. 58, 217n. 31, 218n. 34, 227n. 81, 228n. 93, 228n. 95

Russell, D. A., 17, 32, 200n. 29, 200n. 31, 202n. 1, 202n. 3, 205n. 47

Rutter, N. K., 221n. 1

Saïd, S., 211n. 59, 223n. 32

Saintillon, D., 215n. 17

Salvioni, L., 18, 199n. 26, 199n. 28, 200n. 34, 200n. 35, 202n. 4, 205n. 54, 230–231n. 17

Sappho: Fr. 1 L–P, 88–89; Fr. 2 L–P, 88; Fr. 16 L–P, 154–156, 160, 164, 191, 223n. 31, 232n. 24; argumentation in, 231n. 21, 231n. 22; visual impact and, 88–89, 154–156

Sauppe, H., 230n. 16

Schechner, R., 198n. 17

Scheid, J., 217n. 32, 218n. 33

Schein, S., 229n. 106

schêma, 6, 111; cf. 35–36

Schiappa, E., 197n. 4, 199n. 26, 200n. 29, 200n. 30, 229n. 3, 230n. 12, 231n. 20, 232n. 31, 233n. 46

Schiassi, G., 225n. 50, 226–227n. 69

Schmitt-Pantel, P., 211n. 59

Schütrumpf, E., 206n. 57

Schwyzer, 205n. 51

Scodel, R., 128, 223n. 30, 223n. 36, 224n. 38, 224n. 40, 224n. 41, 225n. 53, 225–226n. 60, 226n. 64

Scotti, F. P., 204n. 36

Second Sophistic, figures of the, 197n. 5

Segal, C. P., 161, 202n. 56, 213n. 71, 217n. 31, 221n. 2, 227n. 81, 228n. 86, 228n. 95, 229n. 105, 232n. 24, 232n. 35, 233n. 43, 233n. 45, 233n. 48, 234n. 53, 235n. 73

Seibel, A., 211n. 57

Semonides, 84–85, 215n. 9

set speeches, 8, 150–151, 170

Shapiro, H. A., 215–216n. 20, 216n. 21, 216n. 22, 220–221n. 58

Shewan, A., 214n. 81

Shipp, G. P., 213n. 77, 219n. 49

Simonides, 20

Sirens, 45–46, 208n. 19, 219n. 41

skênographia, 27

Skutsch, O., 202n. 56, 211n. 55

Slater, W. J., 221n. 3

Snyder, J., 217n. 32

Socrates: Antisthenes and, 170, 236n. 97; on cosmetics and rhetoric, 152, 229n. 107; as deinos speaker, 25–26, 179, 226n. 68; on Gorgias, 122, 228n. 87, 235n. 75; on Helen, 113; kosmos and, 25–26, 204n. 28; on Odysseus, 189; oral style and, 37, 38; as a sophistic type, 170, 206n. 64, 230–231n. 17; on theatrical effect, 9–10, 162–163, 233–234n. 49; visible type and, 35–36, 206n. 59, 218n. 40, 233–234n. 49

Solmsen, F., 208n. 10, 215n. 19

Solon, 234n. 62

sophistês, 183, 185

sophistic style: character impersonation and, 170, 171, 175–176; deceitful techniques of, 119, 120, 121–122, 137–139, 142; development of, 10, 18–19; dramatic enactment and, 108, 110–112; versatility of, 151–154, 189–190, 196, 201n. 29; visual effects and, 24, 25–26, 151, 164–169, 197n. 2; written versus oral, 37, 154, 200–201n. 41. See also oral style, visualizing style

Sophists, 13–14, 18, 35–36, 116, 123, 126, 147, 153–154, 222n. 11, 228n. 93, 230n. 6, 230n. 12, 230–231n. 17

Sophocles: Ajax, 118, 120, 121, 136, 174, 185, 186, 188, 205n. 45, 227n. 79, 234n. 50; êthos in, 32, 205n. 49; kosmos in, 25; Philoctetes, 25, 31, 94, 122, 138, 139–148, 173–175, 177, 180, 202–203n. 10, 229n. 103; poikilos in, 25, 31, 144, 205n. 43; on visible type and deception, 106–107

sôphrosunê, 26

Sparkes, B. A., 221n. 1

Stanford, W. B., 202n. 56, 212n. 66, 212n. 68, 217n. 32, 223n. 35, 235n. 77

Stanley, K., 211n. 57, 218n. 39

Stehle, E., 215n. 8, 215n. 14, 232n. 24, 234n. 57

Steiner, D., 221n. 1, 223n. 29

Stesichorus, 113, 121, 168, 222n. 13, 223n. 34, 231n. 21

suitable and unsuitable style, 59–60, 65–74, 93–94, 121–122, 199n. 26. See also under Helen; Odysseus; oral style

Süss, W., 204n. 36, 206n. 68

Suter, A., 209n. 29, 209n. 30, 214–215n. 7, 225n. 58

Suzuki, M., 202n. 56, 208n. 18, 208n. 19, 215n. 13, 219n. 42, 220n. 52

Svenbro, J., 217n. 32, 218n. 33

Szarmach, M., 227n. 84

technê, 80, 183, 233n. 43; cf. *technai*, 142, 150–151, *technê rhetorikê*, 38

Teisias, 18, 122, 181, 199n. 26

Telemachus, 23, 56, 63, 64, 74, 78, 80, 95, 99, 105–106, 219n. 42

terpsis, 165

Thalmann, W. G., 207n. 1, 207n. 4, 211n. 57, 211n. 58

Theander, C., 231n. 21

theatai, 112

thelgô, 80; cf. *thelxis*, 219n. 43

Theoclymenus, 224n. 42

Theodorus, 9, 26, 179, 183, 204n. 27

Theognis, 29–30, 45

Theophrastus, 197n. 2, 230n. 16

Thersites: abusive style of, 28, 66–67, 94, 145, 152, 209n. 28, 210n. 56, 210n. 57, 218n. 40, 229n. 103; bodily *hexis*, 66–67, 91–92; as iambic type, 93; physical violence and, 92, 146; visible type of, 85, 91–93, 218n. 34

Theseus, 166–167, 180, 235–236n. 83

Thetis, 211n. 59

Thrasymachus, 26, 38, 154, 179, 183, 195, 224n. 41, 230n. 16

Thucydides, 9–10, 37, 111, 142, 152, 178, 235n. 69

Todorov, T., 201n. 48

Too, Y. L., 200n. 31

topos, 54, 76, 157, 174; cf. *topoi*, 48, 75, 171, 215n. 8, 223–224n. 36

Tordesillas, A., 235n. 67

Trahman, C. R., 213n. 76

tricolon, 129; cf. *tricola*, 128

tropos, 6, 188–189

tupos, 6, 199n. 25; cf. *tupikos*, 199n. 25, *tupeomai*, 164

Turner, V., 198n. 17

Tyndareus, 231n. 21

Ubersfeld, A., 221n. 5

Untersteiner, M., 230n. 10

Usher, S., 199n. 26, 200n. 30, 200n. 36, 200n. 39

Vellacott, P., 224n. 37

Verdenius, W. J., 215n. 19, 235n. 69

Vermeule, E., 209n. 25, 219n. 41

Vernant, J. P., 83–84, 202n. 7, 209n. 25, 210n. 38, 214n. 1, 215n. 17, 217n. 32, 219n. 41

Viansino, G., 228n. 89, 228n. 92, 228n. 95, 228n. 96

visible type: character and, 1–2, 29–40, 201n. 47; deception and, 86–90, 97–107; delivery and, 197n. 3, 198n. 15; in dramatic enactment, 108–112; gender stereotypes and, 83–85; *kosmos* and, 5–7, 21–29; oral style and, 8–10, 20, 41–44, 90–101, 123–135, 203n. 15; *poikilos* and, 30–31. *See also* character type; corporeal style; *hexis*; *kosmos*

visualizing style, 98, 120, 127, 131–132, 135, 149–150, 158–161, 164–165, 168, 192, 195–196, 197n. 2, 201n. 52. *See also under* Helen; Odysseus; oral style

Vlastos, G., 236n. 89, 236n. 92

Volkman, R., 200n. 29

Von Reden, S., 203n. 11

Walcot, P., 213n. 73

Walker, J., 200n. 30

Walsh, G. B., 218n. 38, 223n. 34, 233n. 42, 233n. 43, 233n. 48, 234n. 50

Webster, T. B. L., 228n. 89, 228n. 96, 229n. 100

West, M. L., 231n. 21

Whitman, C. H., 211n. 58, 228n. 93

Wilamowitz, U. von, 231n. 21

Wiles, D., 221n. 1, 229–230n. 5

Wilshire, B., 198n. 17

Winkler, J. J., 217n. 28

Wisse, J., 204n. 36

Wohl, V. J., 208n. 19, 210–211n. 44, 215n. 13, 222n. 21

Woodbury, L., 223n. 34

Woodruff, P., 204n. 25, 235n. 76

Worman, N., 202–203n. 10, 205n. 41, 205n. 45, 205n. 52, 208n. 16, 212n. 68, 221n. 1, 228n. 83, 234n. 61, 236n. 95

written style, 2–3, 7–8, 27–28, 37–38, 154, 200n. 41. *See also* oral style

xenia, 45, 94

Xenophon, 36, 152, 170; *Memorabilia*, 35

Zeitlin, F. I., 83, 153, 202n. 7, 211n. 52, 214n. 3, 215n. 11, 215n. 17, 217n. 31, 220n. 53, 221n. 1, 221n. 2, 222n. 14, 223n. 34, 224n. 43, 230n. 9

Zeller, E., 230n. 10

Zeus, 46, 61, 62, 66, 87, 88, 166, 209n. 23, 222n. 19

Aelian
  Varia Historia
    12.32, 222n. 11
Aeschines
  Against Timarchus, 190
Aeschylus
  Agamemnon
    411, 113
    414, 113
    416–419, 113, 119
    689–690, 224n. 44,
      225n. 58
    705–708, 114
    709–712, 114
    717–736, 114
    727, 32
    740–742, 114
    741–743, 115
    742, 119
    743, 114
    745–749, 114
    750–756, 115
    779–780, 115
    923, 31
    926–927, 31
  Eumenides
    52, 83
  Libation Bearers
    854, 228n. 88
  Persians
    649, 32
    833, 222n. 10
  Prometheus Bound
    11, 199n. 22
  Seven against Thebes
    559, 199n. 27
  Suppliants
    282, 199n. 25
  Fr. 175 N², 223n. 26,
    236n. 96
Alcaeus
  Fr. 111 L–P, 217n. 26

Fr. 134 L–P, 217n. 26,
  217n. 27
Fr. 283 L–P, 223n. 31
Fr. 347 L–P, 215n. 9
Alcidamas
  Odysseus on the Betrayal of
    Palamedes
    (Ps.-Alcidamas)
    1–3, 182
    4, 182
    12, 183
    13, 183
    21, 183
    22, 184
    23, 184
    27, 184
    29, 180, 182, 184
  On the Sophists
    3, 222n. 12
    22, 222n. 12
    27, 37
    28, 233n. 41
    32, 37
    34, 222n. 12
Alcman
  Fr. 73 (40 D), 225n. 58
Ps.-Andocides
  4, 237n. 2
Antiphon
  1.1.3, 199n. 26
  2.4.8, 199n. 26
  5.26, 199n. 26
  DK 87B44, 228n. 93
Antisthenes
  Ajax
    1, 186
    3, 186, 188
    4, 186
    5, 186, 187
    6, 186, 187, 188
    7, 186, 187
    8, 186, 187

    9, 186, 187
    10, 187
  Odysseus
    1, 187
    2, 187
    6, 187
    7, 187, 188
    8, 187, 188
    9, 187, 188, 189,
      199n. 22
    10, 187, 188
    14, 188
  Fr. 47a C, 190
  Fr. 47b C, 190
  Fr. 51 C, 38, 188–190,
    199n. 22
Apollodorus
  3.12.5, 225n. 56
Archilochus
  Fr. 114 W², 85
Aristophanes
  Acharnians
    407–89, 221n. 3
    716, 201–202n. 55
  Ecclesiazusae
    120, 201–202n. 55
  Frogs
    91, 201–202n. 55,
      206n. 64, 230–
      231n. 17
    131–133, 230–231n. 17
    815, 201–202n. 55,
      206n. 64, 230–
      231n. 17
    826–829, 206n. 64,
      230–231n. 17
    841, 201–202n. 55,
      206n. 64, 230–
      231n. 17
    907–913, 236n. 94
    909–910, 231n. 19
    927, 235n. 81

943, 201–202n. 55,
206n. 64, 230–
231n. 17
1063, 221n. 3
1069, 201–202n. 55,
206n. 64, 230–
231n. 17
1071, 201–202n. 55,
206n. 64, 230–
231n. 17
1122, 235n. 81
1160, 201–202n. 55,
206n. 64, 230–
231n. 17
1451, 138, 181
1492, 201–202n. 55,
206n. 64, 230–
231n. 17
Knights
1056, 185
1331, 230n. 6
1381, 201–202n. 55
Lysistrata
155–156, 220n. 58,
226n. 63
Peace
220, 205n. 50
Thesmophoriazusae
121, 222n. 7
159–170, 18
528–530, 223n. 30
Aristotle
Categories
8b25–9a13, 198n. 6
Nicomachean Ethics
1103a26–b25, 198n. 6
1103b17, 198n. 7,
228n. 92
1104a11–b3, 198n. 6
1105b19–1106a13,
198n. 6
1113a10–12, 232n. 28
1144a23–28, 178–179
1152a30, 228n. 92
Poetics
1445a17, 176
1447a19, 199n. 23
1447b, 158
1448a1–9, 34
1448a23–24, 110
1448b15–17, 108
1449a28, 28
1449b8, 202n. 8

1449b32, 27
1450a15–32, 108
1450a18–19, 34
1450a38–b4, 34
1450b8, 34
1450b34, 202n. 8
1454a4, 234n. 52
1454a15–16, 34
1454b8–14, 34
1455a17, 176, 234n. 52
1455a21–30, 34
1457b2, 28
1457b33, 28
1459b22–29, 229–
230n. 5
1460b8–12, 34
Politics
1457b2, 204n. 30
Rhetoric
1355b, 214n. 84
1355b–1356a, 214n. 83
1356a9–10, 33
1356a13, 217n. 30
1357a–b, 236n. 85
1361a28, 180
1363a16–19, 169,
232n. 28
1366a9–10, 34
1366a10–12, 34
1366a38, 180
1370a6–7, 228n. 92
1377b20–78a5,
226n. 68
1376a17–23, 199n. 26
1378a8, 33
1378a11, 222n. 8
1388b12, 180
1395b–1396a, 233n. 36
1399a1–3, 169, 232n. 28
1401a5–8, 129
1402a17, 199n. 26
1402a17–28, 199n. 26
1403b1, 18
1403b21–24, 229n. 4
1403b35, 9, 27
1403b–1404a, 9, 197n. 3
1404a, 191
1404a8, 9, 27
1404a20–26, 229n. 4
1404a24–28, 27
1404a26, 236n. 91
1404a34, 27
1404a35, 9, 27

1404b4, 236n. 91
1404b4–8, 27
1404b18–19, 34
1404b18–20, 234n. 50
1404b18–23, 204n. 27
1404b20, 190
1404b20–26, 9
1404b24, 228n. 88
1404b35, 27
1405a, 158
1405a13–14, 199n. 21
1405b35, 161, 206n. 65,
233n. 44
1406a32, 236n. 91
1406a33, 235n. 81
1406b6–8, 235n. 81
1406b12, 206n. 65,
206n. 67
1407a, 235n. 79
1408a, 190, 199n. 26
1408a10, 135
1408a14, 204n. 30
1408a–b, 228n. 88
1409b5–6, 129
1410a–b, 235n. 79
1410b14–15, 213n. 77
1413b–1414a, 200n. 41
1414b27–29, 234n. 55
1415a, 170
1416b25, 205n. 44,
223n. 28, 236n. 100
1417a, 199n. 26
1417a15–25, 34
1417a22–24, 34
1417a21–35, 204n. 36
1425a9, 202n. 8
Rhetorica ad Alexandrum
1441b9, 202n. 8
Arrian
Epicteti Dissertationes
322.80, 205n. 53
Athenaeus
1.21d, 221n. 3

Cicero
Brutus
46–48, 199n. 26
Orator
23–32, 237n. 1
36, 35, 197n. 3, 205n. 53
39, 26, 179
43–44, 194
54–60, 197n. 3

62–64, 206n. 64, 230–
231n. 17
71, 205n. 55
75–78, 237n. 1
97–99, 237n. 1
134, 35, 205n. 53
De Oratore
3.43, 237n. 1
3.59, 198n. 15
Corinna
Fr. 654 *PMG*
20–21, 116
27, 116
Cypria
Fr. 1, 211n. 59
p. 104.23–24 Allen
(Proclus, *Chrestoma-
thia*), 211n. 59

Damon
DK 37B6, 162
Demetrius
On Style
14, 197n. 3
27–28, 197n. 3
36, 202n. 1
173, 197n. 2
243–286, 179
Democritus
DK 68B21, 203n. 17
DK 68B228, 199n. 25
Demosthenes
Against Aphobus 111 (29)
1, 207n. 69
Against Boeotus I (39)
14, 226n. 68
Against Lacritus (35)
40–43, 226n. 68
Against Meidias (21)
1–8, 190
On the Crown (18)
10–11, 236n. 104
251–255, 234n. 62
253, 234n. 62
255, 234n. 62
On the False Embassy (19)
98, 235n. 71
121–127, 236n. 104
246–248, 236n. 103
Dio Chrysostom
52, 137
59.5–6, 227n. 77
59.9, 137

Diogenes Laertius
Lives of the Philosophers
6.15, 33, 200n. 37
6.17, 229n. 2
6.1–19, 235n. 64
Dionysius of Halicarnassus
Demosthenes
2, 206n. 64, 230–
231n. 17
3, 230n. 16
9, 202n. 1, 205n. 53
18, 194
21, 194
25, 204n. 30
50, 194
52, 204n. 30
53, 197n. 3, 201n. 42
Epistula ad Pompeium
4, 199n. 25
Isocrates
3, 169
On Literary Composition
3, 204n. 30
4, 193
10, 193, 197n. 3
12, 193, 197n. 3
18, 179
23, 194, 197n. 3
Lysias
11, 202n. 1
Dissoi Logoi
DK 90, 232n. 29

Empedocles
DK 31A86, 158
DK 31A92, 158
DK 31B17, 4–5
Euripides
Andromache
147–148, 25
148, 31
189, 25
289, 223n. 33
629–630, 220n. 58,
226n. 63
930–938, 201n. 55
936–937, 201n. 54
937, 25, 31
956, 25, 203n. 22
Bacchae
270–271, 201n. 55
453–459, 214n. 4
832, 199n. 23

Cyclops
317, 227n. 73
Electra
362–363, 205n. 48
368–369, 205n. 51
384–385, 205n. 48
1071, 227n. 71
Hecuba
130–135, 201n. 43
131, 223n. 33
131–132, 214n. 85
133, 31
256–258, 201n. 55
266, 130
269, 222n. 10
269–270, 130
309–320, 121
379, 205n. 51
441–443, 118, 201n. 55,
214n. 6, 220n. 53,
224n. 43
687, 224n. 43
891, 226n. 67
1187–1191, 201n. 55
Helen
77, 199n. 27
238, 223n. 33
294–296, 227n. 70
926, 224n. 43
1053–1054, 225n. 48
Heracles
40, 32
157–161, 214–215n. 7
180, 32
188–203, 214–215n. 7
358, 222n. 16
425, 222n. 16
570, 32
582, 32
659, 205n. 51
681, 32
788, 32
877, 235n. 83
961, 32
1252, 235n. 83
1309, 235n. 83
Hippolytus
486–489, 201n. 55
616–617, 222n. 21
631–632, 203n. 22
642, 201n. 54
642–648, 201n. 55
862, 199n. 25

Ion
237–238, 6
239–240, 205n. 48,
228n. 92
834, 203n. 22
Iphigenia in Aulis
75, 223n. 31
526, 31, 214n. 85
583–586, 119–120,
224n. 43
1300, 223n. 33
Medea
103, 205n. 48
300, 31
402, 233n. 43
519, 205n. 51
576, 203n. 22
576–578, 203n. 24
1072, 199n. 23
1159, 31
1162, 199n. 27
Orestes
128–130, 225n. 48
128–129, 121
220, 214n. 4
249, 231n. 21
823, 205n. 43
889–894, 201n. 43
902–906, 201n. 43
903–904, 152
907–908, 152
1145, 222n. 10
1383–1387, 201n. 55,
214n. 6, 220n. 53,
224n. 43
1426–1436, 121
1467, 121
Phoenician Women
469–470, 205n. 43,
223n. 28
469–472, 205n. 44
526–527, 201n. 55
1130, 199n. 25
Rhesus
305, 199n. 25
841, 222n. 10
894, 223n. 33
Suppliants
902–908, 205n. 49
Trojan Women
282, 223n. 33
282–287, 201n. 43
283–287, 119, 222n. 25

651–652, 226n. 69
651–653, 201n. 55
860, 124
881–882, 124
886, 124
889, 124
891–893, 118
891–894, 124–125,
201n. 55, 214n. 6
895, 126
896–897, 125
901, 126
914–915, 127
917–918, 225n. 52
919–920, 128, 234n. 55
919–930, 128
920, 127
922, 129
924, 127, 129
924–928, 127
924–937, 129
925–928, 12
929, 129, 132, 165, 174
929–930, 127, 131
929–937, 131
931, 225–226n. 60
933–934, 129–130
935–936, 129
935–937, 127, 131
936–937, 130
937, 129
940, 130
940–942, 127
941, 130
941–942, 130, 225n. 52
942–943, 127
943, 130
946–950, 127
946–947, 225n. 52
948–950, 234n. 56
950, 130
951, 130, 222n. 10
952, 128
955–957, 128
955–958, 131, 225–
226n. 60
957–958, 127
958, 131, 220–221n. 58
959–960, 128
961–963, 131
962–964, 127
963, 131
966–967, 125, 132

966–968, 13, 201n. 43
967, 133
967–968, 122, 225n. 50
968, 133, 179
982, 6, 13
987–988, 134
987–992, 214n. 5
991–992, 134
991–997, 227n. 70
1021–1023, 125
1022–1024, 125, 134
1025–1027, 121, 134
1030–1031, 134
1035, 133, 135
1038, 135
1033, 227n. 72
Fr. 439 N², 228n. 88
Fr. 472e N², 227n. 70
Frs. 578–590 N², 137
Fr. 583 N², 132

Galen
7.471, 199n. 25
Gorgias
Encomium of Helen
1, 128, 157
2, 222n. 8
3, 157, 162, 224n. 41,
234n. 59
4, 157–158, 160
5, 159
6, 142, 160
6.1–2, 225n. 55
7.10–11, 225n. 55
8, 160, 162, 202n. 66,
234n. 59
8–14, 159
8–19, 160
9, 161, 224n. 44,
230n. 15
9.22–23, 225n. 55
9.28, 225n. 55
10, 162
11, 163, 231n. 19,
232n. 32, 236n. 94
12, 163
13, 164
14, 163
15, 164
16, 127, 132, 165, 174,
226n. 66
17, 163, 164
18, 165

19, 132, 163, 165
21, 165
On Not Being
  DK 82B3, 158, 162, 164,
    228n. 94, 232n. 29
Palamedes' Defense
  1, 235n. 81
  3, 173, 235n. 81
  4, 175, 180, 218n. 40,
    226n. 66
  5, 173, 181, 235n. 81
  7, 225–226n. 60
  8, 235n. 81
  9, 176, 225–226n. 60
  10, 131, 235n. 81
  11, 235n. 81
  12, 235n. 81
  13, 225–226n. 60
  15, 176
  16, 177
  18, 177
  19, 177, 235n. 81
  22, 173, 177
  22–24, 181
  24, 173, 177, 235n. 81
  25, 177, 178
  26, 178
  28, 178, 179, 180,
    225–226n. 60
  29, 179–180
  30, 175, 180, 204n. 28
  30–31, 180
  31, 175, 181, 235n. 81
  33, 180, 235n. 81
  35, 235n. 81
  36, 175, 180, 235n. 81
DK 82A4, 165, 174, 226n. 66
DK 82A24, 181
DK 82B23, 231n. 19,
  236n. 94

Hermogenes
 On Style
  2.11, 199n. 25
  3.21, 197n. 3
Herodotus
 Histories
  1.57, 205n. 50
  1.60, 222n. 10
  1.107, 199n. 22
  1.116, 205n. 50
  1.132, 233n. 47
  1.142, 205n. 50

2.112–120, 112
2.37, 222n. 10
2.47, 222n. 10
2.86, 199n. 25
2.116, 113
2.128, 199n. 25
2.130, 199n. 27
3.72, 222n. 10
7.69, 199n. 27
Hesiod
 Theogony
  24–34, 46
  26, 208n. 15
  27, 210–211n. 44
  41, 45
  83, 45
  83–84, 45
  84, 45
  86, 45
  90, 45
  92, 199n. 27
  94–97, 45
  97, 45
  205, 88
  206, 88
  511, 30
  521, 30
  570, 203n. 19
  573, 87
  587, 87, 203n. 19
  589, 87
 Frs. 196–204 W², 231n. 21,
  237n. 106
 Fr. 204.56–63 M–W,
  234n. 58
 Works and Days
  7, 87
  9, 87
  42, 87
  47, 87
  51, 87
  65, 83
  67, 29, 87
  72, 87, 203n. 19
  73–74, 87
  76, 87, 203n. 19
  78, 29, 87, 117
  83, 87
  203–208, 205n. 40
  582–588, 215n. 9
Hippocrates
 On Nourishment
  34, 198n. 6

On Setting Joints
  41, 198n. 6
Hipponax
 Fr. 26 W², 208n. 15
 Fr. 128 W², 208n. 15
Homer
 Iliad
  1.248, 211n. 57
  1.249, 45
  1.286, 211n. 47
  1.599–608, 85
  2.56, 78
  2.189, 66
  2.190, 66
  2.195, 66
  2.198, 66
  2.199, 66, 218n. 39
  2.201, 66
  2.202, 66
  2.213, 66
  2.213–214, 203n. 13
  2.217–219, 85, 91
  2.226–234, 67
  2.239–242, 67
  2.245, 67
  2.246, 66–67, 203n. 21,
    209n. 28, 211n. 56,
    211n. 57
  2.251, 67
  2.255, 67
  2.258–268, 91–92
  2.258–264, 92
  2.259, 146
  2.264, 218n. 40
  2.265–266, 92
  2.270–277, 92
  2.484–759, 211n. 49
  2.485, 210–211n. 44
  2.488, 211n. 49
  2.489–490, 211n. 49
  2.645–652, 214n. 79
  2.796, 209n. 28
  3.39, 51
  3.40, 51
  3.45, 214n. 4
  3.48, 51
  3.52–55, 51
  3.54, 210n. 32
  3.54–64, 167
  3.55, 51
  3.64, 210n. 32, 214n. 5
  3.125–129, 105
  3.126, 220n. 57

3.141, 104, 214n. 5
3.141–142, 103
3.152, 45
3.156, 210n. 42
3.156–158, 103, 214n. 6,
    224n. 43
3.158, 133
3.159–160, 103
3.160, 47
3.171, 209n. 22
3.172, 49
3.173–174, 49
3.180, 49
3.195–198, 91
3.197, 90
3.220, 91
3.221–223, 91
3.212, 217n. 32
3.212–224, 45
3.229, 48
3.234–242, 48
3.371, 104, 214n. 4
3.380–382, 104
3.382, 214n. 4, 221n. 61
3.383–420, 50
3.385, 104, 214n. 4
3.391–394, 50
3.392, 105, 214n. 5,
    219n. 47
3.394, 209n. 29
3.395, 105
3.396, 221n. 60
3.396–397, 105,
    214n. 5, 214n. 6
3.399, 51
3.404, 49, 210n. 43,
    224n. 43
3.405, 89, 223n. 33
3.406, 50
3.407–409, 50
3.410, 210n. 43
3.411, 47
3.412, 48, 50
3.415, 132, 174,
    234n. 52
3.419, 104, 105
3.419–420, 103, 214n. 5
3.420, 211n. 50
3.427, 50, 209n. 22
3.428–429, 50
3.429, 51
3.432, 50
3.432–436, 51

3.434–436, 50
3.436, 51
3.442, 221n. 61
3.443, 221n. 61
3.446, 88
5.127–128, 208n. 13
5.252–254, 208n. 13
5.331, 214n. 4
5.423, 132, 174,
    234n. 52
5.425, 214n. 4
5.759, 203n. 13
5.815–816, 208n. 13
6.5, 188
6.187, 217n. 32
6.214, 208n. 13
6.289–292, 106
6.295, 106
6.311, 106
6.318–322, 214n. 5
6.324, 220n. 57
6.335–336, 210n. 43
6.337, 45, 52
6.343, 45, 52, 209n. 22
6.344, 49, 53, 210n. 43,
    224n. 43
6.345–348, 53
6.350, 53
6.351, 210n. 43
6.352, 47
6.356, 49, 53
6.357, 47
6.358, 54
6.407–439, 208–
    209n. 20
6.460–461, 210n. 40
7.11, 188
7.324, 217n. 32
8.12, 203n. 13
9.50–54, 208n. 13
9.93–94, 208n. 12
9.111–113, 208n. 11
9.160–161, 70
9.223, 67
9.225, 71
9.225–227, 212n. 69
9.225–228, 68
9.225–230, 68
9.229, 69
9.230, 69
9.230–231, 69
9.231, 69

9.231–232, 69
9.231–235, 69
9.237–238, 69
9.239, 69
9.241–242, 69
9.244, 69
9.246–251, 69
9.249–250, 69
9.252, 67
9.256–57, 68
9.261, 70
9.280, 70
9.284, 70
9.297, 70
9.299, 70
9.303, 70
9.308–313, 189
9.309, 71
9.311, 71
9.311–312, 71
9.318, 71
9.422–423, 217n. 32
10.169, 208n. 13
10.227, 208n. 13
10.316, 92
10.374–377, 92
10.405, 93
10.413, 93
10.427, 93
10.454–457, 92
11.380–381, 209n. 26
11.383, 210n. 42
11.482, 30, 223n. 33
12.104, 199n. 27
13.830, 45
14.84–85, 209n. 26
14.133, 208n. 13
14.161–186, 219n. 43
14.166–221, 89
14.170–186, 214n. 4
14.178, 104, 220n. 56
14.178–179, 227n. 71
14.187, 87
14.197, 89
14.214–215, 221n. 59
14.215, 89
14.216–217, 87, 117
14.300, 89
14.328, 88
14.329, 89
14.343, 221n. 61
14.359, 88
18.595, 220n. 56

19.154–183, 72
19.164, 212n. 68
19.165, 212n. 68
19.169, 72, 212n. 68
19.174, 212n. 68
19.178, 212n. 68
19.179–180, 72
19.186, 72
19.211, 72
19.214, 72
19.216–237, 72
19.221, 73
19.225, 73, 212n. 68
19.229, 212n. 68
19.233, 212n. 68
19.256, 73
19.285, 221n. 60
19.314, 73
19.315–337, 73
19.319, 72
19.366–383, 83
19.338, 73
19.352–353, 73
19.365, 73
19.367, 73
19.410, 73
19.421–422, 73
20.197, 51
21.507, 220n. 56
22.450–459, 208–
    209n. 20
22.494–501, 54
24.253–254, 209n. 26
24.725–745, 208–
    209n. 20
24.764, 55, 209n. 25
24.766, 55
24.767–768, 48
24.767–772, 55
24.774–775, 55
24.775, 224n. 43
24.777, 209n. 22
Odyssey
1.1–5, 63–64
1.56–57, 117, 215n. 16
1.131, 94
1.434, 215n. 11
2.183–184, 209n. 26
3.163, 30, 223n. 33
4.42, 221n. 62
4.73, 221n. 62
4.116–118, 56
4.121, 221n. 61

4.130, 105
4.140, 210–211n. 44
4.141, 56
4.143, 56
4.145, 63, 209n. 23
4.204–205, 57
4.219–264, 45
4.220, 219n. 42
4.221, 56
4.234, 209n. 22
4.235–264, 95
4.239, 56, 60
4.240, 211n. 49
4.240–243, 61
4.242, 57, 60
4.244, 58
4.244–251, 57–58
4.245, 584.246, 58
4.247, 58
4.249, 58
4.251, 96
4.252–253, 219n. 41
4.256, 59, 96
4.259–260, 59
4.261, 226n. 62
4.264, 59
4.265–289, 59
4.266, 23, 56, 59, 64
4.267–273, 60
4.271, 57, 60
4.274–275, 61–62
4.277–279, 62
4.279, 56, 62
4.287–288, 62
4.383, 213n. 77
4.399, 213n. 77
4.441–442, 214n. 4
4.677–678, 217n. 32
5.126, 219n. 45
5.177–179, 211n. 45
5.230, 104
5.230–232, 96
5.262–264, 211n. 45
5.264, 96, 219n. 41
5.308, 97, 209n. 24
5.308–309, 78
5.321, 97
5.323–324, 97
5.346–347, 97
5.356–357, 217n. 32
6.127–136, 97
6.131, 97
6.132–133, 97

6.137, 214n. 4
6.141–210, 89
6.143, 52, 219n. 49
6.145, 97
6.146, 52, 219n. 49
6.148, 45, 52, 98,
    219n. 49
6.152, 98
6.157, 98
6.158–159, 98
6.162–169, 98
6.187, 98
6.188–189, 98
6.195–197, 98
6.203, 99
6.205, 219n. 45
6.207–208, 98
6.229–237, 98
6.230, 220n. 50
6.232, 101
6.235, 220n. 50
6.236, 98
6.237, 220n. 51
6.241, 99, 219n. 45
6.242–243, 98
7.107, 220n. 56
7.168, 30, 223n. 33
8.72–82, 67
8.73, 174
8.134–137, 93
8.153–157, 93
8.158–164, 146
8.158–185, 22
8.159–164, 93
8.166–185, 93
8.170, 22
8.172, 199n. 27
8.174–175, 93
8.175, 22
8.179, 22, 93, 211n. 47
8.266–366, 209n. 29
8.314–320, 209n. 23
8.364–366, 23, 214n. 5
8.480, 46
8.489, 203n. 15, 203–
    204n. 24, 211n. 47
8.492, 203–204n. 24
9.14, 174
9.39–59, 78
9.422–423, 217n. 32
10.213, 219n. 42
10.235, 219n. 42
10.236, 219n. 42

10.299–301, 96
10.305, 96
10.316–320, 96
10.318, 219n. 43
10.325–335, 96
10.341, 88, 96
10.342–344, 211n. 45
10.343–344, 96
10.347, 96
10.348–370, 96
10.358–365, 211n. 45
10.360–367, 219n. 41
10.367, 94
10.398, 219n. 42
10.480, 96
10.487–495, 219n. 42
10.503–540, 219n. 42
10.543, 104
11.152, 215n. 11
11.339–353, 182
11.367, 203n. 15
11.547, 209n. 24
11.628, 215n. 11
12.161, 215n. 11
12.187, 45
12.434, 215n. 11
13.254, 76
13.255, 76
13.262–266, 76
13.269–270, 213n. 75
13.273, 78
13.279–282, 78
13.287–295, 77
13.291, 219n. 46
13.293, 30, 223n. 33
13.303–304, 217n. 32
13.386, 217n. 32
13.435, 214n. 4
14.122–125, 213n. 72
14.122–132, 229n. 102
14.127–132, 208n. 15
14.131–132, 80
14.156–157, 77
14.192, 213n. 77
14.192–359, 146
14.193–195, 77
14.274–275, 78
14.296–297, 77
14.321, 22, 80
14.340, 77
14.361–365, 229n. 102
14.362–365, 208n. 15
14.363, 22, 80, 211n. 47

14.363–368, 80
14.395–397, 208n. 15
14.463, 78
14.463–466, 78
14.468, 215n. 11
14.495, 78
14.500, 203n. 21
14.503, 215n. 11
14.508–509, 78, 213n. 72
14.508–517, 208n. 15
14.509, 23, 80, 203n. 21, 211n. 47
15.105–108, 220n. 57
15.108, 106
15.126, 106
15.160–178, 63
15.167–169, 64
15.169–170, 64
15.172–178, 219n. 42
15.176–177, 63
16.175–176, 99
16.183, 99
16.187, 99
16.194–195, 80, 99
16.202–212, 99
16.419–420, 93
17.215–218, 80
17.385, 159
17.415–418, 208n. 15
17.415–444, 146
17.416, 94
17.445–465, 93
17.454, 94
17.464, 215n. 11
17.514, 80, 159
17.521, 80
17.525, 80
17.559–560, 208n. 15
17.580, 80
18.192–193, 220n. 50
18.195, 220n. 50
18.196, 99
18.251–256, 100
18.394–397, 94
18.401, 209n. 26
19.54, 99
19.56, 99
19.108–114, 100
19.118–120, 100
19.124–129, 100
19.165–202, 79
19.171–185, 79

19.172–173, 79
19.181, 214n. 81
19.184, 214n. 81
19.185, 100
19.190, 214n. 81
19.215–217, 229n. 102
19.221–248, 100
19.225–234, 100
19.235, 100
19.246, 218n. 40
19.248, 218n. 40
19.457, 233n. 47
19.535–558, 63
20.61–65, 210n. 38, 220n. 54
20.285–300, 215n. 10
21.426, 215n. 11
22.115, 30, 223n. 33
22.202, 30, 223n. 33
22.226, 215n. 11
22.281, 30, 223n. 33
23.156–163, 220n. 51
23.157, 220n. 50
23.159, 101
23.162, 220n. 50
23.163, 100–101
23.173, 101
23.175, 101
23.200, 101
23.222, 220n. 52
24.246–279, 135
Homeric Hymn to Aphrodite
5.1, 214n. 5
5.2, 88
5.7, 88
5.33, 23, 88
5.45, 88
5.57, 88
5.58, 221n. 61
5.58–59, 214n. 4
5.59, 221n. 61
5.60–65, 214n. 5
5.61–90, 219n. 43
5.65, 23
5.66, 221n. 61
5.82, 88
5.84–85, 88
5.85–90, 214n. 5
5.88, 88, 89, 221n. 60
5.91, 88
5.102, 88
5.109, 23
5.117–118, 209n. 29

5.143, 88
5.162, 23
6.11, 23
6.12, 23
6.14, 23
6.57, 174
Homeric Hymn to Delian Apollo
162–164, 62
Homeric Hymn to Hermes
13–14, 23
155, 30
255, 203n. 13
265, 23
433, 23
479, 23
514, 30
Horace
Epodes
14, 216n. 25

Ibycus
Fr. 268 *PMG*, 217n. 27
Ilias Parva
Fr. 2, 211n. 47
Isaeus
10.1, 226n. 68
Isocrates
Against the Sophists
17, 202n. 8
Antidosis (15)
45, 199n. 22, 236n. 98
74, 202n. 8
Demonicus (1)
15, 38–39
40, 236n. 88
Evagoras (9)
5, 168
5–8, 39, 199n. 22
5–11, 232n. 30
9, 204n. 30
73–75, 36
Helen (10)
1, 166
1–13, 166
6, 166
13, 166
16, 166
18–38, 166
25, 235–236n. 83
37, 235–236n. 83
38, 167
39–41, 167
43–44, 167

48, 167
54, 167
54–55, 168
59–60, 234n. 56
61, 168
64, 168
65, 158, 168
Nicocles (3)
32, 39, 199n. 26
Panathenaecus (12)
1, 236n. 88
4, 207n. 69
246, 207n. 69
Philippus (5)
25–27, 9, 38
27, 207n. 69
To Nicocles (2)
48, 202n. 8

Lycurgus
1.20, 226n. 68
Lysias
1.26, 204n. 29
7.38, 199n. 26
7.41, 204n. 29
12.27, 199n. 26
19.16, 204n. 29
21.19, 204n. 29
24.16, 199n. 26

Orphica
Argonautica
391, 198n. 6

Parmenides
DK 28B8.52, 203n. 17
Philodemus
On Music
p. 9K, 236n. 98
Volumina Rhetorica
2.137S, 205n. 53
Philostratus
Vita Apollonii
6.11, 221n. 3
Pindar
Nemean Odes
2.8, 24
3.21, 222n. 16
6.53, 24
7.20–21, 115
7.22–24, 115
7.24–26, 116
8.24–26, 116
8.27, 116, 222n. 16

8.33–34, 117
8.35–36, 117
Olympian Odes
1.29–30, 31
1.30–32, 116
2.86–87, 201n. 53
3.13, 24
6.87, 205n. 42
8.13, 203n. 20
9.36–37, 24
11.13, 24
Pythian Odes
4.249, 233n. 43
4.384, 233n. 47
Fr. 194.2, 24
Plato
Alcibiades I
103–105, 230n. 7
Apology
17a, 214n. 84
17b1, 26, 179
17b3, 26
17b4–5, 26
17b5, 25
17b8, 25
17b15–c1, 25
17c2, 25
17c3, 25
17d, 202n. 2
18a5, 25
18a6, 25
18b1–d7, 225n. 60
41b, 223n. 29
Cratylus
393d, 207n. 69
417e, 207n. 69
424b–425a, 206–207n. 68
Epistle VII
340d7, 207n. 72
344b4–7, 206–207n. 68
Euthydemus
289e–290a, 224n. 44
Gorgias
453a, 226–227n. 69
461d–462a, 228n. 87
465b, 39
465b1–c2, 39
465b2–c2, 229n. 107
465b3–4, 152
465b4–5, 39
483c8–d2, 224n. 41
493c6, 204n. 28, 235n. 75

493d2, 204n. 28
494a1, 204n. 28
502b, 233–234n. 49
502b–d, 9
504a1–d1, 204n. 28
506e1–e7, 204n. 28
509–510, 226n. 68
513a, 207n. 69
513c1, 207n. 69
523e6, 26

Hippias Minor
363c, 222n. 11
364e, 189
364e–365b, 212n. 66
365e2–5, 236n. 101
368b–d, 189
368d7, 230n. 6

Ion
530b, 229n. 4
530b–d, 236n. 102
530b5–d8, 202n. 5
535d, 207n. 69

Laws
816d, 202n. 2

Menexenus
236d7, 204n. 28
236e2, 204n. 28
237c3, 204n. 28
237c4, 204n. 28
239c1, 204n. 28
246a3, 204n. 28
248c5, 204n. 28

Meno
76c4–d1, 162
76e3, 163
95c, 179

Phaedrus
239d1, 235n. 75
239d1–d2, 204n. 28
243a3–b2, 113, 222n. 13
245a4, 204n. 28
246c2, 204n. 28
247a1, 204n. 28
253d4–e5, 206n. 59
256b2, 204n. 28
257c, 38, 236n. 103
261b, 229n. 3
261b6–8, 183
261c, 38, 154, 179
261d, 184
264c, 233n. 41
266c, 38
266e4, 26, 179
267a, 199n. 26

267a6–8, 122, 232n. 29
267b, 181
267c, 38, 183
267c–d, 179
267c9–d1, 154
272d–273d, 199n. 26
273a10, 222n. 8
275d, 37
277c2–3, 38
278d4–5, 207n. 71

Philebus
12c, 207n. 69
53e, 207n. 69

Protagoras
315b6, 204n. 28,
    235n. 75
320d5–e1, 204n. 28
322c3, 204n. 28
334c–335a, 228n. 87
337a, 236n. 93
347d7, 204n. 28

Republic
341a, 224n. 41
343c, 224n. 41
396e, 199n. 25
398c, 199n. 22, 236n. 98
400d, 236n. 98
402d, 199n. 25
402d1–4, 198n. 11,
    206n. 59
424c, 236n. 98
601a4–b6, 39

Sophist
223c, 207n. 69
226a, 207n. 69
234b, 207n. 69

Symposium
182e, 236n. 88
212d–223a, 230n. 7
215d5, 218–219n. 40

Theatetus
146d, 207n. 69
153b, 198n. 6
171e, 199n. 25
192a, 199n. 25

Plutarch
Alcibiades
1.26, 230n. 7
16.25, 230n. 7
23, 230n. 8

Moralia
2.442c, 199n25

Theseus
31.2, 209n. 29

Quintilian
Institutio Oratoria
6.2.8–9, 35
11.1.3, 197n. 3
11.3, 198n. 15

Sappho
Fr. 1 L–P, 88, 217n. 27
1, 223n. 33
2, 223n. 33
11, 155
18–19, 89
Fr. 2 L–P, 88
Fr. 16 L–P, 214n. 6,
    217n. 26, 222n. 23,
    223n. 31, 231n. 21
12–14, 217n. 27
18–19, 217n. 27

Semonides
Fr. 7 W²
4, 84
18, 84
35, 84
73, 84
91, 84
108–109, 84

Sextus Empiricus
Against the Logicians
65–87, 232n. 29

Simonides
Fr. 43 *PG*, 223n. 33
Fr. 122 *PG*
81, 20, 199n. 27

Solon
Fr. 1 W², 203n. 17
Fr. 13 W²
11, 203n. 13
39–40, 204n. 39

Sophocles
Ajax
29, 186
47, 186
60, 188
148, 120, 234n. 50
151–152, 120
188, 120, 222n. 23
198–199, 120
349, 186
379–382, 120
381, 120
388, 120
389, 120
445, 174
461, 186

467, 186
511, 186
582, 233n. 47
594–595, 205n. 49
796, 186
914, 205n. 45
1276, 186
1283, 186
1349, 121
1358, 218n. 40
1365, 121
1367, 121, 223n. 35,
    235n. 77
Antigone
705, 32
1046, 201n. 55
Oedipus at Colonus
762, 205n. 43
Oedipus Tyrannus
545, 179
Philoctetes
9–10, 140
11, 140
12, 140
14, 140
26, 228, 87
54–55, 141
55, 222n. 23
56, 228n. 89
57, 141
65, 141, 144, 147
66, 141
72, 228n. 89, 229n. 99
77, 142
79–80, 142
80, 174
82, 145
88, 142, 147, 148, 174
99, 142
100–134, 223n. 33
101, 223n. 33
102, 142
108, 143
110, 143, 147, 228n. 96
130, 25, 31, 146
223, 199n. 23
223–224, 139
224, 145
254, 143
258, 143
260, 143
265–266, 229n. 98
266, 143

273, 143
276–278, 144
281, 143
314, 143
315–316, 144
319, 143
321, 143
340, 143
343–344, 146
344, 143
346, 229n. 98
347, 143
355, 143, 229n. 100
359, 143
367, 143
368, 143
374, 143
384, 144, 147, 175
387–388, 175
389–390, 144
407–408, 120, 144
407–409, 13, 145,
    201n. 43
408, 122, 174
431, 145
440, 144, 145, 179,
    218n. 40
440–442, 218n. 40
448, 144, 174
563, 146, 592, 146,
    493–594, 146
607–608, 190
608, 223n. 33
614–619, 146
622, 146
633–634, 177
670, 235–236n. 83
875–876, 214n. 4
927, 174
971–972, 175
984, 147
994, 147
1006, 147
1015, 148
1025, 139
1063–1064, 25
1135, 148
1136, 148
1357, 174
Trachiniae
308–309, 205n. 48,
    228n. 92
Fr. 176 Radt, 205n. 50

Fr. 325 N², 228n. 95
Stesichorus
Fr. 26.1, 113, 222n. 13
Syrianus
On Hermogenes
1.112, 202n. 8

Theocritus
Idylls
22, 220n. 57
Theognis
119–120, 205n. 51
213, 29
215–216, 204n. 38
221–226, 217n. 29
365–366, 45
947–948, 203n. 20
965–967, 29, 205n. 51
1071, 30
1259–1260, 30
1259–1262, 203n. 14
1261–1262, 30
1386, 217n. 29
Thucydides
History of the Peloponnesian War
1.22, 235n. 69
2.41, 205n. 45
2.65, 201n. 43
3.38, 201n. 43, 214n. 85
3.38.16–17, 111
3.38.20, 111
3.38.24–25, 111, 178
3.38.33, 111
3.38.33–34, 111
3.53.2, 225n. 60
6.12.2, 230n. 6
6.15, 201n. 43
6.16.3, 230n. 6
6.16.5, 230n. 6

Xenophon
Apology
26, 223n. 19
Memorabilia
2.1.21–33, 35
2.1.22, 35, 36
2.1.27, 36
2.1.28, 36
2.1.34, 36
2.5.1–4, 235n. 64
2.12–47, 230n. 7
3.11.17, 235n. 64